EDITED BY SUZANNE CONKLIN AKBARI
AND AMILCARE IANNUCCI
With the assistance of John Tulk

160101

Marco Polo and the
Encounter of East and West

UNIVERSITY OF TORONTO PRESS
Toronto   Buffalo   London

© University of Toronto Press Incorporated 2008
Toronto   Buffalo   London
www.utppublishing.com
Printed in Canada

ISBN 978-0-8020-9928-0 (cloth)

Printed on acid-free paper

Library and Archives Canada Cataloguing in Publication

Marco Polo and the encounter of east and west / edited by Suzanne Conklin
Akbari and Amilcare Iannucci; with the assistance of John Tulk.

Includes bibliographical references and index.

ISBN 978-0-8020-9928-0

1. Polo, Marco, 1254–1323?. Travels of Marco Polo. 2. East and West. 3. Polo,
Marco, 1254–1323. 4. Travelers' writings–History and criticism. 5. Travel,
Medieval. 6. Geography, Medieval. I. Akbari, Suzanne Conklin II. Iannucci,
Amilcare A. III. Tulk, John

G370.P9M37 2008   915.04'2092   C2008-905543-8

University of Toronto Press acknowledges the financial assistance to its publishing program of the Canada Council for the Arts and the Ontario Arts Council.

University of Toronto Press gratefully acknowledges the financial assistance of the
Centre for Medieval Studies, University of Toronto, in the publication of this book.

University of Toronto Press acknowledges the financial support for its publishing activities of the Government of Canada through the Book Publishing
Industry Development Program (BPIDP).

For
Anna, Matthew, and Emily Iannucci
and
Yasin, Sara, Camilla, and John Akbari

Contents

Preface

In 2001, Amilcare Iannucci and I decided to embark upon a project that would integrate my current research on medieval depictions of the Orient with his ongoing work on medieval Italian literature, as well as enrich our common interest in comparative literary history: this initiative resulted in a symposium, 'Marco Polo and the Encounter of East and West,' held at the University of Toronto on 24–6 May 2002. Along with an exhibition and published catalogue titled 'Expectations and Experience: The World of the Medieval and Renaissance Traveller,' curated and written by Pam Gravestock, the symposium marked one of the first major events organized by the newly founded Humanities Centre, housed at University College under the directorship of Amilcare Iannucci. We worked together to solicit presentations by a formidable range of scholars, including those whose contributions are represented in this volume (John Larner, Marion Steinicke, Debra Strickland, Susan Whitfield, Suzanne Yeager, and Longxi Zhang) and planned to round out the volume with essays by each of us as well as additional solicited contributions.

The project was harshly interrupted by the illness that ultimately took Amilcare Iannucci's life. Through strength of will, he was able to further the project by recruiting an essay from Martin McLaughlin and co-authoring an essay with his longtime collaborator and friend, John Tulk; I solicited additional essays from Yunte Huang and Sharon Kinoshita, edited the volume, and wrote the introduction we had originally hoped to co-author. I had hoped to learn a great deal from Amilcare's long experience in editorial work; instead, I learned a great deal about how a brave human being faces suffering with dignity and grace. *Marco Polo and the Encounter of East and West* is a tribute to

Amilcare Iannucci's ability to draw together scholars from a wide range of disciplines, working in institutions scattered across the globe, and to unite them in a common search for humanistic understanding. It was his belief that the study of the humanities could do much to bridge the differences separating societies and peoples in the world today. If the volume succeeds in this goal, it will be fitting tribute to the man.

Thanks are due to the persons and organizations who so generously supported the initial conference, as well as to those who nurtured the volume during its preparation. These include Alex Kisin, Amilcare's dear friend and executor; Paul Perron, of University College; Roland Le Huenen, of the Centre for Comparative Literature; André Schmid, of the Department of East Asian Studies; Carlo Coen, of the Italian Cultural Institute; Anne Dondertman, of the Thomas Fisher Rare Book Library; Klaas Ruitenbeek, of the Royal Ontario Museum; the Connaught Committee of the University of Toronto; and the Social Sciences and Humanities Research Council of Canada. Warm thanks to Elizabeth Watkins, for editorial assistance, to Andrew Reeves, for work on the bibliography, and to Sara Akbari, for work on the index. A publication subvention was provided as a memorial to Amilcare Iannucci by the Faculty of Arts and Science of the University of Toronto, led by Dean Pekka Sinervo; additional support was provided by the Centre for Medieval Studies, under the acting directorship of Lawrin Armstrong. Finally, for permission to reproduce the works of art included in this volume, I would like to gratefully acknowledge the Bibliothèque Nationale, Paris; the Bodleian Library, Oxford; the British Library, London; the Parker Library of Corpus Christi College, Cambridge; the Morgan Library, New York; and Ryukoku University Library, Japan. For her generous help in helping to obtain image permissions from the Ryukoku University Library, I am very grateful to Mariko Liliefeldt, Chief Librarian of the Japan Foundation, Toronto. In the last conversation I had with him, Amilcare and I decided that we would like to dedicate this book to his children and to mine.

Marco Polo and the Encounter of East and West

1 Introduction: East, West, and In-between

SUZANNE CONKLIN AKBARI

The title of this collection contains a binary opposition – that of 'East' and 'West' – which many readers will at once recognize as being both reductive and essentialist. To talk of the 'encounter of East and West,' moreover, is to use this essentialist binarism in order to represent the history of cultural encounter as if it were fundamentally an exchange of equals, devoid of the imbalance of power that, historically, has characterized colonial experience. This volume, however, deliberately begins with this formulation in a kind of 'strategic essentialism.'[1] To employ this phrase is to echo the very terms used by writers of historical narratives of encounter to portray that experience, thus using their own essentialist binarism as a starting point from which to develop more complex accounts of cultural interaction. Accordingly, the essays contained in this volume begin with the arbitrary dichotomy of 'East and West,' but quickly move beyond it. In several of the essays that follow, this dichotomy is historicized as a medieval construct; other essays elaborate the dichotomy of East and West into more complex theoretical models based not on static opposition, but on the phenomena of currency, mobility, and flow. All of the essays in this volume, however, share the common ground of the late thirteenth-century travel narrative of Marco Polo, even as they range from historically nuanced explorations of medieval textuality to creative postmodern theoretical interventions.

It is appropriate, in the introduction to this volume, to begin by illustrating the 'strategic' nature of the binarism of the title, showing how the binary opposition of 'East and West' can actually enable a kind of 'binocular' vision of the cultural encounter of Marco Polo, illustrated here in two medieval maps, one produced in late twelfth-century

England, one in early fifteenth-century east Asia. Each of these maps represents the known world, and each of them reveals a great deal concerning the way in which its creator and its first readers understood their place in that world. Figure 1.1 shows the twelfth-century *mappamundi* long attributed to Henry of Mainz, now more commonly referred to as the Sawley Map.[2] It is among the earliest of the great medieval world maps produced in Europe, whose heyday extended from soon after the First Crusade until the fifteenth century, when the increase of exploration and territorial expansion rendered such 'symbolic geographies' largely redundant.[3] Like the majority of these *mappaemundi*, the Sawley Map places Jerusalem at the centre of the world, reflecting its role in salvation history, and locates Eden at the top of the map, in the far East, with the rivers of paradise extending downward to water the world with spiritual blessings. In the upper right-hand corner of the map (at one o'clock, if the map were a clock face), we find the island of 'Taprobana,' the name used by medieval cartographers and encyclopedists to designate Sri Lanka, a place believed to harbour fabulous riches and extraordinary marvels, and to be located at the very fringe of the world.[4]

Figure 1.2 is also a world map, this one produced in Korea in the early fifteenth century, compiled (according to its prefatory inscription) with the aid of two earlier maps of China and the surrounding regions. Titled the 'Honil kangni yŏktae kukto chi to' ('Map of Historical Emperors and Kings and of Integrated Borders and Terrain'; hereafter 'Kangnido'), this world map places the large land mass of China at the centre, the peninsula of Korea at the upper right, and the islands of Japan on the lower right.[5] What is extraordinary about the Kangnido, however, is its inclusion not only of the western portions of Asia and the Middle East, but of Africa and Europe as well: the landmass extending downward at the left side of the image is the continent of Africa, with the Arabian peninsula beside it, and Europe above it. The Arabic source of the place names of these western regions attests to the cultural transmission of cartographic knowledge hand-in-hand with the mercantile interaction that linked east Asia with the Islamic world and, through the Middle East, with Europe itself.

On the Kangnido, Sri Lanka appears not as the tiny remote island at the fringe of the world that Europeans knew as 'Taprobana'; instead, it appears as a round island immediately to the east of the Arabian peninsula, in a relatively central location on the map, near the sprawling amalgam of India and China that dominates the Kangnido. It is Europe

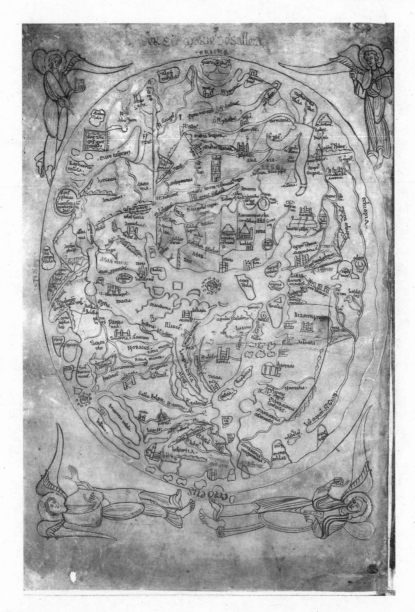

Figure 1.1: Sawley Map, late twelfth century; Cambridge University, Corpus Christi College MS. 66, fol. 2. Reproduced by permission of the Master and Fellows of Corpus Christi College, Cambridge.

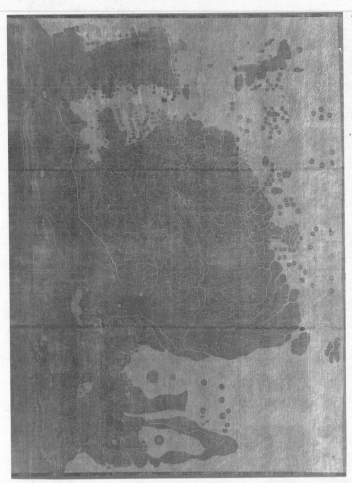

Figure 1.2: Kangnido Map ('Honil kangni yŏktae kukto chi t'o' ['Map of Historical Emperors and Kings and of Integrated Borders and Terrain']), early fifteenth century; Omiya Library, Ryukoku University Academic Information Center, Kyoto, Japan. Reproduced by permission of Ryukoku University.

that trails off into mysterious ambiguity at the upper left portion of this map, a location that was just barely within ken for those living in fifteenth-century Korea who created and read the Kangnido. Placing these two maps side by side allows us now to imagine these two world views superimposed upon each other, sharing features in common – Africa, India, Arabia, Sri Lanka – but seeing them from very different perspectives. For European readers of the Sawley Map, the east Asian lands of China, Korea, and Japan were unimaginably distant, beyond the already exotic and unreachable island of Taprobana. For Asian readers of the Kangnido, the remote lands of Europe lay at the very edge of the world, physically unreachable but still imaginable, linked through an infinitely long chain of mercantile links spanning the breadth of the linked continents of Eurasia.[6] Seeing through the medium of these paired maps permits us a glimpse of the 'binocular vision' that is offered by the essays of this collection, in which the binary opposition of 'East and West' opens the door to exchange, reciprocity, and dialogue.

In order to adequately introduce the collection of essays contained in this volume, it is necessary to comment on their relationship to the conceptual framework of 'Orientalism,' a theoretical construct that for three decades has dynamically shaped the way in which cultural encounter is described. The fact that it is now commonplace to refer to 'the East' as a construct is owing, in no small measure, to the transformative effect of Edward Said's study of *Orientalism*, which from its publication in 1978 served to make clear the extent to which the Orient had, in Said's words, served as a 'stage' on which the West both portrayed and viewed its most vivid fantasies and fears. Said's characterization of the Orient, however, was strongly centred on the Middle East, in keeping with the geographical regions which were indeed the object of western scrutiny in the classical and medieval world – Babylon and Jerusalem chief among them. This focus makes itself manifest throughout *Orientalism*, so much so that formulations such as 'Islam and the West' or 'the Orient and Europe' come to be used interchangeably. To put it another way, in Said's *Orientalism*, the Orient and the Islamic world are co-terminous.[7] In turn, postcolonial theorists (beginning with the work of the Subaltern Studies collective of the 1970s) have sought to understand the construction of western views of the Orient not only through different modalities, political and economic, but also with a different geographical focus. The Portuguese and British colonization of India and east Asia have been the target of much of the most dynamic work carried out over the last few decades. Such work has yielded rich insights into the interrelation of ideological, economic, political, and cultural modes of domination during periods of colonization, from the fifteenth century to the twentieth.

This volume's focus on the 'encounter of East and West,' then, is further complicated by the question of which 'East' one refers to: The Orient, variously centred on Babylon and Jerusalem, of Said's great work? Or the stereotypically 'despotic' Orient of the Ottoman Empire, variably seen as being an ally of European nations (notably, Elizabethan England) and a perpetual threat to the integrity of eastern European borders?[8] Or the Orient of the Indian sub-continent, which was crucial to the development of Portuguese dominance in trade, and subsequently to British colonial expansion?[9] Or the regions further east, particularly the region of China – then called, following Roman practice, 'Cathay'? Rarely visited and hence scarcely known to medieval travellers, China was nonetheless vividly imagined; today, by contrast, this region has become an economic and political world power, linked globally through technology and the dynamic currents of cultural production. For all these reasons, the eastward voyage of Marco Polo along the Silk Road, narrated during the last years of the thirteenth century, makes a fitting starting point for an inquiry into the encounter of East and West: an encounter which began many centuries ago and still has not concluded. The essays contained within *Marco Polo and the Encounter of East and West* therefore trace the paths of exchange and interaction not only as they are mapped out within the text, but also as they are re-enacted in subsequent cross-cultural readings of the work. Accordingly, the volume begins with detailed studies of Marco Polo's narrative in its many medieval forms (including French, Italian, and Latin versions) that place the text not only in its material manuscript context but also in its generic context, considering the place of Marco Polo's account within the conventions of the emergent genre of travel literature. Reception of Marco Polo's work, both medieval and modern, characterizes the second group of essays, while the volume concludes with historiographical and poetic accounts of the place of Marco Polo in the context of a truly global world literature. By the volume's end, the foundational binarism of East and West emerges as a strategic dichotomy that enables the reader to theorize the very nature of encounter and the role of the text in mediating cultural difference.

The origins of the work known as Marco Polo's *Travels* are rooted at once in oral narrative and the written tradition of medieval romance.

The story was first recorded, its writer tells us, in an Italian prison cell. Recounted from his own experiences by the traveller and merchant Ser Marco Polo, the story was given written form by a writer of romances called Rustichello and rapidly redacted in a number of versions; the nature of the lost original text remains tantalizingly elusive. The language of the earliest surviving version of the *Travels* is a hybrid of French and Italian, a vernacular tongue that would have made its story accessible to a wide range of readers, both learned and unlearned.[10] The appeal of the *Travels* is attested by the extraordinary rapidity with which it would go on to be translated into a range of other vernaculars as well as Latin, the common language of learned culture during the Middle Ages. Old French and Tuscan renditions were soon followed by the Venetian version as well as the influential Latin translation of Francesco Pipino, as well as subsequent versions in German, Aragonese, Catalan, Castilian, Irish, Czech, and Portuguese. While the title 'Travels' is the one most familiar to modern readers, appearing on the first page of virtually all translations, this title only came to be commonly attached to Marco Polo's work (like that of John Mandeville) in the course of the seventeenth century, with the rise of travel literature as an established genre. Before that time, the book of Marco Polo was known under a variety of names. The earliest, Franco-Italian version is usually described in manuscripts as *Le Devisement dou monde*, or *The Description of the World*, a title that attests to the work's simultaneous celebration of diversity and eagerness to classify that same heterogeneous reality.[11] As Katherine Park has memorably put it, the *Devisement* is at once 'a hymn to the world's diversity' and 'a sermon naturalizing and justifying trade.'[12]

Later Italian versions usually title the work *Il Milione*, sometimes thought to mean 'the liar,' but now more commonly believed to be an adaptation of the Polo family name.[13] One medieval French version titles the work *Le Livre des merveilles du monde* (*The Book of the Marvels of the World*), while another titles it *Li Livres du Graunt Caam* (*The Book of the Grand Khan*). The Latin version of Pipino, very widely disseminated throughout Europe during the Middle Ages, refers to the work as *De mirabilibus mundi*. The heterogeneous range of narrative genres through which Marco Polo's voyage was recounted during the thirteenth and fourteenth centuries went on to become even more diverse, as the work – now dubbed *The Travels of Marco Polo* – came to be rendered in a wide range of editions, scholarly and popular, published in expensive luxury editions and in popular press versions. Editions printed in the British colonies of Hong Kong and Shanghai [*sic*] attest to the paradox of the record of a medieval encounter of Europe and China becoming a luxurious artifact of Victorian colonialism in British-controlled east Asia. During the last century, film adaptations, ranging from children's cartoons to pornography, have recast Marco Polo's account into new forms, to suit the tastes of very different audiences. It is appropriate that a book which filtered into so many vernaculars and genres, and whose text spans such a wide range of geographical locations, should have been known under such a wide range of names. This heterogeneity is reflected in the various editions of the work cited in the essays included here, some of which focus on one or more of the medieval redactions, while others select one of the modern versions of the text: for example, in his study of Calvino, Martin McLaughlin uses the modern edition of *Il Milione* that the novelist himself is known to have owned. In most cases, the role of the editor is to harmonize the various versions of the text discussed in the volume's essays; in this case, however, to do so would be to undermine the very principle of textual heterogeneity essential to the ongoing interpretive fecundity of Marco Polo's book. The multiple 'textual isotopes' of the *Devisement dou monde*, both medieval and modern, embody the mediating properties of a text as it multiplies across linguistic, cultural, and temporal boundaries.[14] The work is singular only temporarily and provisionally, in the eye of the individual during the moment of reading.

This collection begins with studies of the earliest versions of Marco Polo's book, while subsequent essays delve into the historical background that lies behind the semi-fictional account of the Venetian merchant. The essays that close the volume return to the paradigm with which it began, provocatively exploring the question of whether Marco Polo's *Travels* offers a reflection of the West in the mirror of the Orient, a sidelong view of the East in the eye of the western observer – or something in-between. The first section of this collection, 'Marco Polo and the Experience of Wonder,' sets the narrative of the *Devisement dou monde* in its medieval context. The essays contained in this section (by Strickland, Kinoshita, Steinicke, and Akbari) both explore the manuscript tradition of the work and place it within the framework of other travel literature and descriptions of the so-called 'wonders of the East.'[15] Debra Higgs Strickland's 'Text, Image, and Contradiction in the *Devisement dou monde*' reflects the ways in which illustrated manuscripts 'do not simply reflect the texts they accompany, but may complement, contradict, augment, diminish, or even ignore them.' This essay, written from the perspective of a historian of art, sensitively explores the interrelation of text and image in two of the four extant illustrated Marco Polo manuscripts of the French text of the *Travels*: Bibliothèque nationale MS French 2810, commissioned by John the Fearless, Duke of Burgundy, in the early fifteenth century; and Bodley 264, an early fifteenth-century product of the London workshop of the master artist Johannes. These manuscripts lend themselves to detailed comparison, not only because both are productions of the great age of illuminated painting, both centred on the vernacular French text of the *Devisement*, both of them deluxe commodities produced for courtly patrons, but also because both depict the inhabitants of remote lands using conventions for the representation of 'Saracens' and 'monstrous races.' Strickland's monograph on these very conventions, *Saracens, Demons, and Jews*, makes her especially well suited to place the *Devisement dou monde* in this pictorial context: she demonstrates, for example, that the Mongolian soldiers featured in Bodley 264 are depicted in ways that correspond to the European Christian conventions for the portrayal of Muslims, a 'visual conflation' that makes the Mongolians into what Strickland terms 'functional Saracens.'[16] Following a comparative analysis of the manuscripts' iconographic strategies for the depiction of Tartars, monstrous races, Mongols, and Saracens, Strickland turns to an exploration of how the 'city functioned as an especially relevant pictorial symbol' in the luxury manuscripts devoted to the *Devisement dou monde*. Like Marco Polo and Rustichello, the illuminators 'fully participated in the goal of marketing the East to the West,' yet did so within the narrower, more focused framework of satisfying their patrons.

Like Strickland, Sharon Kinoshita focuses her study on the French text of Marco Polo represented by the *Devisement dou monde*. Unlike Strickland, however, Kinoshita seeks to locate the work not in the cultural and pictorial context of the late Middle Ages, but in its twelfth- and thirteenth-century literary and historical milieu. 'Marco Polo's *Le Devisement dou monde* and the Tributary East' is, in Kinoshita's words, a 'thought experiment' that recognizes the centrality of the figure of the Grand Khan, an imperial leader of nations in the mould of Alexander the Great and Charlemagne. Kinoshita's recent study of ethnic and racial alterity in Old French literature, *Medieval Boundaries*, provides a broad comparative context for this essay's close examination of the 'thematics of crusade' that informs Marco Polo's text.[17] Using literary and historical sources ranging from the twelfth-century *Voyage de Charlemagne* to the mid-thirteenth-century *Ystoria Mongalorum* of John of Plano Carpini, Kinoshita illustrates the way in which the *Devisement dou monde* can be read as a reflection of that pivotal period of 'first contact' between Europeans and Mongols, even as it constructs an imaginative fantasy of eastern wonders. Significantly, as Kinoshita emphasizes, these wonders are not located in the 'monstrous races' long associated with the remote Orient; on the contrary, the greatest wonder of them all is the Grand Khan himself, and the magnificent 'tributary power' over which he presides. The narrator's exploration of the empire of the Grand Khan gradually reveals two concomitant features of the empire of the Mongols: first, the 'effacement of clear lines of difference' between the Oriental other and the western self; and, second, the growing prominence of the figure of the merchant, who proves to be able to move effortlessly across national, linguistic, and cultural boundaries through the transformative power of the commodity.

While Strickland and Kinoshita historicize the encounter with the other narrated in the *Devisement dou monde*, Marion Steinicke instead provides a psychoanalytical context. She interprets the encounter with the other in Freudian terms as an intellectual trauma that first negates the 'unbearable discovery,' and only subsequently accepts and assimilates it. In the case of Marco Polo's narrative, Steinicke argues, the 'unbearable discovery' is precisely the recognition of oriental cultural, scientific, and economic supremacy, and the consequent 'decentralization' of the Occident. Central to Steinicke's reading of the text is the *Letter to Prester John*, a twelfth-century forgery that – for its European Christian audience – at once forecast the ascent to power of the Mongols and encouraged Christian hopes for a successful reconquest of Jerusalem. Steinicke argues that the figures of Prester John and his putative ancestors, the three Magi, serve to underpin the *Devisement dou monde*'s narrative of the eastern assimilation of western might. The variable locations assigned to the tomb of the three Magi, ranging from Milan and Cologne, on the one hand, to Baghdad and Persia, on the other, map out a trajectory of displacement that testifies to the 'narcissistic trauma' played out in the mercantile myth of Marco Polo. Steinicke's essay closes by comparing the *Devisement* with the travel narrative of John Mandeville, a text that integrates the wonders of the East into western categories of knowledge and thus reaffirms the ideological supremacy of the Occident.

In 'Currents and Currency in Marco Polo's *Devisement dou monde* and *The Book of John Mandeville*,' Suzanne Akbari places into dialogue the late thirteenth-century account of an actual voyage and the mid-fourteenth-century account whose author is unlikely to have travelled beyond the walls of his library. Any consideration of the genre of medieval travel literature has recourse to the paired texts of Marco Polo and Mandeville; to place them in a single category, however, is to elide the extraordinary gap that separates their visions of the world. Akbari's essay seeks to locate their distinct visions in a semiotics of space, in which the definition of centre and periphery serves to delineate borders, create hierarchies, and generate symmetries. Through the polysemous notion of 'currency,' Akbari seeks to use a single set of terms to articulate both the devotional discourse that structures the *Book of John Mandeville* and the mercantile discourse that pervades the *Devisement dou monde*. While the rivers and streams emanating from Eden nourish the world both physically and spiritually, the system of watercourses and canals that permeate the lands of the Grand Khan facilitate economic and cultural exchange. In Akbari's reading, currency – both the flow of liquids and the stream of paper money emanating from the treasury of the Grand Khan – is the lifeblood of empire. The sacred centres of Jerusalem and Eden found in the *Book of John Mandeville* find their counterpart, in the *Devisement dou monde*, in the variable and temporary centrality of the great cities of the Grand Khan's empire. While both texts participate in a pre-modern discourse of Orientalism, they do so in very different ways, reflecting the variable intersection of the discourse of Orientalism with the distinctive vectors of religious and national alterity.

The essays in the second section of this volume are gathered under the heading 'The Reception of Marco Polo: Medieval and Modern.' Appropriately, the section begins with an essay by John Larner, whose recent book on *Marco Polo and the Discovery of the World* has had a transformative effect on studies of the historical context of the *Devisement dou monde*.[18] In 'Plucking Hairs from the Great Cham's Beard: Marco Polo, Jan de Langhe, and Sir John Mandeville,' Larner, like Akbari, places the works of Marco Polo and John Mandeville into dialogue. Larner, however, addresses the relationship of these writers in terms of a third, Jan de Langhe, who together with his more famous counterparts participated in the generation of geographical knowledge that shaped late medieval and early modern perceptions of the world. Using a familiar, discursive style that reflects his intimate knowledge of these authors and their cultural environment, Larner spins a narrative web that places each writer in his historical context and illuminates his place in late medieval imaginings of the East. Larner boldly suggests that Jan de Langhe may be identified as the author of the *Book of John Mandeville*, a work whose apparently eponymous author has long been known to be a myth, noting the close correspondence of source materials in the *Book of John Mandeville* with works known to have been translated by Jan de Langhe, including the *Relatio* of Oderic of Pordenone. Curiously, however, as Larner remarks, the *Book of John Mandeville* largely abandons the pragmatic geography of Oderic in favour of a fantastical narrative of wonders which 'makes no attempt to deal with coherent space.' For Larner, the relentless abandonment of realistic geography and well-grounded historiography found in the *Book of John Mandeville* renders it epistemologically incompatible with the *Devisement* of Marco Polo, which ignores the world of marvels to focus instead on 'what is sternly factual.'

Following in the footsteps of Larner, Suzanne Yeager continues the dialogue of Marco Polo and Mandeville in 'The World Translated: Marco Polo's *Devisement dou monde, The Book of John Mandeville*, and Their Medieval Audiences.' Yeager brings a wealth of knowledge of the manuscript tradition and the patterns of dissemination of these travel narratives, generating a thick description of late medieval reading practices that reveals a great deal about how these works were understood by their fourteenth-century readers. Because Yeager focuses particularly on English readership, the Latin version of Marco Polo produced by Francesco Pipino assumes a special prominence. While the numerous vernacular redactions of the *Book of John Mandeville* ensured that it was transmitted as a popular text in England, Marco Polo's narrative was known only through the learned, didactic Latin of Pipino. Yeager's survey of manuscript collation patterns reveals the context within which medieval readers interpreted Mandeville, on the one hand, and Marco Polo, on the other. While Mandeville's *Book* appears as commonly in devotional collections as in miscellanies devoted to the wonders of the East, Pipino's translation of Marco Polo generally appears in collections of scientific treatises and historical chronicles. This distribution, Yeager argues, both reveals the nature of medieval 'tastes' and illustrates the extent to which an appetite for marvels influenced late medieval reading practices. Yeager offers a close reading of the depiction of Jerusalem in the *Book of John Mandeville*, contrasting that work's privileging of the Holy City with the portrayal of Venice – Marco Polo's native city – and Khanbaliq – the Grand Khan's imperial city – in the *Devisement dou monde*. Like Strickland, Kinoshita, and Akbari, Yeager uses the city as a spatial point of orientation around which the travel narrative is constructed. In her reading, however, biblical models and the practice of devotional reading are the crucial elements that serve to locate medieval readers' experience of both Mandeville's *Book* and Pipino's translation of Marco Polo.

With Martin McLaughlin's essay 'Calvino's Rewriting of Marco Polo: From the 1960 Screenplay to *Invisible Cities*,' Marco Polo is revealed as an author who has influenced modern imaginations of the city as pervasively as those of the Middle Ages. Perhaps the most famous modern work of literature to have been inspired by Marco Polo's travel narrative is Italo Calvino's 1972 novel *Invisible Cities*. The book became Calvino's best-known work in North America, and quickly acquired cult status not just among readers of literature, but also among architects and practitioners of a wide range of visual arts. It is less well known, however, that Calvino first became interested in Marco Polo's text in the summer of 1960, exactly ten years before he embarked upon *Invisible Cities*, when he wrote a substantial draft screenplay for an Italian film about Marco Polo (a film which, in the end, was never made). Calvino's screenplay has only recently become available for study by scholars, and has received comparatively little attention during that time. McLaughlin's essay examines in full for the first time the two-stage process by which Marco Polo's original text led, first, to the 1960 screenplay of *Marco Polo* and, subsequently, to *Invisible Cities*. McLaughlin thus charts the different kinds of inspiration that the medieval account of Marco Polo exercised on the modern author Calvino, tracing a creative route that led from an abortive screenplay to one of the great modern works of poetic prose. Like the twinning of Mandeville and Marco Polo in Yeager's essay, the twinning of Calvino and Marco Polo in McLaughlin's work reveals the dynamic poetic processes at work in the creative imagination, whether in the fourteenth century or in the twentieth, and illustrates the extraordinary fertility of Marco Polo's *Devisement*.

McLaughlin's essay is followed by another meditation on modern appropriations of Marco Polo's narrative. Co-authored by Amilcare Iannucci and John Tulk, 'From Alterity to Holism: Cinematic Depictions of Marco Polo and His *Travels*' illustrates the range of creative reworkings of the late thirteenth-century text, ranging from children's cartoons to orientalist pornography. This essay's unusual length is justified by its status as a unique resource for the study of cinematic adaptations of the Marco Polo story: it provides summaries of films rarely seen and, in some cases, obtainable only with great difficulty. Iannucci and Tulk provide an overview of these adaptations, focusing particularly on their tendency to characterize their protagonist within two general categories: the adventurous romantic hero, and the historical ethnographer. The former model, unsurprisingly, is on full display in the 1938 *Adventures of Marco Polo* directed by Archie Mayo, starring Gary Cooper and a nubile Lana Turner; the latter model is unfolded in elaborate detail in Giuliano Montaldo's lavish 1982 historical mini-series, *Marco Polo*. Iannucci and Tulk argue that the latter adaptation features an extraordinarily nuanced depiction of alterity, in which the experience of travel transforms the traveller to such an extent that his 'exotic' environment becomes a new homeland. They discuss in detail the extent to which contemporary historical circumstances exerted a formative influence on the Orientalism of the Marco Polo films, focusing particularly on the perspectives of American film-makers and the viewing public on the on-going social and political reforms taking place in China. This history reaches its pinnacle, for Iannucci and Tulk, in the extraordinary co-operation and cultural interaction between Italian and Chinese institutions that enabled the realization of Montaldo's ambitious mini-series.

The volume's final section, 'Cross-Cultural Currents,' reaches out broadly to consider the extent to which the occidental self finds itself reflected in the oriental other, and the ways in which the Orient speaks back to its past colonial masters. The essays in this section include Susan Whitfield's historiographic approach to cultural exchange in terms of 'ebb and flow,' Yunte Huang's meditation on the poetic currents engendered by Marco Polo's text, and Longxi Zhang's synthetic evocation of what lessons might be drawn from Marco Polo's experience in order to enable 'an alternative model of East-West encounter.' In 'The Perils of Dichotomous Thinking: A Case of Ebb and Flow Rather Than East and West,' Susan Whitfield argues persuasively that it is impossible to understand Central Asian history if we continue to articulate that history in terms of an encounter of East and West. Whitfield is extraordinarily well-placed to comment on methods of theorizing cultural relations in Asian historiography: renowned for her numerous publications on the Silk Road, Whitfield is director of the International Dunhuang Project housed at the British Library.[19] She argues that the terms 'East' and 'West' are expressions of a dichotomous model of thinking that is fundamental to much modern historiography of both China and Central Asia. While to a large degree such thinking emanates from the modern theoretical framework of Orientalism, it is deployed by means of a wide range of dichotomous terms. In terms of contemporary Chinese history, it is seen in the ubiquitous use of 'Han' versus 'non-Han' by both Chinese and western historians and journalists; such usage perpetuates a misleading homogeneous model of Chinese (or 'Han') history. In terms of Central Asian history, this model is expressed in terms of the prevalent discussion of 'sedentary' versus 'nomad,' or 'civilized' versus 'barbarian.' The pitfalls of such dichotomous thinking are demonstrated amply by the reaction to the discovery of the Shu finds in what is now south-western China, and European mummies in what is now western China: both of these were hailed as astonishing, simply because they did not fit the conventional dichotomous model. In this essay, Whitfield argues that, instead of trying to shoehorn such data into an ill-fitting dichotomous model, we must reject the model as too limited and instead find new models that are able to accommodate and help us to better understand and analyse these complex data. Whitfield's groundbreaking work on computer models for cultural movement, extrapolated from computer models centred on oceanographic phenomena, enables her to suggest bold new frameworks for how we might discuss Central Asia – and, by extension, other regions – without the distorting binarism of 'East' and 'West.'

Yunte Huang's 'Marco Polo: Meditations on Intangible Economy and Vernacular Imagination' is an evocative essay that employs Marco Polo's text as the central point of an argument that, in Huang's words, 'proceeds in incomplete circles.' The circular mode of meditative argument allows Huang to draw together literary texts and cultural phenomena into a postmodern investigation of the 'vernacular imagination.' Focusing on visual image and audible utterance as dual modes of perception, Huang argues, permits a reading of Marco Polo's *Devisement* that provides a template for broader considerations of 'visual space' and 'acoustic space.' This theoretical framework, which is indebted to the work of Marshall McLuhan and Bruce Powers, is applied by Huang to other literary texts including Calvino's *Invisible Cities* and Eugene O'Neill's *Marco Millions*, placing these modern works into dialogue with the thirteenth-century text. The oral origins of Marco Polo's narrative re-emerge, in Huang's reading, in the 'acoustic space' of these twentieth-century literary refashionings. The 'universal language' of currency, evoked in the famous passage concerning paper money in Marco Polo's text and recalled in the Calvino novel and O'Neill play, corresponds to the linguistic vernacular, so that the reader is always also a listener, and what he sees/hears is at once financial currency and the currency of the word. Linguistic exchange, like financial exchange, proves to be fraught with pitfalls, gaps that separate word from meaning and threaten to cancel the transaction. Huang's recent monograph on the overlapping and conflicting demands of Chinese and North American identity offers a rich foundation for his extended meditation on the role of poetic language in the global economy, whether in the medieval world of Marco Polo or the postmodern world in which we live.[20]

To close the volume, eminent cultural theorist Longxi Zhang provides a synthetic overview of issues raised in this introduction, and explored in several of the essays.[21] 'Marco Polo, Chinese Cultural Identity, and an Alternative Model of East-West Encounter' begins with an effort to seek out Chinese documentary sources that offer evidence relating to the circumstances of Marco Polo's historical journey, thus providing a contemporaneous look back at the European self through the eyes of the oriental other. Such inversion of the conventional subject-object relationship reappears in Zhang's reading of Marco Polo's narrative, in which Zhang suggests that Marco Polo self-consciously adopts a 'Mongolian perspective,' enabling him to present an extremely positive 'picture of China and the East blessed with incredible wealth.' Like Huang, Zhang explores the complementary relationship of the visible and the audible as they are reflected in Marco Polo's text, comparing eleventh-century Chinese poetic evocations of the unintelligible 'language of the south' with Marco Polo's own description of the foreign place-names he encounters. While Zhang continues to draw upon the binary opposition of 'barbarian' and 'Chinese,' a formulation that Susan Whitfield suggests should be superseded, he complicates that dichotomous relationship by pointing out how 'porous' the boundaries of 'Chineseness' prove to be. In Zhang's view, ethnicity, religious affiliation, national identity, family structures, and cultural forms all participate to varying degrees in the construction of identity, which is itself an ongoing process that has the capacity to result in 'dialogue and exchange rather than antagonism or confrontation.' In Zhang's essay, as in the many voices collected together in this volume, the encounter of East and West is reframed in terms of reciprocity rather than conflict, generating a fertile cross-cultural ground to nourish other future endeavours. The legacy of

Marco Polo's journey is a continuation of the Silk Road followed long ago by the merchant/explorer/storyteller, a path that leads into a future of continued exchange.

NOTES

1 The phrase 'strategic essentialism' is adapted from its original use in connection with some strands of post-humanist feminism; see Fuss, *Essentially Speaking*.

2 On the reattribution of the so-called Henry of Mainz map and its re-dating to the late twelfth century (from 1100), see Harvey, 'Sawley Map.'

3 The phrase 'symbolic geography' was made widely current by its use in Greenblatt, *Marvelous Possessions*.

4 On the identification of Taprobana, its variant spellings, and its appearance on a range of world maps, see von den Brincken, '*Fines terrae.*'

5 On the Kangnido, see Ledyard, 'Cartography in Korea' and 'The Kangnido.'

6 On the arbitrariness of how continents are designated and the connotations of where their boundaries are drawn, see Lewis and Wigen, *The Myth of Continents*.

7 For an overview of critiques of Said's theory and on its relevance for studies of medieval Europe, see Akbari, *Idols in the East*, especially 'Introduction: Medieval Orientalism?'

8 See Matar, *Turks, Moors, and Englishmen*; Bisaha, *Creating East and West*.

9 See Rubiés, *Travel and Ethnology*; Raiswell, 'Before the Company.'

10 On the status of Franco-Italian (or, as it is sometimes called, Franco-Veneto) as 'a literary language, learned from books, but often presented to a listening public' (Cornish 320), see the influential work of Aurelio Roncaglia, 'Le Letteratura franco-veneta'; see also Alison Cornish, 'Translatio Galliae,' esp. 315–21, 328–9. On the Franco-Italian compositions of Rustichello da Pisa, see Vitullo, *The Chivalric Epic*; see also the discussion of the Franco-Italian text of Marco Polo and Rustichello da Pisa to appear in Simon Gaunt's forthcoming monograph.

11 A combined edition of the earliest version of the text, the *Devisement dou monde* (based on the edition of L.F. Benedetto), together with the first Tuscan version, *Il Milione*, can be found in *Milione / Le Divisament dou monde. Il Milione nelle redazioni toscana e franco-italiana*, ed. Gabriella Ronchi (Milan: Mondadori, 1982). A detailed, multi-volume edition of the Old French *Devisement* is currently appearing under the general editorship of

Philippe Ménard (2001–); see the detailed listing of editions and translations of Marco Polo in the Bibliography below, pp. 297–8.

12 Park, 'The Meanings of Natural Diversity' 146. On natural diversity in
medieval encyclopedias and travel literature, see Suzanne Conklin Akbari,
'The Diversity of Mankind.'

13 See the discussion in the introduction to Valeria Bertolucci Pizzorusso's edition of Marco Polo, as well as the original hypothesis as presented by
Benedetto in 'Perché fu chiamato *Milione* il libro di Marco Polo,' *Il Marzocco*
35 (14 September 1930) and 'Ancore del nome *Milione*,' *Il Marzocco* 35
(16 November 1930).

14 The evocative phrase 'textual isotope' was coined by Iain Macleod Higgins
to describe the medieval 'multi-text' of the *Book of John Mandeville*; see
Higgins, *Writing East*.

15 On wonder in medieval narrative, see Katherine Park and Lorraine Daston,
Wonders and the Order of Nature; Caroline Walker Bynum, 'Wonder' (revised
version in *Metamorphosis and Identity*).

16 Debra Higgs Strickland, *Saracens, Demons, and Jews*.

17 Sharon Kinoshita, *Medieval Boundaries*.

18 John Larner, *Marco Polo and the Discovery of the World*.

19 See especially Susan Whitfield, *Life along the Silk Road* and *The Silk Road:
Trade, Travel, War and Faith*, ed. Susan Whitfield with Ursula Sims-Williams.

20 Yunte Huang, *Transpacific Displacement*.

21 Among his many publications, see especially Longxi Zhang, *Allegoresis* and
Mighty Opposites.

PART ONE

Marco Polo and
the Experience of Wonder

2 Text, Image, and Contradiction in the *Devisement dou monde*

DEBRA HIGGS STRICKLAND

One of the main debates in current Marco Polo studies concerns the original function of the *Devisement dou monde*. Most recently, the problem has been examined in detail by John Larner (68–87), who evaluates different theories that by turn interpret the work as a travel itinerary, a merchant's handbook, a book of marvels, a chivalric tale, or a call to crusade. The nature of a Latin version made before the year 1341 by the Dominican friar Francesco Pipino of Bologna has also prompted the hypothesis that it fulfilled an essentially Christian goal as a guidebook for missionaries (Critchley 137–57; Larner 111–15). However, what the debate has largely overlooked is the role of pictorial images in the *Devisement*; specifically, their ability to shape reader perceptions of the lands and inhabitants of the exotic East. Because painted miniatures were an integral part of the presentation of the text to at least a small number of late medieval aristocratic patrons, any discussion of the book's function for these readers must also consider the nature and power of its images.[1]

This thesis is underpinned by the theoretical conviction that images in illuminated manuscripts do not simply reflect the texts they accompany, but may complement, contradict, augment, diminish, or even ignore them. The responsibility for conceiving and executing these relationships in a given manuscript lay with medieval authors, artists, patrons, patrons' agents, or some combination of these (Green 62). By whatever means such relationships were enacted, it was the combined force of text and images that generated meanings impossible to communicate by either words or pictures alone. This essay seeks to examine a selected series of such text-image interdependencies in two fifteenth-century deluxe copies of the *Devisement*, BNF fr. 2810 and Bodley 264.

The extent to which artists were familiar with the texts they illustrated is another issue rightly considered in the assessment of any
illustrated book, but it is by no means a solvable problem or even a
straightforward question. This is because knowledge of a text does not
necessarily inspire a visual response to it, nor does apparent pictorial
evocation of a text automatically signify artistic understanding. Superficial text-image correspondences may be achieved through someone
else's instructions or pictorial models; while meaningful contradiction
of a text, just as much as detailed adherence to it, requires knowledge
of it (Runte; Alexander, *Medieval Illuminators* 52–71). Author-illustrated
manuscripts are among the very few about which the artist's knowledge of the text is absolutely certain.[2]

Rejecting the claim that medieval miniaturists were by definition
artisanal automatons who simply followed instructions (Hindman),
we may hypothesize that verbal-visual disjunctions in BNF fr. 2810
and Bodley 264 were carefully planned glosses on the text and not simply examples of 'artistic error.' I shall argue that well-informed and
commercially motivated artists responsible for the execution of the
Devisement illustrations responded to the text in ways that may be
explained through reference to specific interests and beliefs current
among their aristocratic patrons.[3]

Precious few illuminated copies of the *Devisement* have survived, but
it is very likely that others have been lost. In theory, a contemporary
inventory reference to a *livre des merveilles* or a *roman* might refer to a
lost copy of the *Devisement*, although in the absence of corroborating
external evidence, the significance of such references is impossible to
assess. However, the survival of even a few illustrated copies suggests
that for some readers, pictorial images were an inseparable part of
their experience of the *Devisement*, an especially popular book in the
French court (Benedetto xlv–xlvii; Ciccuto 6). That painted images were
an integral component of many other types of books in aristocratic and
royal libraries is the best evidence that courtly readers preferred not
just texts but also images for maximum edification, contemplation, and
entertainment – as well as conspicuous consumption (Buettner). It is
to such a courtly audience that Marco Polo's prologue is in fact
addressed: 'Seignors enperaor et rois, dux et marquois, cuens, chevaliers et b[o]rgio[i]s, et toutes gens que volés savoir les deverses jenera-
sions des homes et les deversités des deverses region dou monde, si
prennés cestui livre et le feites lire' ['Emperors and kings, dukes and
marquises, counts, knights, and townsfolk, and all people who wish to

know the various races of men and the peculiarities of the various regions of the world, take this book and have it read to you'] (Ronchi 305; Latham 33).

The luxury manuscript compilations to be examined here represent two out of only four extant that contain extensively illustrated versions of the *Devisement*. BNF fr. 2810 in the National Library in Paris is the famous travel anthology commissioned in 1412 by the Duke of Burgundy, John the Fearless, as a gift for his uncle, Jean, Duke of Berry. Jean of Berry was a travel literature enthusiast, as were a number of his contemporaries in the French court. He kept another copy of the *Devisement* in his own collection and in 1412 he gave still another to Pierre des Essarts, provost of Paris. A few years earlier he had given a copy of the *Travels* of Sir John Mandeville to his valet, Jean Barre. In addition, he owned six large tapestries of scenes of the Great Khan (Meiss, *The Boucicaut Master* 43; Porter 9–11). BNF fr. 2810, his most spectacular book of travels, bears the title *Livre des Merveilles du Monde* (*Book of the World's Marvels*). In addition to the *Devisement*, it contains several other illustrated travel texts, including those of Odoric of Pordenone, the Mandeville author, and Hetoum (Porter 2). The illustrations have been attributed to the atelier of the Boucicaut Master in collaboration with another atelier working in the style of the Bedford Master.[4]

The second lavishly illustrated copy of the *Devisement* was bound into Bodley 264, housed today in the Bodleian Library in Oxford. The portion of Bodley 264 that bears the title *Li Livres du Graunt Caam* was executed between 1400 and 1410 by the master artist Johannes and members of his London workshop (Christianson 124; Scott 2: 70–3). In this case, the original patron is unknown and the *Livres du Graunt Caam* was added to an earlier collection of Alexander romances of Flemish origins dated to 1338 (Scott 2: 68–70; James, *Romance*). This fact of later addition does not rule out original English ownership of the manuscript, however, as Edward III and a good number of his retinue were in Flanders for most of 1338–40, at which point the Alexander romances could have been commissioned (Dutschke, 'Truth' 298). In any case, the earliest known mention of Bodley 264 appears in a 1397 inventory of the library of Edward's youngest son, Thomas, Duke of Gloucester, and an inscription of 1466 indicates that by the time the *Livres du Graunt Caam* was added, the manuscript was owned by Richard Wydevill, Lord Rivers, father-in-law of Edward IV (Pächt and Alexander 70; Dutschke 298).

As noted, only two more surviving manuscript copies of the *Devisement* contain lavish pictorial cycles. Royal 19.D.I, a Parisian manuscript of the first quarter of the fourteenth century housed today in the British Library, was probably made for Philip VI and was the model for Bodley 264.[5] However, the images in this manuscript bear little stylistic or iconographical relation to those of Bodley 264, and their technical level of execution is considerably lower. This last judgment is based on the fact that many of the relatively simplified images exhibit a perfunctory and repetitive stock quality, certain important subjects are not represented, and the folios lack the gold leaf and elaborate decoration characteristic of Bodley 264. The sixteenth-century French 5219 in the Arsenal Library in Paris was made for an unknown patron, and while its pictorial cycle is highly accomplished, its relatively late date precludes its inclusion in the present discussion.[6] In addition to the four luxury manuscripts, there are also a number of other fourteenth- and fifteenth-century copies of the *Devisement* that contain much more modest pictorial programs, mostly in the form of historiated initials or line drawings.[7]

I have chosen to focus on Bodley 264 and BNF fr. 2810 for three reasons. First, these two manuscripts contain independently conceived pictorial cycles that contrast in style and iconographical content, and are therefore interesting from a comparative point of view (Ménard, 'L'Illustration' 17–31). Second, the fact that they are both deluxe manuscripts written in vernacular French for courtly patrons makes them analytically compatible (Ménard, ed., *Devisement* 1: 40–50). Third, and most importantly, these are the two medieval copies of the book with the most artistically impressive, carefully planned, and extensive pictorial programs, and thus represent the height of contemporary artistic attempts to realize – and, as we shall see, to modify – Marco Polo's vision.

The *Devisement dou monde* is certainly a text that cries out for pictures. Marco and his collaborator, Rustichello of Pisa, were at continual literary pains to create vivid mental images of eastern lands, peoples, fauna, and cultural practices. Because its power derives from the novelty of unseen things, it is perhaps not too far-fetched to hypothesize that if there had been an artist imprisoned in Genoa alongside Marco and Rustichello, the *Devisement* in its original draft would have included drawings or paintings of some kind. This was information too novel to communicate through conventional, written modes of description; what was needed was a way of putting the colours and forms of the marvellous before the very eyes of the audience, something that artists accomplished by modifying existing pictorial models with exceptional creativity and awareness of the interests of their aristocratic viewers.

Unlike other books popular at court, such as bibles, psalters, Books of Hours, or Arthurian romances, most of which include variations on familiar iconographical cycles, the *Devisement* was a new text filled with observations about persons, places, and events unknown in the West. Most significantly, the tenor of most of these observations flew in the face of long-held western beliefs concerning the nature of the East and its inhabitants. These two factors spelled major challenges for artists, who had to find ways of 'translating' into visual form concepts unfamiliar to their western readers in a manner that retained narrative coherence and the high entertainment value that aristocratic patrons had come to expect from their illustrated books.

A few specific examples will demonstrate how the artists of Bodley 264 and BNF fr. 2810 demonstrated extraordinary skill and creativity in meeting these artistic challenges. An image from Bodley 264 accompanies the extended description of the Great Khan's birthday party held annually in his palace in Canbaluc (Khanbaliq, today Beijing; figure 2.1). In their verbal description, Marco and Rustichello were mainly trying to communicate something of the overwhelming splendour of the Khan's court (Latham 135–40). But western courtly readers already knew how a splendid court should look, both from their own experiences and from images in other types of books. This is why the Bodley 264 artist situated the Khan's elaborate celebration in a contemporary western Gothic interior, complete with golden goblets, a golden fountain that dispenses wine, and court musicians positioned in upper towers. The text mentions all of these things specifically, as well as the attendants who kneel before the Great Khan as a show of humility. The Khan and the seated ladies – probably his four wives – all wear golden crowns and sit in Gothic-style chairs. The artist did not depict the jugglers and other entertainers described in the text, or the two huge men with staves who guard the threshold, perhaps because these specifics are not crucial to a presentation of splendour, which in this image is signified primarily by the colour gold, the ultimate sign of sumptuosity in western art and thought.

The image in BNF fr. 2810 of the surrender of the Queen of Mangi to the Khan's baron, Baian Cinqsan, is another good example of the artistic translation of the foreign into the familiar (figure 2.2). Although situated in southern China, this consequence of the siege of the city is

Figure 2.1: The Great Khan's birthday feast, *Li Livres du Graunt Caam*, London, ca. 1400–10. Oxford, Bodl. Lib. MS Bodley 264, fol. 239r. Photo: Bodleian Library, University of Oxford.

Figure 2.2: Surrender of the Queen of Mangi, *Livre des merveilles du monde*, Paris, 1412. Paris, Bibl. Nat. MS fr. 2810, fol. 64r. Photo: Bibliothèque Nationale de France, Paris.

rendered visually in western chivalric terms (Latham 202–3). With its whitewashed exterior, towers, crenellations, and city gate, the castle would not look out of place in another of the Duke of Berry's prized books, the *Belles Heures* (Meiss and Beatson). The crowned queen, elegantly dressed in pink and riding sidesaddle on her dapple-gray, is handing over the silver city keys to Baian, identified by his gold crown. Although not described in the text, handing over keys was the standard ritual following siege in the West (Keen 119–33), and the artist relied on the viewer's familiarity with this practice to understand the meaning of this scene. Such an iconographical addition also ensured that the image was comprehensible even if the viewer did not read the text. This characteristic, observable in this and other images, in combination with the statement in the Prologue ('prennés cestui livre et le feites lire' ['take this book and have it read to you']) and other rhetorical evidence from the text, supports the hypothesis that the book was read aloud to the patron and probably also to others.[8]

A second image from BNF fr. 2810 depicts Kublai Khan's four wives and eldest sons (figure 2.3). Although in many ways a conventional

Figure 2.3: The four wives and eldest sons of Kublai Khan, *Livre des merveilles du monde*, fol. 36r. Photo: Bibliothèque Nationale de France, Paris.

image, it becomes more compelling once the viewer realizes that the four sons represent only a sixth of the total number of offspring the Khan reportedly sired by these four women (Latham 123–4). It remains to explain why, of all the numerous personages mentioned in the *Devisement*, the artist and/or patron elected to include a portrait of the Khan's four anonymous wives and eldest sons. I believe the answer lies in both the importance of lineage in the West, and also in a well-documented prurient western interest in eastern sexuality. It has already been observed that the eastern practices of keeping multiple wives and of making wives available to travelling strangers are given repeated emphasis throughout the *Devisement* (Westrem, 'Medieval Western' 141–56). Especially titillating must have been the discussion that follows this particular image of the Khan's sexual rota of six young women, every three days (Latham 122–3). There is some intriguing manuscript evidence of reader enthusiasm for these customs. In Hunter 458 (fol. 115v), today in the Glasgow University Library, and Garrett 157 (fol. 41v), now at Princeton University, contemporary readers made a visual *nota bene* either in the form of a pointing finger or a note in the margin beside the description of the Khan's women. In his annotations to his Latin edition of 1485, even Christopher Columbus expressed particular interest in the text passages concerning the Tibetan preference for non-virginal wives as well as wife-sharing in Camul, characterizing the latter as 'an admirable way of showing hospitality to strangers.'[9]

An aristocratic audience may have responded to the story of the Khan's women as they did to other popular stories with a sexual dimension. These would have included the tales of lust, adultery, and multiple sexual partners scattered throughout the Old Testament, illustrated versions of which were regularly commissioned by members of the French and English courts, as well as copies of such risqué literature as the *fabliaux* and Boccaccio's *Decameron*. That the four wives are rendered in the BNF fr. 2810 image not with a concern for empirical accuracy but rather according to a western, courtly ideal is highly conducive to vicarious, viewer participation in the Khan's world of women. Accordingly, the figures are elongated and slender, with white skin and demure postures, wearing contemporary French gowns and golden crowns adorned with pearls and coloured gems.

All three of the images examined so far depict subjects familiar to their western readers from their experience not only of courtly life, but of romance imagery. Court-commissioned illuminated manuscripts, panel paintings, tapestries, and precious objects of ivory or metal routinely pictured courtly interiors, castle sieges, and gatherings of dainty women. It therefore appears that the subjects included for illustration in luxury copies of Marco's book were selected for their potential for visual translation into familiar subjects that made eastern personages and experiences tangible and accessible to a western, courtly readership.

Bodley 264 continues this trend with an image of the Garden of Paradise, located in Mulecte (Persia) and administered by the Old Man of the Mountain (figure 2.4). According to the text, the Old Man uses this wonderful garden, populated with beautiful women and other sensual delights, to lure young men into his company of murderous Assassins.[10] But to western viewers, this was an image of the *hortus deliciarum* ['garden of delights'], an aristocratic emblem of luxury, leisure, and courtly love that was depicted often in tapestry, luxury objects, and popular texts such as the *Roman de la Rose* (Fleming 54–103; Huot). The castle setting, private garden, fruit trees, elegant ladies, contemporary costumes, and even musical instruments are all characteristic of a conventional garden of delights; the only way to

Figure 2.4: Old Man of the Mountain, *Li Livres du Graunt Caam*, fol. 226r. Photo: Bodleian Library, University of Oxford.

know that this garden represents something rather different is to read the accompanying text.

We may turn again to Bodley 264 for still another example of an oriental episode transformed into an occidental event. The subject of this image is the battle between Chinggis Khan and Prester John, fought on the plain of Tenduc following Prester John's refusal to hand over his own daughter for marriage to the Khan (figure 2.5). During the ensuing conflict, called 'the greatest battle that was ever seen,' Prester John was slain by the Great Khan himself (Latham 93–6). Close observation reveals that the fallen Prester John is the light-skinned figure in the foreground slumped over his horse, and that the tall, dark-skinned, bearded figure wearing a crown over his helmet and waving a blood-stained scimitar represents Chinggis Khan.

Iconographically and in its pictorial details, this image is similar to numerous battle scenes found in illustrated chronicles and *chansons de gestes* which normally pit western Christians against Muslims, known

Figure 2.5: Battle of Chinggis Khan and Prester John, *Li Livres du Graunt Caam*, fol. 231v. Photo: Bodleian Library, University of Oxford.

pejoratively as 'Saracens.' In the Bodley 264 image, the western-style arms, armour, and standards employed by Prester John's army contrast with the costume and eastern scimitars wielded by the Khan and his men. Most notable is the eccentric white beehive headgear worn by the latter group, an odd cross between a turban and a helmet. The visual distinction between the Mongolian and Christian armies makes sense in the context of the *Devisement* narrative, which reiterates contemporary belief in the legendary Prester John as a powerful Christian leader, albeit still a vassal of the Great Khan (Latham 105–6; Hamilton 177–91). Although clearly an inhabitant of the East, the fact that he is Christian earns for Prester John an essentially western identification, expressed visually through white physiognomy and western armour. Members of the Mongolian army in this image might be viewed in light of the more familiar Christian-Muslim battle imagery as 'functional Saracens.' They are accordingly represented as small, dark, and

inappropriately dressed for battle, just as Saracens are often so rendered in contemporary chronicle and romance illustrations (Lejeune
and Stiennon; Strickland, *Saracens* 179–82).

The resulting visual conflation of Muslims with other 'pagans,' such
as Mongols, is an artistic phenomenon that is in keeping with the
broader medieval Christian tendency to conceive of all non-Christians
as more or less ideologically interchangeable as God's rejected. However, in the case of the *Devisement* illustrations, this visual conflation is
at odds with the accompanying text, in which Marco and Rustichello
normally characterize Mongols positively and Muslims negatively,
and in so doing draw sharp distinctions between them. While the
Devisement was highly unusual in expressing a favourable view of
Mongols, its anti-Muslim stories and remarks are consistent with the
stereotype promoted by many other contemporary writers during the
long period of the crusades.[11]

Marco's desire to portray Kublai Khan as an ideal ruler informs
details of the Khan's appearance and the activities in which he is
involved in both Bodley 264 and BNF fr. 2810. For example, the Great
Khan's love of hunting is translated in both manuscripts into a western
courtly idiom, doubtless because this skill was such an important hallmark of the western monarchy and aristocracy (Cummins). In an
image from BNF fr. 2810, the Khan engages in his weekly hunt in the
private park that surrounds his summer palace in Ciandu (Shangdu),
on the northeast coast of China (figure 2.6). The text indicates that the
hunting reserve is stocked with animals that provide food for the
Khan's falcons (Latham 108), and so he is shown luring one of them.
The image also contains some exotic additions: the Khan wears not
conventional western hunting gear, but a bright red robe and fanciful
eastern headgear as he prepares to ride across the river on his white
horse, not with dogs, but with a trained leopard in tow (Kubiski 172–4).
In its basic outlines, however, to western viewers this was a recognizable scene of a huntsman luring his falcon in a northern European forest setting, with a northern Gothic castle and even a windmill visible in
the distance.

A comparable image in Bodley 264 shows a crowned Khan consulting his hunting party as a huntsman blows a horn before the charging
hounds in a representation of an apparently simultaneous deer, boar,
and bear hunt (figure 2.7). The accompanying text describes the hunt in
great detail, from the hounds to their baronial keepers to the treatment
and distribution of the hides (Latham 141–7). Compositionally, the

Figure 2.6: Kublai Khan hunting in Ciandu, *Livre des merveilles du monde*, fol. 31v. Photo: Bibliothèque Nationale de France, Paris.

Bodley 264 image closely resembles many other western hunting scenes depicted in virtually all artistic media, especially tapestry and manuscript painting, such as that found in fifteenth-century copies of Gaston Phébus's *Livre de chasse*, a hunting manual well known at court (Thomas et al.). The same iconographical elements of aristocratic hunters, huntsmen on foot, hounds, and wild animals bounding into the forest against a decorative gold background may be observed in many such images. The only element that signifies Elsewhere in the Bodley 264 scene is the dark-skinned figure wearing the white turban, partially visible on the far left.

We have observed how the process of translating eastern customs into a western courtly visual parlance not entirely devoid of the exotic was a major creative challenge for artists. A considerably more formidable one was the task of satisfying reader expectations, of resolving the disjunction between contemporary received wisdom about the East and its inhabitants and Marco's radical, revisionist text. Most revolutionary were the implications that the East – even the Far East – was not an entirely craggy wasteland rife with only savage beasts and danger; and that the Mongols, known pejoratively as 'Tartars,' were not the uncivilized, conspiratorial agents of Antichrist dreaded since the

Figure 2.7: Kublai Khan hunting stags, boars, and bears, *Li Livres du Graunt Caam*, fol. 240v. Photo: Bodleian Library, University of Oxford.

mid-thirteenth century. Rather, the image of Mongols that emerges from Marco and Rustichello's report is of highly civilized people with an organized system of government and a powerful and just ruler, an image completely at odds with centuries of western literary and pictorial tradition.

A sumptuously illustrated book of marvels executed in Angers around 1460 for the court of René d'Anjou is one of many that contains images that reinforce the conception of the East that Marco and Rustichello sought to overturn.[12] Throughout this manuscript, the artists have insisted on the long-entrenched view of a mythical, hostile East full of monstrous men and fabulous fauna. One such image represents Scythia, said to include Cathay (northern China), the land of the Great Khan that Marco wrote about with such admiration (figure 2.8). However, unlike in Marco's Cathay, in this place things are not going well at all. On the left, three men flay another man alive in order to use his skin for saddles and pavements. To their immediate right are werewolves in

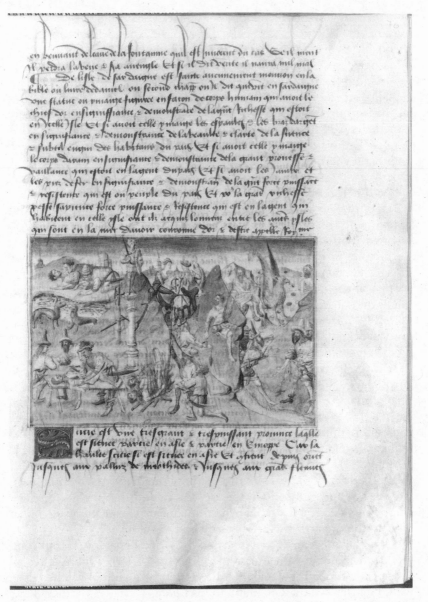

Figure 2.8: Scythia/Cathay, *Livre des merveilles*, Angers, ca. 1460. New York, Pierpont Morgan Library, MS M. 461, fol. 70r. Photo: The Pierpont Morgan Library, New York.

human form worshiping an idol of Mars to which human sacrifices are burning in a holocaust. On the far right, a vampiric group pledge friendship by letting the blood they plan to imbibe. Here and there are fantastic beasts, such as the griffin eyeing the cyclops in the right background and the man-faced manticore squaring off with another quadruped beside the stream in the middle distance. All the while, in the far left background, ferocious Anthropophagi feast on human flesh, and armed, mounted Amazons converse between twin mountains. It is notable that this *Livre des merveilles* was illustrated about fifty years *after* both Bodley 264 and BNF fr. 2810 and for a similar courtly readership. Clearly this was a view of the East that was going to die very hard, and it would take much more than the *Devisement* to finally kill it.[13]

Not only their lands but also the Mongols themselves were the stuff of myth and legend. The traditional, fearful, western view of Mongols inspired the name *Tartars*, because they were believed to have burst forth from *Tartarus*, the infernal regions (Connell 115–37; Bezzola). This belief emerged as a western European reaction to the devastating Mongol invasion of eastern Europe during the early 1240s.[14] In later medieval sources concerned with events to take place at the end of time, the Tartars are identified with Gog and Magog, the ferocious hordes locked up behind gates by Alexander the Great, now guarded by the Queen of the Amazons but scheduled to burst forth during the Last Days to wreak havoc on all of Christendom.[15] Marco himself encouraged this eschatological tradition, perhaps unintentionally. That is, even though the *Devisement* initially dismisses the association between the Tartars and Gog and Magog by claiming that the enclosed peoples are actually a different group, it later indicates that the names 'Gog' and 'Magog' are translations of 'Ung' and 'Mungul (=Mongols?),' provinces inhabited by the Ung and the Tartars, respectively (Latham 106). It is easy to see how this passage could be used later to support rather than dispute the notion that the Tartars *were* Gog and Magog, an idea to which medieval world maps also bear witness (Baumgärtner 248–52), as discussed below.

Cannibalism was without question the worst behavioural trait commonly attributed to non-Christian groups by western writers, and so it became an important element of the western view of the heathen East, including the Tartars (Guzman). In his *Chronica majora*, Matthew Paris provided a contemporary illustration of man-eating Tartars to accompany his sensationalized account of their alleged barbaric customs and war atrocities (figure 2.9).[16] In this image, ugly Tartars eat human flesh,

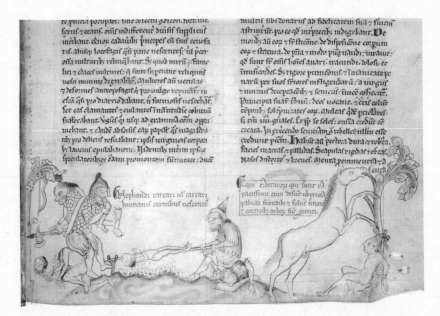

Figure 2.9: Tartar cannibals, Matthew Paris, *Chronica majora*, St. Albans, ca. 1240–53 and later. Cambridge, Corpus Christi College MS 16, fol. 167r. Photo: by permission of the Master and Fellows of Corpus Christi College, Cambridge.

not unlike their monstrous brethren in the *Livre des merveilles* image of Cathay discussed above (figure 2.8). Such cannibalistic images were based on representations of the Anthropophagi, imaginary man-eaters depicted in many contemporary artistic contexts concerned with the monstrous men of the East. By the thirteenth century, Anthropophagi were familiar inclusions on *mappaemundi*, such as the Hereford Map, and were also favourites in illustrated treatises on the Monstrous Races.[17] Informed by this tradition, images of cannibalism were a popular feature of many illustrated travel accounts. For example, in the section of BNF fr. 2810 containing Odoric of Pordenone's travel report (which follows on directly from the *Devisement*), there is a graphic image of man-eaters on the island of Dondin chopping a man to pieces and hastily consuming his flesh at table.[18]

Although Matthew Paris's drawing of man-eating Tartars probably was not widely viewed outside of St Albans where he painted it, it is entirely consistent with contemporary literary descriptions of Tartars that were very well known, such as those of John of Plano Carpini and of Simon of Saint-Quentin.[19] These reports assert that Tartars are small, filthy, and unattractive, with large, slanted eyes, wide faces, and wide and flat noses. They wear odd clothing; their speech is rapid, guttural, and horrible; and their women are extremely ugly. They live in tents rather than in villages or cities, and because they are pastoralists, they have no bread. Instead they eat unspeakable things, such as lice and the afterbirth of mares. Usurious, oversexed, and idolatrous, they had no place in western courtly or mercantile culture.

Or did they? Although the western view of Mongols was a decidedly negative one based on a combination of myth and polemical accounts, it could be argued that Italians might have been better informed, as Italian merchants maintained regular contact with them in the course of business transactions. Moreover, there were many Asiatic immigrants in Italy during Marco's time who were sold in slave markets in key cities, including Venice, for distribution to the rest of Italy (Olschki, 'Asiatic Exoticism'; Origo). Marco himself kept one such slave, known as Peter the Tartar, whose freedom after Marco's death was a condition of his master's will (Moule and Pelliot 1: 539). However, it is unlikely that fifteenth-century French and English aristocratic patrons drew any meaningful connection between Mongolian slaves in Italy and the dreaded Tartars of lore. As was the case with most ethnic and religious outsiders, such as Black Africans, Jews, and Muslims, there were at least two different types of medieval Mongols: one informed by reality, and the other by the Christian imagination.

To late medieval courtly readers, Tartars were a de facto Monstrous Race, ideologically comparable to Anthropophagi, Panotii (huge-eared people), and Cynocephali (Dogheads). Literary as well as pictorial evidence supports this view. Both Monstrous Races and Tartars functioned symbolically in didactic western Christian literature. In moralizing bestiaries and *exempla*, Monstrous Races were held up as either positive or negative examples of Christian behaviour. For example, the Panotii were said to use their large ears to hear evil, or else to hear the word of God, depending on the particular slant the preacher needed for his sermon. Pygmies were compared to the humble, Giants to the proud, and Cynocephali to nay-sayers.[20]

The imaginary Tartars sometimes figured into Christian sermons, where they, too, provided either positive or negative examples for Christian edification. In the mid-thirteenth century, Berthold of Regensburg preached that even the polygamous, pagan Tartars still punish each other severely for adultery, while Christian adultery runs rampant and goes unpunished. On a still darker note, as a means of dissuading Christian idolatry, Berthold in another sermon mocks Tartar idolatry and its obvious futility. If the idol itself can burn in the fire, Berthold says, how could it possibly save anyone's soul from *eternal* fire (Ruotsala 443)? Tartar idolatry is, therefore, another of the continuing themes in the *Devisement* and so it is the frequent subject of illustration in both BNF fr. 2810 and Bodley 264. In BNF fr. 2810, one image of idol-worship puts a familiar, visual spin on the text description of the annual White Feast, said to take place every February (figure 2.10). According to the text, the Great Khan dresses himself in gold and twelve thousand of his Tartar subjects in white because white is considered an auspicious colour with which to begin the new year. All rulers and lords then assemble to offer costly gifts to the Khan and to worship him as a god (Latham 138–9). This act has been translated by the artist into a more conventional form of idolatry involving the veneration of a golden image, even though this contradicts the text description. However, the Great Khan's golden robe connects him visually with the golden idol, thereby implying that his subjects' reverence for his royal person is tantamount to idolatry. Again, artists had in mind a ready model for such a scene: men in exotic headgear kneeling before a golden idol is iconographically similar to pejorative images of Jews and other 'pagans' worshipping idols, such as the Golden Calf, found in many types of medieval books, from bibles to bestiaries (Camille 165–75). Like cannibalism, idolatry was a definitive sign of the non-Christian, and was therefore assumed common practice among Jews, Saracens, Tartars, and any other 'pagan' group. This explains why the artist in BNF fr. 2810 ignored the details of the text in order to render a recognizable scene of idol-worship to accompany the description of the White Feast. It also explains the repeated scenes of idol-worship in both this manuscript and in Bodley 264, which between them illustrate this practice no fewer than eight times in their respective *Devisement* sections.[21]

In Marco Polo's account, the practice of idolatry is sometimes linked with that of cannibalism. For example, the text states that the inhabitants of Ferlec on the island of Lesser Java (Sumatra) practise cannibalism (Latham 252–3), as pictured in BNF fr. 2810 at the head of the relevant chapter (figure 2.11). In this image, the cannibals are provided with a degree of acceptability through relatively good dress, perhaps because man-eating in the text is interpreted not as a savage crime but as an unusual custom, part of the islanders' proclivity for eating just

Figure 2.10: Idol-worship during the White Feast, *Livre des merveilles du monde*, fol. 40r. Photo: Bibliothèque Nationale de France, Paris.

about anything. That they tend to worship whatever they see first in the morning is indicated by the figures kneeling in reverence before the dog and the horse. Such an association between idolatry and cannibalism recalls the medieval Christian conception of idolatry as a vital link in a progressively worsening chain of sin. For example, in the thirteenth-century *Bibles moralisées* executed for Louis IX, this concept takes visual form in a carefully co-ordinated pictorial sequence that links idolatry to both usury and the worship of Antichrist (Lipton 31–53). In the secular context of the *Devisement*, the link between idolatry and cannibalism as conceived by artists or patrons identifies the islanders as both non-Christian and non-civilized, or as both pagan and barbaric, thus maintaining the wide cultural gap between Us and Them.

A final comparison between Tartars and Monstrous Races may be drawn on the basis of physical location. Geographically speaking, they were neighbours. That is, according to medieval belief, both monsters and Tartars inhabited the periphery of the known universe, where only a few had ever experienced them directly. In the case of Monstrous Races, this belief is clearly expressed on world maps on which they are located along the eastern and southern peripheries, as observable on

Figure 2.11: Inhabitants of Lesser Java (Sumatra), *Livre des merveilles du monde*, fol. 74v. Photo: Bibliothèque Nationale de France, Paris.

the thirteenth-century Ebstorf, Hereford, and London Psalter maps (Harvey, *Medieval Maps* 18–37; von den Brincken, *Fines Terrae* 77–96). As a result of their conflation with Gog and Magog, Tartars – including the Great Khan – also featured on *mappaemundi*, usually in the far northern reaches of Asia.[22] The legends that accompany these figures on the maps make clear the conflation between the Alexander legends, Tartars, Anthropophagi, and the unclean biblical hordes, a phenomenon fuelled especially during the thirteenth century by western fears of Mongol conquest. An especially good example of this conflation may be observed on the Catalan world atlas of c. 1375 produced by a Majorcan Jewish cartographer, Abraham Cresques, for Charles V of France.[23] One of the legends in the section that represents Cathay proclaims that Alexander, with the aid of Satan, enclosed the Tartars – identified as Gog and Magog – in the Caspian Mountains along with other nations who eat raw flesh and with whom Antichrist will emerge. To the left of this legend is an image of a crowned Alexander pointing to a dark, winged demon (Freiesleben 32 and pl. 6). Just above this is a portrait of the Great Khan himself, rendered as a crowned, white-skinned, and bearded figure holding a sceptre enthroned beside the city of Cambelech (Beijing). The legend positioned above this figure is a laudatory one based on a description in the *Devisement* that emphasizes the Great Khan's power and authority.[24] That the Khan, 'the mightiest prince of all the Tartars,' enjoys a flattering rendering and description on the same map that identifies the Tartars with Gog and Magog is testimony to an important transitional phase in cartography, during which older, conventional ideas were juxtaposed with empirical information derived from a small number of contemporary travel accounts, including Marco's.[25]

On the whole, however, traditional views of the Tartars prevailed. Because they were thought to be of similar nature and behaviour, dwelling together in the far reaches of the exotic East, it is no wonder that courtly patrons expected to find both Tartars and Monstrous Races in their illustrated copies of the *Devisement*, and that the artists responsible for Bodley 264 and BNF fr. 2810 met these expectations. Even though no such fabulous beings were recorded by Rustichello – presumably because Marco Polo neither witnessed nor described them – canonical Monstrous Races find their place among pictorial representations of eastern lands. While such imagery may appear to be a wilful disregard for the text, it was perhaps not quite as independently conceived by artists as previous assessments of it have implied (Wittkower, 'Marco Polo' 77–9, 81–4; Larner 110–11). This is because Marco and Rustichello do not altogether dispense with the traditional monsters and marvels: they simply rationalize them. Hence, unicorns become rhinos, man-eating by some groups is explained as a religious practice, griffins are identified as large and aggressive birds of prey, and Pygmies become monkeys dressed up to resemble men. But the fact that unicorns, cannibals, griffins, and Pygmies are included at all indicates that the authors as well as the artists recognized that patrons would expect to read about those marvellous things that everyone knew inhabited the exotic East.

This is why monsters and marvels in luxury copies of the *Devisement* are illustrated in traditional ways rather than the new, rationalized ones. Unicorns look like unicorns, not rhinos; and griffins look like griffins, not eagles. Familiar, fabulous inhabitants of India appear in Bodley 264, and Monstrous Races also turn up in the wild region of Bargu (on the Russian/Mongolian border) in BNF fr. 2810 (Friedman 154–8; Tesnière et al. 194n87) (figures 2.12, 2.13). Iconographically and compositionally, either of these images would be at home in a traditional *livre des merveilles*. The Bodley artist has situated his monsters on

Figure 2.12: Monstrous Races in India, *Li Livres du Graunt Caam*, fol. 260r. Photo: Bodleian Library, University of Oxford.

what appear to be three small islands, and has emphasized their aggressive qualities by arming the headless Blemmyae and the one-legged Sciopod with clubs, and the Cyclops and Doghead with spears (figure 2.12). Three of the four also carry shields. In addition, all are covered with hair which identifies them with Wild Folk – savage, sylvan types familiar to courtly readers from medieval romance.[26] In BNF fr. 2810, a Blemmyae, Sciopod, and twin-bearded Cyclops are distributed evenly across the foreground of a rocky and semi-forested background (figure 2.13). All three are rendered nude; the Cyclops alone is armed with a club and shield. The text describes their habitat, Bargu, as a deserted plain, but the artist has provided the traditional craggy, even mountainous, landscape that so commonly serves to situate Monstrous Races in other contemporary pictorial contexts.

However, both of these images of Monstrous Races are at odds with their accompanying texts. It has been long observed that the most

Figure 2.13: Monstrous Races in Bargu, *Livre des merveilles du monde*, fol. 29r.
Photo: Bibliothèque Nationale de France, Paris.

monstrous people in the *Devisement* are the inhabitants of the Angaman (Andaman) islands in the Bay of Bengal, said to have heads, eyes,
and teeth like dogs (Latham 258). This may be interpreted as a pejorative description that conveys conventional western notions of ugli-
ness, because by this time, both literary and pictorial referrals to
outside groups as 'dogs' as a form of moral condemnation were well-
established, cross-cultural practices (White). Based on anticipated
reader response to this description, however, the BNF fr. 2810 artist
has transformed the inhabitants of Angaman into the familiar Monstrous Race of Cynocephali (figure 2.14). Curiously, the artist has
attempted to 'civilize' these monstrous types in contradiction to both
the text description of the Angaman islanders and the traditional conception of Cynocephali, both of which emphasize Doghead bestiality
and cruelty (Lecouteux). But here, genteel Dogheads outfitted fashion-
ably in colourful robes and boots converse politely, gesturing with
human hands. The city outside of which they are conducting their
mercantile transaction visible in the far distance is rendered, as in
other images, in northern Gothic architectural style.

Figure 2.14: Dogheads in Angaman, *Livre des merveilles du monde*, fol. 76v. Photo: Bibliothèque Nationale de France, Paris.

Bodley 264 includes still another representation of Monstrous Races, this time located on the islands of India (figure 2.15). Three giant, hirsute, horned men are involved in an incident described in the accompanying text, which states that the Indian islanders dine on their captives in lieu of ransom payments demanded of the victims' families (Latham 247–8). Accordingly, the figure on the left is devouring the limbs of a cadaver from an open sepulchre, while the single-horned, hoofed one in the foreground has just taken down a stag. The third figure stands holding a shield and spear, guarding the pink castle populated with three more armoured knights waiting to be ransomed.

Pictorial details in all four of these images reveal that location plays an important role in viewer perception of monsters (figures 2.12, 2.13, 2.14, 2.15). As already noted, the inhabitants of Angaman are clearly situated outside of the city, visible in the far background, a visual clue that this is an outside, alien group (figure 2.14). In Bodley 264, the monsters in both images are situated in forest settings (figures 2.12, 2.15), while in BNF fr. 2810, the wild inhabitants of Bargu amble across a craggy plain (figure 2.13). The forest location may function in these images as it does in medieval romance, as a place symbolic of various

Figure 2.15: Monstrous men of India islands, *Li Livres du Graunt Caam*, fol. 262r. Photo: Bodleian Library, University of Oxford.

themes ranging from adventure to misfortune (C. Saunders 132–3). Besides forests, islands, deserts, swamps, mountains, and caves were other typically monstrous locations featured in treatises on Monstrous Races. Ominous location is given particular emphasis in the Anglo-Saxon *Liber monstrorum* (*Book of Monsters*) and in the illustrations of the eleventh- and twelfth-century manuscript copies of the *Marvels of the East* (James, *Marvels*; Orchard 175–203). The objective was to position the monsters as far away as possible from civilization; in particular, well outside of the city, the natural home of the civilized.

The concept of the city as the locus of civilization was one of a series of medieval ideas inherited from antiquity that sought to separate the civilized from the barbaric, or Us from Them.[27] In the ancient Greek world, all Greeks were assumed civilized and all non-Greeks barbarians. Therefore, civilized people wore stylish clothes, ate a Mediterranean diet, spoke Greek, drank wine, ate cooked food, and, most importantly, lived in cities. During the Middle Ages, the idea of the city as the physical locus of civilization continued to hold sway during the long period of urban growth and development in western Europe. This is why so many depictions of Monstrous Races show them as naked and cannibalistic, but also locate them with the city clearly visible in the background, thus emphasizing their barbaric, outsider status.

The architectural city was also a powerful, pictorial symbol in religious books patronized by the court, including illuminated Apoc-alypse manuscripts. In these manuscripts, very ubiquitous are repre-sentations of the New Jerusalem, often depicted as either a Gothic cathedral or as an elaborate and colourful, highly ornamented com-plex of northern Gothic buildings (Stookey; Frugoni 19–28). To ren-der the New Jerusalem in contemporary, impressive architectural terms was an effective means of conveying not only the future splen-dour of the New Age as described in Scriptures, but also the fact that the Last Days were at hand. Other religious symbols that lent them-selves well to architectural form in books patronized by the court include the biblical Babylon, the Tower of Babel, and St Augustine's *City of God*. In a secular context, Christine de Pizan's *Cité des dames* (*City of Ladies*) inspired urban imagery in illuminated manuscripts that were especially popular at court (Dufresne). The Duke of Berry, for example, counted among his illuminated manuscripts three cop-ies of the *Cité des dames*, six copies of the *City of God*, and two Apoca-lypses (Meiss, *Late Fourteenth Century* 1: 312–15). In general, the city functioned as an especially relevant pictorial symbol in both sacred and secular pictorial contexts during a period in western Europe of unprecedented urban growth and development.

That Marco Polo and Rustichello of Pisa fully grasped the ideologi-cal significance of the city helps to explain why so much of the *Devise-ment* is organized around detailed descriptions of the urban Orient. It is also true that during the thirteenth century, urban description as a distinct literary genre had reached its apogee, especially in Italy, and to some extent, the city descriptions in the *Devisement* follow a famil-iar rhetorical format (Hyde, 'Medieval Descriptions'). The authors' emphasis on the beauty and sophistication of eastern cities was there-fore an effective way of convincing readers of the high level of civili-zation in this previously unknown part of the world. On the other hand, bearing in mind his readership's preconceived, negative ideas about the nature of the Tartars and their lands, Johannes's famous image of Venice in Bodley 264 might be interpreted as a sign that the

Polos are *leaving* civilization in order to journey to lands impossibly far outside any known, civilized boundaries (figure 2.16). The idea of departure is clearly the image's subject, as the Polos are pictured at three different stages of their leave-taking: approaching the canal near the centre of the scene, stepping out of a dinghy docked across the canal on the lower right, and finally sailing eastward in the flotilla disappearing to the far right (Scott 2: 70–1). In fact, the Polos departing from a western city is the subject of miniatures in all four of the extensively illustrated copies of the *Devisement*, which suggests the importance placed on the notion of departing civilization for unknown, distant lands.[28]

Bodley 264 contains several images of eastern cities in which it is again possible to observe artistic interpretation and modification of oriental exoticism for an occidental audience. One of these represents Quinsai (Hangzhou), capital of Mangi, described in the text as the 'city of heaven,' and 'the finest and most splendid city in the world' (Latham 213–29) (figure 2.17). It is said to be surrounded by water with twelve thousand bridges with wide and spacious streets, watercourses, and large market-places. Quinsai is given unusually extensive treatment in a lengthy text section that describes its magnificent palaces, municipal buildings, artisan and luxury shops, bath-houses, and parks; as well as the Quinsanians, who work as magistrates, doctors, astrologers, businessmen, and prostitutes (Moule).

Given the artistic tendency to translate exotica into the familiar, it is not surprising that many of the architectural features in the Bodley 264 image of Quinsai are recognizably western, such as the crenellated city walls, the towered gatehouse, the pitched red tile roofs, chimneys, and the projecting garderobes (latrines) (figure 2.17). However, the round form of the central building, presumably a place of worship, is a visual device by which the artist has evoked the East, as it is reminiscent of other round buildings in the West modelled on eastern architecture, such as copies of the Holy Sepulchre. On the whole, this is a quite modest rendering in spite of the passionate text proclamation that this is the finest city in the world. This was perhaps a deliberate attempt by the artist or patron to ensure that viewers realized that Quinsai, however grand, could never approach the greatness of Venice (figure 2.16). Alternatively, the artist may have felt unable to represent the full extent of the splendour described in the text and so found more emblematic ways of doing so. For example, the single, very prominent bridge may stand for all twelve thousand of them.

Figure 2.16: Venice, *Li Livres du Graunt Caam*, fol. 218r. Photo: Bodleian Library, University of Oxford.

It is significant that the artist has chosen to emphasize the only two negative aspects of Quinsai recorded in the text. The first is that the people of Quinsai are idolaters, made plain visually by the prominent golden idol positioned on an altar at the centre of the image. Second, Quinsanians are said to eat all sorts of flesh, including that of animals 'which Christians would not touch for anything in the world,' such as dogs (Latham 220); hence the dog's head visible just at the foot of the idol. The dog may also function independently from the text as a general pejorative sign, as noted above. One final reminder that Quinsai, however urban and splendid, is still emphatically Elsewhere is the presence of the ubiquitous stereotypical Tartars wearing the white turbans.

Figure 2.17: Quinsai, *Li Livres du Graunt Caam*, fol. 257r. Photo: Bodleian Library, University of Oxford.

It is important to recognize that dark-skinned, stereotyped renderings were not used indiscriminately for all Tartar figures in either Bodley 264 or BNF fr. 2810. In particular, such renderings were usually avoided in representations of either of the Khans or of high-ranking members of their courts. There are two important reasons for this. First, in order to remain consistently within a western pictorial idiom, it was necessary to represent the Khan in sumptuous dress with recognizable accoutrements of office; mainly a throne and golden crown, as faithfully rendered in the image of the coronation of Chinggis Khan from BNF fr. 2810 (figure 2.18). For this purpose, a majestically elongated, tall figure is a more appropriate vehicle for splendid costume and attributes.

The Khan's white European as opposed to dark-skinned physiognomy featured in this image suggests a second and more culturally important reason for contrasting portrayals of the Khan and his subjects. By this time in western art and literature, there was a long tradition in place that sought to differentiate by physical appearance socially

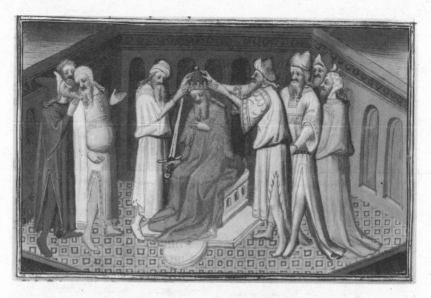

Figure 2.18: Coronation of Chinggis Khan, *Livre des merveilles du monde*, fol. 25v. Photo: Bibliothèque Nationale de France, Paris.

important or divine personages from others (Mellinkoff 1: 119–44; Hassig). This differentiation is especially marked in Bodley 264 in the image of Kublai Khan condemning to death his uncle, the traitor, Naian (figure 2.19). Naian is shown twice, first kneeling before the Khan on the left while awaiting judgment, and again as a small, dark, nearly nude figure hanging from the scaffold near the centre. His hanging contradicts the text, which reports that Naian was executed by being violently dragged while wrapped tightly in a carpet so that the blood of the imperial lineage might not be spilled upon the earth (Latham 118). But in this image, the artist substituted hanging for dragging because the former was the typical contemporary punishment for treason in the West, a substitution that may be compared to the western interpretation of the surrender of Mangi discussed above (figure 2.2). The choice of hanging as Naian's punishment is at the same time not totally unrelated to the text, in that the contemporary western punishment of hanging was normally preceded by dragging (drawing) the condemned through the streets, albeit for different reasons (Bellamy 18 and passim).

What is especially significant in this image is the fact that Naian is rendered as physiognomically distinct from the Great Khan, even

Figure 2.19: Condemnation and execution of Naian, *Li Livres du Graunt Caam*, fol. 236v. Photo: Bodleian Library, University of Oxford.

though the two men were understood to be related by blood. In this and other images, concern for expressing the Khan's supreme rank outweighs any biological relationship, and so he is rendered white-skinned as opposed to dark, and tall as opposed to short; in relation not only to Naian but to the Khan's own officers. The portrait of Chinggis Khan in the image of the battle with Prester John discussed above appears at first to contradict this visual code (figure 2.5). However, although the Khan is dark-skinned, he is equal in size and costume with Prester John, and thus ranks symbolically higher than members of his small, dark-skinned, turbaned army, yet below the legendary Christian leader. In this case, the image carries pejorative force because it is the 'pagans' who are dark and the Christians who are white. This cannot be explained by empirical observation of different skin colour, because the Christian portrayed is in the first place imaginary, and in the second a native of the same land as the Great Khan.

An image in BNF fr. 2810 reveals an even more striking physiognomical contrast, this time between the small, dark pepper harvesters of

Coilun (Quilon, in India) and the tall, white European merchant shown tasting the quality of a pepper berry (Latham 287; figure 2.20). This is a type of visual ethnocentrism, an example not just of contrasting physiognomies but of hierarchical scaling, whereby the personage representing the group thought to be the most important and valuable is the physically largest (Bunim 7–8). The BNF fr. 2810 image of the Indian pepper harvesters was also informed by medieval climatic theory, in particular, the belief inherited from antiquity that great heat has an enervating effect, causes the skin to darken, and the hair to dry and frizzle (Tooley 73–5). The effects of the environment on physical form and moral character are detailed in other medieval travel accounts, encyclopedias, and literary works; and reveal the general consensus that inhabitants of the West are superior in both realms (Akbari, 'Due East'; Strickland, *Saracens* 29–39). In the *Devisement's* description of Coilun, the authors comment on the blackness and scanty dress of the inhabitants, and also attribute the non-western characteristics of the flora, fauna, and fruit to the extreme heat (Latham 288). Earlier in the narrative, they also record the presence in India of physiognomists (Latham 267). Most importantly, the image of the Coilun pepper-harvesters met courtly reader expectations of the physical appearance of the inhabitants of India in a manner which, through reference to physiognomical theory, emphasizes the subordination of Indians to western Europeans.

The *Devisement* text-image relationships examined above show how both authors and artists provided an account of eastern culture for consumption by a western audience, but they also highlight ways by which the images consistently diminish the narrative's 'scientific' or ethnographic value (Hyde, 'Ethnographers'). I suggest that Marco and Rustichello organized their account around descriptions of cities not only because this is an obvious mercantile interest, but also because it is a traditional way of expressing the concept of advanced civilization. Marco's admiration for the Mongol empire was after all immense, and he must have hoped that his report of sophisticated urban development would help to overturn the deeply ingrained, traditional medieval view of a barbaric East peopled with unorganized, uncivilized savages.

Artists participated fully in the goal of marketing the East to the West, but not in the same ways that Marco and Rustichello did. While the authors were interested in creating an image of the East favourable enough to be respected in the West, artists working out of commercial

Figure 2.20: Pepper harvest in Coilun, *Livre des merveilles du monde*, fol. 84r. Photo: Bibliothèque Nationale de France, Paris.

workshops were concerned primarily with satisfying patron demand (Doyle; Rouse and Rouse). Toward this end, they rendered eastern architecture, battles, celebrations, customs, personages, flora, and fauna in a familiar, western pictorial idiom. Moreover, in order to feed the seemingly insatiable courtly appetite for the marvellous, they supplied imagery of the imaginary exotic that transcends textual boundaries. While it has been well noted that images of Monstrous Races constitute one such attempt to meet patron demand, these extraneous monsters fulfilled still another function, which was to push the *Devisement* into a conceptual niche between fiction and empiricism, in which images supply the 'truth value' seemingly missing in Marco's text. Indeed, the restoration of monsters and other 'facts' about the East has been held up as one of the principal reasons why the Mandeville author's later report was more popular than Marco's.[29]

But perhaps another reason why conventional marvels continued to be perpetuated in travel literature was because contemporary readers wanted assurance that they still existed. If viewed from this perspective, images of Monstrous Races and other fabulous creatures in the *Devisement* were 'evidence' that the new East-West diplomatic relations made witnessing these marvels possible once again, just as they had been experienced long ago by ancient travelers such as Alexander the Great (Cary). The great irony was that by the time both Bodley 264 and BNF fr. 2810 were produced, these diplomatic ties had essentially shut down, and travel from West to East along the customary trade and missionary routes was both dangerous and illegal (Richard, 'Les Navigations'). Of course, owners of luxury copies of the *Devisement* would have been fully aware of this situation, but awareness would not necessarily have precluded an intense desire for its resolution, a desire that may have been satisfied vicariously through perusal of the *Devisement* imagery.

With this we may return to the problem of function posed at the beginning of this essay. There is much to recommend a reading of the *Devisement* not only as a book of marvels, but as chivalric romance, given that it was actually written down by a romance writer and exhibits many literary characteristics of this genre (Goodman 83–103; Larner 132). While discussions to date do not marshal pictorial evidence in support of this thesis, we have seen that the pictures do support it, emphasizing as they do a number of romance themes, such as royal splendour, the garden paradise, lovely ladies, and heroic battles. Reasons for the selection of these particular subjects include the very pragmatic one that the same artists responsible for illustrating the *Devisement* were also illustrators of romance, and this was the visual idiom in which they already worked. Such imagery appealed to the tastes of royal and aristocratic patrons who were adamant consumers of vernacular romances and other works of art that depicted similar themes (Alexander, 'Painting' 156–62). Again, we may take the Duke of Berry as a representative of these interests, whose surviving inventories list a number of romances, including copies of Lancelot and the *Roman de la Rose* (Meiss, *Late Fourteenth Century* 1: 312–15). That the *Devisement* was bound in with romances, such as the Alexander stories, in Bodley 264 and other manuscript anthologies, alone suggests a strong conceptual link between the two genres.

Before interpreting the *Devisement* as romance, however, the hypothesis that it functioned as pro-crusading propaganda should also be considered. This view is supported by the fact that certain manuscript anthologies group together the *Devisement* with other texts that express this interest, and that crusading was an ongoing concern of their French and English courtly patrons (Ross 63–5; Porter 91–157). Justification for crusade is one of the functions assigned to medieval travel literature as a genre because so much of it presents an image of a heathen East ripe for Christian conquest and the introduction of the True Faith, one of the ostensible crusader goals (Porter 86–90; Ciccuto 5–6, 34). It is also true that crusading themes are not incompatible with romance, as demonstrated in the *chansons de geste* as well as in other romance genres that emphasize the Christian conquest of the 'infidel.' In other words, romance may function as pro-crusading propaganda to which both texts and images may contribute. In the illustrated *Devisement* manuscripts, battle images modelled iconographically on Christian-Saracen conflicts may be read as references to the ongoing struggle against the Ottoman Turks, in which the Burgundian French nobility in particular were active organizers and financiers (Housely 80–117).

At this point, it is necessary to distinguish between form and function: a romance can *function* as a souvenir, or a call to crusade, or as courtly entertainment, or as all three at once. So rather than try to pigeonhole the *Devisement* into a single genre, it is perhaps better to recognize that it had different functions for different audiences: for Pipino of Bologna, as a missionary guide; for Columbus, as a geographical guide to natural resources; for Marco Polo himself, as a souvenir of his extraordinary experiences (Larner 85). For late medieval courtly readers whose manuscripts contained an essential visual gloss, I suggest the *Devisement* functioned as a multivalent, marvellous romance that provided a vicarious experience of the exotic East otherwise inaccessible to the western world.

Finally, the evidence assembled here demonstrates that *Devisement* images were by no means dictated by or merely reflective of the text they accompanied. Rather, text and images are interrelated translations of an utterly alien world in which the whole is greater than the sum of the parts: neither on their own could communicate the foreign couched in the familiar as effectively as they could together. Unillustrated copies of Marco Polo's *Devisement dou monde* were therefore severely impoverished, and so were their medieval readers.

NOTES

1 Following the completion of this preliminary study, I published a more extended analysis of text-image relationships in the same manuscripts examined here, but with a rather different focus. Whereas in the present article I am concerned with the processes of artistic 'translation' of the text

and its functions for courtly readers, in the subsequent study I focus more closely on the ways in which artists actively undermined authorial projects, as well as how both artists and authors participated in the creation of reader 'wonder.' See Debra Higgs Strickland, 'Artists, Audience, and Ambivalence.'

2 De Clercq; Harris 183; Pächt.
3 Wittkower, 'Marco Polo'; Lawton 47–50; Ménard, 'Réflexions' 80–92.
4 Meiss, *Boucicaut Master* 34–46, 116–22; Ciccuto 20–1; Avril 204–15.
5 Warner and Gilson 2: 339–41; Ross 63–75; Dutschke 'Truth.'
6 Martin 163; Benedetto, xliii–xliv; Ménard, ed., *Devisement* 1: 48.
7 For examples, see Ménard, ed., *Devisement* 1: 40–1, 43; Young and Aiken 378–9; and Thorp 101–2.
8 Crosby 95–8, 102–7; Joyce Coleman 109–47; Saenger 265–72.
9 Latham 172–3, 88; Giovannini 103n1; 183n2; Heers, 'De Marco Polo' 138–42.
10 Latham 70–3; Nowell 475–89; B. Lewis.
11 Olschki, *Marco Polo's Asia* 232–52; Larner 103–4; Tolan; Strickland, *Saracens* 157–92.
12 Friedman 159–62; Plummer 32–3; Beaugendre 81–2.
13 Elliott 28–53; Bucher 75–91; Mason; Pochat 113–46.
14 Stakosch-Grassman; J. Saunders, *History*; Morgan, 'Mongols'; Jackson.
15 Von den Brincken, 'Gog und Magog' 27–9; Burnett and Dalché; Gow 74–88; DiMarco.
16 S. Lewis; J. Saunders, 'Matthew Paris'; Bezzola 63–5.
17 Friedman (passim); Tattersall; Westrem, *Hereford Map* 100–1.
18 BNF fr. 2810, fol. 107r; Omont, pl. 94; Yule 2: 173–6.
19 Menesto; Richard, *Simon de Saint-Quentin*; Spuler.
20 Oesterley 575; Hilka 36, 53; Friedman 124.
21 BNF fr. 2810, fols. 22v, 40r, 74v; Bodley 264, fols. 232r, 235r, 252v, 257r, 262v.
22 Von den Brincken, 'Gog und Magog' 27–9; Gow 75–88; Westrem, 'Against Gog and Magog' 61–2; 66–7.
23 Freiesleben; Baumgärtner 239–44; Gow 75–7.
24 Freiesleben 33; Baumgärtner 242–43 and fig. 4; Latham 135.
25 Cordier; Baumgärtner 252–3.
26 Bernheimer; Husband; Sprunger.
27 Jones; Bartlett, *Gerald* 158–77; Hall; John Coleman.
28 Other initial departure scenes depict Niccolò and Maffeo Polo leaving Constantinople for Sudak (Royal 19 D.I, fol. 58r; BNF fr. 2810, fol. 1; and Bibl. Arsenal 5219, fol. 9r).
29 Campbell, *Witness* 153–8; Phillips 205–11; Gosman 77; Larner 106.

3 Marco Polo's *Le Devisement dou monde* and the Tributary East

SHARON KINOSHITA

The Old French version of Marco Polo's *Le Devisement dou monde* is best known in magnificent manuscript versions from the turn of the fifteenth century, the same milieu that produced the *Très Riches Heures* of that great royal bibliophile, Jean, duc de Berry. The most famous of these is the so-called *Livre des Merveilles du Monde* (BNF fr. 2810), commissioned in 1412 as a gift for Jean by his nephew John, duke of Burgundy (Polo, *Livre des Merveilles*). In consequence, the *Devisement* is typically considered in its late medieval context – its manuscripts analysed alongside lavish volumes like the *Très Riches Heures* and its text alongside wonder tales like Mandeville's *Travels*. This essay returns the *Devisement* to its thirteenth-century context, reconsidering it not among those texts and trends it anticipates but among those it draws on and transforms. Since its emergence as a literary language in the mid-twelfth century, Old French had become the vehicle for (among other things) the representation of Latin Europe's contact with the cultures of the Mediterranean and west Asia. From its inception, vernacular French constituted an alternative to Latinate traditions of the representations of the other. In the twelfth and thirteenth centuries, *chansons de geste*, for all their violence, displayed toward the Saracen 'other' a variety of attitudes ranging from brutal intransigence (as in Roland's famous war-cry, 'Pagans are wrong and Christians are right!') through fascination, desire, accommodationism, and outright co-operation (Kinoshita, *Medieval Boundaries*). In the thirteenth century, the eruption of Mongol power in the East vastly extended the scope of the European imaginary: tales of the Mongol conquest of the Russian steppes and of Baghdad became inextricably linked with legends of Prester John and tapped into the Plinian tradition of the 'monstrous races,' derived from Greek antiquity and transmitted to the medieval West through encyclopedic compilations like those of Isidore of Seville. In contrast, my thought experiment locates the *Devisement* in a vernacular tradition elaborated by and for a francophone nobility actively engaged in conquest and expansion, and, increasingly, for a Mediterranean commercial élite for whom the true 'marvels of the East' were less the monstrous races traditionally taken to populate farthest Asia than the great tributary empires controlling fabulous emporia like those of Baghdad, Samarcand, and Khanbaliq. This essay, then, approaches the *Devisement* not in its fifteenth-century textualization as a 'Livre des merveilles' but – as its earliest manuscripts proclaim it to be – 'le livre du Grand Khan' (Ménard, ed. *Devisement* 1: 96).[1]

I

When *Le Devisement dou monde* was composed c. 1298 through Marco's jail-cell collaboration with romance writer Rustichello da Pisa, its language of composition was neither Tuscan nor Venetian but Old French. However puzzling this may seem from a modern perspective, in contemporary terms it was a perfectly logical choice: having emerged as a written vernacular in the mid-twelfth century, by the second half of the thirteenth Old French was 'at once a national and a supranational language' of 'prestige and dominance' (Brownlee 266). Dante's elder contemporary Brunetto Latini, for example, famously composed his *Livres dou Tresor* in French 'por çou que la parleure est plus delitable et plus commune a tous langages' ['because that language is more delightful and more widespread than all others'] (Brownlee 266; see also Larner 56);[2] between 1267 and 1275, Marco Polo's countryman and contemporary Martin da Canal likewise composed *Les Estoires de Venise* in French 'porce que lengue franceise cort parmi le monde et est la plus delitable a lire et a oïr que nule autre' ['because the French language goes throughout the world and is more delightful to read and to hear than any other'] (2, I.5). Beyond the rarefied world of northern Italian letters, Old French was the *lingua franca* of Latin Europe's expansion into the Mediterranean, carried by an 'aristocratic diaspora' (Bartlett 24–59) to the crusader states of Outremer,[3] Norman Sicily, Lusignan Cyprus, and Frankish Morea.

By the late thirteenth century, literary activity in vernacular French included allegories and dream visions, like the two parts of the *Roman de la Rose*; the 'realist' literature associated with the bourgeois milieux of northeastern France; prose historiography, like the *Grandes chroniques de France;* and the great Arthurian prose cycles like the *Lancelot-Graal* and the *Tristan en prose,* to which Rustichello da Pisa's one surviving romance text, *Méliadus,* is related (Kay 57–68). To varying degrees, these texts participated in the totalizing and often moralizing impulse of the time – an age of encyclopedias and summas, in contrast to the more free-wheeling and fragmented literary production of the previous century (Zink 81).[4] On the one hand, the *Devisement* clearly partakes of the spirit of its age: its densely textured mapping of the known world and beyond manifests the same will toward totalization evident in the *Prose Lancelot* or Jean de Meun's continuation of the *Roman de la Rose.* At the same time, it shares a great deal with the literature of the previous century. Its casual disinterest in matters of religion, to take one example, seems less out of place among certain twelfth-century texts – 'vernacular' in the strong sense of the word, self-consciously articulating interests at odds with the dominant (clerical) culture of official truths and learning (Kinoshita, *Medieval Boundaries* 4–6).

Among the staple themes of early vernacular literature was that of contact between Christians and 'Saracens,' usually in the heroic mode of the Old French *chanson de geste.* What we might call the 'thematics of crusade' was, however, only a subset of a broader motif: the Franks' contact with the great empires of the medieval Mediterranean.[5] In the twelfth century, as crusaders and other adventurers began making their way in large numbers into the Mediterranean, vernacular texts began reflecting their encounter with the tributary culture of empire. Before the emergence of the capitalist world system in the fifteenth and sixteenth centuries, according to political theorist Samir Amin, advanced precapitalist societies were characterized by the relative transparency of economic relations (surplus being extracted as 'tribute') combined with the mystification of relations of power (5).

The cultural dimension of what Amin calls the 'tributary mode of production' has been most fully elucidated by historians and, especially, art historians interested in the rich court cultures common to a number of medieval empires in the Mediterranean and west Asia. Despite their religious differences, these empires – Byzantine, Islamic, and (as we shall see) Mongol – were linked by their ways of articulating power relations through a constellation of ceremonial practices (the reception of ambassadors and supplicants, the distribution of honours) often marked by the exchange of beautiful precious objects rendered as tribute, bestowed as favours, or given as diplomatic gifts.[6] Between the tenth and twelfth centuries, the circulation of fine silks, carved ivories, rock crystal, and fine metalwork produced what art historian Oleg Grabar has called a 'shared culture of objects,' predominantly secular in nature, linking the Islamic, Byzantine, and Latin Mediterranean worlds. A measure of the symbolic attraction this culture exerted is revealed in the case of Roger II of Sicily: granted the title of 'king' in 1130, this upstart count articulated his royal pretensions in a visual and ceremonial language taken not from Ottonian or Capetian precedents but from Byzantine Greece and Fatimid Egypt (Kinoshita, 'Almería Silk' 173–4). For nobles from more northerly parts of Latin Christendom, on the other hand, contact with the elaborate palace cultures of Constantinople or Cairo elicited varying degrees of awe, incomprehension, desire, and envy.

A striking literary representation of such contact comes from the late twelfth-century epic *Le Voyage de Charlemagne*, a parodic 'prequel' to the *Chanson de Roland* that narrates the western emperor's journey to the East to take the measure of his symbolic rival, King Hugh of Constantinople. Though the patriarch of Jerusalem has recently recognized Charles's greatness – 'Aies nun Charles Maines sur tuz reis curunez!' ['Let your name be Charlemagne, over all crowned kings!'] (l. 158) – once Charles arrives in Constantinople, he is overwhelmed – a literary reflection of the multiple indignities waves of crusaders and other westerners endured in their historical dealings with the Byzantine emperor throughout the twelfth century (Kinoshita, 'Poetics of *Translatio*' 320–37). The city's magnificence is exemplified in its royal palace: 'Karles vit le paleis et la richece grant; / La sue manantise ne priset mie un guant' ['Charles beheld the palace and the great wealth: he cared not a glove for his own possessions'] (ll. 362–3). A moment later, when a sea breeze causes the palace to spin like a mechanical top, the emperor and his retinue are literally floored in terror:

Karles vit le paleis turneer et fremir:
Il ne sout que ceo fud, ne l'out de luign apris.
Ne pout ester sur pez, sur le marbre s'asist.
Franceis sunt tut versét: ne se poent tenir,
E covrirent lur ches et adenz et suvin,
E dist li uns a l'altre: 'Mal sumes entrepris;
Les portes sunt uvertes, si n'en poüm issir.'

Charles saw the palace revolve and quiver:
He did not know what was happening; he had not learned of it from afar.

Unable to stand on his feet, he sat down on the marble [floor].
The Franks were spilled on the ground, not being able to stand.
They covered their heads, some lying face down, others supine,
And said to one other: 'We're in a bad situation!
The doors are open, yet we cannot leave.'   (ll.385–91, emphases added)[7]

A common trope in Mediterranean and West Asian historiography, the motif of the palace that amazes is here turned against the western imperial figure synonymous with power and solemnity.

By the time Marco Polo's father and uncle set out on their first journey in the second half of the thirteenth century, descendants of the Franks who had once been so humiliated in Constantinople now ruled it. In 1204 the Fourth Crusade, originally targeted against Egypt, at Venetian instigation attacked the Byzantine capital of Constantinople instead. In the ensuing sack of the city, crusaders carried off many treasures – most famously, the horses of San Marco – still given pride of place in western collections. More significantly, the Venetians gained territories out of which they constructed a colonial empire giving them 'undisputed maritime preeminence in the eastern Mediterranean' (Frederic Lane 43).

Meanwhile, the geopolitics of the eastern Mediterranean and western Asia had been further reshaped by the advent of the Mongols. Following a first wave of conquest under Chinggis Khan in the early thirteenth century, the Mongols had rapidly expanded their power in all directions. They first burst into the western European consciousness in the late 1230s, in reports of the horrific violence and devastation 'Tartar' attacks wrought on Persia and on eastern Europe.[8] In 1238, according to Matthew Paris's *Chronica Majora*, envoys from the Old Man of the Mountain (leader of the so-called Assassins) reached the court of France to propose a Christian-Muslim alliance against these barbarian invaders. By the 1240s, however, Latin Christendom's leaders foresaw a new possibility: an alliance *with* the Mongols – some of whom were reported to be Christian – *against* the Muslim states of the eastern Mediterranean. In 1245, Pope Innocent IV dispatched the Franciscan John of Plano Carpini 'to the Tartars and the other oriental nations … [with] instructions … to examine everything and to look at everything carefully' (Dawson 3–4). Reaching court just in time to witness Güyük's acclamation as Great Khan, Plano Carpini subsequently wrote his *Ystoria Mongalorum*, a 'spy report' (Morgan, *The Mongols* 24) that, alongside ethnographic descriptions of Mongol customs and practices, detailed their manner of warfare and made recommendations on how they might be defeated.[9] In 1253, Louis IX of France unofficially sent William of Rubruck, another Franciscan, to make contact with the Great Khan and gather as much information about them as possible.

Thus when Niccolò and Maffeo Polo set out from Constantinople in 1260, the realignment of power in west and central Asia was relatively new, yet 'first contact' between Mongols and Latin Europe had already been established. The West's first official impressions came from the Franciscan envoys mentioned above, whose first-person accounts betray a complete misapprehension of the tributary culture of empire. The Mongols, John of Plano Carpini writes, 'never make peace except with those who submit to them.' Rulers of countries are summoned to court, ritually to perform their subservience. 'When they come, they do not receive the honour which is their due but are treated like other low-born people and *are obliged to give substantial presents*' (Dawson 39). Envoys like himself

> are asked for many presents both by the princes and others of high and lower rank and if these are not forthcoming they despise them, indeed they consider them of no account; if they have been sent by men of importance, the Tartars are unwilling to receive a small gift from them, saying, 'You come from an important man and you give so little.' And they refuse to accept it and, if the envoys wish for success in their undertaking, they are bound to give larger gifts. On that account we had no choice but to bestow in gifts a great part of the things given to us by the faithful for our expenses. (Dawson 28)

Subjected to similar demands, William of Rubruck reacts with rather less ethnographic detachment:

> everything they saw on our attendants, knives, gloves, purses, belts, they marvelled at and wanted to have them all. I pleaded as an excuse that we still had a goodly stretch before us and ought not thus speedily to divest ourselves of things necessary for the completion of so considerable a journey. Whereupon they said I was an imposter.
>
> It is true they take nothing away by force but they ask in a most ill-mannered and impudent fashion for whatever they see, and if a man gives to them, then he is the loser for they are ungrateful. In their own eyes they are the lords of the world and consider that nobody ought to

refuse them anything; if he does not give and then afterwards stands in need of their aid, they serve him badly. (Dawson, 106–7)

In the Mongols' demands for gifts, we recognize a central aspect of tributary economies (Cutler); in their importunity, we recognize the bluntness of a people themselves relatively new to the imperial culture of power.[10] Where John expresses resignation and William irritation, other petitioners more familiar with tributary practices take such demands and expectations as a matter of course. When Hetoum I, king of Lesser Armenia, set out in 1254 to seek an alliance with Möngke (newly elected Great Khan), he made special arrangements to assure the safe transport of 'the goods to be used as gifts and presents.' His solicitousness paid off: 'having offered his presents' to Möngke, Hetoum remained at court fifty days and 'was suitably honoured' (Boyle 178–81).[11]

Like Hetoum, the Venetian merchants Niccolò and Maffeo Polo understand how to do business in the Mongol lands. Setting out from Constantinople 'pour gaaignier' ['in order to make a profit'] (1: 1.9), they make a point of taking 'plusours joiaus' ['several jewels'] (1: 1.10) with them as they travel first to Soladaÿe (the Crimean port of Sudak), then onward to the court of Barta (Berke), khan of the Golden Horde.[12] Their foresight, like Hetoum's, pays off; upon their arrival, Barta

> fist grant hounour aux .II. freres et ot moult grant alegrece de lor venue. Et il li donnerent touz les joiaus que il avoient aportez. Et il les reçut moult volentiers: si li plorent moult, et il leur fist donner .II. *tans* que ce ne valoit qu'il li avoient donné.

> greatly honoured the two brothers and was very happy at their coming. And they gave him all the jewels they had brought. And he very gladly accepted them; they pleased him very much, and he gave them *double* the worth of what they had given him. (1: 2.6–11)

The syntax is ambiguous: both the antecedent of 'les' (in 'il *les* reçut moult volentiers') and the subject of 'plorent' could plausibly be construed as *either* the jewels *or* the brothers. In the end, the two are inseparable: the brothers' fine welcome is inseparable from the favourable impression created by their unstinting generosity. Unlike Friar William, they have mastered the basic principle of tributary largesse: that one must give in order to receive. Though their adventures are just beginning, they have already amply realized their ambition of making a profit, doubling their investment not by buying and selling silks, spices, dyes, wool, grain, soaps, or the other commodities in which merchants typically trafficked but by exploiting the inexorable logic of tributary largesse.

The seven years separating William's journey from that of the elder Polos hardly seems adequate to explain the disparity in their respective interactions with their Mongol hosts. Of course, since William is a Franciscan, his rejection of acquisitiveness and his disdain for worldly goods is to be expected. But despite the aura of 'first contact' conveyed by both Plano Carpini and William of Rubruck, their accounts offer a peek at lands under Mongol rule already teeming with Latin merchants. From the time of the First Crusade (1096–9), westerners had insinuated themselves into the politics of the region, often through the mediation of eastern Mediterranean Christians like the Byzantine Greeks and the Armenians.[13] These political connections helped the Latins' commercial expansion into Mongol lands. Journeying through Kiev (incorporated into the Khanate of the Golden Horde around 1240), John of Plano Carpini encountered merchants 'from Constantinople' who included 'Michael the Genoese ... Manuel the Venetian, James Reverius of Acre, [and] Nicolas Pisani' (Dawson 71). Eight years later, in the Crimean port of Sudak, William of Rubruck encounters 'merchants from Constantinople' – likely also a mixed group of Italians – who advise him on everything from posing as an envoy to what sort of transport to hire for his journey (Dawson 91–2). Two decades and more before Marco Polo's journey, countrymen like 'Manuel the Venetian' were already pursuing the commercial potential within the Mongol empire's ever-expanding borders. If Niccolò and Maffeo Polo, like Hetoum, understand how to do business in the Mongol lands, it is because of their double identity as merchants and as Venetians.

II

Though Rustichello's prologue begins by evoking the 'les grandesimes merveilles' ['the very great marvels'] (1: 1.3) the book contains, in the *Devisement* traditional marvels like those associated with India are in remarkably short supply (Larner 82–3).[14] Those that remain are highly rationalized: 'unicorns become rhinos, man-eating ... is explained as a religious practice,' and so forth (Strickland 44, in this volume) in a kind of 'workaday geography and anthropology' (Larner 83). Most strikingly, 'none of the monstrous races are to be found in the Book' at all – a 'staggering omission' (Larner 82) that sharply distinguishes Marco's *text* from the lavish manuscript *illustrations* like those found in BNF fr. 2810.

In the late thirteenth century, when the Mongol empire was at the height of its power, the greatest source of wonder was in fact Kublai himself. As Marco describes:

> Or vous veul commencier en nostre livre a conter les granz faiz et toutes les granz merveilles du Grant Caan qui ore regne, qui Cu[b]lay Caan est appelez, qui vaut a dire en françois le grant seigneur des seigneurs et des seignours empereours. Et il a bien ce non a droit pour ce que chascuns sache en verité que c'est *le plus puissant homme* de gent et de terre et de tresor *qui onques fust au monde ne qui orendroit soit* du temps d'Adam nostre premier pere jusques au jour d'ui. Et ce vous mousterrai je tout apertement en nostre livre que c'est tout voir ce que je vous ai dit – et que chascuns y sera [content] – comment il fu li plus granz sires qui onques fust ne qui orendroit soit.

> Now [at this point] in our book I want to begin to tell you the great deeds and all the great marvels of the currently reigning Great Khan – Kubilai Khan is his name – meaning 'the great lord of lords' and 'emperor of lords' in French. And he has every right to this name, for everyone should know, in truth, that he is *the most powerful man* – in peoples, lands, and riches – *who ever was or ever has been*, from the time of Adam, our first father, through today. And in our book I will clearly show you – to everyone's satisfaction – that what I have said is completely true: that he was the greatest lord that ever was or will be. (3: 75.1–13)

In the Latin Middle Ages, Alexander of Macedon was the king against whom all others were measured; in Alexandre de Paris's mid-twelfth-century *Roman d'Alexandre*, the titular protagonist – having conquered the Armenians, Persians, Syrians, Indians, Africans, Egyptians, Babylonians, and Tyrians – is hailed by Julius Caesar as 'tous li mieudres des princes terrïens' ['the greatest of all earthly princes'] (1: 5.204).[15] But in the wake of the 'currently reigning' Kublai Khan, the power and splendour of Alexander and Caesar, of Charlemagne and Arthur, are quickly forgotten – swept away as if nothing. In a literature accustomed to marking superlatives through vivid (if conventional) comparison – mightier than Roland, fairer than Iseut – the Great Khan is a world unto himself. There is nothing exceptional about his appearance:

'Il est de belle grandesce, ne petit ne grant, mais il est de moienne grandesce. Il est charnus, de belle maniere, et est trop bien tailliez de tous
membres et si a le vis blanc et vermeil, les ieux noirs, le nex bien fait et
bien seant' ['He's of fair size: neither small nor large, but of middle
size. He is plump in an attractive way, his limbs very well-shaped, his
face white and red, his eyes black, his nose well-formed and regular']
(3: 81.2–7). Rather, what occasions marvel is the unprecedented extent
of his rule: 'le plus grant et le plus poissant' ['the greatest and most
powerful'] of all the Mongol khans, he is lord over 'touz les Tartars du
monde' ['all the world's Tartars'] in both East and West, such that all
the world's Christian and Saracen kings together 'n'aroient pooir a lui
ne tant ne porroient faire comme cestui Cublay le Grant Caan porroit'
['would have no power over him or be able to do as much as this Great
Khan Kublai'] (2: 68.4–15).

The fascination exerted by Kublai's unprecedented tributary power
may be measured by its effect on the syntactico-cultural distribution of
wonder. At the same time that the Great Khan displaces all other wonders that 'inspire the amazement of the Western world' (Harf-Lancner
236), through much of the *Devisement*, the Mongols themselves are cast
as the prime consumers of marvels. The first 'marvel' evoked in the text
occurs when envoys sent by the Il-khan Hülegü to his brother Kublai
encounter Niccolò and Maffeo Polo in the city of Bukhara, in Transoxi-
ania: 'Et quant li message virent ces .II. freres, si *orent grant merveille* pour
ce que onques n'avoient veu nul Latin en celle contree' ['when the
envoys saw these two brothers, *they marvelled greatly* because they had
never seen a Latin in this country'] (1: 3.11–13). They immediately invite
the Venetians to accompany them, for the Great Khan, they explain, has
never seen a Latin and 'a grant desir de veoir ent aucun' ['greatly wishes
to see one'] (1: 3.18). In return, they promise, the Polos will garner 'grant
pourfit et grant hounour' ['great profit and great honour'] (1: 3.15). It is
an offer they can't refuse. Once they reach Kublai's court, however,
Niccolò and Maffeo are treated not as wonders but as privileged informants. After welcoming them 'a grant hounour et ... moult grant joie'
['with great honour and ... very great joy'] (1: 5.2–3), the Great Khan
questions them at length 'de maintes choses' ['about many things']
(1: 5.4): how their emperors maintain justice and make war; who their
kings and princes are and what they are like; about the pope, the Roman
Church, and 'toutes les coustumes des Latins' ['all the customs of the
Latins'] (1: 6.2–3). Having in the meanwhile become well acquainted
with the 'Tartar' language, the brothers 'dirent toute la verité de chascune

chose par soi, bien et ordeneement et sagement comme sage homme qu'il estoient' ['told the whole truth about everything in turn, in a good, well-ordered, and wise fashion befitting the wise men that they were'] (1: 6.3–5). Where the worthy friars John of Plano Carpini and William of Rubruck had made the journey to the East to gather intelligence on the Mongols for the pope and the king of France, the Great Khan turns Niccolò and Maffeo into native informants, brought to the heart of empire to supply information on their own people.

The image of the ruler obsessed with assembling knowledge from all corners of the earth is not unique to the Great Khan. In the medieval romance tradition, Alexander the Great's voyages to the ends of the known world result at least as much from his desire for knowledge as from his lust for conquest. Others chose not to roam the world themselves but to have knowledge brought to them. Consider the example of one twelfth-century Mediterranean king: 'it pleased him to know the nature of his land and to know it with certainty and precision... He also wished to know about other lands, their division into the seven climate zones upon which the scholars agree and which the translators and authors confirm in their registers' (Mallette 146). He began by consulting the books of many learned authors – including a *Book of Marvels* by the tenth-century author al-Mas'udi and a *Description of the World* (whose title anticipates our *Devisement dou monde*) by the ninth-century mathematician al-Khwarizmi. However, finding these textual sources to be unclear, incomplete, and 'rather simpleminded ... he summoned to his presence experts in these things ... and sought their knowledge on the subject.' This, too, proves a disappointment: 'he did not find among them any more knowledge than he had found in the books mentioned above' (Mallette 146–7). So he

> summoned those who ... had traveled in these lands, and he had them questioned by an intermediary... When their accounts ... corroborated each other, he recorded what was most reliable and most trustworthy. When they varied among each other, he put their information aside and disregarded it. He worked in this manner for about fifteen years. Not for a single moment during this time did he neglect his research and his search to uncover the truth, until his work became complete as he wished it. (Mallette 147)

The resulting work, completed in 1154 by the North African scholar al-Idrisi, was entitled *Nuzhat al-mushtaq fi ikhtirak al-afaq* (*Amusements for those who long to traverse the horizon*). It is more commonly known, however, as the *Book of Roger* (*Kitab Rujar*) after the king who commissioned it: Roger II of Sicily (ruled 1130–54), the Norman king known for his multilingual, multiconfessional court and kingdom.[16] Nearly a hundred years later, Roger's grandson Frederick II (emperor 1220–50) – that outsized personality whose quarrels with the papacy rent Italy, the Empire, and much of Latin Europe in the first half of the thirteenth century – himself authored a treatise called *De arte venandi cum avibus* (*On the art of hunting with birds*), in which he, too, presented himself as 'a seeker and a lover of knowledge' (Mallette 164):

> over a long period of time we investigated, with care and diligent attention, those things that pertained to this art, dedicating ourselves to the theory and practice of it, in order that we might at last be able to collect in a book those things that we have learned through our own experiences or those of others. We summoned from a great distance – at great expense to ourselves – those who were experienced in the practice of this art … taking advantage of whatever they knew best and commending their words and deeds to memory. (Mallette 163)

What these examples show is that the *Devisement*'s representation of Kublai Khan (whose reign, 1260–94, takes up almost exactly where Frederick's leaves off) is at least in part a literary topos meant to convey the grandeur of the tributary ruler. In the days before fellowships and foundation grants, before microfiche and interlibrary loan, only the great and very powerful could command the resources to research and compile a 'Book of Marvels' or a 'Description of the World,' when such projects were cast not simply as the collation of existing texts but of new accounts based on first-hand experience. In a sense, the tales travellers and informants bring to the ruler at the heart of empire are of a piece with the pearls, silks, spices, and other treasures rendered by subject peoples in homage to their tributary lord.

We are now better placed to understand Marco's unique position at Kubilai's court. When he first arrives with his father and uncle on their return visit to the Khan, Marco's linguistic and cultural adaptability make him an object of wonder: 'aprist si bien la coustume des Tatars et lor langage et lor lettre et lor archier que *ce fu merveilles*. Et sachiez vraiement, il sot en pou de temps de pluseurs langages et sot de .IIII. lettres de lor escriptures' ['he learned the Tartars' customs, languages, writing, and archery so well that *it was a wonder*; know, truly,

that in a short time he learned many languages and four scripts']
(1: 15.2–6). Dispatched on his first embassy, he impresses even further:
having previously noted the Great Khan's disappointment when
envoys returning from 'diverses parties du monde ... ne li savient
autre [chose] dire que ce pour quoi il estoient alé' ['different parts of
the world ... were unable to tell him about anything other than the
mission on which they had been sent'] (1: 15.15–17), Marco makes a
special point of noting 'novelties and the ways of different lands' to
feed Kublai's wide-ranging curiosity: 'pour ce, alant et venant, y mis
moult s'entente de savoir de toutes diverses choses selonc les contrees, a ce que a son retour le puisse dire au Grant Caan' ['Thus, in his
comings and goings, he put great effort into learning about all the different things in each region, so that on his return he could recount
them to the Great Khan'] (1: 15.21–4). His effort pays off: 'il conta
toutes les nouveles et toutes les estranges choses que il avoit veu et
seu bien et sagement, si que le Seignour et touz ceulz qui l'oïrent le[17]
tindrent a merveilles' ['he related all the news and all the strange things
he had well and wisely seen and learned about, in such a way that the
Lord and all those who heard him marvelled at him'] (1: 16.4–7).

Located near the end of the prologue of the Devisement, this passage
is meant to convey the favour Marco enjoyed at Kublai's court and to
explain how he came to make the voyages described in the main body
of the text. Thanks to his skills as an envoy and storyteller, 'le Seignour
l'ama moult et li faisoit moult grant hounor' ['the Lord loved him
greatly and showed him great favour'] (1: 16.25–6). For seventeen
years, Marco roamed the world on his behalf; so it was that he 'en sot
plus et en vit des diverses contrees du monde que nul autre homme'
['came to know more about and saw more of the world's different
lands than any other man'] (1: 16.29–30). It also amounts to a significant disruption of western narrative logic. Where John of Plano
Carpini and William of Rubruck had taken pains carefully to 'examine
everything' (Dawson 4) in Mongol lands to report back to Pope Innocent IV and King Louis IX of France, respectively, Marco does the same
with the goal of pleasing Kublai himself: 'metoit il moult s'entente a
savoir et a espier et a enquerre pour raconter au Grant Seignour' ['he
put great effort into finding out, observing, and inquiring – in order to
[have something to] tell the Great Lord'] (1: 16.31–2). As Italo Calvino
intuits (see McLaughlin, in this volume), Marco's true audience is in
some sense less the Latin European readership of the Devisement than
the Great Khan himself. Formerly the object of western intelligence,

Kubilai here becomes the *subject* of wonder, with Marco as his eyes and ears.[18] Whether we marvel over the pearls of Malabar or the barking, dog-headed men of Andaman, we are in a way only eavesdropping on the tales Marco has collected like tribute to be rendered up to the Great Khan. Ironically, the ruler of the greatest nomadic empire ever known assembles his knowledge not (like Alexander) through constant travel, but by staying home and letting news of the world come to him.

Of all the narrative and narratological complications created by the text's multiple layers – Marco's voice versus Rustichello's, the plurality of potential *destinataires* – I wish to focus on two. The first is the gradual effacement of clear lines of difference between Latin Christians and their cultural and confessional others; the second, related to the first, is the emergence of merchants not as the excluded figures marginal to the world of epic and romance but as key agents of travel, interaction, and exchange.

III

From the outset of the *Devisement*, the formulaic nature of early French prose helps level the sense of cultural difference. When the newly elected Pope Gregory X receives the Polos 'a moult grant hounour et a moult grant feste et a moult grant joie' ['with very great honour, celebration, and joy'] (1: 12.3–5) as they first prepare to set out from Acre, for example, his greeting – except for the 'beneïson' ['blessing'] (1: 12.5) tacked on at the end – reproduces virtually verbatim the reception previously accorded the elder Polos by the Great Khan himself: 'il les reçut a grant hounour et leur fist moult grant feste et moult grant joie de lor venue' (1: 5.1–3). As the text unfolds, any clean division between Latin Christians and their others is complicated, as we have seen, by the perspectival shifts making Mongols rather than Latin Europeans the ultimate consumers of wonder. Thus when Kublai's brother Hülegü captured Baghdad, 'ot moult grant merveille' ['he was amazed'] (1: 24.28–9), we are told, to find the caliph ensconced in a tower filled with silver and gold. Incredulous, he demands to know why the conquered leader had not used his massive treasure to hire 'saudoiers et … chevaliers et … gens d'armes pour toi deffendre et ta cité!' ['mercenaries and knights and armed men to defend yourself and the city'] (1: 24.35–6). Re-routed through Mongol eyes, western tropes of Muslim wealth (and avarice?) are recoded as military incompetence. This scene is followed by the anecdote of a caliph of Baghdad who tested the faith of his Christian subjects (1: 25–8). At the end of this long parable demonstrating the power of Christianity, the text serves up a conventional swipe at Islam:

> Et *ne vous merveilliez* se li Sarrazin heent les Crestiens, car la maloite loy que Mahoms leur donna si commande que touz les maus que il pueent faire a toutes manieres de gens et meïsmes aus Crestiens ... Et veez con sanglante loy et com mauvais commandemens que il ont. Et tous les Sarrazins du monde se maintiennent en ceste maniere.

> And *do not be surprised* if Saracens hate Christians, for the accursed law Muhammad gave them commands them to do all the ill they can to all kinds of people and even to Christians ... And you see what a bloody law and bad commandments they have. And all the Saracens in the world behave in this way. (1: 28.46–54)

If the audience is told *not* to be surprised – 'ne vous merveilliez' – it is because this violent and perfidious behaviour is precisely the *opposite* of a marvel: it is the predictable, the to-be-expected, the always-already known. Yet the anecdote in question is set in 1275 (1: 25.3) – twenty years after the supposed Mongol conquest of Baghdad (erroneously situated, as we have seen, in 1255); 'Et puis ça avant,' we had been told, 'n'i ot nul caliphe n'en Baudas ne en autre lieu' ['from then on, there hasn't been any caliph, either in Baghdad or anywhere else'] (1: 24.51–2). Despite the Middle Ages' characteristic looseness with numbers and disregard for the straight narrative line (Kinoshita, *Medieval Boundaries* 139–40), this blatant evocation of a Christian-hating caliph ruling twenty years *after* the Mongol overthrow of the caliphate (and surely within living memory of some in the *Devisement*'s first audience) marks this story as an *exemplum* whose ties to historical reality are, as Ménard notes, 'très lâches' (*Le Devisement* 199n.).

As the narrative takes us further and further into Asia, the clear binary opposition between Christians and Saracens proves increasingly difficult to maintain. The province of Mosul, for example, is inhabited by 'pluseurs generations de genz ... Il y a unes gens qui sont apelez Arrabi, qui aourent Mahommet. Encore y a une autre maniere de gent: Crestiens, [Nestorins] et Jacopins; il ont patriarche que il apelent Jocolit' ['several races of people ... There are some people called Arabs, who worship Muhammad. There is also another kind of people: Christians, [Nestorians] and Jacobites; they have a patriarch they call

Jocolit'] (1: 23.3–7). What is striking in this account is that it is the Arab Muslims who require no explanation; eastern Christians, on the other hand, necessitate a kind of comparative sociology, highlighting their similarity-in-difference:

> Et cestui patriarche fait evesques et archevesques et abbez et touz autres prelez, et les envoie par toutes pars, en Ynde et em Baudas et [au Cata], aussi com fait l'Apostoile de Romme par les contrees des Latins, car sachiez que touz les Crestiens de celle contree dont il y a moult grant quantité sont touz Jacopins et Nestorin crestiens, mais non pas si que commande l'Apostoile de l'Eglyse de Romme, car il faillent en pluseurs choses de la foy.

> And this patriarch names bishops, archbishops, abbots, and all other prelates and sends them everywhere – to India and Baghdad and [Cathay], just like the pope of Rome in Latin lands; for know that all the Christians of that country – of which there are a great many – are all Jacobite and Nestorian Christians, but not ruled by the pope of the Roman church, for they are wanting in several matters of faith. (1: 23.8–17)

Still in the area around Mosul, another kind of complication is presented by the Kurds – a people (like the Mongols) professing more than one faith, thus troubling the easy equation between religion and 'ethnic' identity: 'Encore y a une autre maniere de gens qui habitent es montaignes de cele contree, qui s'apelent [Curd], *qui sont crestien et sarrazin*' ['There is also another kind of peoples who live in the mountains of this region, who are called [Kurds], *who are Christian and Saracen*'] (1: 23.22–5).[19] Pausing not a moment over this multiconfessional diversity, Marco instead hurries on to what all Kurds have in common: they are 'moult mauvaise gent, qui robent volentiers les marcheanz' ['very bad people who readily rob merchants'] (1: 23.25–6).

As the narrative progresses, the Christian-Saracen binary is further attenuated by different sorts of idolaters. In the province of Tangut, for example, there are some Nestorian Christians and Saracens; otherwise, its inhabitants are 'tuit ydres' ['all idolaters'] (2: 57.4). Adopting a tone of 'scientific' detachment, Marco goes on to explicate the funerary customs of 'tuit li ydolastre du monde' ['all the world's idolaters'] (2: 57.26), including cremation, the burning of paper cut-out men and beasts to serve the departed in the afterlife, and offerings of food placed before the dead. This broadening of cultural perspectives –

Larner's 'workaday anthropology' – produces a series of dislocations, as when the familiar tale of the Magi is recast through the eyes of its Zoroastrian protagonists. In the Persian city of Sarra, Marco comes across the tombs of Caspar (or Jaspar), Balthasar, and Melchior, the three kings who had come with 'offrandes' ['offerings'] (1: 30.25) to 'aourer Jesus Crist' ['adore Jesus Christ'] (1: 30.6). Entering his presence one at a time, each is astonished to find a man his own age. 'Et quant il furent touz .III. ensamble, si dist chascuns ce que il avoit veu et trouvé. De ce se firent il moult grant merveille' ['And when all three of them got together, each one said what he had seen and found. They marvelled greatly at it'] (1: 30.39–41). On their way home, they open a box the child has given them and find a stone: 'Quant il la virent, si orent moult grant merveille que ce pooit estre que l'enfant leur avoit donné et pour quele senefiance' ['When they saw it, they greatly wondered what this could be that the child had given them, and what (its) meaning (could be)'] (1: 31.4–6). Casting the stone into a well, they are stupefied at the sudden descent of a fire from the heavens: 'Et quant les .III. roys virent ceste merveille, si demourerent tout esbahi et furent moult repenti de ce que il avoient la pierre jetee, car bien aperçurent adont la senefiance qui grant estoit et bonne' ['And when the three kings saw this marvel, they were completely amazed and greatly repented of having thrown the stone away, for now they saw its meaning, which was great and good'] (1: 31.18–22). The wonder of Christianity is made new through the eyes of the idolater kings of Persia.

As they penetrated the eastern Mediterranean and west and central Asia, Latin Christians found themselves in a world increasingly characterized not just by its strangeness but by its internal diversity. In the high Middle Ages, western 'Europe' emerged as a common culture based on programs of standardization initiated in the time of Charlemagne (Bartlett, *The Making of Europe*; see also Kinoshita, *Medieval Boundaries* 8). The nascent sense of imagined community thus produced was further crystallized during the crusades – exemplified in Fulcher of Chartres's famous claim that 'we who were diverse in languages, nevertheless seemed to be brothers in the love of God and very close to being of one mind' (Peters 49). In contrast, the empires of the eastern Mediterranean and beyond thrived on difference. Under the tributary system the Mongols adopted from the peoples they conquered, the greatness of empire is manifested precisely in the variety – of peoples, products, and customs – of the lands that compose it. This privileging of diversity accounts for the trope of the *collection*: of the innumerable foreign princes permanently housed at court or making regular visits to mark special ceremonial occasions; of the profusion of precious objects amassed in imperial treasuries – an objective correlative of the wealth of empire; even of the crowds of women populating the harems of polygamous kings, reinforcing the centripetal pull of empire by their marriages to the daughters of local indigenous rulers.[20] (In this sense, in the *Devisement* as in Calvino's *Invisible Cities*, the Great Khan is a collector of stories, harvesting the wealth of wonders his great empire has to offer.) And in the great markets and emporia from Cairo to Samarcand and beyond, no Latin Europeans were better prepared to benefit from the diversity of empire than the enterprising merchants of Venice.

IV

In the second section of *Les Estoires de Venise*, Marco's compatriot Martin da Canal sings the praises of their native city, 'la plus belle et la plus plaisant dou siecle, ploine de biauté et de tos biens' ['the most beautiful and agreeable in the world, filled with beauty and good things of all kinds'] (2: 1–2). At first glance, we might assume that 'biens' refers to the town's civic virtues or to its incomparable treasures (exemplified by the recently rebuilt basilica of San Marco). The subsequent passage, however, suggests he may have had something more concrete in mind:

les marchandies i corent par cele noble cité, con fait l'eive des fontaines. Venise est desor la marine: si cort l'eive salee parmi et environ et par tos autres leus, fors que es maisons et es voies; et lors quant li citeïns sont es places, si povent retorner lor maison que par terre que par eive. De tos leus vient marchandies et marcheans, qui achatent les marchandies de quel maniere que il veulent et les font condure en lor païs.

merchandise flows through this noble city like the water from [its] fountains. Venice is situated on the sea: every place (except the houses and roads) has salt water running through and around it; when its citizens are in the squares, they can return home either by land or by water. Merchandise and merchants come from everywhere, buying whatever merchandise they desire and shipping it back to their country. (2: 2–5)

Here, the description of the city's most distinctive feature – its innumerable waterways and its location on the Venice lagoon – is bracketed by and inseparable from the merchants and merchandise it draws from all over the world.[21] It would be small wonder if men from such a place found much to admire in a city like Tabriz, capital of the newly conquered Mongol Il-khanate of Persia. Its inhabitants, Marco reports, 'vivent de marcheandise de dras' ['live by the cloth trade'] (1: 29.7–8); the city itself is

> [si] bien assise que d'Ynde et de Baudas et de Masal et de Tremesor et de mains autres lieus y viennent les marcheandises, si que pour ce y vient maint marcheant latin et proprement Genevois pour acheter et pour faire leur afaires, car on y trueve aussi moult grant quantité de perrerrie. Ele est citez que li marcheant y font moult de leur pourfit.

> so well located that merchandise comes there from India, Baghdad, Mosul, Hormuz, and many other places; for that reason, many Latin merchants – specifically, the Genoese – come there to buy and to do business, for you also find great quantities of stones there. It is a city where merchants make a lot of profit. (1: 29.9–15)

For Martin da Canal's audience, a more enticing description can hardly be imagined.[22]

The Mongol empire to which Tabriz belonged was in many ways a merchant's paradise. Traversed by the Silk Road, Central Asia had of course long prospered from long-distance trade (Foltz 35).[23] Before the advent of the Mongols, the Soghdians, the Uighurs and the Qara-Khitai had successively played key roles in East-West exchange, linked to crossroad centres such as Kashgar, Samarcand, and Bukhara (Tucker 165–6; Foltz 12–14, 108–9). In the late eleventh century, a Uighur chancellor had counselled his prince to treat merchants well: 'It is these who will carry your name through the world, / who will spread your reputation, good or bad … / If you want to be sure to become famous, / let the merchant have just pay for his goods' (Tucker 166).[24] A century and a half later, Genghis Khan's son and successor Ogödei encouraged trade in his newly built capital of Qaraqorum by protecting roads with permanent garrisons, standardizing weights and measures, abolishing local tariffs, introducing a system of paper money, and, not least, paying 'extremely high prices for all manner of goods' – textiles, ivory tusks, pearls, hunting falcons, golden goblets, jewelled belts, willow whip handles, cheetahs, bows and arrows, garments, hats, exotic animal horns – 'whether he needed them or not and whether they were of high or low quality' (Weatherford 136).

By the second half of the thirteenth century, the *pax mongolica* had enabled an unprecedented expansion of Latin commercial activity.[25] In the Mediterranean port of Laias, gateway to the overland routes through West and Central Asia, 'les marchans de Venise et de Gennes et de tous autres paÿs' ['merchants from Venice and Genoa and all other countries'] (1: 19.16–17) could be found buying and selling a multitude of goods. Further inland, the Genoese, as we have just seen, had taken the lead in establishing themselves in places like Tabriz and on the Caspian Sea – the half-century from 1257 to 1311 marking the high point of Genoa's medieval prosperity (Epstein 140); around the turn of the fourteenth century, an anonymous poet captured the adventurous spirit driving his compatriots' expansionism: 'E tanti sun li Zenoexi / e per lo monde si distexi, / che und'eli van o stan / un'atra Zenoa ge fan' ['so numerous are the Genoese / and so spread out throughout the world, / that wherever one goes or stays / he makes another Genoa there'].[26]

As a careful reading of the narratives of John of Plano Carpini and William of Rubruck suggests, in the thirteenth-century Latin expansion into Mongol-dominated lands, 'missionaries largely followed in the footsteps of merchants' (Larner 119). When Niccolò and Maffeo Polo returned from their first expedition in Mongol lands, they brought back a message for the pope that included the Great Khan's request for 'cent sages hommes de vostre[27] loy crestienne' ['a hundred wise men of your Christian faith'] (1: 7.22–3) and some oil from the lamp of the Holy Sepulchre. (As Anthony Cutler points out, merchants frequently served as envoys: 'a foreigner's designation as "ambassador" or "merchant" [was] a function of the purpose of his visit rather than a clear-cut distinction in the minds and attitudes of those upon whom he called.')[28] When the elder Polos set out a second time, in 1271 – this time with Marco in tow – they were accompanied not by a hundred wise men but by two rather reluctant Dominicans, Nicholas of Vicenza and William of Tripoli, who proved much less intrepid than the Venetian merchants. Finding Lesser Armenia under threat by the Mamluks of Egypt, the two friars 'orent moult grant peour d'*aler avant* et distrent qu'il ne vouloient plus *aler avant*' ['were very afraid of *going on* and said that they didn't want to *go on*'] (1: 12.22–4), handing their letters of privilege over to the Polos and beating a hasty retreat to Acre. The

merchants, in contrast, venture forth without hesitation. On their earlier journey, the elder Polos, having reached the Crimea, '[il] lor sembla
bon *d'aler plus avant*' ['thought it would be good to *go further on*']
(1: 2.2); then, arriving at the court of Berke and finding their way back
home blocked by hostilities between the rival Mongol states of the
Golden Horde and Persia, they simply shrugged and decided it would
be 'bon *d'aler encore avant*' ['good to keep going further'] (1: 2.22–3). In
the *Devisement*, in other words, merchants go where missionaries fear
to tread.

As the narrative progresses, merchants assume an increasingly visible role. Already in Lesser Armenia, Marco had contrasted the craven-
ness of the nobility – 'anciennement ... preudomme d'armes et vaillant,
mais orendroit ... chetif et vil, ... mais il sont bon buveour' ['formerly
... brave and valiant fighters, but now miserable and low ... if good
drinkers'] (1: 19.8–11) – with the energy and initiative of the merchants
from every country who flock to Laias to buy and sell goods and
arrange transport to the interior. As the *Devisement* takes us further into
Asia, however, something curious occurs: 'merchants,' whom Marco
initially takes pains to identify as (for example) Genoese or Venetian,
gradually come to form a group linked by commonalities of interests
that supersede differences of ethnicity, citizenship, or even religion. The
merchants 'de tous ... paÿs' ['from all countries'] (1: 19.16–17) Marco
describes doing business in the Mediterranean port of Laias might
possibly (if not necessarily plausibly) be limited to a mix of Latin and
Eastern Christians. On the other hand, those exporting locally made
silk 'pour faire lor afaire et lor pourfit' ['for business and for profit']
(1: 33.4–5) from the Persian city of Jasoy (Yezd) or those who 'vont par
tout le monde feisant marcheandise' ['traverse the world, buying and
selling'] (2: 50.7–9) from their base in Casar (Kashgar) in Chinese
Turkestan clearly belong to supranational cohort unbound by constraints of nationality, language, or religion. In the Persian Gulf port of
Hormuz, for example, merchants from India unload 'leur ne[s] chargies
d'espiceries et de perrerie et de peles et de dras de soie et dorez et de
dens d'olifans et d'autres pluisours marcheandises et si les vendent aus
marcheans, qui puis les portent par universe monde, vendant aus
autres marcheans' ['ships loaded with spices, stones, skins, silks and
gold cloth, elephant tusks and many other kinds of merchandise which
they sell to merchants, who then carry them throughout the world, selling to other merchants'] (1: 36.13–18). As a group, merchants fear
bandits and highwaymen, irrespective of religion. Thus in Mosul, the

Kurds (the same people described, as we have seen, as both Christian *and* Saracen) are 'moult mauvaise gent, qui robent volentiers les marcheanz' ['very bad people who readily rob merchants'] (1: 23.24–6). Merchants appreciate strong rulers who can curb banditry and impose order. Thus Marco praises the rule of the Persia Il-khans, for without their lordship [seignourie], the cruel and murderous people of their lands (who happen to be Saracens) 'feroient granz maus as marcheans … car se il ne trouvaissent les marcheanz bien appareilliez d'armes, il leur oteroient et roberoient tout; et aucune foiz, quant il ne se prennent pas bien garde, si les destruient touz' ['would do great harm to merchants … for if they come across merchants who are not well-armed, they rob them of everything; and sometimes if [the merchants] are not careful, [the attackers] destroy them all'] (1: 32.25–31). Their prosperity dependent on the order and security provided by the *pax mongolica*, merchants were among those who had the most to gain from Mongol success.[29] If the Il-khans of Persia sometimes fell short of being able to guarantee full order in their realm, the same cannot be said of Kublai, source of all the Mongols' power and authority.

V

At the conclusion of his lengthy exposition (sections 64–9) on the Mongols, Marco alludes to Kublai but defers a full-fledged presentation: 'Or vous ai moustré et dit toutes les usances et les coustumes des Tartars, mais non mie que je vous ai conté du Grant Caan, qui est sires de touz les Tartars ne de sa grant emperial cort. Mais je le vous conterai en ce livre quant temps et lieus en sera *car moult sont merveilleuses choses* a metre en escript' ['Now I have shown and told you all the Tartars' practices and customs, but have told you nothing of the Great Khan (lord of all the Tartars) or his great imperial court. But I will describe [them] to you in this book in due time and place, *for these are wondrous things* to put into writing'] (2: 69.130–5). These marvels are first hinted at in Marco's account of Ciandu (Coleridge's fabled Xanadu), the Great Khan's summer residence with a wondrous walled garden enclosing not one but two palaces: the first in marble – its walls adorned with images of animals, birds, trees, and flowers so subtly rendered that it's 'un delis et une merveille a veoir' ['a delight and a wonder to see'] (2: 74.9–10) – and a second made 'tout de cane' ['all of cane'] (2: 74.25–6), gilded and watertight.[30] But the real objective correlative of Kublai's power is the superlative palace in his capital of Khanbaliq:

Sachiez que il est le greingneur qui soit jamais veus ... Les murs dedenz les sales sont toutes couvertes d'or et les chambres aussi et d'argent, et y a [pourtrais] dragons, bestes, oisiaux, chevaliers et ymages de plusieurs autres generations de choses. Et la couverture est ainsi faite si que il n'y a autre que or et argent et painture. La salle est si grant et si large que bien y mengeroient .VI.M personnes. Il y a tant de chambres que *c'est merveilles a veoir*. Il est si biaux et si granz et si riches que il n'y a homme au monde qui mieulz le sceüst ordener.

Know that it is the greatest that was ever seen. Inside the halls as well as the rooms, the walls are all covered with gold and silver, with depictions of dragons, animals, birds, knights, figures and many other species. The ceilings are completely [covered with] gold, silver, and painting. The hall is so big and wide that a good 6000 people could eat there. There are so many rooms that *it's a marvel to see*. It [the palace] is so beautiful and rich that no man in the world could devise a better one. (3: 83.43–4, 46–56)

In the *Voyage de Charlemagne*, Constantinople and Hugh the Strong's marvellous palace were the end point of Charlemagne's journey, the ultimate instantiation of the wonders of the East. In the *Devisement*, on the other hand, Constantinople is the mere point of departure for an even more fabulous journey – one in which Kublai Khan appears as a tributary lord to make a Byzantine emperor tremble, an eastern *stupor mundi* who outstrips anything the West could heretofore have imagined.

By the early fifteenth century, when the 'Livre des Merveilles' (BNF fr. 2810) was produced, the Mongol empire no longer represented either a clear and present danger or a source of enticement to merchants and travellers. As abruptly as it had arisen in the thirteenth century, Mongol power collapsed in the mid- to late fourteenth: 1335 in Persia and 1368 in China. Dependent on 'the quick and constant movement of people, goods, and information,' the empire was unable to survive the results of political instability and the Black Plague: 'With each group cut off from the other, the interlocking system ... collapsed' (Weatherford 241–51; see also Morgan, *The Mongols* 171–4; Abu-Lughod 237). With its dissolution, the Mongol empire became available for resignification – rescripted and domesticated through Gothic court iconography..For by the early fifteenth century, courtly patrons 'expected to find *both* Tartars *and* Monstrous Races in their illustrated copies of the *Devisement*' (Strickland 44, in this volume; emphasis mine). The illuminations produced to gratify these expectations thus resulted in a striking 'verbal-visual' disjunction between the text and its accompanying 'illustration.' The resurgence of the monstrous races may be linked to the late fourteenth-century revival of interest in classical antiquity at the court of French king Charles V the Wise (brother of the bibliophile duc de Berry), who sponsored numerous translations of Greek and Latin works and established a royal library in the Louvre. Thus the fascination for the 'monstrous races' evinced in texts such as BNF fr. 2810 should perhaps be understood less as a symptom of medieval credulity, remnant of an earlier age, than as a cutting-edge trait of the humanist 'renaissance' touching French as well as Italian letters in the late fourteenth century.[31]

NOTES

1 On the various titles given Marco's text over the centuries, see Larner 77–8, 105–7.
2 Brownlee thus describes Dante's *Commedia* as a 'profoundly aggressive' claim on behalf of the new Italian literary vernacular, one that 'strategically ignores the fact of French cultural primacy in the vernacular' (286). On the emergence of the Lingua Franca as a 'contact vernacular,' particularly in the eastern Mediterranean, see Kahane and Kahane.
3 The vestigial crusader kingdom of Acre was captured by the Mamluk Egyptians in 1291, just before the Polos' return to Venice.
4 On the distinction between twelfth- and thirteenth-century literatures, see Kinoshita, *Medieval Boundaries* 2–3 and 135–8.
5 I use 'Frank' here in Bartlett's sense of 'aggressive westerner' far from home. Overlapping with but not identical to 'Latin Christian,' it was produced in large measure by the experience of the crusades, which brought men of many different languages and allegiances into contact (Bartlett, *The Making of Europe* 101–5).
6 On the way ambassadorial functions were often fulfilled by merchants, see Cutler.
7 Here and throughout, emphases are mine unless otherwise indicated.
8 The khanate of the Golden Horde was established through the conquests made between 1237 and 1240 by Genghis Khan's nephew Batu; in 1241 Batu entered Hungary, only to be 'recalled' to the famous *kuriltai* [council] occasioned by the death of the Great Khan, Ogödei (Morgan, *The Mongols* 136–41). In 1258, Genghis's grandson (Kublai's younger brother) Hülegü conquered Baghdad, overthrowing the Caliphate. Though the Mongols' westward expansion was checked by the Mamluk victory at Ain Jalut in

1260, Hülegü and his successors established the 'Il-khanate,' a vassal state subordinate to the Great Khan, centred in Khorasan and Azerbaijan. Hülegü's great-grandson Ghazan converted to Islam c. 1295, facilitating the political and cultural reabsorption of the Persian empire into the Islamic world. For recent positive reassessments of the Il-khanate, see Komaroff and Carboni, and George Lane.

9 The *Ystoria Mongolorum* was subsequently incorporated into Vincent of Beauvais's *Speculum Historiale* (Dawson 2).

10 Presents loomed large in Mongol foreign relations. In 1289, Arghûn, Il-khan of Persia (Kubilai's great-nephew), wrote to French king Philip IV, ostensibly to propose a Frank-Mongol alliance against the Mamluks of Egypt; the deal, Arghûn hinted, would be considerably advanced if Philip were to send 'rare objects from the land of the Franks, falcons and precious stones of various color.' In 1305 his successor Oljaitu, who had become Il-khan the previous year, again wrote to Philip to complain of the lack of presents. In the past, he begins, Philip had sent envoys bearing 'peace gifts' to Oljaitu's 'noble Great-Grandfather' (Hülegü), 'noble Grandfather' (Abaqa), 'noble Father' (Arghun), and 'noble elder Brother' (Ghazan). 'Why,' he continues, 'do you neglect to do this [now]?' (Spuler 141–4).

11 On the Mongols' diplomatic relations with the Christian rulers of Armenia, Georgia, and Trebizond, see Bryer.

12 I cite from Philippe Ménard's critical edition of the French version of the *Devisement*, currently at five volumes. (References refer to volume, section, and line numbers, with my translations unless otherwise indicated.) This edition takes as its base text manuscript B1 (British Library, Royal 19 D 1, fol. 58–135), made in Paris after 1333; in it *Le Devisement* is preceded by a *Vie d'Alexandre* (fol. 1–46) and *La Vengeance d'Alexandre* (fol. 46–57) and followed by Jean de Vignay's *Merveilles d'Outremer* (a translation of Odoric de Pordenone's *Directorium ad faciendum passagium transmarinum*, fol. 135–43), excerpts from Vincent de Beauvais's *Miroir historial* (fol. 148–65), Guillaume Adam's *Directoire* (fol. 165–92), Primat's *Chronique* (fol. 192–251), and excerpts from the biblical *Book of Kings* (fol. 193–252).

13 By the mid-thirteenth century, for example, the Lusignan kings of Cyprus were closely related to the kings of Lesser Armenia (Boase 25–6).

14 At the beginning of the thirteenth century, Gervaise of Tilbury had defined 'marvel' as 'that which, *although natural*, escapes our understanding' (Harf-Lancner 236). In displacing focus from India to China, the *Devisement*, as Harf-Lancner notes, highlights wonders of *culture* rather than nature (Harf-Lancner 236, 245).

15 References are to branch, laisse, and line numbers of Alexandre de Paris, *Roman d'Alexandre*.

16 Elsewhere I have suggested that Norman Sicily, often mar
   tories of the medieval West, may (like Christian Iberia) be re
   Latin Europe's privileged points of access to the cultures of t
   Mediterranean (Kinoshita, 'Almería Silk' 174).

17 Here I read the singular direct object 'le' as referring to Marco h.
   rather than more loosely to the wonders (plural) he describes.

18 The prologue, for example, recounts that on their way to the Great
   the elder Polos found 'moult de granz merveilles de diversetez [des
   choses' ['many great marvels of different kinds'] (1: 4.6). However, sa
   Rustichello, 'we will not tell you about them now because my lord Ma
   who also saw everything, will tell you about them fully later in this book
   (1: 4.7–10).

19 Compare the Mongols' reluctance to be called 'Christian,' even when they
   believe 'something of Christ.' As William of Rubruck reports, 'they are
   proud to such a degree that … they are unwilling to be called Christians,
   wanting their own name, that is, Mongol, to be exalted above every other
   name' (Dawson 121).

20 See Kinoshita, *Medieval Boundaries* 91–3. I further develop this analysis in
   my book-in-progress, *Paying Tribute: Eastern Empires and the Medieval French
   Imaginary.*

21 In a subsequent description of Venice's varied population, Martin's praise
   of the city's nobles is likewise bracketed by mentions of 'li marchans de tos
   païs qui vendent et achatent' ['merchants from all countries who sell and
   buy'] on the one hand and 'li marcheants…qui vendent et achatent' ['merchants who sell and buy'] – along with moneychangers, 'citaïns de tos mes-
   tiers' ['citizens of every profession'], sailors, and richly dressed ladies
   (2: 5–7) – on the other.

22 The mention of Genoese activity in Tabriz would surely have read as an
   irritation and a challenge to Marco's Venetian readership.

23 The term 'Silk Road' 'Seidenstraße' was coined by Ferdinand von Rich-
   thofen in the late nineteenth century (Foltz 1–2; Tucker 15). I use it to refer
   to the network of routes spanning Asia.

24 The Uighurs were among the predecessors whose practices and expertise
   the Mongols most readily assimilated; John of Plano Carpini describes their
   appropriation of the Uighur alphabet as if it were a spoil of war (Dawson
   20–1; Morgan, *The Mongols* 108–11).

25 Nicola di Cosmo underscores the Mongols' key role in encouraging commercial activity around the Black Sea, in part to redress the (over)emphasis
   on European, especially Italian, agency (di Cosmo 393).

26 Cocito 566, cited in Epstein 166. Marco notes the new Genoese presence on
   the Caspian Sea in 1: 22.48–9. In 1290, hundreds of Genoese spent the

winter on the Sea of Basra, building a fleet of galleys for the Mongol Il-khan to use to disrupt the Indian Ocean trade of his rivals, the Mamluks of Egypt (Ashtor 12).

27 Ménard amends the reading 'vostre,' found in ms. B1, to 'nostre,' found in A1, A3, C1, and C2 (123n31).

28 This was especially so since both roles involved the exchange of 'gifts' (Cutler 266).

29 In quieter moments, merchants 'prennent moult de leur delis' ['take great enjoyment'] (1: 33.12–13) from beautiful woods filled with game birds and wild asses and other pleasures of the road.

30 The wonders of Ciandu also include a large herd of white mares whose milk is reserved exclusively for the Khan and his lineage, and a cohort of Tibetan and Kashmiri 'sages enchanteeurs astrenomiens' ['wise astrono-mer-magicians'] (2: 74.75) who roast and eat executed prisoners and levi-tate tableware in the Great Khan's palace.

31 We should not forget that Christine de Pizan, whose *Livre des fais et bonne moeurs du sage roy Charles V* contributed to the king's reputation as a patron of letters, was the daughter of the king's court astrologer (Willard 20, 126–8).

4 Marco Polo's *Devisement dou monde* as a Narcissistic Trauma

MARION STEINICKE

When, at the beginning of the twentieth century, Sigmund Freud tried to place a value on the importance of psychoanalysis for science of the future, he posited three narcissistic traumas that humanity in its recent cultural developments had collectively and progressively suffered:

> Zwei große Kränkungen ihrer naiven Eigenliebe hat die Menschheit im Laufe der Zeiten von der Wissenschaft erdulden müssen. Die erste, als sie erfuhr, daß unsere Erde nicht der Mittelpunkt des Weltalls ist, sondern ein winziges Teilchen eines in seiner Größe kaum vorstellbaren Weltsystems. Sie knüpft sich für uns an den Namen Kopernikus, obwohl schon die alexandrinische Wissenschaft ähnliches verkündet hatte. Die zweite dann, als die biologische Forschung das angebliche Schöpfungsvorrecht des Menschen zunichte machte, ihn auf die Abstammung aus dem Tierreich und die Unvertilgbarkeit seiner animalischen Natur verwies. Diese Umwertung hat sich in unseren Tagen unter dem Einfluß von Ch. Darwin, Wallace und ihren Vorgängern nicht ohne das heftigste Sträuben der Zeitgenossen vollzogen. Die dritte und empfindlichste Kränkung aber soll die menschliche Größensucht durch die heutige psychologische Forschung erfahren, welche dem Ich nachweisen will, daß es nicht einmal Herr im eigenen Hause, sondern auf kärgliche Nachrichten angewiesen bleibt, von dem, was unbewußt in seinem Seelenleben vorgeht.

> Humanity has in the course of time had to endure from the hands of science two great outrages upon its naïve self-love. The first was when it realized that our earth was not the centre of the universe, but only a tiny speck in a world-system of magnitude hardly conceivable; this is associated in our minds with the name of Copernicus, although Alexandrian

doctrines taught something very similar. The second was when biological research robbed man of his peculiar privilege of having been specially created, and relegated him to a descent from the animal world, implying an ineradicable animal nature in him; this transvaluation has been accomplished in our time upon the instigation of Charles Darwin, Wallace and their predecessors, and not without the most violent opposition from their contemporaries. But man's craving for grandiosity is now suffering the third and most bitter blow from present-day psychological research which is endeavouring to prove to the ego of each one of us that he is not master in his own house, but that he must remain content with the veriest scraps of information about what is going on unconsciously in his own mind. (Freud, *Vorlesungen* 283–4; tr. 562)

These 'outrageous' discoveries have a thoroughly traumatic character as experiences that overwhelm the intellectual capacity and, consequently, the emotional balance of individuals as well as of a whole society by annulling *in toto* the axioms of their knowledge and epistemological systems. The three narcissistic traumas of humankind named by Freud radically put into question not only certain scientific ideas which have been taken for granted but the whole order of things that grounds the cultural identity of any given society. The usual reaction to an intellectual trauma of this kind entails, according to Freud, first, a complete negation of the unbearable discovery; second, recognition of its fact by offering instead a diverse and more traditional interpretation of it; and, finally, acceptance of both the fact and its correct interpretation, while reducing or denying its importance and consequence for cultural self-image and social life.

From this perspective, it is possible to discern another trauma to western society which (like the Mongol invasion at the beginning of the thirteenth century) might have been successfully repressed and replaced by the later discoveries of unknown parts of the world that were yet to be conquered: namely, the experience manifested in Marco Polo's travel report that the Occident is by no means, either geographically or culturally, the very centre of the world. It cannot be regarded as the central destination of the universal history of salvation, because beyond the horizons of the Christian world it is possible to find cults and religions that lay claim to the same traditions for their own purpose, as well as entire realms at the remotest margins of the world that display higher levels of technical and cultural sophistication than that found in any western society, and that consequently consider Europe and Christianity to be phenomena of relatively small importance, hidden away at the occidental margins of the world.

Among the many writings that imparted 'Indian' information and projections to the Middle Ages, most important was the *Romance of Alexander*, especially the adventurous Greek version of Pseudo-Kallisthenes translated into Latin in the ninth or tenth century by the Archpresbyter Leo of Naples, and revised and expanded during the eleventh century to include some smaller treatises including Alexander's famous *Letter to Aristotle* and his *Conversation with the Brahmans*. These fantastic, so-called 'Indian' treatises were particularly popular and are preserved in a significant number of manuscripts. Other important sources of information about the Far East were the encyclopedias of Roman compilers such as Pliny and Solinus and the bestiaries deriving from the late antique *Physiologus*. In each of these texts, the Orient figures as an ambiguous wonderland where an exotic abundance harbours immeasurable treasures and a proliferating nature creates gigantic shapes, fabulous animals, and monstrous nations. Derived from antiquity, this supposed knowledge about far distant lands was made to correspond to the testimonies of Holy Scripture, in particular to the prophetic books. Whereas ancient writers such as Pliny regarded the Marvels of the East as a manifestation of 'ingenios ... natura' ['inventive nature'] (*Nat. his.* VII, ii, 32), Christian epistemology interpreted the oriental world according to eschatological patterns, considering Asia to be at once the noblest and most privileged of the three known continents (being geographically proximate to the Earthly Paradise) and the home of Antichrist, from whence would emanate his diabolic hordes bent on demolishing Christianity at the end of the time. As the seat of historical time's beginning and end – of Edenic expulsion and apocalyptic horror – the East occupied an important and fundamentally ambiguous role within salvation history.[1]

Western conceptions of the Far East were confirmed and actualized in the midst of the twelfth century by the so-called *Letter of Presbyter* (or *Prester*) *John*.[2] The author, of course, was neither (as the letter maintains) king of India nor king of any other eastern country; instead, he might more profitably be sought among Friedrich Barbarossa's civil servants. The letter was addressed to the Byzantine Emperor Manuel Komnenos, but also circulated among the important courts of the West. The mythical Indian 'rex et sacerdos' John confirmed all the well-known Indian topoi, and therefore was thought to give trustworthy evidence of the actual situation in the eastern parts of the world (*La lettere del Prete Gianni* 18). His realm reaches from the Tower of Babel to India Magna, where the Apostle Thomas is buried, and is irrigated by one of the four rivers of Paradise. It harbours immense treasures that have not only material value but also magical powers. Monstrous races and the apocalyptic nations Gog and Magog live under his rule. His dominion is the earthly equivalent to the heavenly and messianic Jerusalem described in the Revelation of John (Rev. 20–1): lies, envy, and murder are completely unknown. The royal and priestly descendant from the three Holy Kings knows about the loss of the Christian realm of Jerusalem and promises to support his brethren in the fight against evil, seeking to destroy their common enemy, the Islamic Saracens, and reconquer the Holy Land:

> Quando procedimus ad bella contra inimicos nostros, XIII cruces magnas et praecelsas, factas ex auro et lapidibus pretiosis, in singulis plaustris loco vexillorum ante faciem nostram portari facimus, et unamquamque ipsarum secuntur X milia militum et C milia peditum armatorum, exceptis aliis, qui sarcinis et curribus et inducendis victualibus exercitus deputati sunt. ...
>
> Palatium vero, quod inhabitat sublimitas nostra, ad instar et similitudinem palacii, quod apostolus Thomas ordinavit Gundoforo, regi Indorum, in officinis et reliqua structura per omnia simile est illi. Laquearia, tigna quoque et epistilia sunt de lignis cethim. Coopertura eiusdem palacii est de ebeno, ne aliquo casu possit comburi. In extremitatibus vero super culmen palacii sunt duo poma aurea, et in unoquoque sunt duo carbunculi, ut aurum splendeat in die et carbunculi luceant in nocte. ...
>
> Semel in die comedit curia nostra. In mensa nostra comedunt omni die XXX milia hominum praeter ingredientes et exeuntes. Et hi omnes accipiunt expensas singulis diebus de camera nostra tam in equis quam in aliis expensis. Haec mensa est de pretioso smaragdo, quam sustinent duae columpnae de ametisto.

When we go to war against our enemies, the wagon before us instead of carrying banners has thirteen huge crosses made out of gold and decorated with precious stones, and to each of these crosses are assigned 10,000 knights and 100,000 foot soldiers, without counting the other people making part of the baggage train and taking care of the wagons and the supplies. ...

The palace in which our Majesty resides is really identical to the palace that the Apostle Thomas constructed for Gundoforo, King of India; it perfectly resembles it, both inside and outside. The ceiling and the beams and architraves, too, are manufactured of Cyprian wood; the roof is made out of ebony instead, so that it can in no way catch fire. On the very top of the palace, on the top of the cupola, there are two golden apples, and inside them there are two carbuncles, so that the gold shines during the day and the carbuncles glow at night. ...

At our court, we are accustomed to eat once a day, and 30,000 persons get their daily meal upon our table, without counting the hosts that are present. These others receive daily all the resources they need, including horses and other equipment, out of our treasure chamber. The table consists of noble emerald and lies upon two pillars of amethyst. (*La lettere del Prete Gianni* 74ff.)

The epistemologically well-known territory, to which the Christian side assigned so many hopes and fears, was to be seriously shattered by a new and unexpected 'description of the world' being elaborated at the end of the thirteenth century in a prison in Genoa. After an absence of nearly twenty-five years, the son of a Venetian merchant, Marco Polo, his father Niccolò, and his uncle Maffeo returned to Venice from a long stay in the oriental world.[3] Soon afterwards, Marco was imprisoned as a result of one of the martial conflicts that, at the end of the century, took place frequently between the two rival sea powers of Genoa and Venice. While in prison, he met the cultivated *homme de lettres* Rustichello da Pisa, a compiler of romances, who had been captured – as most scholars assume – during the battle of Meloria in 1284 (Larner 47). It is not very clear (and probably never will be) whether Marco Polo really dictated the experiences of his journey, as Rustichello assures us in the prologue to 'our book,' or whether Rustichello instead based his book on a now-lost Italian manuscript (Emersleben 110). The oldest existing manuscript, however, seems to have been entitled 'Le Devisement dou monde,' and is related in an idiom commonly known as Franco-Italian or Franco-Venetian (Segre xv–xvi; Larner 46). This purely literary language is one of the several mixed forms of Italian and French that was used in northern Italy from the end of twelfth to the end of the fourteenth century, particularly for the adaptation of chivalric romances. Within the lifetime of Marco Polo, the experiences of his journey were compiled in French, Tuscan, Venetian, and Latin versions, which often differed substantially from one another. The narration of the 'Meraviglie del mondo' ['Wonders of the world'], as the text was entitled in several Italian manuscripts,

spread over the occidental world in the following centuries, reproduced in almost every language.[4]

In hardly any other writing has the western view of the world been
challenged· so much. The *Devisement dou monde* shows the Far East,
with its incredible wonders, as a cultural hemisphere of its own,
instead of regarding it – as was generally the case in the past, and as
the *mappaemundi* with Jerusalem at the very centre apparently demonstrated – as located at the very margins of the known world. Thus
'notre livre' ['our book'] differs from all other travelling reports of this
period: it still keeps close to the literary topoi and commonplaces
about the East, but it differentiates and mingles them with new and
as yet unheard descriptions (ch. 1).[5] The contradictions that arise
between the expectations caused by a providential interpretation of the
world and its empirical encounters are manifest in the narrative itself.
In contrast to other travelling reports of the late Middle Ages, the
Devisement does not succeed in putting the far eastern marvellous
world in a rational relation to Christian concepts or in harmonizing the
discrepancies that inevitably arise. Whenever the text faces experiences
that are radically different from the ideas of western tradition and do
not fit into conventional patterns of interpretation, a moment of
profound disorientation appears. It is this hiatus that causes the fascinating and anxious atmosphere of the *Devisement*. The text does not
give documentary information, as might be expected, but is instead an
authentic document of a borderline experience in language and literature: by rendering the conception of a bewildering counter-world that
does not make up part of the western cultural dominion but lies
beyond the ecumenical perspective of the Occident, it consequently
puts into question Christian universality. It threatens not only to split
off 'our book' and the community of 'our' narrators but also the whole
'Description of the world,' as the story of 'our' three Holy Kings will
paradigmatically show.

The story of the Magi, which was to become very important in later
Christian theology and art, is recounted in the gospels only by Matthew
(Matt. 2: 1–12). At the time of Jesus' birth, some astrologers from the
East, having seen a new star rising, come to Jerusalem and ask Herod
where they may find the newborn king of the Jews. Herod and the
people of Jerusalem are frightened, and the Jewish scholars are immediately asked where the birth of the Messiah is expected to take place.
They find out that, according to the prophecies, the Messiah will be
born at Bethlehem. Herod therefore sends the Magi to this town and

asks them to return to Jerusalem on their way home. During their journey, the astrologers are guided by a star that leads them directly to
Christ and his mother. They recognize the child as the coming ruler of
the world and demonstrate their adoration by offering their gifts: gold,
frankincense, and myrrh. A dream tells them not to return to Herod, so
they choose another route to the eastern parts they set off from. Herod,
deceived by the Magi, who do not return, decides to kill the newborn
king by murdering all the children of Bethlehem younger than two
years of age.

The three Holy Kings are representatives of the 'ecclesia ex genti-
bus,' and in this sense are already in the Gospel of Matthew clearly
opposed to the Jews (Luz 2, 2; Sand 1384). In contrast to the Jews of
Jerusalem, the Magi from the East are not frightened by the birth of
the new king; while the Jews know the place of his birth but do not
recognize the time of his coming, the Magi are alerted by the appearance of the new star, follow it joyfully, and by searching for the place
where the Messiah has been born they arrive just in time to adore him.
The adoration of the Kings was understood as the first epiphany of
Christ, the appearance of God in human form, and it was evidently of
great importance that this revelation was realized by the pagan 'Magi'
and not by the Jewish priests, since (in the words of the *Golden Legend*)
'the Jews' indifference was condemned by the Magi's zealous search'
(Voragine 80). The 'right' adoration of the newborn Messiah by the
pagan astrologers was also seen in relation to the three men from
Chaldaea who refused to perform the sinful worship of the golden
idol set up by Nebuchadnezzar, and for this reason were condemned
to death (Schiller 107).

Besides the Gospel of Matthew, the traditional liturgy of epiphany
also includes Isaiah 60: 1–4 and Psalms 72: 10–11, both of which feature
a strong metaphorical system focused on light. The exegesis of the
Psalm 'citation' encouraged the reinterpretation of the oriental Magi as
kings, a status that was probably thought to be more suitable to honour the newborn Messiah and ruler of the world, and which lacked the
ambiguous significance of sorcerers and swindlers that weighed on the
word 'Magi': a term that, other than in the Gospel of Matthew, was
employed in the New Testament only in the Acts of Apostles, and there
in a pejorative sense (Monneret de Villard 4). In Christian art, the Magi
were from the tenth century represented as kings; before this time, they
were often depicted in Persian clothes, wearing Phrygian caps to indi-
cate their foreign status. Their representation followed the late antique

model of the so-called *aurum coronarium,* in which barbarian people offer golden wreaths to victorious commanders or emperors. In later tradition, the Magi were thought to represent the three known continents of Asia, Africa, and Europe. The number of the Kings, not mentioned in Matthew, was derived from the quantity of their gifts, while their names – Melchior, Balthasar, and Caspar – appear for the first time in an Egyptian text around 500. The festive day of the three Holy Kings, the feast of Epiphany, probably has its origin in Egypt, where it took the place of a festival of Isis celebrated on 6 January. At the beginning of the fourth century, the day of Epiphany became widespread throughout the oriental world and served to celebrate the birth, adoration, and baptism of Christ. In the western parts, conversely, the birth of Christ and the adoration by the Magi were celebrated together on 25 December. Only at the end of the fourth century was a separate festive day of Epiphany introduced in order to recall the revelation of the Christian God to the pagan kings, marking the fulfilment of ancient expectations of salvation (Schiller 105ff.).

In the *Devisement,* the story of the three Magi is introduced after a long account of the city of Baudac (today's Baghdad) and of the marvels that took place there (chs. 25–9). At first glance, the mention of Baghdad – a city that Marco Polo never visited – and especially of the legendary Kings, seems to be somewhat puzzling. The city had been taken in 1258 by a cruel assault of the Mongols, and a great part of the population had been massacred. The bloodiest deeds during the invasion, however, had been carried out by Christians who profited from the opportunity to take revenge on the passionately hated Muslims (Weiers 195). In Marco Polo's story of the 'Miracle of Baudac,' nothing is said of this matter, but the 'exemplum' could be interpreted as a subsequent justification of the Christian crimes. In 1275, we are told, the Caliph of Baghdad, a mean-spirited and malicious man, read in the Gospel of Matthew that true Christian faith would be able to move mountains. As a result, he cynically decided to ask the Christian community to perform this wonder, declaring that, in case of failure, all Christians would be sentenced to death. Miraculously, the event takes place, and after this striking demonstration of the power of the Christian God, a great number of Saracens become Christians, and even the Caliph himself decides to be baptized secretly. Yet – as happens so often in 'our book'[6] – only a few chapters later a contradictory story is told. The account of the three Holy Kings, though very similar in its legendary character and also describing a divine revelation, does not correspond at all to the first example of the splendid and convincing supremacy of Christianity, but presents different and somewhat less convincing results of Christendom:

> En Persie est la cité qui est apelé Sava, de la quel se partirent les trois mais, quant il vindrent ahorer Jesucrit; en ceste cité sunt soveliz les trois mais en trois sepouture mout grant et beles, et desor la sepouture a une maison quarés. ... Les cors sunt encore tuit en[t]iere et ont ch[e] voilz et barbe. Le un avoit a nom Beltasar, le autre Gaspar, le terço Melchior. Mesere Marc demande plusor jens de cel cité de l'estre de ces trois mais, mes nul ne i ot qu'il en sause dire ren, for qu'il disoient qu'il estoient trois rois que ansie-nament i furent soveliz. Mes il en apristent ce que je vos dirai.

> There is a town in Persia called Sava [Saba], from which the three Magi set out to adore Jesus Christ, and in this city the three Magi are buried, in three very large and beautiful monuments, and above them there is a square building. The bodies are still entire, with the hair and beard remaining. One of these was called Balthasar, the second Caspar, and the third Melchior. Messer Marco asked several people of this town about those three Magi, but he did not find anybody who could tell him any-thing about this matter, except that it was said they were three kings who were buried there in days of old. But then he learned about them what I am going to tell you. (ch. 31)

In the West, the names of the three Holy Kings and of the places they came from had been spread by the famous *Historia Scholastica* of Peter Comestor, completed around 1170. The even more important *Legenda Aurea*, written in the 1260s by the Dominican Jacobus de Voragine, also relates that the Kings 'came from the borderland of Persia and Chaldaea ... where the Saba river flows, so that the region is called Sabaea' (Voragine 83). So far, the *Devisement* is in complete correspondence with western tradition. But the fact that the 'premitiae gentium' ['firstlings of pagans'] to whom God revealed himself (Augustine, *Sermones* 1026ff) were unknown at the place where their holy bodies were interred must have been quite startling to a contemporary reader who was convinced that these Kings, in the influential retelling of the *Legenda Aurea*, had spread the *euangelion* or 'good news' of Christian salvation throughout the eastern parts of the world after their baptism by the Apostle Thomas (Voragine 35).[7] Even more scandalous, however, was the asser-tion that the mortal remains of the ancestors of Prester John should still rest in Persia: it was widely known that their bodies had long ago been transported from Constantinople to Milan and, after the conquest of the Italian city by the German Emperor Friedrich Barbarossa, brought in triumph to Cologne.

In the midst of the twelfth century, the city of Milan, the most important community in the Italian territories of the Holy Roman Empire, was opposed to Friedrich Barbarossa. During the first siege of the town, the relics of the three Holy Kings had been moved from the church of Saint Eustorgio near Milan into the city itself. After the capitulation of Milan in 1162, Barbarossa offered the relics to the Imperial Chancellor and archbishop of Cologne, Reinald von Dassel, known as a most obedient servant of the Emperor, and the bodies of the Holy Kings were brought to Cologne in 1164, where the transfer was celebrated each year with a triumphal procession.[8] The legend of the Magi served to reinforce the imperial politics against the papacy because the Holy Kings had been witnesses to the revelation of God without any intercession of the Church. Iconographically this concept is expressed in a relief on the front side of the famous Cologne shrine that was finished around 1220, where Otto IV is represented within the adoration scene as the fourth of the Holy Kings (Stehkämpfer 39–40). Pope Alexander III, who tried in vain to stop Reinald von Dassel on his way back to Cologne in order to seize possession of the relics, was probably already aware of the political importance that the Holy Kings could gain as a pro-imperial argument in the investiture contest.

The translation of these relics had a large 'international resonance' (Schäfer 73), and was widely publicized by the chronicles of the time. The bodies were exhibited in the nave of the old Cathedral at Cologne where they were devoutly adored by the crowd. It was believed that gazing upon the relics could prevent unhouseled death, a quality otherwise attributed only to the fourteen auxiliary saints. Immediately after their translation, the Magi began to work miracles as the *Relatio de tribus Magi*, written in 1200, recounts. They were said to protect against misfortune, especially against fire disasters, bad weather, and epilepsy. Later, they came to be honoured as patrons of merchants and travellers (Brückner 1388–9). Cologne consequently became a very important centre of pilgrimage and was named, together with Rome, Santiago de Compostela, and Canterbury, as one of the four 'peregrationes maiores' that granted the believer a great reduction of penance (Gui lvi). Milan, trying desperately to reclaim the Kings' relics and asserting that it still held a small finger of one of the Magi and a gold piece that had fallen out of one of their pockets during the transport, propagated the Cult of the Holy Kings as well (Hofmann 218 ff.). The significance of the holy bodies is also demonstrated by the fact that several chronicles talking about the terrifying Mongolian invasion in 1236 seriously suggested that the frightening horsemen had come to Europe only to regain the relics of their descendants and to bring them home to their realm (Monneret de Villard 158ff). For these reasons, the Holy Kings' presence at Saba, as reported in the *Devisement*, must have been most inexplicable to a contemporary audience, taking into consideration the important role of these relics within the popular imagination, as well as their role within the theological system. It is not amazing that Marco Polo, as he continues his report, insistently tries to clear up these strange facts. At the 'Cala Ataperistan' ('que vaut a dir en françois castiaus de les aoraor do feu' ['that is to say, in French, castle of the worshipper of fire']) (ch. 21), three days' journey further on, he finally obtains more information about this puzzle:

[L]es homes de cel caustaus dient que jadis ansienemant [trois lor] rois de cele contree aloient aorer un profete qui estoit nes, et aportent trois ofert – or, encens et mire – por connoistre se celui profet estoit dieu ou rois tereine ou mirre. Car il dient: se il prant or, qu'il est roi tereine, et se il prient encens il est dieu et se il prient mire qu'il est mire.

The people of this castle relate that, in days of old, three kings of that country went away to worship a prophet that had been born, and they carried with them three manner of offerings – gold, frankincense and myrrh – in order to ascertain whether that prophet were a God, or an earthly king, or a physician. For, they said, if he takes the gold, then he is an earthly king; if he takes the incense, he is a god; if he takes the myrrh, he is a physician. (ch. 31)

It is striking that the biblical star guiding the Kings to the crib is not even mentioned, for it played an important role in the theological debate and was interpreted as enlightenment in several different modes: as the *Legenda Aurea* puts it, 'the star the Magi saw was a fivefold star – a material, a spiritual, an intellectual, a rational, and a supersubstantial star' (Voragine 82). In particular, the concept of the 'spiritual star' as a manifestation of true faith in God and internal devotion to his glory and light was very important to the spirituality of the late Middle Ages (Luz 2, 2, 5c). The legend related by Marco Polo, however, pays much more attention to the gifts that the three Kings took with them. In contrast to western tradition, the Magi do not appear as tributaries or fervent devotees of the King and Messiah, but instead seem far more interested in assaying the true nature of the newborn prophet by their offerings. The symbolic value that the oriental version gives to these gifts corresponds in many ways to the interpretation of occidental theologians, who emphasize the disjunction between the poverty of the new King and the precious offerings brought by the Magi. The myrrh is, however, in early western tradition a symbol for death, and thus figures as a sign of the Messiah's human nature and mortality rather than his role as a physician, a meaning which was particularly widespread in Manichaeism (Monneret de Villard 92–8) and later became important for Renaissance iconography. The story related to Marco Polo by the people of Ataperistan continues most strangely: when the Kings approach the child with their offerings, one after the other, they find the child to be always of their own age. Only when they decide to enter all together do they behold the child in his actual state. They adore the child and offer their presents, and the child takes all their offerings at once. In return, the child gives a small sealed box to the Kings. On their journey homeward, they cannot resist the desire to open the box; inside they find nothing more than a simple stone. The Kings, showing themselves to be less wise and clairvoyant than western tradition expected them to be, do not grasp the deeper meaning of the stone, which symbolizes their firmness in the Christian faith, and, obviously disappointed, throw it into a well. At this moment, a fire descends from heaven into the well. Seeing this marvel, the Kings finally understand the importance of the gift and deeply repent their hasty act. They take the fire home to their country and carry it into a sanctuary, where it is adored as if it were God himself. The people of the place take care that the fire will never go out; if it happens to go out by accident, they go to their brethren, take some of their fire, and bring it back to their own church. 'Et vos di,' the narrator concludes his bewildering account, 'qu'il sunt mantes jens' ['And I tell you that they are many people'] (ch. 32).

In spite of the apparent similarities, the oriental version of the legend of the Holy Kings related by Messer Marco – which is, in fact, an etiological legend about the origins of Zoroastrianism – differs widely in its religious tendency and its theological meaning.[9] From the western point of view, the Kings' loss of spirituality and holiness would evidently weaken the status and effects of their relics. In contrast to the 'Miracle of Baudac,' the legend does not demonstrate the supremacy of Christianity, but rather creates an atmosphere of confusion and anxiety. The Magi, said to have propagated the Christian faith in the East, are seen at the same time as founders of a deeply heretical cult that split off from Christianity in *statu nascendi*, and which bears throughout it diabolic tendencies. It is significant that this scandalous taking over of 'our' three Kings by a completely different tradition is not even mentioned in the Latin version of the *Devisement dou monde* elaborated by the Dominican monk Fra Pipino between 1310 and 1314. The story of the heretical Kings and their many followers, who darken the light of the true faith by worshipping fire, did not find any reception in the Occident (Cardona 658–62). It is mentioned neither by the Franciscan Odoric nor by the great and ingenious compiler Sir John Mandeville. Even the narrator of 'our' book, who distinguishes himself explicitly from his protagonist 'mesiere Marc Pol' in only a few cases, seems to keep his distance here. Before these incredible and intolerable indications, the text splits off in two positions: Messer Marco Polo, who insists that he heard this bewildering account with his own ears, and the narrator, who insistently confirms that it is Messer Marco (and not the narrator himself) who relates those facts, and consequently refuses to take any responsibility for their heretical meaning. As he puts it, 'Et toute ceste chouse content et distrent, celç dou chastel, a mesiere Marc Pol' ['And all this was related by those of the castle to Messer Marco Polo'] (ch. 32). It remains uncertain whether by withdrawing himself from this account the narrator weakens or reinforces its authority. According to an early Christian concept, all magic should have come to an end with the Incarnation. The Magi, in fact, were said not to be scientific astrologers but rather devout Christians when they returned to their homelands (Luz 2, 2, 5a). In the *Devisement*, conversely, the revelation of the divine nature of the Son of Man leads to the foundation of the 'magic' cult of fire worship. From now on, the ambiguous glow of fire from the community *in ignibus* begins to cast its bright light on the whole *Description of the World*, and the heretical Magi that arise (instead of disappear) with the birth of Christ will remain insistently present in 'our' book.

The perplexity that arises for the Christian *imago mundi* in its description (the *Devisement dou monde*) is clearly reflected in the narrative functions and competences separating Messer Marco Polo from the narrator. As Bertolucci Pizzorusso in her seminal article (4–30) and Rieger in his more recent study (289–312) have pointed out, in general, the narrative 'I' or 'we' oscillates, and it remains unclear precisely who is speaking. The few cases where the narrative positions are made explicit, therefore, are of special interest for textual analysis. While the narrator of the heretical story about the Holy Kings insists on the difference between himself and Messer Marco, there is no such separation, for example, in the case of the description of the town of Quinsai.[10] Instead, we find a strong identification of Messer Marco and the narrative 'I' that repeatedly confirms the truth and authenticity of the experience but which can hardly find adequate words for it, thus leading the narrating subject to the very edge of communicability. The exceptional character of this episode is indicated by a strikingly unusual opening in the chapter concerning the 'City of Heaven,' located in the prosperous province of Mangi, the former state of the Sung Dynasty. Right at the beginning, a letter is mentioned which was apparently written by the Queen of the Sung to prevent the Mongolian conquerors from demolishing the town. This document, which makes reference to detailed internal knowledge, serves as a direct source for the city's description. Its citation is legitimized by an external eyewitness who calls himself Marco Polo and who vouches for the correctness and precision of the information: 'Et selonc que en celle escripture se contenoit ... fu verité selonc ce que je Marc Pol vit puis apertemant a mes iaux' ['And what this writing contained ...was the truth, according to what I, Marco Polo, afterwards saw directly with my own eyes'] (ch. 152).

This double authentication – that is, the necessity of a surplus of authentication – seems rather strange precisely because Quinsai (today's Hangzhou) at first sight may appear quite familiar. The town of Quinsai clearly resembles Venice: 'Et nulz se face mervoille se il ha tant de pont, por ce que je vos di que ceste ville est toute en eve, et est environ[é] de eve, et por ce convient que maint pont hi aie por aler por toute la vi[ll]e' ['And there is no wonder that there are so many bridges, for you see the whole city stands as it were in the water and surrounded by water, so that a great many bridges are required to give free passage about it'] (ch. 152). From the very beginning of this unusually detailed account, however, Quinsai is described as something entirely different: it is not merely the far eastern equivalent of the famous European centre of commerce, but is far more than that. In quantity as well as in quality, Quinsai is superior to Venice, being of greater beauty and far richer; it has many more bridges, twelve thousand in number, all of which are made of stone, some with high arches so that even large ships can easily pass under them. Although the Franco-Venetian manuscript of the *Devisement* does not explicitly compare Venice to Quinsai, the similarities and thus the differences are obvious. Taking into consideration the fact that the largest bridge of Venice was built out of wood and connected by a drawbridge which had to be opened in order to give passage to ships with a higher superstructure, there could be no doubt about the inferiority of European techniques. Only at the end of the sixteenth century was the old bridge of the Rialto replaced by a construction made of stone (Hubala 143).

The question 'Et que je voç en diroie?' ['And how can I say this to you?'], which is insistently repeated and varied in the *Devisement*, is in this context far more than a mere rhetorical figure. Facing the incredible nature of what it tries to describe precisely, the narrative 'I' interrupts its discourse and hesitates, as if searching for the right words, and at last gives up – only to immediately return to the argument which it can neither explain sufficiently nor leave alone.[11] There are the very rich and luxurious palaces with all their comfort and beauty, and the countless abbeys and monasteries of the town. Further, Quinsai is known for its very beautiful public baths, in which a hundred persons can bathe at one time, and it possesses towers of stone, where people can take refuge in case the city catches fire. The roads of Quinsai, indeed of the whole province, are paved with stones and with baked bricks, so that one can walk or ride without becoming dirty – an unheard-of luxury for Europeans of that time! More and more the narrative develops a peculiar dynamic of its own that urges the narrator even against his intention to keep on narrating:

> Et sommeemant vos di con tute verité que l'afer de la provence dou Mangi est si tres grant couse, e de richese et de rende e de profit que n'a le grant kan, que ne est home que l'oisse conter e ne le veisse que le peust [c]roire; et a poine se poroit escrivere la grant nobilité de ceste provence e por ce m'en tarai atant, que ne vos en dirai grantment desormés, me si voç en dirai aucune couse encore e puis nos en partiron.

> And, in short, I tell you with all truth that the business of the province of Mangi is so very great a thing both in wealth and in revenue and in profit which the great Khan derives from it that there is not a man who heard it told and did not see it who could believe it; and one can hardly describe

the great and noble things of this province. And therefore I shall be silent about it then, that I shall not tell you much about it henceforth. But yet I will tell you something more again about it, and then we shall leave it. (ch. 152)

Notwithstanding this determined resolution of the narrator, the narration goes on and on, and subsequently the next chapter insistently turns to the description of the city and its marvellous riches. The attempt to give an impression of the magnitude and richness of the occupied town by calculating the revenue that the great Khan collects from salt taxes, however, leads simply to an abstract enumeration of quantities. The sums of income appear even more immense and monstrous, reported as they are in a tone of distinguished impartiality and cool merchant logic (Greenblatt 47). In contrast to the treasures of Prester John, the revenues of the Great Khan do not conduce toward symbolical, allegorical, or anagogical interpretation. They do not give any further information beyond their concrete meaning, which refers only to number:

> Or sachiés tuit voiremant que le sal de ceste ville rente chascun an cons[u]etudemant LXXX tomain d'or: e chascun tomain est LXXX^M sajes d'or; que montent, les LXX t[o]main, MMMMM^M et DC^M de sajes d'or, que chascun sajes vaut plus de un florin d'or o de un ducato d'or. E ce est bien une merveiose couse e grandismes enonbre de monoie.

> Now you may know quite truly that the salt of this town produces every year, in round numbers, fourscore tomans of gold; and the toman is worth 70,000 saggi of gold, so that the total value of the fourscore tomans will be five millions and six hundred thousand saggi of gold, each saggio being worth more than a gold florin or ducat. And this is quite a marvellous thing and a very great sum of money. (ch. 153)

Instead of being a marvellous wonderland, with its four rivers of the Earthly Paradise and its fountains of youth, Quinsai turns out to be a real town under foreign rule, where the citizens are engaged in their various trades and enjoy themselves in the evening. At the same time, the southern Chinese capital with all its 'demesuré' ['immeasurable'] (ch. 152) goods and riches and its infinite number of inhabitants appears as an abstract noun that cannot be reproduced or explained by conventional terminology or images, because it is beyond any terms and imagination. Most surprising is the frighteningly small dimension allotted to Christianity in this great metropolis: in the crowded city, with its multitude of temples and monasteries, there is 'une gliese de cristienz nestorin solement' ['one church only, belonging to the Nestorian Christians'] (ch. 152). In fact, although the Christian religion can be practised without any obstructions at Quinsai, as in the rest of the realm, Christianity plays a very limited, even an exotic, role. The spiritual power of the state and its Mongolian ruler, who assembles many representatives of different cults at his court, is attributed in the *Devisement* almost completely to the lamaistic monks. These Magi are at least as extraneous and terrifying as the perverted Holy Kings that founded the cult of the fire-worshippers. The description of the powerful *bacsi* from Kashmir and Tibet, who can conjure up darkness and bad weather, who make their idols speak, and who can even cause cups full of wine to rise from the pavement and float through the hall, oscillates in the *Devisement* between horror and fascination:[12]

Et sajés tout voirmant que cesti bacsi que je voç dic desovre, que sevent tant de enchantemant, font si grant mervoille com je voç dirai. Je voç di que quant le grant kaan siet en sa mestre sale a sa table, qui est aut plus de VIII coves, e les coupes sunt emi le paviment de la sale, longe de la table bien X pas, e sunt plene de vin et de lait ou d'autres buen bevrajes, et ceste sajes encanteors que je voç ai dit desovre, que bacsi sunt només, il font tant por lor encantement et por lor ars que celes coupes pleinnes por lor meesme se levent [desus] le paviment ou elle estoient et s'en vont devant le grant kan san ce que nulz ne le toucent; et ce font voiant X^M homes, et ce est voir et vertables sanz nulle mensogne.

And you may know quite truly that those *bacsi*, of whom I have been speaking before as knowing so many enchantments, perform a great marvel as I am going to tell you. And I tell you this: when the Great Khan is in his main hall, seated at his table, which stands on a platform some eight cubits above the ground, his cups are set before him on the paved floor of the hall, at a distance of some ten paces from his table, and filled with wine and milk or other good spiced beverages. And these wise enchanters who are called *bacsi* and of whom I have already told you before, by the power and the art of their enchantment, cause the filled cups to move by themselves from their place on the floor without being touched by anybody, and to present themselves to the Great Khan. And they perform this in front of 10,000 persons. And this is true and real, without any lie. (ch. 75)

The magical practices and their weird performers seem so dangerous that the narrator even in faraway Genoa prefers not to talk in detail of these enchantments and marvels. By refusing to put into language the incredible performances of the *bacsi*, however, he also declines to appropriate this part of the world by his description, to annex and to usurp it epistemologically with his categories and terms. The explicit attempt to not talk about the incomprehensible acts of the *bacsi* produces an odd attraction, an attraction that neither the narrator nor the reader of 'our book' can withdraw from. Precisely because the magic arts of the lamaistic monks are not put into language, and are not comprehensively described in words in order to be rejected as demonic jugglery, their enchantment remains an inexplicable, latent menace:[13]

> Et encore voç di qu'il ont les plus sajes encanteor et les meior astronique, selonc lor usanç que soient en toutes celles provences que entor euç sunt, car il font les plus fere encantemant et les greignor mervoiles a oir e a veoir por ars de diables, que ne est pas buen a contere en nostre livre por ce que trop se mervelieront les jens.

> And I tell you again that there are the wisest sorcerers and best astrologers of their tradition, according to the practice of those who reside in the surrounding provinces, for they perform the most magic enchantments and the greatest marvels that you may ever hear and see by means of diabolic arts, so that it is not good to retell this in our book, for people would be too much amazed. (ch. 116)

In the hidden background of this silence, les 'jens' – that is, the European people reading this report – may discern at least the gloomy shadows of a counter-world where occidental culture has lost all significance. It makes no sense to regard these magic practices as a conspiracy of Antichrist, and it does not correspond in any way to the common Christian topology and topography of evil. The well-known wonderland, considered to be located merely at the periphery of salvation history and upon the distant horizon of western thinking, turns out to be an autonomous centre of civilization. Looking back from the Far East to the Occident, the latter appears as a region of little importance: as to riches and goods, it is a *quantité négligeable*, while as to culture and religion, it is only one cult among many others, and is even marginal. In later western travel literature, however, different strategies can be found which can be identified as reactions to this radical change of perspective and to the related traumatic offence of cultural narcissism.

In the *Itinerary* of the Franciscan Odoric da Pordenone, written in 1330, the narration of the telekinetic powers of the lamaistic monks is placed in another context and is compiled with some descriptions of high festivities at the court of the Great Khan. In contrast to the accounts of the *Devisement*, where these celebrations demonstrate the magnitude and power of the Mongolian Khan and his assemblage, Odoric's description of the Great Khan's birthday celebration displays ridiculous and grotesque features. Upon command, the henchmen of the Great Khan fall to the ground, put their fingers into their ears, and start – as reported in some manuscripts – to grind flour! At the end of this amazing spectacle, jugglers come in and cause cups to fly through the air. The threatening magicians turn out to be merely minstrels and buffoons, their troubling enchantments unmasked as simply Chinese acrobatics:

> Hoc facto et ordinato, tunc aliqui ystriones ad ipsum accedunt et etiam alique ystrionatrices; ante ipsum tam dulciter cantant quod quedam iucunditas est audire. Deinde ystriones faciunt venire leones que reverenciam faciunt Imperatori. ... Deinde ystriones vehi faciunt ciphos aureos per aerem, plenos bono vino, et sic ad ora omnium volencium bibere de isto vino porigunt istos ciphos. Sic hec et multa alia coram domino isto faciunt.

> When all this has been done in order, some artists (and among them also women) come forward, and they sing so sweetly before the Emperor that it is a pleasure to hear them. Then the artists bring in some lions that make their reverences to the Emperor. ... Then the artists make golden cups filled with noble wine fly through the air, and in this way they offer the cups to everyone who cares to taste the wine. And they perform this and many other things in front of their lord. (Odoric 29.7, 30.482)

This tendency to impart only a curious and far from menacing character to the far eastern wonderworld is characteristic of Odoric's *Itinerary*. The representative of the divine *logos* never lacks for a suitable comparison, never misses a decisive judgment, and describes the exotic world through amusing anecdotes. By demonstrating his sovereignty over language, Odoric's *Itinerary* (which is clearly inspired by hagiographic motives) also demonstrates the primacy of Christian religion and western culture. The text communicates a consoling and calming message: that even in the queer world of far eastern marvels, 'our' own cultural self-consciousness is not menaced at all.

Sir John Mandeville, who is himself (as Greenblatt [47–83] emphasizes in his important study) just as fictitious as his travel report compiling a great number of written sources, gives another account of the ceremonies that take place on the occasion of the Great Khan's birthday. In contrast to the Franciscan missionary, the knight-errant Mandeville does not content himself with what he knows about the queer and foolish performance of the Mongol entourage. The exemplary curious pilgrim insists upon asking – here and everywhere else throughout the exotic lands he travels – the inhabitants themselves to explain their strange habits, and they obligingly describe whatever he desires to know. The double affirmation that combines the outside perspective of an eyewitness with the exclusive knowledge of an insider is characteristic of the *Book of John Mandeville*. Like Odoric, Mandeville never loses sovereignty over his language; moreover, he even makes exotic people speak in terms and categories that sound familiar to western ears. In contrast to the *Devisement*, the occidental perception is never called into question but is rather confirmed as the only right and valuable interpretation of the world, which naturally includes within it the exotic and peripheral regions of the Far East. The explanation that Mandeville gives for the strange behaviour of the Mongols, for example, is absolutely convincing:

> Ie demanday a eulx quelles misteres ne quelles significacions ces choses auoient; et il me respondirent que le bessier la teste a telle heure dadont celle honneur estoit telle mistere, que tous ceulz qui lauoient baissie seroient a tousiours mais obeissans et loial a lempereur et que pour dons ne pour promesses il ne pourroient estre corrumpus ne incliner pour nul auoir a lui faire trahision. Et du doy mectre en loreille ilz disoient que nulz de ceuls ne pourroient oir parler ne dire chose qui fust contraire a lempereur, que tantost ne lalast dire ou noncier a lempereur, et fust ses peres ou ses freres.

> I asked them what secret meaning or significance these things had, and they replied that the bowing of the head during this hour of celebrations had the secret meaning that everyone who had bowed would always remain obedient and loyal to the Emperor, and that by neither gifts nor promises could he be corrupted or inclined to do treason. They said that

putting their finger into the ear means that none of them would ever listen or say anything against the Emperor without their referring and announcing it to him immediately, even if it were their fathers or brothers. (Mandeville, ed. Deluz 361)

Mandeville appropriates the long distant wonderworld anew following a double strategy: confirming, on the one hand, the traditional *mirabilia*; and, on the other, giving them a 'new' (that is, reasonable) explanation. The menacing and troubling wonders of the far eastern world are consciously stylized and thus reduced to conventional topoi. A striking example of this strategy appears at the end of the birthday ceremonies, when jugglers enter the hall. They enter not in order to make cups or other things fly around, or to spread dark and bad weather, but to make the sun and moon appear in person, right in the middle of the hall, as if 'they presented their reverence to the Great Khan.' The weird powers of the lamaistic monks turn out to be nothing but an allegorical masquerade, alluding to the trees of sun and moon in the *Romance of Alexander* that prophesy the protagonist's fate, thus reducing the whole performance to merely an occidental tale of the Orient. The incomprehensible far eastern world of the *Devisement* is once again annexed to western tradition:

> Et apres viennent iugleours et enchanteurs, qui font trop de merueilles; car il font venir en lair le soleil et la lune par semblant pour lui faire reuerence, qui donnent si grant clarte que a paine veoient ilz lun lautre. Et puis font la nuit venir, si que on ne voit goute; et puis font il reuenir le iour.

> And afterwards jugglers and enchanters come in, who work many marvels; for they make the sun and the moon rise into the air as if to show reverence to him [the Emperor], which give forth such brightness that only with difficulty could they distinguish one [light] from the other. And after that they make night fall, so that one cannot see a thing; and then they make the day come again. (Mandeville, ed. Deluz 362–3)

Thus Mandeville, after Marco Polo's traumatic loss of language, succeeds in reintegrating those dangerous wonders and figures and sites into the former map of western epistemological territories, satisfying both conventional literary expectations and sceptical attitudes toward traditional knowledge. As we know, Mandeville also satisfied many scientists, travellers, and philologists who long continued to give more credence to him than to Marco Polo and to his disquieting *Devisement*. Perhaps this was simply because Mandeville, explaining all those bewildering marvels in plain words, was able to replace the traumatic effects of Marco Polo's broken language and thus reassuringly confirmed the superiority of western culture.

NOTES

1 The literature about the Marvels of the East and their reception is exhaustive; still fundamental for the subject are Wittkower; LeGoff, 'L'Occidente medievale' and *Phantasie*; Perrig. The nexus between monstrous nations and apocalyptic hordes is worked out in detail in my dissertation, 'Apokalyptische Heerscharen und Gottesknechte.'

2 On this mythical king, see, for example, Olschki, 'Der Brief'; Knefelkamp; Zaganelli, 'La Terra Santa'; *La lettere del Prete Gianni*; Milanesi; Silverberg.

3 Some recent studies of Marco Polo include Haw, *Marco Polo's China*; Wood; Larner; Emersleben; Münkler.

4 A still useful study of the very complex redaction of the text is Benedetto. For a shorter overview, see Segre xv–xxi; Reichert 181–8; Wunderli 131–6.

5 All citations of the *Devisement* are taken from *Milione/Le Divisament dou monde*, ed. Ronchi.

6 It seems to be part of the narrative strategy of the text to juxtapose contradictory or inconsistent information. See, for example, the unicorn and the tailed men whose existence is negated in ch. 166, but who reappear in ch. 169.

7 On the southern choir in the Cathedral at Cologne, the Apostle is represented in the act of consecrating the Holy Kings.

8 The importance of the Holy Kings in politics, culture, and theology of this time is especially accentuated by Hofmann, Engels, Stehkämpfer, and Schäfer.

9 Allsen emphasizes the importance of the Muslim, especially Persian, imprint on the *Devisement* which might have been underestimated: 'Polo clearly carried European and Christian cultural baggage to the East, but the new baggage that he acquired along the way is what makes the Description so challenging' (Allsen 382).

10 For the representation of Quinsai in illustrated copies of Western fifteenth-century manuscripts, see Strickland, *Saracens* 511–15.

11 This argument is developed in further detail in my forthcoming paper 'Souveränität und Ohnmacht des Erzählens in spätmittelalterlichen Reiseberichten.'

12 Rossbach interprets the flying cups as 'phantastisches schlaraffisches Motiv' ['a fictional motive alluding to the land of Cockaigne'] (31), and therefore as a phenomenon of pure Western literariness, without taking into consideration the menacing traits of the powerful *bacsi* that formed the religious elite at the court of Kublai. A general tendency of denying the disquieting experiences articulated in the *Devisement* may, however, be observed in Park and Daston 27–34.

13 This menace is sensible, however, in the bewildering encounter with the dark-spreading Caraunas (*Div.* XXXVI) and the acoustic demons in the desert of Lop (*Div.* LVII). While the *Divisament* does not succeed in translating these lethal experiences into common terms and traditional patterns, later 'travel literature' (Odoric, Mandeville, John Bunyan) will reinterpret these traumatic episodes allegorically in Christian terms, in the trope of the 'Valley of the Shadow of Death' (Steinicke, 'Apokalyptische Heerscharen' 140–237).

5 Currents and Currency in Marco Polo's *Devisement dou monde* and *The Book of John Mandeville*[1]

SUZANNE CONKLIN AKBARI

It is scarcely possible to discuss the 'travels' of Marco Polo without also discussing the 'travels' of Sir John Mandeville, and vice versa. These two works were composed within sixty years of each other, both of them forerunners (or very early exemplars) of the emerging genre of travel literature; in this sense, they are two texts of a single kind. At the same time, the so-called travels of Marco Polo and John Mandeville are almost invariably seen as fundamentally different, both in terms of their authors' intentions and in terms of their medieval reception. One was written by a real merchant and traveller, who tells of places he has actually been, even if he exaggerates somewhat in the retelling; the other was written by a person who seems to have simply adopted the name 'John Mandeville' as a pseudonym, and to have 'traveled no further' (in the words of one critic) 'than the nearest library.'[2] Paradoxically, the more 'authentic,' reality-based account of Marco Polo was less popular with medieval readers than the more fantastical book of John Mandeville, which was within fifty years of its composition translated into a range of medieval vernaculars as well as Latin, and which survives in literally hundreds of manuscripts.[3] In spite of the ease with which the works of Marco Polo and John Mandeville are contrasted, however, few efforts have been made to analyse the structural principles of these works, that is, the discursive basis for the geography in each one. The most notable efforts in this direction have focused on the phenomenon of 'diversity,' a spatial and narrative ordering principle in both the *Devisement dou monde* and the *Book of John Mandeville*, as Katherine Park and Iain Higgins have shown.[4] This essay, by contrast, will explore the interrelation of spatial and narrative order in terms of mediation, that is, the process by means of which disparate elements in the world are drawn together in the process of flow, dispersal, and reintegration.

Both Marco Polo's *Devisement dou monde* and the *Book of John Mandeville* – to use the titles by which they were known to medieval readers – use what we might call 'currency' to link together the disparate parts of the world into a coherent whole. In the *Book of John Mandeville*, this is carried out in a devotional context, where the rivers of paradise are thought to flow throughout the whole of the created world. On a literal level, the rivers of Eden water the dry land of the world, while on a figurative level, these watercourses bestow heavenly blessings upon the earth's spiritually parched inhabitants.[5] In the *Devisement dou monde* of Marco Polo, currency functions in quite another way. Here, waterways appear not as the conduits of spiritual blessings, but rather as the means by which travellers (especially merchants) can make their way from one port to another, from one trading place to another. Once there, the traveller can participate in the act of exchange, trading goods (and knowledge) with the travellers he meets. In this discourse of commodity exchange, currency is the blank slate that allows for the transmission of value, as well as the transmission of meaning.

By juxtaposing these two discourses – one devotional, one mercantile – I will try to show how the process of synthesis and unification is described very similarly throughout medieval travel literature, whether the goal of the particular piece of literature is to enable trade, or to facilitate conversion. In the concluding parts of this paper, I will argue that the discourse of currents and currency in the *Devisement dou monde* and the *Book of John Mandeville* allows us to draw certain conclusions about the role that orientation plays in the medieval manifestation of Orientalism. To put it briefly, a world oriented toward sites which are eternally significant in Christian salvation history – Eden and Jerusalem – is fundamentally different from a world oriented toward a whole series of interchangeable, variable centres of trade and exchange, scattered throughout the islands and ports of India and China.

Throughout the Middle Ages, the rivers of paradise were featured prominently on world maps and in prose geographies. Their earliest description, found in the opening chapters of Genesis, had been elaborately expounded by Church fathers such as Ambrose, who (building upon the exegetical strategies of Philo) declared that the four rivers of paradise can be interpreted allegorically, and that each of them – both literally and figuratively – continues to flow throughout the world today. The river Phison (or 'Pishon,' Gen. 2:11), for example, signifies prudence: this river flows to the ends of the earth because, through wisdom, all humanity is redeemed. Within the confines of paradise, Ambrose explains, the river is called 'Phison'; outside Eden, however, it is called the Ganges. Similarly, the river called 'Gihon' in paradise appears elsewhere in the world as the Nile; this river represents temperance. The Tigris and Euphrates are known by the same names both within Eden and outside it; but these watercourses, too, submerge themselves within the ground and re-emerge elsewhere, and are consequently called by different names in different places.[6] In his commentaries on Genesis, Augustine follows the interpretive path of Ambrose; his account of the rivers of paradise in the *De Genesi ad litteram* was reproduced in the *Glossa Ordinaria*, a manual of scriptural interpretation widely used for preaching throughout the Middle Ages, and by this means became very widely disseminated.[7]

Medieval maps similarly use the rivers of paradise to provide a holistic, unifying structure to the world. These maps are generally oriented toward the east, with a schematic representation of Eden at the very top of the map. Spreading outward and downward from Eden, four watercourses wander throughout the world, re-emerging to form the rivers that divide the land mass of the world into the three known continents of Asia, Africa, and Europe.[8] In medieval encyclopedias, the rivers of paradise function very similarly: just as the rivers appear at the top of the map, they also appear at the beginning of the geographical sections of medieval encyclopedias, delimiting the boundaries between continents and the various regions of the world. For example, in Pierre d'Ailly's *Imago mundi*, a geographical survey composed in the early fifteenth century, the rivers of paradise are explicitly identified with the rivers of the world. His description of the river Phison segues effortlessly into a wide-ranging description of the wonders of India, for (as d'Ailly explains) the Phison is actually the Ganges, just as the Gihon is actually the Indus.[9] For Pierre d'Ailly, to venture into farthest India is to enter the gates of Paradise. So far, it seems, the early fifteenth-century description of Pierre d'Ailly is basically similar to that produced in the fourth century by Ambrose and Augustine. Interestingly, however, this very passage in the *Imago mundi* is simultaneously very modern, in the sense that it integrates its description of the rivers of Eden with a detailed account of the known geography of India. D'Ailly's more detailed knowledge of far eastern geography explains why he identifies the river Gihon not as the Nile (as Ambrose and Augustine do), but as the Indus. The geography of the *Imago mundi* is so up to date (at least, by fifteenth-century standards), including a whole series of maps and diagrams, that it was among the texts carried by Columbus on his early voyages; a copy which includes Columbus's abundant annotations survives today.

The *Book of John Mandeville* appeared in or around 1356, about sixty years before Pierre d'Ailly composed his *Imago mundi*. Although one of these works is a geographical treatise and the other a wide-ranging, highly fictional account of one man's travels throughout the world, they both employ the rivers of paradise as an organizing principle, in keeping with the rich medieval tradition I have just outlined. Mandeville states that all the rivers of the world come from a single spring, which is located in Eden: 'Et el plus haut lieu de Paradiz el droit mylieu est la fontayne qe gecte les IIII fluvies qe courent par diverses terres' ['In the highest part of Paradise, right in the middle, is the fountain from which issues the four rivers which flow out through different lands.'][10] Mandeville identifies the first of these as 'Physon ou Ganges' ['Phison, or the Ganges'], which 'court parmy Ynde' ['flows through India']; the second is Gihon, or the Nile, which rises out of the earth near Mount Atlas, 'vait par Ethiope et puis par Egipte' ['passes through Ethiopia and then through Egypt']. The other two rivers, the Tigris and the Euphrates, similarly pass through various lands, sink down into the earth and re-emerge, known under other names, until they too run into the ocean. Mandeville concludes, 'Et dit homme par dela qe toutes les eawes douces du mounde dessure et dessous prignent lour naissance de cel fontaigne de Paradis, et de celle fontaigne toutes y viegnent et issent' ['And men everywhere say that all the sweet waters of the world, both above and below, have their origin in this fountain of Paradise, and all of them flow and issue from this fountain'] (ch. 33; 468–9).

Clearly, this account is at once practical and symbolic – practical, in that it accounts for the physical relationship between various waterways, connected by underground streams; symbolic, in that it posits a single point of origin for all the disparate waterways of the world. However heterogeneous the world may be, the reader is assured, all of its disparate elements are joined at their root by the abundant fountain located deep within the cradle of mankind. This balance of the practical and the symbolic pervades all descriptions of waterways in the *Book of John Mandeville*. The account of the Nile, for example, includes the very useful information that the river floods annually, including the dates when it floods, and how deeply: 'Celle rivere de Nil toutz les aunz quant le solail entre en signe de Cancre elle comence a crestre, et crest toutdis tant come le solail est en Cancre et en Leoun, et crest en tiel manere qe elle est ascune foiz si grande qe elle ad bien XX cubitz ou plus de parfond, et fait adonques grant damage as biens desour terre ... Et quant le solail entre en signe de Virgine adonques comence la rivere a descroistre petit et petit si qe quant le solail entre en signe de Libre adonques elle entre dedeinz ces rives' ['Every year, this river Nile begins to rise when the sun enters into the sign of Cancer, and it rises continually until the sun is in Cancer and in Leo, and it rises in this manner until it is sometimes as deep as twenty cubits or more, and it accordingly does great damage to the land ... And when the sun enters the sign of Virgo, the river at once begins to fall, little by little, and when the sun enters into the sign of Libra, it keeps once again within its banks'] (ch. 6; 144). In the same passage, however, this eminently practical information is counterbalanced by the symbolic significance of the river, which is (Mandeville writes) rightly called the 'Gihon,' for it 'vient courrant de Paradis par my les desertz de Ynde' ['comes flowing from Paradise, through the deserts of India'], before it makes its way underground to Ethiopia, through Egypt, to Alexandria, and at last into the sea (ch. 6; 144–5).

Nowhere in the *Book of John Mandeville* is the practical and the symbolic unified as fully as in the itinerary of the city of Jerusalem. Here, a whole series of wells appear which are imbued with profound significance, owing to their sacred origin. Near the Temple of the Lord (that is, the Dome of the Rock), Mandeville writes, is 'ly bain Nostre Seigneur. En ceo bain soloit entrer l'eawe de Paradis et unqore elle degoute' ['the bath of Our Lord. Into this bath there used to flow the water of Paradise, and still now it drips there'] (ch. 11; 205). Near it is the *probatica piscina* or Pool of Bethesda, where 'soloient les angeles descendre et baigner dedeinz et ly primer qe se baignoit après estoit garriz de quecunquez maladie q'il eust' ['the angels used to come down and bathe, and the first one who bathed there afterwards would be healed of whatever illness he had had'] (ch. 11; 206). Not far away, in the Valley of Jehosaphat, there is a church of Our Lady: 'Et la delez vers occident a dessouz d'un autier y ad une fontaigne qe vient del flun de Paradis' ['And near there, toward the west, under an altar, there is a spring that comes from a river of Paradise' (ch. 11; 212). Each of these sites is holy, not just because of its intersection with specifically Christian salvation history – touched by Jesus, or by his mother – but because of its connection to the ultimate source, located at the birthplace of humanity. These sites emanate both from the place of mankind's birth – Eden – and mankind's spiritual rebirth – Jerusalem.

Even in the regions located further east in the *Book of John Mandeville*, the rivers of paradise continue to appear as the source of all abundance, both material and spiritual. Near the Indian city of Polumbum, the narrator encounters a fountain with extraordinary properties: it is 'une bele fontayne et grande qe ad odour et savour de toutes espices et a chascun hour del jour change odour et savour diversement' ['a beautiful and great spring, which has the odour and flavour of every spice, and each hour of the day it variously changes its smell and flavour']. This fountain not only pleases the senses, but has the power to affect the body more substantially as well: 'Et qy boit troiz fois jeun de celle fontayne il est curez de queconquez maladie q'il ait. Et cils qe demoerent et boivent sovent ils n'ount unques maladie et semblent toutdis estre jeovenes' ['And whoever drinks three times, fasting, from this fountain, he is healed of whatever malady afflicted him. And those that stay there and drink often, they never have any illness and forever seem to be youthful']. As a result, 'Ascuns l'appellent la Fontayne de Juventé ... et dit homme qe celle fontaigne vient de Paradis et pur ceo est elle vertuouse' ['Some call it the Fountain of Youth ... and men say that this fountain comes from Paradise, and this is why it has such power'] (ch. 18; 320–1). Here, physical health is assured by the revivifying spring; because its source is the waters of Eden, however, it offers spiritual benefits as well. It is noteworthy that, like the wafer of Holy Communion, this water makes the one who receives it healthy and whole when it is received 'jeun,' that is, taken on an empty stomach.

Still further east, in Ceylon ('Silha'), is found a lake, brimming over with waters, marvellously located at the very top of a mountain. This water has its source in Eden, too, though not through the usual means. Its source is not the fountain at Eden's centre, but the watery fruits of the Fall: 'Et dient cils de païs qe Adam et Eve ploroient sur celle montaigne C aunz quant ils furent gectez de Paradis. Et celle eawe dient ils estre de lur lermes, qar tant ploroient ils sur celle montaigne qe cis lac fust ensi fait' ['And those of that land say that Adam and Eve wept on that mountain for a hundred years after they were cast out of Paradise. And that water, they say, comes from their tears, for they wept so much upon that mountain that this lake was made of it']. These waters, in other words, are the overflowing tears of repentance. It is appropriate, therefore, that the lake abounds in jewels whose material value reflects the spiritual value of the tears in which they are bathed: 'Et al founz de cel lac troeve homme moultz des pierres preciouses et grosses perles ... Et ly roys du pays touz les aunz une fois donne congee as povres a entrer ou lac et amasser celles pierres en almoigne et pur l'amur de dieu Adam' ['And at the bottom of that lake men find many precious stones and great pearls ... And, every year, the king of that land gives permission to the poor people to enter into the lake and gather up these precious stones, for alms and for the love of the God of Adam']. The overflowing lake generates a river running down one side of that mountain, where one can find 'pierres et des perles grant foisoun' ['great abundance of precious stones and pearls'] (ch. 21; 352–3). Spiritual riches give rise to material riches, which are polished (so to speak) with the charity and love that continues to govern their use.

As the itinerary of the *Book of John Mandeville* moves further eastward, the narrator continues to approach nearer to Eden itself. This is made evident not just by the direction of his journey, but by the marvels he sees, which include rare spices and woods, exotic gems, and even rivers literally flowing with jewels. In the land of Cathay, the narrator discovers that the Grand Khan rides in a chariot made entirely of a luxurious wood called *lignum aloes*. Its source, unsurprisingly, is Eden: the chariot's coach or 'chambre' is 'faite d'un manere de boys qe vient de Paradiz terrestre qe homme appelle *lignum aloes*, qe les fluvies de Paradiz meynent hors en la saisoun ... Et si est celle chambre mult odorant pur cause de ceo bois, et est la chambre toute coverte par dedeinz des plates de fin or ovesqez pierres preciouses et ovesques grosses perles' ['made of a type of wood that comes from the Earthly Paradise, that men call *lignum aloes*, which the rivers of Paradise carry outward at a certain time of year ... And this coach is wonderfully scented because of this wood, and the coach is entirely covered inside with plate of fine gold, with precious stones and with fat pearls'] (ch. 25; 398). In Prester John's Land, which is located even nearer to Eden, the narrator discovers an even greater marvel. In this land, Mandeville writes, 'y ad ... multz des merveilles, qar en soun pays est la mer Arenouse qe est toute d'areyne et de gravelle sanz goute de eawe et vait et vient as grandes undes auxi comme l'autre mer fait' ['there are ... many marvels, for in his land is the Sandy Sea, which is entirely of sand and of gravel, without a drop of water, and it ebbs and flows in great waves just as the other sea does']. Beyond this sea are mountains, between which flows 'une fluvie qe vient de Paradiz, et est tout des pierres preciouses sanz eawe, et court aval parmy le desert a undes si qe fait la mer Arenouse, et se fiert en cel mer et la se piert' ['a river that flows from Paradise, and it is full of precious stones, without water, and it flows through the desert in waves just like the Sandy Sea, and it comes to that Sea and disappears into it'] (ch. 30; 435–6). The lands ruled by the Grand Khan and by Prester John are located so far east that they actually lie on the borders of Eden; they are even connected to Eden by way of the rivers that flow outward. The abundant material riches of the East, then, are presented in the *Book of John Mandeville* as a physical manifestation of the spiritual riches planted by God in Eden. The borders that separate these far eastern lands from Eden are clearly permeable, because treasures flow outward; it is important, however, that the flow is exclusively one-way.

This may seem like a small point, but it is a crucial one. Mandeville himself emphasizes the one-way current of the rivers of Eden in a subsequent passage. He writes, 'Et sachez qe nul homme mortel ne poait aler ne approcher a ceo Paradiz, qar par terre nul n'y porroit aler pur les bestes savages qe sont as desertz, et pur les roches ou nuls n'y porroit passer par les lieux tenebrous … Et par les riveres nuls n'y porroit aler qar l'eawe court si roidement pur ceo qe elle vient de haut, et si vient a si grandes undes qe nul nief ne porroit vagir encontre' ['And you must know that no mortal man can approach or enter Paradise, for by land no one can pass through owing to the wild beasts in the wilderness, and because of the rocks where no one can pass through the shadowy paths … And by the rivers no one can pass, because the water courses so strongly that it springs up, and so rises in such great waves that no ship can sail against them']. The same waters that flow outward from Eden bearing spiritual blessings are, simultaneously, an impassible barrier: 'nul mortel ne poet approcher si ceo n'estoit d'especial grace de Dieu. Se que de cel lieu ne vous saveroie jeo plus qe dire ne diviser' ['no mortal man may approach except by the special grace of God. And so of that place I can teach you no more, or say, or describe'] (ch. 33; 470). This is the single moment, in all of the *Book of John Mandeville*, where the narrator admits defeat: I couldn't go there, he admits, so I cannot tell you about it. Eden remains a sacred space, a geographical *sanctum sanctorum*, cut off completely from exploration and travel. One cannot penetrate there; but one can be penetrated by it, as the world is inundated by the rivers that eternally flow outward from Eden.

The one-way flow of material wealth and spiritual blessings found in the *Book of John Mandeville* is altogether different from the two-way, variable traffic carried out by means of the many waterways that run throughout the *Devisement dou monde* of Marco Polo. Different, yet complementary; for currents and currency unify the world of Marco Polo just as surely and coherently as they do the world of John Mandeville. Rivers regularly appear in the *Devisement dou monde* as geographical features, as when the great city of Canbaluc is said to be divided by the river, with the old city on one bank, and the new city on the other (ch. 85; 420).[11] Similarly, the province of Gheindu [Kain-du] is said to be delimited by 'un grant flun que est apelé Brius, au quel se fenist la provence de Gheindu' ['a great river called Brius, which marks the boundaries of the province of Gheindu'] (ch. 117; 468). Such rivers provide not only identifiable borders, but (if wide enough) security from invaders as well. For example, the kingdom of Mangi is said to be enclosed by great rivers that insulate its cities from invaders. In the city of 'Singiu,' the ruler of Mangi has ingeniously augmented the natural protection offered by the city's 'great river' by dividing this natural moat into two: 'de cest grant flunz en ont fait II: car il font l'une moitié aler ver levant et l'autre moitié ver ponent, ce est que le un vait au Mangi e le autre por le Catai' ['of this great river they made two, for they made one half of it go in one direction and the other half in the other direction, that is, one flowing toward Mangi and the other toward Cathay']. These rivers facilitate the passage of trade, but they also serve as protective barriers against invasion, manned as they are by 'si grant navile ... que ne est nul que ne veisse que peust croire' ['so great a fleet ... that there is no one who, seeing it, could believe it'] (ch. 135; 494). Rivers both demarcate territory and repel aggression, preserving the integrity of the lands bounded by the waterway.

Throughout the *Devisement dou monde*, waterways are universally described as facilitators of commerce. This is the overwhelming and super-abundant norm in Marco Polo's account, although only a few examples are included here. Before entering the realms of Mosul and Baghdad, Marco describes the great sea of Glevechelan, which is enlarged by the many great rivers that empty into it, including the Euphrates ('Eufrautes'). This sea is navigated not only by local traders, but by European merchants as well: 'Et novelemant les marchians de Jene najerent por cel mer ... Et d'iluec vint la soie ke est apellé Ghelle' ['And recently the Genoese merchants have begun to navigate this sea ... And from that place comes the kind of silk called "ghelle"'] (ch. 23; 328). Here we find the name of one of the rivers of paradise, the Euphrates; it appears not in a devotional context, however, as in the

Book of John Mandeville, but in a mercantile connection. Where this river flows together with others, traders congregate from all over the world, from as far away as Genoa. Many similar cases ensue: for example, ten miles west of the city of Canbaluc, 'adonc trove un grant flum qui est apellés Pulisanghinz, le quel flus ala dusque a la mer osiane; et qui alent mant mercanz con mantes mercandie' ['at once you find a great river called Pulisangan; this river goes as far as the great ocean, and along it sail many merchant vessels, with lots of merchandise'] (ch. 105; 450–1). The city of Ciangli, in the south of Cathay, is pierced by a waterway laden with goods: 'por mi la cités de Ciangli vait un grant flum et large por le quel se portent et en sus et en jus grandismes quantité de mercandies de soies et de speceries e de autres chieres couses' ['in the midst of the city of Ciangli flows a wide and deep river, upon which are carried here and there great quantities of merchandise, silks and spices and other expensive goods'] (ch. 133; 491–2). Throughout the text, watercourses both natural and artificial serve to mediate the two-way transport of goods, serving the great capital city that lies at the heart of the empire.

Even in cases where the mediating properties of the waterway might symbolically convey other values, the mercantile imperative remains front and centre. The city of Coygangiu, for example, lies on the 'great river' of Caramoran, upon which 'maintes cités hi font aporter lor mercandies, por ce que les respandent por cel flum a maintes autres cités' ['many cities have their merchandise transported, because they are linked by this river to many other cities'] (ch. 140; 501). This river of Caramoran 'vient de la terre dou Prestre Joan' ['flows from the land of Prester John'] (ch. 138; 497). In the *Book of John Mandeville*, nearness to the land of Prester John, seen as a Christian king and potential ally in the crusader effort to retake Jerusalem, is a clear indicator of spiritual as well as temporal wealth; in the *Devisement dou monde*, by contrast, the material abundance of Prester John's land is paramount, and the river that flows from his land offers not devotional riches but the potential for ever-expanding mercantile exchange.

But perhaps the most expansive description of how waterways facilitate trade appears in the *Devisement*'s lengthy and detailed description of the city of Singiu, which is not a tremendously large city but is one 'de grant naives e de grand mercandies' ['of great fleets and abundant merchandise'] due to its situation upon the great river 'Quian' (Kiang). This river is 'le greignor flum que soit au monde' ['the greatest river in the world'], up to ten miles in width, and requiring one hundred days to navigate. It flows through more than sixteen provinces, and is banked by over two hundred cities 'que toute ont plus naives de ceste' ['which all have even more fleets [upon the river] than that']. The city of Singiu is not alone in reaping the benefits of the trade carried out upon the great river: 'por achaison de cest flum cest cité a mout grand-isme quantités de naves qui portent por ceste flun maintes couses et maintes mercandies, e por ce est ville de coi le grant can en a grant rende e grant treu' ['as a result of this river, this city has a very great quantity of fleets, which carry upon this river many goods and much merchandise, and consequently it is a town from which the Grand Khan receives great income and great tribute'] (ch. 147; 507). The wealth generated upon the river rewards the city upon its banks, but it also rewards all those engaged in trade, as well as the magnificent fig-ure at the head of them all: the Grand Khan, who receives a portion of all revenues engendered upon the waters. It is unsurprising, then, that the Grand Khan should wish to further expand upon the waterways provided by nature, and develop a system of canals: 'Et si voç di que le grant kaan a fait ordrer celle voies de l'eive da ceste cité jusque a Canbalu: car il a fait grandismes fosee et large et porfund da le un flum a l'autre e da le un lac a le autre; et fait aler l'eive si que senblent grant flun' ['And so I tell you that the Grand Khan established these water-ways from this city as far as Canbaluc: for he had made great ditches, wide and deep, from one river to the next, and from one lake to the next; and he made the water run so that it seemed to be one great river'] (ch. 148; 508).

As is apparent from just these few examples, throughout the *Devise-ment dou monde*, waterways are (as it were) the life-blood of mercantile exchange. Where they flow together, cities arise in which the ebb and flow of trade mimics the flow of the watercourses themselves. It is therefore unsurprising that we find, elsewhere in the *Devisement dou monde*, description of cities that do not feature watercourses, but which seem themselves almost to flow with currency, if not with currents. For example, the city of Toris (Tabriz) is said to be perfectly situated for the confluence of traders: 'la cité si en si buen leu que de Yndie et de Bau-dac et de Mosul et de Cremosor et de maintes autres leus hi vient les mercandies, et iluec vienent maint mercaant latin por acater de celes mercandies que hi venent des estranges pais' ['the city is in such a good location that merchants come here from India and Baghdad and Mosul and Kerman and from many other places, and many European merchants come here to obtain the merchandise that comes here from exotic places'] (ch. 30; 337). Further east one finds 'Cormos' (Hormuz), which is an island at the centre of a great confluence of trade routes, visited by traders who bring 'toutes especeries et pieres presieuses et perles et dras de soie et d'ores et dens d'olifant et maintes autres mercandies' ['every kind of spice and precious stones and pearls and cloth of silk and of gold and elephants' tusks and many other types of merchandise']. These goods flow into the port city and flow back out again, as regularly as the tides: 'en cel cité le vendent a les autres homes que puis l'aportent por tute universe monde, vendant a les autres gens' ['in this city they sell [these goods] to other men, who then carry them out into the wide world, to sell them to still other people'] (ch. 37; 347).

The capital city ('mestre vile') of Canbaluc, further east, experiences a similar tidal flow of goods and of travellers, 'si grant moutitude' ['so great a multitude'] of merchants and travellers, continually arriving and departing, 'que ne est homes que peust conter le nonbre' ['that there is no man who could count their number']. The multitude of traders is matched by the multitude of goods brought to the market, as all manner of 'pieres presiouses et perles et toutes autres chieres chouses sunt aportés a ceste ville' ['precious stones and pearls and all other valuable things are carried to this town']. Both the quality and the quantity of merchandise exchanged at Canbaluc exceed that found anywhere in the world: 'a ceste ville vienent plus chieres chouses et de greignor vailance et les greignor quantités que en nulle ville dou monde, et plus merchanties hi si vendent et achatent' ['to this town come the most valuable things, and of greater value, and in greater quantities, than in any other town in the world, and more merchandise is bought and sold here'] (ch. 95; 437–8).

In one curious case, the city of Sindanfu located on the border separating Cathay from Mangi, the watercourse that runs within the city almost appears to contain another mini-city upon it. This great river is so wide that 'il ne senble flum mes mer, tant est large' ['it does not seem to be a river but a sea, it is so large']. Dotted with merchant ships upon its surface and by trading posts along its banks, the river is crossed by a bridge that is itself a locus of dynamic exchange: 'encore ha sus ceste pont maintes maiçonnet, es quelz se font mercandies et ars asez' ['upon this bridge are many shops, in which there are many merchants and craftsmen']. This tiny marketplace generates not only trade revenues for the individual merchants but also tribute money for the ruler (ch. 114; 461). The dynamic flow of the waterways is mirrored not only in the cities, but in the stream of trade conducted upon the bridges. The distinction between city and waterway is similarly almost invisible in the account of 'la tre nobilisme cité qui est apellé Quinsai' ['the very noble city called Quinsai']. This case is rendered particularly interesting by the fact that Kin-sai appears to be something of a paradise itself, for its name signifies '"la cité dou ciel"' ['"the celestial city"']. Unlike the paradise of Eden described by Mandeville, however, the traffic on the river, and the goods in the streets, flow in every possible direction. The city is a hundred miles around, permeated with twelve thousand bridges over its canals: 'ceste ville est toute en eve, et est environé de eve' ['this town is entirely filled with water, and is surrounded by water']. The many bridges are necessary to serve the abundant population that gathers there, buying and selling: 'Il hi a tant mercaans et si riches que font si grand mercandies que ne est homes que peust dir la verité' ['There are so many merchants there, and so rich, selling so much merchandise, that there is no man who could tell the whole of it'] (ch. 152; 513–14)]. Though Quinsai may seem to be a kind of paradise, this 'celestial city' is not like Eden in that its pre-eminence is transitory, not permanent. Its stature is dependent upon imperial power, a power which (as history teaches us) is mutable. Quinsai may be a centre of trade, for now; the same is true even of the Grand Khan's imperial centre of Canbaluc, which is at the centre of a whole web of trade networks – for now. The status of these cities is ephemeral, however, compared with the enduring pivotal role of Eden, and of Jerusalem, as portrayed in the *Book of John Mandeville*.

In the *Devisement dou monde*, cities are the places where the paths of travellers and traders converge, where exchange takes place. Most often, these paths are waterways, though even in examples like those noted above where waterways are not emphasized, cities still continue to be described in terms of the swift currents and little eddies generated by the dynamic flow of trade. This ebb and flow featured in the *Devisement dou monde* can be profitably juxtaposed with the depiction of one-way flow we saw in the *Book of John Mandeville*. There, we will remember, the rivers of Paradise may bear material wealth, but such gems and jewels are simply physical manifestations of the spiritual goods that flow outward from Eden. In Marco Polo's account, by contrast, wealth flows in more than one direction; and, significantly, this wealth is reproductive, multiplying in the form of profit margins and in the form of revenues generated from trade and flowing backward into the coffers of the Grand Khan.

There is a sense, however, in which the spiritual currents that pervade the devotional geography of the *Book of John Mandeville* do indeed flow in more than one direction. The watercourses emanating from Eden, certainly, flow in only one direction; Mandeville makes this quite clear. The spiritual blessings conveyed by those waters, however, do in a sense return to their point of origin – not to the cradle of mankind's first birth, Eden, but to the origin of mankind's rebirth, Jerusalem, through the redemption of Christ. The pilgrimage itinerary which makes up the first fifteen chapters of the *Book of John Mandeville* (almost half the whole work) traces just this flow of believers to the Holy Land, and to the sacred places. This journey inward ends, appropriately, at the centre of the world: Mandeville states that, in the Church of the Holy Sepulchre, there is a perfect circle drawn upon the floor that marks the point where Christ's body was lowered from the Cross. This location, he says, is 'the mid-point of the world' (79; ch.10). The blessings which flow outward from Eden, borne upon the waters, eventually flow backward toward the site of mankind's redemption in the form of faithful pilgrims, whose 'way' (or *via*) is as surely guided by God as the watercourses that flow outward from Eden.

This two-part movement found in the *Book of John Mandeville*, where the flow of the rivers of Paradise outward from Eden is mirrored in the reciprocal flow of pilgrims inward toward Jerusalem, is very different from the dynamic, constantly changing flow which unifies the mercantile universe depicted in the *Devisement dou monde*. While the symbolic geography of Mandeville is devotional, the symbolic geography of Marco Polo is mercantile: consequently, materials and men flow both ways, up and down the rivers and canals. In Mandeville's devotional geography, however, time is conceived of in terms of teleology, where mankind moves inexorably forward on a one-way journey from Eden, through Jerusalem, to the plain of Har-Megiddo where the Day of Judgment will begin. In Marco Polo's mercantile geography, locations are relative, each city contributing both to the supply of the market and to the demand for goods. Time is not teleological but cyclical, organized about the day-to-day exigencies of exchange, and patterned around the weekly, monthly, and seasonal cycles of the market itself. In Mandeville's account, the rivers coursing violently outward from Eden mirror the teleological flow of time. In the *Devisement dou monde*, however, the one-way flow of water current has a rather different set of connotations. Only on one single occasion in the *Devisement* is water said to flow strongly in one direction. In his description of Madagascar and its surrounding islands, Marco states that only two of the islands are regularly visited by merchants, 'por ce que la mer hi cort si ver midi que a poine s'en poroient venir; e por ceste achaisonç ne i vont les nes ... [L]a corent vait toç jorç ver midi; e ce avint toutes foies que jamés ne cort en autre mainere que ver midi' ['because here the sea runs so toward the south that one can move forward only with great difficulty; and for this reason the ships do not sail here ... The current always flows toward the south, and it always happens that it does not flow in any direction except southward'] (ch. 191; 594). This singular case of one-way current is described emphatically as an unusual (and dangerous) exception to the rule, notable not for its symbolic value but for the very practical obstacle it poses to the efficient practice of trade.

Similarly, the cases where Marco Polo describes waterways running with gems or gold are notable not for the reasons given in the *Book of John Mandeville*, but for very practical reasons. In Mandeville's account, as noted above, rivers flowing from paradise abound in gems which are material manifestations of the spiritual blessings that emanate from Eden. In Marco Polo's account, by contrast, the gems in the rivers are simply sources of wealth, pure and simple. For example, through the province of Ciarcian run rivers 'qui moinent diaspes et calcedon' ['which carry jaspers and chalcedonies'], which are carried away by merchants and sold at great profit, 'car il en ont aseç et bones' ['because they are so many and so good'] (ch. 56; 369). In the case of the city of Gaindu, the acquisition of the gems to be found in the waterways is dependent upon the imperial authority of the Grand Khan: near the city is a lake, 'ou se treuvent maintes perles' ['where many pearls can be found']. The quantity of pearls is so great that, if the Grand Khan allowed everyone to take them, 'eles seroient molt viles et ne vaudroient noiant' ['they would become very debased and would be worth nothing'] (ch. 117; 466). Several other locations, like the province of Caraian, are said to have rivers flowing with flakes and even lumps of gold (ch. 119, 470). This gold is not symbolic of blessings, as it might be in the *Book of John Mandeville*; rather, it is simply a commodity like any other. Marco Polo describes these waterways coursing with gold not for spiritual edification, but to tell the travelling merchant where he might find what he seeks, and make a profit.

In the *Devisement dou monde*, the really significant flow of wealth takes place not by means of the discovery of gold dust, or even the treasure trove of rich lodes of jewels. Instead, wealth is created by trade, a process of exchange that generates revenues not only for the buyers and sellers, but for the ruler who has authority over the places where trade takes place and who receives revenues accordingly. This process is facilitated by the flow of currency, a neutral, quantifiable means of exchange that enables the establishment of practically universal standards. The practice of trade is made far more efficient – and, therefore, more profitable – by the presence of currency. The most famous description of currency in the *Devisement dou monde* is, of course, the description of the paper money minted by the Grand Khan, described in more detail below. Other peoples, however, are also said to mint their own currency, such as the people of Gaindu. They have two currencies, the greater of which is made of gold rods, cut to a particular thickness. Their 'smaller' currency is composed of salt cakes, whose value varies depending upon the region one is in (ch. 117; 467). Several other peoples are said to use a certain kind of white shells for money. In Caraian, west of Gaindu, 'vaillent les LXXX porcelaines un saje d'arjent, que sunt deus venesians gros, et sachiés que les VIII sajes d'arjent fin vailent un sajes d'or fin' ['eighty of the white shells are worth a *saggio* of silver, which equal two Venetian groats, and you should know that eight *saggi* of fine silver are worth one *saggio* of pure gold'] (ch. 118; 469). The value of this particular currency varies depending upon the place where it is used. It is not a stable, fixed currency, but rather a currency that (like the salt cakes used by the people of Gaindu) varies in value almost as much as the commodities themselves.

No such variability can be attributed to the paper money minted by the Grand Khan, whose currency is of fixed value, backed not only by the imperial authority of the ruler but by the gold standard. This famous account is worth summarizing at length: the Grand Khan 'fait faire une tel monoie cum je voç dirai: il fait prendre escorses d'arbres ... et de celes sotil buces fait fer chartre come celle de papir ... Et quant cestes chartre sunt faites, il le fait trinchier en tel mainer, car il en fait une petite que vaut une moitié de tornesel petit; et l'autre est de un tornesel encor petit; et l'autre est d'un mi gros d'arjent, et l'autre d'un gros d'arjent' ['has a kind of money made as I will describe: he has them take the bark of trees ... and from the thin lining [between the bark and wood] he has made documents like those of paper ... And when these documents are made, he has them trimmed in such a manner, that he has made a small one, that is worth half a denier tournois; and another that is worth a denier tournois; and another that is worth half a silver groat, and another that is worth a silver groat'] (ch. 96; 439). The passage goes on to give numerous currency equivalents, relating each measure of currency issued by the Grand Khan to the equivalent value in various European currencies – deniers, groats, and besants. The currency is carefully controlled, with the Grand Khan's own royal seal affixed to each note, and is distributed widely throughout all the lands under the Khan's rule. Use of this paper money is not optional but obligatory: 'nulz ne le ose refuser a poine de pardre sa vie' ['no one dares to refuse it, on pain of losing his life']. It is widely accepted, exchanged freely 'de mercandies et de perles et de pieres presiouses et d'or et d'arjent. Toutes chouses en puent achater' ['for merchandise and for pearls and for precious stones and for gold and for silver. All things can be purchased with it'] (ch. 96; 440). Note the emphasis on the practice of authentication of the paper currency, stamped with the seal of the Grand Khan, with its value guaranteed by the ruler himself. Everyone freely uses this money, not just because its use is the law of the land, but because it can be exchanged without difficulty for gold or jewels – in short, used to purchase 'all things.' It is universal currency, at least within the Grand Khan's borders.

Significantly, the paper currency flows not only outward, from the mint under the authority of the Grand Khan, but inward as well, for damaged or over-used currency can be exchanged freely: 'quant l'en a tenue ceste carte tant qu'ele s'en ronpent et que se gastent, et il le porte a la secque et il sunt cangié a noves et fresches, si voiremant qu'il en lase trois por C' ['when one has used this currency so that it tears or gets thin, he takes it to the mint and they [the notes] are changed for fresh, new ones, as long as he leaves three for every one hundred'] (ch. 96; 440). Note how the coffers of the Grand Khan are directly enriched by the inevitable exchange of currency as his officers collect 3 per cent on every transaction, as well as indirectly enriched by the general facilitation of trade (and therefore of tax revenue). Marco Polo concludes that, certainly, 'tuit les seignor deu seicle ne ont si grant richese come le grant sire a' ['none of the lords of the world has so great riches as the Grand Khan'] (ch. 96; 441), for he controls a source of wealth that is renewable and, at least potentially, infinite. This paper currency circulates everywhere within the realm of the Grand Khan, and even in some of the territories bordering his domain. In the nearby city of Chintigui, for example, the people use the paper money of the Grand Khan ('lor monoie est de carte et sunt au grant kaan' [ch. 138; 496]). The same is said of a whole series of cities, about which Marco Polo identifies only three features worth noting: in each case, he remarks that the people 'are idolaters and burn their dead; they use paper money' (e.g., chs. 131–3, 140–1). These details, apparently, are all the traveller really needs to know.

Money flows not only outward, from the mint of the Grand Khan, but also inward, both in the form of used up paper currency returned to the mint for replacement and, far more importantly, in the form of revenues. These are described in detail in the *Devisement*: some goods are taxed at the rate of three and one-third per cent but others, especially items imported from farther away, are taxed at the rate of ten per cent. The remarkable total of the revenues is summed up, with the added authenticity of eyewitness testimony: 'jeo, Marc Pol, que plusor foies oi faire le conte de la rende de tous cestes couses ... por chascun an, vaut CCX tomain d'or, que vailent XIV m miaia et DCC m' ['I, Marco Polo, who often heard the accounting of all these things ... for each year, [the revenues] equalled 210 gold tumans, which are worth fourteen million seven hundred thousand ducats'] (ch. 149; 520–1).

The last feature of the economy of the realm of the Grand Khan remaining to be pointed out concerns the rare moments of stagnation, moments when the energetic flow of goods and currency comes to an abrupt halt. These moments, I would argue, are significant within the mercantile symbolic geography of the *Devisement dou monde*, for they signal points of vulnerability in the discursive and economic system that is, in general, so highly praised throughout the work. One of these appears in connection with the description of the luxurious palace of the Grand Khan located at Canbaluc. The northern quarter includes an artificial pond, fed by a small river and used to water cattle, which leads in turn to another artificial pond. This pond houses many kinds of fish, waiting to be selected to be served to the king: 'un grant flun hi met et oisse, mes si est si ordrés que nul peisson non poit oissir, et ce est fait con rees de fer et de raim' ['a great river issues from there, but it is built in such a way that no fish can escape, with gratings made of iron and copper'] (ch. 84; 418). Here, the usual function of waterways, to facilitate movement of people, goods, and currency, comes to an abrupt halt: these fish, destined for the Grand Khan's table, have nowhere to go.

Comparable moments of stagnation appear elsewhere in the *Devisement dou monde*, here in connection not with the flow of goods but with the passage of currency. Ordinarily, as we remember, the paper money minted by the Grand Khan is used to make the practice of trade still more efficient (and hence profitable): it flows back and forth, from hand to hand, temporarily taking the place of goods of every kind. On rare occasions, however, paper money passes only in one direction: this occurs when it is used by the dead. In the province of Tangut, Marco recounts, the people cremate their dead with great ceremony, and carry out a peculiar practice: the mourners 'font entailler homes de carte de papir et chevaus et gamiaus et monete grant come biçans; et toutes cestes couses funt ardoir avec le cors: et dient que en le autre monde le mors aura tant escalif et tantes bestes et tantes montons com il font ardoir de charte' ['have the figures of men etched on pieces of paper, and horses, and camels, and money as large as besants; and all these things they burn along with the body; and they say that, in the other world, the dead one will have as many slaves and beasts and sheep as they burned in the form of paper'] (ch. 58; 372–3). These 'pieces of paper' are clearly simulacra which take the place of the objects they depict, whether servants, clothing, or beasts of burden. The paper pieces of money, however, are somewhat different. Presumably they are copies or simulacra of 'real' paper money, for who would want to burn hard currency? If so, they are simulacra of something that is, in a sense, itself a simulacrum, a representative or place-holder for that which has intrinsic value. Another example of this practice is observed among the Tartars, who have so firm a belief in the parallel world of the dead that they carry out marriages uniting their deceased children. In the ceremony, 'il font enpindre et portraire en carte homes a similitude de eles, et chevaus et dras et biçanz et arnois, puis les font ardoir; et dient que toutes celles couses qu'il avoient fait portraire et ardre auront lor enfans en l'autre monde' ['they have drawn and painted on papers the likeness of men, and horses and clothes and besants and equipment, and then they burn them; and they say that their children will have in the other world all these things that they had drawn and then burned'] (ch. 70; 392). Among the Tartars as in Tangut, the flow of currency is one way, for there is no possibility of goods or money returning from the land of the dead. This stagnation of the cycle of exchange, as substance is annihilated through flame, differs strikingly from the circular, liquid economy of salvation that permeates the *Book of John Mandeville*.

If the *Devisement dou monde* of Marco Polo and the *Book of John Mandeville* are works of medieval Orientalism, we must ask whether these texts participate in the construction of the same Orient. The simple answer, of course, is 'no.' The geographical focus of the *Book of John Mandeville* is clearly the Holy Land, especially Jerusalem. Mandeville's description of the regions further east participates in the same devotional discourse, so that, as the birthplace of mankind, Eden serves as a forerunner of Jerusalem, the site of mankind's spiritual rebirth. Although Prester John's land is spatially proximate to Eden, it is temporally remote from it, for Prester John is associated with the Apocalypse and subsequent Day of Judgment. In other words, Prester John's land is located at the end of days, just as Eden is located at the beginning; both, however, are located deep in the Orient.

This Orient is very different indeed from the Orient of Marco Polo, an Orient dominated by Cathay and Mangi, by the magnificent cities of Quinsai and Canbaluc, and by the imperial authority of the Grand Khan. One might argue that this Orient, even though it is centred geographically on a different part of the world, is basically similar to the Orient of the *Book of John Mandeville*. I would object, however, that the impermanence of these Oriental centres of Quinsai and Canbaluc makes them, in the end, very different from Eden and Jerusalem. I would suggest, therefore, that Marco Polo's Orient is – if I can put it this way – differently oriented from the Orient of Mandeville. In terms of the symbolic geography of the *Book of John Mandeville*, the flow of currency, whether in the form of the rivers flowing outward from Eden or the devout pilgrims hastening inward toward Jerusalem, is essentially stable. The devotional economy of Mandeville's world is balanced, with the abundance of grace flowing from God making up for any shortfalls on the part of mankind. Conversely, in terms of the symbolic geography of Marco Polo's *Devisement dou monde*, the flow of currency is not necessarily stable. The value of goods fluctuates, as supply and demand ebb and flow. Currency itself wears out and has to be replaced (at the price of 3 per cent), and sometimes disappears entirely into the parallel world of the dead. While the paper currency minted by the Grand Khan is currently stable, and will remain so as long as his imperial authority lasts, it will not remain so forever, because there will be a time when the power of the Grand Khan has passed away, just as there was a time before his power had come into being. The discursive systems of the *Devisement dou monde* and the *Book of John Mandeville* are comparable, for each is structured in terms of the flow of currents and currency. In each of these texts, the process of mediation – whether devotional or mercantile – is carried out by the waters. For Mandeville, these are the blessed waters of grace; for Marco Polo, they are the dynamic tides of the harbour.

NOTES

1 A version of this essay was given at the Medieval Studies Colloquium 'Travel in the Middle Ages,' University of California at Santa Barbara (12 February 2005). Thanks to Harvey Sharrer and Edward English for the invitation, and to Yunte Huang for his insightful response.

2 M.C. Seymour, *Sir John Mandeville* 23.

3 On the manuscript tradition of *The Book of John Mandeville*, see Susanne Röhl, *Der livre de Mandeville*. A more general overview of the text's circulation can be found in Rosemary Tzanaki, *Mandeville's Medieval Audiences*.

4 On 'diversity' as spatial and narrative principle in each work, see Katherine Park, 'The Meanings of Natural Diversity'; Iain Macleod Higgins, *Writing East*, esp. chapter 5, 'Earthly Symmetry and the Mirror of Marvelous Diversity in and around Ynde' (124–55). For a detailed reading of Mandeville in terms of Park's treatment of 'diversity' in Marco Polo, see Suzanne Conklin Akbari, 'The Diversity of Mankind in the *Book of John Mandeville*.'

5 For a persuasive reading of the *Book of John Mandeville* as devotional itinerary, see Suzanne Yeager, '*The Book of John Mandeville*: Text of Pilgrimage and Spiritual Reform,' chapter 4 of 'England's Quest for Jerusalem'; see also Yeager, *Jerusalem in Medieval Narrative* (Cambridge: Cambridge University Press, 2008).

6 Ambrose, 'De paradiso' 1.3.

7 See Augustine, *De Genesi ad litteram* 8.7, commentary on Genesis 2: 10–14, col. 378. The citation of Augustine's Genesis commentary in the *Glossa Ordinaria* can be found in Walafridus Strabo (attrib.), *Liber Genesis*, ed. J.-P. Migne, col. 87.

8 For an overview of medieval world maps, see Evelyn Edson, *Mapping Time and Space*. For a more detailed account, see David Woodward's 'Medieval Mappaemundi.'

9 Pierre d'Ailly, *Imago mundi*, chs. 56–7.

10 All quotations from the *Book of John Mandeville* are taken from Christiane Deluz's excellent edition of the Continental version of the French text (a reliable version of the Anglo-French text has yet to appear). Quotations are cited in the text by chapter and page number; translations are my own.

11 All quotations from the *Devisement dou monde* are taken from the facing-page Tuscan and Franco-Italian edition of Gabriella Ronchi. Quotations are cited in the text by chapter and page number; translations are my own.

PART TWO

The Reception of Marco Polo: Medieval and Modern

6 Plucking Hairs from the Great Cham's Beard: Marco Polo, Jan de Langhe, and Sir John Mandeville

JOHN LARNER

I

The two most famous European books about Asia, those of Marco Polo and John Mandeville, were written within sixty to seventy years of each other, between 1298 and, at the latest, 1365, which is to say toward the beginning and end of the first direct engagement of Europe with the further East. The work of Jan de Langhe, a Fleming who wrote in Latin under the name Johannes Longus and in French as Jean le Long, and whose life straddled those same years, is much less well known. But he too has importance in our theme, which is to consider the relative importance of their writings to the growth of geographical knowledge in Europe.

First in time was Marco Polo, who, with Rustichello of Pisa, began writing his book, as its preface says, 'in the prisons of Genoa in the year 1298.' Since I have already written about it at some length elsewhere,[1] I will make only a few salient points here. First it is worth stressing that it is a collaborative work. Marco was a man who had spent twenty-four years, most of his life, all his adult life, in Asia. His return to Europe must have been a deeply unsettling experience; he was coming back to a world that he would often have found difficult to understand. It was, in particular, a world of whose literary traditions he knew almost nothing. If he were to write of what he had learned, it was essential that he should find a collaborator, and by good fortune he eventually found him when captured by the Genoese. It is a commonplace that this man, Rustichello, wrote poorly, that his style is singularly lifeless, and many have doubted whether it was indeed such good fortune that it was precisely this man whom Marco met. Yet much the same might be said of some of the best-selling authors of our own or any day; their skill, like Rustichello's, is in having an understanding of what contemporaries will take. Here that ability was of key importance, since the novelty of the book's material was likely to provoke scepticism. What this meant too was that Marco was not a completely free agent. Literary collaboration always exacts penalties; in this instance it is as though it were Marco's western audience which is helping him to write the book, a book he has sometimes to change in order to meet their interests or expectations.[2]

One should add that if it were Rustichello who devised the plan of the work, he had a gift for organization of material. That plan takes the form of a series of imaginary journeys to, within, and from China. Yet, though well developed for its task, it has led to a serious misunderstanding of what the book actually is. It is not a travelogue. One finds a lot of passages which at first sight allow one to think that it is describing real travels. In fact, these are simply an organizing device to present geographical material. There is no description here of the route of the Polos through Asia; the route is just the means by which Marco and Rustichello lead their readers from West to East and then back from East to West, the route of the narrator through his book.

It is worth saying this again, since still today the book is very commonly spoken of as the *Travels* of Marco Polo. In the Middle Ages it was never given that title. What it was normally called was some variant of the *Description of the World*, or the *Book of the Great Khan*. The first to call it the *Travels* was Giambattista Ramusio at the end of the 1550s. Ramusio was a Venetian, the compiler of a great mass of geographical reports, mostly travel literature, which he called *Travels by Land and Sea* (*Navigazioni e Viaggi*). When he included Marco, it was explicable that he should have changed the title of his book to *I Viaggi di Marco Polo*. In doing this, Ramusio almost changed not just its title but its subject. Call a book 'The Travels' and, if it is interesting enough, people will set about discovering the route of these travels. The first whom I know of to attempt this was the learned Jesuit Athanasius Kircher in his *China Illustrata*, published in 1667. Kircher was also the first to highlight a common crux of later scholarship: 'I am staggered [*vehemente miror*] that Marco Polo does not mention the Great Wall of China through which he must have passed.' And, as if that observation was not going to breed enough difficulty, he then went on to discuss Marco's itineraries and to print a map of what he believed was the Polos' journey from the Caspian to Canbaluc.[3]

This proved an attractive game for anyone who knew something about the East. You wrote out all the place names in the order they appeared in the Book, you tried to identify them, and then you said this was the route the Polos took. The more you knew the better you could display all your knowledge. One of the best at it was the Victorian editor, Henry Yule. And his conclusions, refined by his friend, Henri Cordier, became more or less standard.[4] The only difficulty with them – though this wasn't first pointed out until some twenty years ago – was that the results were unbelievable. Here are the Polos carrying a message from the pope, already two years overdue, to the most powerful ruler in the world. By virtue of their possession of the gold *paiza* given to them by the Great Khan, their safety was guaranteed in Mongol lands, and they could have used the Mongol post-system right up to Beijing, which would have brought them to the Khan in, at most, nine months. Instead, if you follow Yule, they decide first to sail to China, which, as a contemporary put it, was 'the most difficult and dangerous way' and which would have taken them at least double the time.[5] Accordingly they make their way to Hormuz on the Indian Ocean. When they get there, they take one look at the Arab ships and timorously decide they'll go by land instead. They set off again, once more studiously seeking to avoid Mongol territory. They arrive at Badakhshan, where they do some mountaineering, traversing a plateau of the Pamir some sixteen thousand feet up. And so on it goes. It is like travelling from Toronto to New Orleans by way of the Rocky Mountains. The first to rebel against this was Jacques Heers in 1984.[6] Since then others have added their contributions to this insight.[7] Yet scholars continue to march along the old itineraries. In 2001, in a new edition of the northern French manuscripts of the Book, we have an editor who once again forces the luckless Polos to make their laborious way up into the Himalayas.[8]

The truth is the Book is not an account of travels: it is a geography. As such, it has very little in common with any geography found previously in the West. There had been very few chorographies, and Marco and Rustichello's book bears no resemblance to them. For instance, and despite what so many writers claim,[9] the book does not serve up a diet of fabulous marvels. None of the 'The Monstrous Races' appear here. The marvels here are above all true marvels, such as the amazing number and wealth of the cities of China, rather than those prodigies which are the staple of most other accounts of the East written in the Middle Ages. To write the book, that is to say, its authors had to create a new genre of western literature.

That genre derived ultimately from Chinese writings. It came from Chinese local topographies, geographical encyclopedias, and anthropological descriptions. Or rather, since Marco himself knew no Chinese, from what of Chinese geographical literature had been taken on board by the Mongol administrative class which at that time ruled China. One thinks here of the reports delivered to the Great Khan Kublai on missions he had sent out in search of strange birds and beasts, or on the expedition he had sponsored to find the source of the Yellow River. Or again the written reports of ambassadors to foreign parts, the road-guides within and outside the Empire, and the maps used by the Mongol government.[10]

This is the tradition that informs the work. Marco's Book is that of a Mongolian civil servant who has taken early retirement, and is telling us about the human geography of Asia, its customs and folklore, and above all, about the political authority of the Great Khan who there holds sway. These things are welded together into a work which is bounded by immensely wide horizons and could only be written because Marco had been the servant of an enormous empire. Within that span, what's remarkable is the variety of what he takes into consideration: trade-goods, artisan production, accounts of animals, birds, fish, vegetation, religions, crops, customs, governments. It should be added that, in modern comments on the book, one quite often meets suspicious, slightly querulous remarks, pointing out that Marco says nothing about architecture, or art, or landscape. But these things were not yet discussed in the Europe of his day; one has to wait until the humanists and the artists of the Renaissance before they become common themes.

Certainly it could be argued that, in what is treated, there is much that is superficial, that the concision is often extreme. Of the seventy Chinese towns which are recorded in the book, only two receive anything beyond a brief one- or two-sentence description.[11] Yet it is because Marco so often merely grazes the surface of his materials that he can take on the whole of Asia. As a result, what the book gave its first readers was a portrait of a new world. Here Europeans received their introduction to the Far East, China, and the East Indies. And they were introduced to this by a book which derived its power from the fact that its author was a man who, having left Venice at the age of seventeen and having spent some twenty-four years of his life in the service of an Asian empire, was someone who had found himself at home in that empire, more so perhaps than he was, on his return, in Europe.

This was Marco Polo's legacy. Was it, in the later Middle Ages, accepted as truth or as a romantic fantasy? Generally, scholars have declared that it was disbelieved and ignored. In my own study, I have concluded that this was not so. Though some readers were sceptical, Marco Polo came to carry general conviction, more particularly when, in the fifteenth century, he was taken up by the humanists. As a result, his was a work which made a major contribution to that European discovery and reconnaissance of the world which took place at the end of the Middle Ages.

II

Back in the fourteenth century, one who believed in the truth of Marco Polo was the Benedictine monk Jan de Langhe. Born at Ypres, he was by 1334 a member of the ancient and celebrated abbey of Saint-Bertin at Saint-Omer, some twenty miles from Calais. Two of its abbots had been canonized; it boasted a vast collection of relics; it had what for the time was a very large library of over eight hundred volumes; and it owned considerable rights and property in northern France, Flanders, and the Rhineland.[12] As a young monk Jan was sent to the University of Paris, where he read philosophy and law. On his return he was appointed legal defender of the Abbey's possessions and eventually, in 1365, elected abbot. These were difficult times, not least because the monks had the English at Calais as their close neighbours and were often caught up in the Hundred Years' War. In the monastery's annals one reads: 'While he lived our Abbot Jan struggled on behalf of his church, but as a result of the wars of the English and French, and the revolts of the Flemings, he could do very little of what he wished to restore its fortunes.'[13]

   In 1383, the last year of his life, we find him writing a chronicle which tells the story of the abbots who had ruled Saint-Bertin. This is set within a universal history, and an account of local circumstances in France and Flanders.[14] It seems at first sight to be just what you would expect from a member of the ecclesiastical establishment. It is written in serviceable medieval Latin; it is serious, level-headed, conventional. Predictably enough for anyone writing in the thick of the Hundred Years' War, it has a lot on 'the good old days.' The good old days were the days of Abbot Guibert, who lived in the thirteenth century: 'All things then smiled and rejoiced; in his time there was peace in the country and if lords went to war, it was in other lands. In those days the young obeyed the old, servants were most punctilious in their service, and were content with little.' You could see that from looking at the accounts for the building of the refectory; the builders in those days were satisfied 'with some bread, a plate of beans, and a penny a day.'[15]

The characteristic tone of an elderly gentlemen in a position of power is broken only at one moment when suddenly, and in impassioned and confessional terms, Jan warns his readers against alchemy:

It promises fair things and gives few; powerfully does it seduce and draw men on, and much are they deceived in that. *Experto crede!* Take it from one who knows. For I who write was deceived in that, and I have seen many others deceived in the same way, and I have never seen anyone who achieved its supposed purpose.[16]

For a brief instant he reveals himself as having at least once in the past been a fantasist, a dreamer.

Just two more things about this man before we look at the big question which hangs over his head. The first, which may just be of importance in considering the big question, is that one of his monks described him as being so large-bellied, so grossly fat, that he was barely able to walk.[17] The second is that he had a strong interest in the East. In his *Chronicle*, after telling of the death of Clement IV in 1268 and the three-year papal interregnum which followed, Jan goes on to say this:

In this interim the great emperor of the Tartars, Cobilaazan, brother of Alahon, sent his emissaries to the pope with letters. These, claiming great devotion to the faith of Christ, asked that the pope should dispatch to him in sufficient numbers men well versed in the Catholic faith and the liberal arts who would know how to prevail in disputations with the unbelievers, Jews, Saracens, and idolaters of his land; at the same time they asked that he should send some of the oil from the lamp burning at the sepulchre of the Lord in Jerusalem.

These emissaries were two citizens of Venice called Niccolò Polo and his brother Maffeo Polo, with Catagal, a certain Baron of the Tartars who died on the way. The two men took three years from the Kingdom of Cathay and the aforesaid Great Khan to Rome. When they arrived they found that the pope had in fact died, and so, while waiting for the election to take place they went to Venice to attend to their family and business affairs. Then, seeing the election to be so long drawn out, and afraid that their lord would blame them for the over-long delay, they took ship to the Holy Land, the lord Niccolò Polo taking with him back to the Tartars his son, a very able young man, twenty years old or thereabouts, called Marco Polo.[18]

He goes on to tell how in the Holy Land the Legate (as he calls him) Tebaldo came to be elected pope, how he sent them off with two friars who then deserted the party, and how, finally, they were warmly received by the Great Khan. He continues:

And then the lords Niccolò and Maffeo were sent back again to these parts [Europe] with other Tartars. But Marco Polo, whom he made a knight, was retained by the Emperor and stayed with him for a period of twenty-seven years. Because of the skill he showed in his affairs he sent him to various parts of India, Tartary and the islands where he saw many marvellous things about which he afterwards wrote a book in French, which *Book of Marvels*, with many others similar, we have in our possession.[19]

This is the only account of the Polos in which Marco's age on leaving Venice is reckoned as 'twenty or thereabouts' instead of, as it is generally given, 'seventeen,' and where his father and uncle go back straightaway to Europe rather than staying on in China and returning with Marco in 1292. De Langhe must either be referring to a version of Marco's book which has been lost or he has misremembered his reading of the Book from perhaps several years back.[20] But what is of most interest here are Jan's concluding words on the 'many other similar' books which are 'in our possession.'

In fact, in 1351, over thirty years before, Jan had produced another book from just these materials. This was a collection of his own translations from Latin into French of six works about the East. The first is a book called the *Flower of the Histories of the East*, which had been written in France in 1307 by Prince Hetoum, a Prince of Little Armenia, a country which had had a lot to do with the Mongols and the realms they ruled. The second is by an Italian traveller in India and China, a Franciscan missionary called Odoric of Pordenone, who on his return from the East in 1330 had dictated an important account of his experiences. And the third is a record of a pilgrimage to Jerusalem through Egypt and Palestine by the German knight William of Boldensele, written about 1336. There are other very interesting works, but these for our purpose are the most important. This compilation survives in six manuscripts. In two of them (among which is the famous, richly illustrated *Livres des Merveilles* given by John the Fearless of Burgundy to the Duc de Berry in January 1413), the books of Marco Polo and of John Mandeville are added to the basic six texts. The earliest surviving manuscript says that it was written by Jan of Saint-Bertin in 1351, and that he is 'at present, 1368, Abbot of that place.'[21]

In itself this collection is sufficient to give Jan de Langhe a position in the history of geography. This is because it established a new genre. It is the first surviving example of those translated compilations of travels beyond Europe which in the Renaissance culminate in the multiple volumes of Giovanni Battista Ramusio and Richard Hakluyt. One tries to imagine what impulse lay behind Jan's work. Translation from Latin to French was a noticeable feature of French culture of the fourteenth century. An important figure here, for instance, is Jean de Vignay, who between the 1320s and 1340s translated at least twelve sizeable Latin books into French, among them some which treat of the East.[22] Yet Vignay's works fit into the traditions of the Parisian book trade. They are all commissioned works, most of them commissioned by the French royal family. De Langhe's collection differs from these in that he does not mention any patrons and does not make any dedications, which would suggest that his book has not been commissioned, that it has not been written to raise money – as an alternative, say, to alchemy – but that it came into existence as a diversion, the satisfaction of a private passion.

Here then is this Benedictine monk, normally tied to his cloister, who in his life never travels anywhere further than Avignon, who in 1351 has just lived through the most terrible events – the Black Death, the pogrom against the Jews who have been accused of spreading it, the opening stages of the Hundred Years' War. His days were already dedicated less and less to the liturgical life or that religious contemplation which perhaps first drew him to the cloisters, more and more to the study of the intricacies of law and the struggle to retain the material possessions of the monastery. He who will never go to Jerusalem, let alone beyond it, thinks it is worth while to translate these works. They do not just describe, as Boldensele's does, the pilgrimage to the Holy Sepulchre – that would be easily comprehensible. That was an already common literary form, a work of sympathetic piety, a mental pilgrimage which allowed the home-stayer to participate vicariously in the great religious experience. They include, too, accounts of much wider journeys beyond Jerusalem to the realms of the Great Khan and the furthest horizons of fourteenth-century Europe. Perhaps what lay behind his interest was some element of escapism.

In which case is it possible that, within at most fourteen years, it is he, Jan de Langhe, who, under the same impulse, wrote, again in French, that classic story of eastern travel, *The Book of Sir John Mandeville*? M.C. Seymour has remarked that Jan would be 'an ideal candidate' to be its author. Seymour thinks of the author as someone who is a fluent French speaker, who compiles his work in a large continental library, a man who is an ecclesiastic with an excellent knowledge of the Bible, fluent in Latin, and someone who has never travelled to the lands he describes.[23] Certainly the three principal sources which *The Book of Sir John Mandeville* draws upon, often word for word, are Hetoum, Odoric, and Boldensele, and the versions of them the author draws upon are precisely those in the French of Jan de Langhe. With two of these, Boldensele and Odoric, it's clear that the author also knew and used the Latin texts. Accordingly one has to ask how many libraries outside Saint-Bertin would, even in northern France, have held by 1365 not only the Latin originals but also the French translations which had been made only a few years before.

As it is, the identity of the original author is still a matter of speculation. Christiane Deluz, who has done so much to illuminate the text and to place it within its fourteenth-century context, holds that the author was an English layman, that he had actually visited, at least, the Near East, and that the original text was written in Anglo-French rather than continental French.[24] If any of these contentions are true, they would be fatal to any claims for Jan de Langhe. I remain drawn to the idea of Langhe's authorship. This is partly, as I've said, because, given the character of book-production of the time, it is difficult to think of the volume written in 1351 as having travelled very far before 1365. But also, I confess, for subjective reasons. I like the idea of a monk who, bound to his monastery as a serf to the glebe, dreams of a freedom which takes him to the ends of the earth. As a man already developing that enormous paunch which will cause him to be remembered as having had great difficulty in walking, who thinks himself into the image of a great traveller. And again as one who, living a few miles from 'the March of Calais' held by the English, in a locality harassed by the intrusions of English soldiers, ironically assumes the body and mind of an English knight, a man to whom he gives his own name, 'John.'

III

What the truth of this is cannot be established until that day when both Jan de Langhe's translations and the continental French version of Mandeville's text have been edited with a full collation of all the manuscripts.[25] In the meanwhile, we have the *Book*, one which in the later Middle Ages was much more popular than Marco Polo's. What sort of book is it? For Josephine Bennett, it was 'a *romance* of travel,' which belonged 'primarily, to the history of literature.'[26] But since she wrote those words, another view has grown up. This has been expressed most emphatically by C.W.R.D. Moseley, who has written of the *Book*'s 'impeccable geographical thought (in the sense that we use the term "geographical" in our methodology),' and goes on to say that it 'embodies as true a picture of the world as anyone in the fourteenth century could have given.'[27] A big claim. The scholar who has looked at the question at the greatest length is Christiane Deluz. Her book bears the subtitle *Une 'Geographie' au XIVe Siécle*, which signals that she comes down firmly on Moseley's side. She argues from such things as that the Mandeville-author offers over sixty place-names from the Far East. She highlights his account of a near circumnavigation of the world, which she sees as an important vulgarization of those proofs, which John of Holywood had given in the thirteenth century, that the earth was a globe. And she has a long section in which she analyses the number of what she calls geographical expressions in the text – these are words like 'weather,' 'river,' 'stream,' 'desert,' and so on – and shows, perhaps not altogether surprisingly, that there were indeed a lot of them.

Yet there are many elements in the *Book* to suggest that it is a geographical fantasy. East of Jerusalem it makes no attempt to deal with coherent space. Its principal source is Odoric of Pordenone; yet the Mandeville-author curiously dispenses with most of the genuine geographic material found in it. Instead, he portrays Asia as a sequence of islands, each with their own marvels. There is an island where mountains of gold are guarded by ants as big as dogs, others where rivers run not with water but with precious stones. There are Isles of Cannibal Giants, of Basilisk-eyed Women, of Apple-Sniffers, and so on. Finally we come to the borders of Paradise, and from there on to the Vale Perilous or Vale of Enchantment. Although it has been tried, all attempts to map the book are doomed.[28] And it is the reverse of the truth to say, as Moseley has said, that the *Book* seeks to exclude fabulous material. In fact, when the marvels don't appear in his sources, the author cannot resist putting them back. After describing an island called Dondin, Odoric had gone on to say this:

> There are many other strange things in those parts about which I will not write, for without seeing them no one could believe them. For in the whole world there are no such marvels as in that kingdom. I have written about only those things of which one can be certain that they are as I have spoken of them.[29]

This note of caution is the reverse of what the Mandeville-author is looking for. It only spurs him on to redress the balance. As Josephine Bennett has pointed out,[30] it is precisely at this point that he decides to treats us to what Odoric has omitted, the whole gamut of 'the monstrous races': headless men with eyes and mouths in their backs, men who use their huge upper lips to shield their faces from the sun, monopeds, Cynocephali, men with ears hanging to their knees, and so on, and so on.

The *Book* is outside geography and anthropology; and it is outside history too. Here in the fourteenth century, Sir John and his companions enlist for sixteen months in the army of the Great Khan, which was, we are told, at war with the King of Southern China.[31] Yet, as Marco Polo and Odoric had shown, the Mongols had already conquered all of China back in the 1270s. Still more striking, this is a world in which the mythic emperor Prester John continues to rule in majesty. On his return from Karakorum in the 1250s, the Dominican missionary William of Rubruck had reported that the Prester was just 'a prosperous shepherd' whom the Nestorians had set up as their king. ('They called him King John and they used to tell ten times more about him than the truth. For the Nestorians of these parts do this kind of thing. Out of nothing they make a great brouhaha.') After Rubruck, Marco Polo again was to make it clear that Prester John was simply just another vassal among Mongol warlords. Then Odoric of Pordenone had gone on to echo and reinforce this by saying that not just one-tenth, as Rubruck had had it, but not one-hundredth part of what was told about his lands was true.[32]

The Mandeville-author ignores all this spoil-sport realism. Instead he throws his weight behind all those in Europe who preferred to retain their dreams. With him Prester John lives on, as Emperor of Greater and Lesser India, Emperor of Upper India, one of the four great Lords of the Earth. He resumes all that splendour which the famous, fabulous twelfth-century Letter of Prester John had bestowed on him. The land over which he rules is four months' journey in breadth, its length measureless. It is divided into seven provinces, each presided over by a subordinate king. His palaces at Nise and Susa are constructed from a dazzling variety of gold and jewels; and here he is attended by the Patriarch of St Thomas as his pope. The mythic resonances are so strong that they cannot be resisted; mere fact must step down before all the pleasures of medieval Orientalism. And writing at a time when most who continued to proclaim the Prester's reality and power were transplanting him from the East to Ethiopia and Abyssinia, the Mandeville book kept him on the borders of the territories of the Great Khan. It is with Prester John that any attempt to portray the book as a geography, as giving 'as true a picture of the world as anyone in the fourteenth century could have given,' must vanish.[33]

What is here instead is a cheerful, exotic travel-fiction with lots of marvels and good stories, plus public-spirited, effortless uplift. Following some moral reformation at home, the crusade will be successful quite soon. Indeed since the religion of the Muslim and all other peoples has so much in common with ours, they may very well become Christians first. Here is a work of escapism, which flourishes on unreality. It is just the thing to take one's mind off the Hundred Years' War, if only for a few hours.

Having said which, it is easy to see why, although its author must have known Marco Polo's book, he never draws upon it. Marco's habitual tendency is to cut down all fabulous marvels and to present what is sternly factual. I write 'sternly' because, as all his readers know, Marco is never in the least touched by any awareness that he might possibly be boring them. There is a marvellous integrity in his determination to tell them all manner of things that they don't want to know. Think of those imagined itineraries through Mangi:

> Now we will quit Suigiu and go to a city which is called Viugiu, and you should know that this Viugiu is a day from Sugiu [sic]. It is a very large city ... But as there is no novelty to be called to mind there we will leave it and I will tell you of another city called Vughin.
>
> And this Vughin is also a very large and noble city. They are idolaters, obey the Great Khan and have paper money ... Now we will part from that city and tell you of the town of Ciangan ...[34]

And so it goes on. One can imagine Rustichello getting very edgy as Marco insists that these passages stay in; the factual density is going to destroy any attempt to make a name for himself as a writer of chivalric literature. The interest of dozens of towns is no more than that: 'their inhabitants are idolaters, obey the Great Khan, and have paper money.' The words run like a litany – yet we have to be told all their names. Our fantasy is shrivelled up. The Mandeville-author does not have any cataloguing of that sort. He is terrified of boring his readers with, as he puts it, 'many places which it would take too long to name and relate,'[35] and this leads him to the constant production of new marvels at the expense of reality.

With that contrast between Polo and Mandeville, I think of the arguments of Francis Wood, who has claimed that Marco Polo never went to China, that he wrote his book after spending twenty-four years hidden away somewhere around the Black Sea or at Constantinople. This thesis has been critically examined and dismissed by several scholars, most thoroughly in a long article by Igor de Rachewiltz.[36] In addition to what they have written, there is something else to be said: if Marco Polo had set down an account of the East which he had invented without going there, what he wrote would not have looked at all like The Book of Marco Polo. What it would have looked like would have been The Book of Sir John Mandeville. It would have been a book which was based solely on sources available in the West, on the West's imagining of the East, and it would have been filled with all those heady marvels which so delight the Mandeville-author. It too would have been a travel romance.

IV

If Mandeville's *Book* is simply a travel romance, does this mean that it had no role in the European discovery of the East? Could it, nonetheless, given its vast popularity, given the vast ignorance of the East in the West, have influenced exploration, have had geographical consequences? Despite the occasional exceptional incident – and despite the arguments of several scholars basing themselves on these exceptions – my own conclusion is that the *Book* was rarely accorded any serious standing in scholarship or cartography. Around 1450, the Bavarian monk Friedrich Ammann gave a list of the sources for his 'Cosmographical Table.' He included Ptolemy, Marco Polo, and Pomponius Mela, but specifically excluded Mandeville as unreliable.[37] This is the first time, as far as I know, that this happens, but it happens a lot thereafter. There is a great contrast here with the way in which, at that very time, the humanists (notably the circle of Toscanelli and Nicholas of Cusa) were taking up Marco Polo.

I say one finds exceptions – for instance, Martin Behaim in 1492 certainly cited Mandeville as one of the sources for his globe.[38] The most famous of these, one often cited, is the appearance of a Latin version of Mandeville in the first edition of Hakluyt's *Principal Navigations*, published at London in 1589.[39] But Sir John was not resurrected here as a result of any geographical considerations, but in order to meet political needs. Europeans who were planning to take over lands outside Europe could at the time seek legitimacy only by claiming, as the Spanish did, to have been their first discoverer – of course, the first discoverers were the indigenous inhabitants, but they did not signify – or by appealing for legal endorsement to the pope, as the French had done but as Protestant England could not now do. This explains the opening section of Hakluyt's work, where one finds documents to prove that back in the sixth century King Arthur had first discovered America, that the Welshman Madoc had colonized it in the twelfth century, that the Bristol merchant, Robert Thorne, had rediscovered it in the fifteenth century, and that 'Sebastian' Cabot (Hakluyt did not get the right Cabot but nobody cared) had then discovered it again on behalf of Henry VII. All this constituted a counter-claim to Spain's assertion of rights over the New World. Britons had got to America long before Columbus. Hakluyt included Mandeville for a similar reason. He was hoping that the early appearance of this Englishman in the East would justify, by the doctrine of first discovery, any English expansion in the East. He gave it in the Latin version because he was appealing to the community of international law. He did not translate it into English – as he does all the other Latin in his book – because, as I would guess, he did not want English sailors or merchants to become confused by it.

Hakluyt follows the text with an Admonition to the Reader, still in the Latin, which ends with the words, 'Vale atque aut meliora dato, aut his utere mecum,' which might be translated as: 'Farewell, and either produce something better yourself, or make use of this as I'm doing.' He continues, in defence of Mandeville's fables, to give some extracts from Pliny's *Natural History* which spoke of the monstrous races.[40] It may just be an unfortunate phrase – 'make use of this as I'm doing' – but one wonders how far it may be a subconscious revelation of cynicism. However this might be, Hakluyt eventually came to realize that it wouldn't carry conviction; nine years later, when he published a second edition, silently, without explanation, our English knight is thrown out. Mandeville thereafter was normally treated as the fiction it is.

Yet, though it seems improbable that John Mandeville ever cut much ice in learned circles, with scholars, with cosmographers, imagination is often more powerful than reason and romance too may be an essential prelude to discovery. In 1512, Ponce de León mounted an expedition from Puerto Rico in an attempt to discover 'the Island of Bimini,' which was said to contain a 'fountain of youth' which washed away the effects of age and which looks very much like that 'Well of Youth' from which Sir John tells us he has drunk. As a result, Ponce became the first white man to discover Florida, to where, of course, today the elderly still flock in search of much the same thing.[41] Seven years later, Diego de Velasquez, governor of Cuba, commanded Cortés to mount an expedition to Mexico, telling him to keep a weather eye out for dog-headed men and those with great flat ears. And it was of course the Amazons who gave their name to America's greatest river.[42] One cannot claim any direct influences in these incidents, but they all derive from that world of medieval fantasy to which Mandeville belongs.

Above all, in the England of Shakespeare, the East was Mandeville's East. It is where Benedick pleads to go to escape Beatrice in *Much Ado about Nothing*: 'I will go on the slightest errand now to the Antipodes ... I will fetch you a tooth-picker now from the furthest inch of Asia, bring you the length of Prester John's foot, fetch you a hair off the Great Cham's beard, do you any embasage to the pygmies rather than hold three words conference with this harpy.' It is from where Othello draws the tales with which he woos Desdemona, stories of:

> the cannibals that each other eat,
> The Anthropophagi and men whose heads
> Do grow beneath their shoulders ...[43]

There is something curiously appropriate in Martin Frobisher having a copy of Mandeville aboard when he picks up fool's gold on Baffin Island.[44] Or that Sir Walter Raleigh's *Discoverie of Guiana*, that archetypical bogus prospectus, should tell us of the anthropophagi dwelling by the river Caora: 'Such a nation was written of by Mandeville, whose reports were holden for fables many yeeres, and yet since the East

Indies were discovered, we find his relations true of such things as heretofore were held incredible.'[45] Adventurers need romance; they need fiction as well as fact.

There are, we have seen, considerable differences in the way in which the three books and their four – or is it three? – authors tell of the East. Jan de Langhe, inventor of a new genre, presents his collection and translation, a work of history, of popularizing scholarship, valuable for those who were trying to discover truth or create fiction. The Mandeville-author offers one of the high points in centuries of European Orientalism, a powerful stimulus to the imagination. Marco Polo and Rustichello gives us simply pages and pages of what was for their world new information, one hair after another patiently plucked from the Great Cham's beard. With these three works, scholarship, fantasy, the narration in chivalric rhetoric of a lived experience, came together to commemorate the first age of European involvement in the Far East and, at the same time, to persuade western minds, in the years that followed, once more to reach out once toward that world.

APPENDIX

The Collection of Jan de Langhe

A.

Jan de Langhe's Book consists of six principal parts:

1. The *Itinerarium*, the account by the Franciscan Odorico da Pordenone of his travels in the Middle East, India (c. 1321), and China (1324/5–28). He was at Padua in May 1330, when he dictated his work to Fra Guglielmo da Solanza, and died there 14 Jan 1331. A copy was sent to Avignon where it was recopied, with some rewriting, by Henry of Glatz.

See: *Sinica Franciscana*, ed. A. van den Wyngaert (Quaracchi, 1929) i, 381–495; *Les voyages en Asie au XIV siécle du bienheureux frère Odoric de Pordenone*, ed. H. Cordier (*Recueil de voyages et de documents*, X, Paris, 1891).

H. Yule, *Cathay and the Way Thither*, 2nd ed. revised by H. Cordier (London, Hakluyt, 1915, photo-reproduction, New York, 1967), vol. 2.

F.E. Reichert, *Begegnungen mit China: Die Entdeckung Ostasiens im Mittelalter* (Sigmaringen, 1992), 148–51.

2. The *Flower of the Histories of the East,* a book on the Mongols and 'The Realms of Asia' by Prince Hetoum of Korykos (otherwise Hethum, Hayton, Haytoun, etc.), nephew of King Hetoum I of Little Armenia. Shortly after becoming a Premonstratensian canon, at the command of Pope Clement V, Hetoum dictated his work in French to Nicholas Faulcon, at Poitiers in 1307. Later Faulcon translated it into Latin. Jan de Langhe retranslated Faulcon's Latin back into French. Since Little Armenia had been a vassal state of the Mongols from the 1240s, Hetoum was in a position to know a great deal about the East. The first part of the book is an account of the realms of Asia. The second gives an history of the 'Emperors' of the continent since the birth of Christ (Persians, 'Saracens,' Khwarazmins, Mongols). The third speaks of the Mongols from the time of Genghis Khan. The fourth part, which consisted of a plan for a crusade, is in Jan's version considerably abbreviated. Using this source, in his *Chronicon S. Bertini, 728,* Jan de Langhe writes of King Hetoum I's embassy to Möngke in the early 1250s.

See: *Die Geschichte der Mongolen des Hetoum von Korkyros (1307) in der Rückübersetzung durch Jean le Long, Traitiez des estas et des conditions de quatorze royaumes de Aise (1351),* ed. Sven Dörper, mit parallelem Abdruck des lateinischen Manuskripts Wroclaw, Biblioteka Uniwersytecka, R 262, Frankfurt a. M., 1998. (= Europaïsche Hochschulschriften, Reihe XIII: Französische Sprache and Literatur, 236).

Hayton, *La Fleur des histories de la terre d'Orient,* ed. C. Kohler (*Recueil des Historiens des Croisades. Documents arméniens, Paris, 1906,* vol. 2).

Hetoum, *A Lytell Chronycle,* ed. G. Burger (London, 1988), reprints Pynson's English version with valuable comment.

3. Two letters written by the Great Khan, Toghon Temur, to Benedict XII in 1338 with the Pope's reply.

See: Jan's translation in 'Notice sur quelques relations diplomatiques des Mongols de la Chine avec les Papes d'Avignon,' ed. M. Jacquet, *Nouveau Journal Asiatique,* 7 (1831), 417–33.

On this incident B.Z. Kedar, 'Chi era Andrea Franco?' *Atti della Societa Ligure di Storia Patria,* n.s. 17 (1977), 369–77.

4. The *Book of the Estate of the Great Khan,* written around 1334 and dispatched to Pope John XXII by either John of Cori or Guillaume d'Adam, successive Archbishops of Sultania in Persia, gave a brief account of the East and missionary hopes there. This is only known in Jan de Langhe's version.

See: Jan's translation in 'Le Livre du Grant Caan,' ed. M. Jacquet, *Journal Asiatique,* 6 (1830), 57–72.

H. Yule, *Cathay,* 3: 89–103, for English version.

5. An account of and guide to pilgrimage through Egypt and Palestine to Jerusalem, written by the German knight William of Boldensele, about 1336.

See: 'Itinerarius Guilielmi de Boldensele,' ed. C.L. Grotefend, *Zeitschrift des Historischen Verein für Niedersachsen*, 1852, rptd. Hanover, 1855, 236–86.

I have been unable to see *Liber de quibusdam ultramarinis partibus*, 1336, ed. C. Deluz, with translation of Jean Le Long, roneotyped, Paris, 1972. An edition of the Latin, French, and German texts is being prepared by Scott D. Westrem; see the introduction to his *Learning from Legends in the James Ford Bell Library Mappamundi* (Minnesota, 2000).

6. *The Book of Travels in Parts of the East* written by the Dominican friar, Ricoldo da Montecroce. Ricoldo was born c.1242 at Montecroce, near Florence, joined the Dominicans at Florence in 1267, and became MA at the convent of S. Caterina at Pisa in 1272. He then travelled to Palestine, and journeyed on as far east as Baghdad. He was back at Florence in 1307, in which year he presented the pope with his *Confutatio Alcorani*. Died 1320. Most of his works (against Muslims, Jews, Eastern Christians) were written at Baghdad.

See: Monneret de Villard, *Il libro della peregrinazione nelle parti d'oriente del frate Ricoldo da Montecroce*, Rome, 1948.

A. Dondaine, 'Ricoldiana: notes sur les oeuvres du Ricoldo de Montecroce,' *Archivium Fratrum Praedictatorum*, 37 (1967) 119–79.

B.

The work survives in six manuscripts, which I give from Dörper's edition of Hetoum, pp. 41–98:

1. Bibliothèque Nationale, fr. Mss. Ancien fonds fr.2810, written on vellum, 297 leaves, 265 large miniatures.

This is the celebrated *Livres des Merveilles* given by John the Fearless, Duke of Burgundy to the Duc de Berry in January 1413. It gives five of the six constituent parts of Jan's translations, but substitutes Faulcon's original French text of Hetoum for Jan's translation. To these are added an Anglo-French version of Mandeville, the northern French version of Marco Polo, and a Life of St Alban of Germany or Mainz.[46]

See: *Le Livre des Merveilles*, ed. H. Omont, 2 vols, Paris, 1904 (Réprod. de man. et min. de la Bibl. Nat., XII).

M. Meiss, *French Painting in the Time of Jean de Berry: The Boucicault Master* (London, 1968), 112–16.

Jean de Mandeville, *Le Livre des Merveilles du monde*, ed. Christiane Deluz (Paris, 2001), 50–3.

Marco Polo, *Le Livre des Merveilles, Manuscrit Française 2810 de la Bibliothèque nationale de France*, commentary of F. Avril, M-Th. Gousset, J. Monfrin, J. Richard, M-H. Tesnière, Th. Reimer, Lucerne, facsimile ed., 1996.

L. de Backer, *L'Extrême Orient au Moyen Age* (Paris, 1877), printed from this manuscript his (not always accurate) transcriptions of the text of Odoric (89–124), Hayton (125–255), Ricoldo of Montecroce (256–334), the Archbishop of Sultania (335–46) and the letters between Toghon Temur to Benedict XII (347–56).

2. Bern, Bürgerbiblothek, Ms. 125.
Parchment of 14th century, which, as in the previous manuscript, substitutes the original French text for Jan's translation of Hetoum and adds copies of the Anglo-French version of Mandeville and the French of Marco Polo.

3. Besancon, Bibliothèque de la Ville, 667
Parchment, consists of the six pieces translated by Jan of Saint-Bertin, adding that he wrote it in 1351 and that he is 'adpresent abbe dicelluj lieu Mi1.CCC.lxUiii.'
See Dörper, 77, who uses it as the base manuscript for his edition of Hetoum.

4. Bibliothèque Nationale, fr. 12202
Paper, 15th century, has the six works of Jan, with some text missing at the beginning.

5. British Library, Cotton, Otho D. II
Parchment, first half of 15th century, severely damaged by fire. Contains the six pieces of Jan, plus an *Histoire de la forteress de Lusignan en Poitou* (86r–150v).

6. Bibliothèque Nationale, fr. 1380
Parchment, 15th century, contains the six pieces of Jan.

The collection, as a whole, was first printed as *Lhystore merueilleuse plaisante et recreative du grand empereur de Tartarie, seigneur des Tartars, nomme le Grand Can*, Paris pour Jean-Saint-Denys, 1529. (According to Backer, above, only two copies survive.)

NOTES

1 Larner, *Marco Polo and the Discovery of the World*.

2 Moreover, in the course of the later Middle Ages – and Iain Macleod Higgins, in *Writing East*, has shown how the same thing happened to the Mandeville book – subsequent transmitters of the text often imposed their own messages upon it.

3 Athanasius Kircher, *China monumentis ... illustrata* (Amsterdam, 1667), Pars secunda, cap. vi, 87–90. The map is between pp. 47 and 48. On the Wall, see Waldron, *The Great Wall of China*.

4 See *The Book of Ser Marco Polo the Venetian*, ed. H. Yule, 3rd edition, revised by H. Cordier (London, 1903); reprinted in 2 volumes (New York, 1993), passim. The most laborious construction of the supposed itinerary is found in N.M. Penzer's edition of John Frampton, *The Most Noble and Famous Travels of Marco Polo together with the Travels of Nicolò Conti* (2nd. ed., London, 1937, 1st ed. 1929), where 'owing to the kindness of Sir Aurel Stein in allowing me to use the maps illustrating his *Third Journey to Innermost Asia*, I have been able, with the help of my expert cartographer, Miss G. Heath, to construct eleven [!!!] entirely new maps which I trust will help to elucidate the itinerary of the great traveller' (xi).

5 *Sinica Franciscana*, ed. A. van den Wyngaert (Quaracchi, 1929) 1: 349 (letter of Fra Giovanni Montecorvino, 1305).

6 In chapter 5 of his *Marco Polo*, Heers advances as an 'hypothèse naturelle-ment hasardée mais, je crois, séduisante' the question as to whether the Book is following 'non pas la route effectivement suivie lors de l'expédi-tion, mais une route exceptionelle, idéale donc imaginaire, encore jamais décrite?' (151). This is hardened in 'De Marco Polo à Christophe Colomb: comment lire le *Devisement du Monde*?' esp. 126: 'Vouloir, par habitude, faire du *Devisement* un recit de voyage est manifestment une erreur. Rien ne milite en ce sens et le *Livre* ne dit jamais rien de pareil.'

7 See, e.g., D. Rieger, 'Marco Polo und Rustichello da Pisa. Der Reisende and rein Erzähler.'

8 Marco Polo, *Le Devisement du Monde*, vol. 1, *Départ des voyageurs et traversée de la Perse*, principal ed. Philippe Ménard, with M.-L. Chênerie and M. Guéret-Laferté.

9 E.g., Ménard, *Le Devisement du Monde* : 'A la façon de ses contemporains Marco Polo est persuadé que l'Orient est une terre de prodiges' (1:106). But cf. Larner 77–83.

10 J. Needham, with Wang Ling, *Science and Civilisation in China*, vol. 3, *Mathematics and the Sciences of the Heavens and the Earth* passim; Larner 84–5.

11 C. Deluz, 'Villes et organisation de l'espace: La Chine de Marco Polo.'

12 J.G. Nichols, 'Inventory of Reliques at St Omer 1465'; G.W. Coopland, *The Abbey of St Bertin and Its Neighbours 900–1350*; D. Nicholas, *Town and Countryside* 92, 100, 102.

13 'Johannes Iperii Continuatum S. Bertini Chronicon,' in *Veterum scriptorum et munimentorum historicorum… opera*, vol. 6 (Paris, 1729), col. 619 (of 614–32). The Abbey's 'border' character is underlined by the fact that in 1360 it became the centre for the collection of the ransom for the release of King John II; E. Perroy, *La Guerre de Cent Ans* 114. This was to lead to accounting disputes between the Abbot and the French monarchy; see 'Johannes Iperii Continuatum' 618–19.

14 *Chronica monasterii Sancti Bertini auctore Iohanne Longo*, ed. O. Holder-Egger; Holder-Egger's life of Jan, etc. 736–47; chron. 747–860. The life of St Erkembode, fourth abbot of Saint-Bertin, found in *Acta Sanctorum* (1863), 12 April, 93–5, has also been attributed to him. L. van der Essen, 'Jean d'Ypres ou de Saint-Bertin,' argued that it is a work displaying particular historical insight and is to be distinguished from the standard hagiography of the age. But M. Coens, 'L'auteur de la vita Erkembodonis' shows that this is to confuse our John V the Long of Ypres with the true author, John III, also of Ypres, abbot from 1187 to 1230.

15 *Chronica monasterii Sancti Bertini* 853.

16 *Chronica monasterii Sancti Bertini* 853.

17 Iacopus Mayer, *Commentarii sive annales rerum Flandricarum Libri septendecim* ed. Antonius Mayer (Antwerp, 1561), p. 200r; J.F. Foppens, *Bibliotheca Belgica* (Brussels, 1739), 2: 669–70 (under Joannes Iperius).

18 Holder-Egger, the editor of the text in the *Monumenta Germaniae Historica*, omitted passages, among them this, which he held to be of no interest. Here one must consult the older edition, Johannes Longus, *Chronica sive Historia Monasterii sancti Bertini* from E. Martène and U. Durand in *Thesaurus novus anecdotorum*, vol. 3 (Paris, 1717, reprint Farnborough, 1968), 746.

19 *Chronica sive Historia monasterii*, 746–7.

20 Neither the northern French version (in Ménard), which has 'Alaü,' 'Cogatal,' and 'Cablay,' nor the Franco-Italian (Marco Polo, *Milione/Le Divisament dou monde*, ed. G. Ronchi), which has 'Alau,' 'Cogatal,' and 'Cublai,' has the form of names that Jan gives in his chronicle. All the manuscripts of Pipino's Latin version that I have seen have 'Alau,' 'Cogatal,' 'Cublay.'

21 See Appendix for a fuller account of the Collection.

22 C. Knowles, 'Jean de Vignay,' and D.A. Trotter's introduction to his edition of Jean de Vignay's *Les Merveilles de la Terre de Outremer*.

23 M.C. Seymour, *Sir John Mandeville* 23–4. On the date of composition,

see 5–7. The first northern French and Anglo-French versions of the text say that it was written in 1356 and 1357 respectively, which seems probable.

24 Christiane Deluz, *Le Livre de Jehan de Mandeville*, passim, and in the introduction to her critical edition of the Insular text: Jean de Mandeville, *Le Livre des merveilles du monde*. Against Mandeville as an Englishman and as dying at Liège, see Seymour, *Sir John Mandeville* 11–15, 25–36.

25 In her edition of the Insular text (note 24), Deluz gives suasions for an English origin by citing some different Continental versions of words used in the Insular text of 1371, but concludes: 'seule une édition critique de la version continentale permettrait d'arriver à des certitudes' (33–6).

26 Josephine W. Bennett, *The Rediscovery of Sir John Mandeville* 19.

27 C.W.R.D. Moseley, 'Introduction' to his translation of *The Travels of Sir John Mandeville* 15; and his 'The Metamorphoses of Sir John Mandeville,' esp. 7. Christian K. Zacher, who broadly follows him in *Curiosity and Pilgrimage*, tells us that Moseley 'is currently [1976] preparing a lengthy study of the strong influence Mandeville had on Renaissance voyagers' (184).

28 Compare *Mandeville's Travels: Text and Translations*, ed. M. Letts, end-paper to vol. 1, with Deluz, *Le Livre*, 400–1 and Jean de Mandeville, *Le Livre*, 88–9, 'Mappemonde de Mandeville.' To draw such maps requires knowledge of much later maps than those available in the 1340s. In the Deluz vesion, based confessedly on Behaim's globe, one sees for instance a representation of 'Cipangu' or Japan (found in Marco Polo but not in Mandeville) and a coastline of Africa which cannot have been suspected before the fifteenth century.

29 H. Yule, *Cathay and the Way Thither*, 2nd ed. revised by H. Cordier (London: Hakluyt, 1916, photo-reproduction, New York, 1967), ii, 176.

30 Josephine Bennett 37–8. See also Mary B. Campbell, *The Witness and the Other World* 154; *Mandeville's Travels: Text and Translations*, ed. M. Letts, ch. 22, 342–4.

31 'Et sachiez que my compaignon et moy avecques nos valles le servismes en soudees xv. mois contre le roi de Marchi, a qui il auait guerre' (*Mandeville's Travels*, ed. M. Letts, 353).

32 'Itinerarium Willelmi de Rubruc,' in *Sinica Fransicana* 1: 206–7; Yule, *Cathay and the Way Thither* 2: 245, n.1 for Jan de Langhe's version of Odoric: 'Il n'en est mie la centisme par de ce que on dit comment soit riche terre et noble pais.'

33 'Ci commence a parler du pays et des ylles de lempereur Prestre Iehan' (*Mandeville's Travels*, ed. M. Letts, ch. 30, 383–7). And see 499–506 for translated extracts from Prester John's Letter, probably used by the Mandeville-

author. Cf. Bernard Hamilton, 'Continental Drift: Prester John's Progress through the Indies,' esp. 247–55.

34 Marco Polo, *Milione/Le Divisament dou monde*, ed. G. Ronchi, ch. 151.

35 'mointe pays qe trop serroient long a nomer et diviser.' Jean de Mandeville, *Le Livre*, ed. Deluz, ch. 20, 331.

36 Igor de Rachewiltz, 'Marco Polo Went to China.' See also J.P. Voiret, 'China, "Objektiv" Gesehen'; Jørgen Jensen, 'The World's Most Diligent Observer'; U. Tucci, 'Marco Polo, andò veramente in Cina?'; D.O. Morgan, 'Marco Polo in China – or Not.'

37 D.B. Durand, *The Vienna-Klosterneuburg Map Corpus of the Fifteenth Century* 176.

38 C.W.R.D. Moseley, 'Behaim's Globe and Mandeville's Travels'; E.G. Ravenstein, *Martin Behaim* 62–71.

39 R. Hakluyt, *The Principal Navigations, Voiages and Discoveries of the English nation, made by Sea or ouer Land* 23–79.

40 Hakluyt 77. I do not think it has been pointed out that the wording is influenced by Horace, *Epistles*, I, vi, 67–8: 'Vive, vale! si quid novisti rectius istis, candidus imperti; si nil, his utere mecum.' It may have been simply the attempt to produce a modish classical echo which gives the unhappy tone.

41 L. Olschki, 'Ponce de Léon's Fountain of Youth.'

42 L. Weckmann, 'The Middle Ages in the Conquest of America'; K.N. March and K.M. Passman, 'The Amazon Myth and Latin America' (see 292–4 for Amazons in Prester John; 294–5 for Amazons in Alexander romances).

43 *Much Ado about Nothing* 2.1.246–53; *Othello* 1.3.143–4.

44 E.G.R. Taylor, *Tudor Geography, 1485–1583* 36–7.

45 Sir Walter Raleigh, *The Discoverie of the Large, Rich, and Bewtiful Empyre of Guiana* 178.

46 Supposedly martyred at the beginning of the fifth century; see *Bibliotheca Sanctorum*, ed. F. Caraffa 1: 659–62. On five occasions, this Life is bound together with the Anglo-French version of the *Book of Sir John Mandeville*; see Josephine Bennett 170–1. On 271 she cites from BN. fr. 5633 the explanation offered there: 'Pour ce que je suis nés de Saint-Alban, et maintes gens de nostre pais cuide qu'il ne soft nul autre Sain Albain que celui de nostre pais, je vueil que vous sachires qu'il y a ung autre Saint Albain en Almagne.'

7 The World Translated: Marco Polo's *Le Devisement dou monde, The Book of Sir John Mandeville,* and Their Medieval Audiences

SUZANNE M. YEAGER

Questions of veracity have long surrounded two closely related medieval travel narratives: the fourteenth-century compilation *The Book of Sir John Mandeville,* and Marco Polo's earlier *Le Devisement dou monde.* One debate concerns Polo in particular, whose reputation suffered posthumously in 1553 when Giovanni Battista Ramusio published his first edition of Polo's work in his *Navigazioni e viaggi.* The *Navigazioni,* both a translation and a substantial abridgment of Polo's *Devisement,* cast doubt on the veracity of Polo's account by commenting that Polo's family name, 'Il Milione,' in fact meant 'the liar.'[1] This interpretation, now known to be inaccurate, caused subsequent commentators to doubt the truthfulness of the account originally assembled in 1298 by Polo and Rustichello of Pisa. Yet even before Ramusio's translation, a contemporary of Polo's, Jacobo of Acqui, wrote in his *Imago Mundi* that Polo himself was aware of the incredible nature of his work:

> because of the tongues of detractors who easily impose lies on others, and rashly condemn as a lie whatever they cannot believe or will not understand ... And because great and vast and almost incredible things are found there, [Polo] was asked by friends when he was dying to correct his book and take back what he had written ... ; and he answered, I did not write half of what I saw.[2]

Regarding the content that Polo and Rustichello did include, some manuscripts of the *Devisement* contain the authors' own explanations for memorializing Polo's travels – that the book's audiences from every level of society may learn something about 'the East.'[3] Polo and Rustichello effectively reinscribe then-traditional views of 'eastern' sites and peoples – no longer the uncivilized denizens of monstrous locales, Polo's inhabitants operate in a world of sophisticated cities, commerce, and intellectual development. Those things deemed stereotypically 'heathen' are 'corrected'; for instance, the Great Khan becomes a reasonable ruler who is said to harbour secret preferences for Christianity – a position which, in the time of the texts' circulation, would have proven his wisdom and civilized manner.

With its primary focus on practical matters of life in eastern and western Asia, India, and adjacent environs, along with its relative lack of 'miraculous' content, the *Devisement* does much to revise the prior, more fabulous depictions of exotic peoples and regions. If this revision of Asia and India were indeed part of the design of the work, it is significant that some late medieval audiences seemed to prefer the comparatively more marvel-filled account offered by the above-mentioned Mandeville-writer. In recent assessments of Mandeville's book, Mary B. Campbell, Iain Macleod Higgins, John Larner, and others have speculated that its writer's apparent restoration of marvellous content added to the audience perception of *The Book of John Mandeville*'s reliability, for the Mandeville-writer was, after all, describing exactly the kind of content medieval audiences expected to see.[4] Expectations of this type were shaped over centuries by sources ranging from antiquity, including Pliny's and Solinus's encyclopedias, to later, medieval productions such as Alexander's *Letter to Aristotle*, the *Liber monstrorum*, and the so-called *Letter of Prester John*. While Polo and Rustichello may have prepared the *Devisement* for a critical reception, *The Book of John Mandeville*, hereafter *Mandeville*, contained information twice as 'incredible' as that in the *Devisement*, yet was received as fact by most western European and English audiences.[5] While present-day logic may suggest a contradiction in the perceptions of *Mandeville* and the *Devisement* as 'true' representations of the East, this essay will show the bifocal nature of late medieval, European audience reception of travel literature; that is, differently as 'the East' and its inhabitants are often portrayed in these two works, certain audiences nevertheless employed both texts to define the Christian morality of their European readers. It is with this context in mind that this essay explores the comparatively different receptions of the texts.

The distinction between audience reception of the two books is nowhere more clear than in England. Medieval manuscripts of *Mandeville* circulated across England and Europe in many versions; all of them portrayed their writer and narrator as an Englishman. The work itself was linguistically more accessible than the *Devisement*, for it circulated in Latin, French, and the vernacular in medieval England while Polo and Rustichello's account remained in Latin. Because of the special relationship between *Mandeville* and the Middle English vernacular language, along with the more limited pattern of the *Devisement*'s transmission into England, the reception of both the *Devisement* and *Mandeville* by English audiences deserves further assessment regarding what factors distinguished these books, making one a 'best-seller' in England and the other, not. Indeed, judging from the many extant English *Mandeville* manuscripts, from those produced cheaply to the finest production copies, *Mandeville*'s audience occupied a broad social range. No doubt other variables such as the different cultural moments in which each text was produced must have affected popular reception. However, this study focuses primarily on content, and seeks to comment on the subjectivity of medieval audiences in the fourteenth century. As I discuss, medieval audiences may have favoured *Mandeville* for being at once more 'incredible' and more devotionally focused than the *Devisement*; moreover, one suspects that Mandeville's inclusion of a description of Jerusalem (and Polo and Rustichello's omission of it) may have played a crucial role in encouraging *Mandeville*'s popularity.

Reception of the Texts

The *Devisement* circulated in continental Europe long before it appeared on the scene in England. There, the Dominican friar Francesco Pipino's translation and adaptation of the *Devisement* appeared in the mid-fourteenth century as *De miribilibus mundi*, written between 1314 and 1324. This translation was the most common: of the seventeen extant manuscripts of Polo's account in England, fourteen are from Pipino.[6] By comparison, Consuelo W. Dutschke's survey of Polo manuscripts shows that as of 1993 there were 135 known extant manuscripts of the *Devisement* in Europe, and 43 per cent of these stem from the translations made by Pipino.[7] In comparison with other manuscripts of the *Devisement*, such as the widespread Franco-Italian version, Pipino adapted his translation from the Venetian version, which was already abbreviated in relation to its sources. Both John Critchley and John Larner have hypothesized that Pipino's Latin version was produced as a guidebook for missionaries.[8] As is later discussed, the more sophisticated version of Polo's East may not have been viewed as the appropriate type of material for imparting a Christian orientation of the world to a popular audience, but rather as reading suitable for a more expert group of theologians. Notably, neither the Pipino translation nor the other medieval Latin manuscripts of Polo in England were ever translated into English.[9] Indeed, the *Devisement* may never have appeared in England in English until 1579.

Among medieval manuscripts, Pipino's version of the *Devisement* featured in collections of scientific treatises and devotional works.[10] Some Pipino manuscripts in England derive from monastic communities and also contain treatises designed for crusade and pilgrimage, including Hayton's *Flos historiarum terre orientis*, appearing in three English manuscripts.[11] Similarly, it also features in a single manuscript together with William of Tripoli's *De statu saracenorum*, Jacques de Vitry's *Historia Hierosolymitana abbreviata*, and Odoric of Pordenone's *Relatio*.[12] At times the *Devisement* appears in English manuscripts with Odoric's *Relatio* alone, leading one to speculate on the close relationship between the two texts. Moreover, Dutschke discusses a manuscript of Odoric and Polo whose heavy annotation in different hands shows that both the *Devisement* and the *Relatio* were read as books of factual information.[13] Pipino manuscripts from fourteenth-century monastic scriptoria also place Polo alongside historical works, such as Ranulf Higden's *Polychronicon* – there are four extant manuscripts which show this practice; moreover, all four manuscripts are of English origin and represent the Pipino version.[14] The *Devisement* also appears with another well-known historical text, Geoffrey of Monmouth's *Historia regum Brittaniae*; it is also found accompanying devotional works like *Piers Plowman*; and even along with the Defective version of *The Book of Sir John Mandeville*.[15] As Dutschke has shown, the appearance of Polo's account with so many contemporary histories and devotional works suggests that his narrative was accepted for its facts; it was perceived as an account of actual events, rather than as a fantastic story.

Along with collation practices, accounts by English medieval readers of the *Devisement* show how the book was received. For instance, Pipino's translation in Oxford, Merton College, MS 312 belonged to Thomas Bradwardine (c.1290–1349); the theologian and philosopher was also one of Merton College's famous mathematicians as well as archbishop of Canterbury. Around 1344, Bradwardine completed a book entitled *De causa Dei contra Pelagium* in which he used Polo and Rustichello's description of non-Christian faiths in order to uphold the merits of Christian orthodoxy against other religions.[16] Among other ecclesiastical authorities in England who read the *Devisement* were Simon Bozoun, prior of Norwich; John of Tynemouth, Benedictine monk at St Albans; and Richard Exeter, Benedictine monk and prior at Westminster. Clearly this sample represents a specialized audience, and, in the case of Bradwardine, shows the *Devisement*'s use in sophisticated theological arguments. Moreover, Polo and Rustichello's work does not seem to have circulated extensively among English fourteenth-century laity.

In contrast to Polo's work, *Mandeville* enjoyed a popular reception in England among clergy and laity alike.[17] The writer appears sympathetic to this particular audience, presenting himself as a fourteenth-century Englishman, 'Ioon Maundeuyle kni?t,' born in St Albans, England (5/6). Although the writer says he is English and calls himself the book's narrator, nineteenth-century through present-day scholars have speculated that Sir John Mandeville may have been a fictitious persona, and, likewise, may not have been English. The suggestion has been made that the Mandeville-persona may have been the invention of a French writer who never, in fact, travelled.[18] In spite of what present-day scholars have deduced about Mandeville, it is clear that much of the book's contemporary medieval audience accepted its author as a real, historical person and the actual narrator of the text. His work was not only popular in England, but also in continental Europe, where the fact that the number of extant *Mandeville* manuscripts is greater than that of the *Devisement* suggests that *Mandeville* enjoyed a wider readership and greater circulation. Over three hundred manuscripts of *Mandeville* survive in a variety of languages, with Czech, Danish, Dutch, English, French, German, Irish, Italian, Latin, and Spanish among them; chronologically, these span the fourteenth through seventeenth centuries.[19] Like *Mandeville*, the *Devisement* was translated into several languages; yet fewer copies of each language are represented. Moreover, in places further afield, such as England, Ireland, and Portugal, more copies of *Mandeville* exist. Extrapolating from the numbers of extant manuscripts which survived in non-Reformist countries, Josephine Waters Bennett and Susanne Röhl submit that the present number of manuscripts in England is small in comparison to the number that existed prior to the Reformation; even so, the numbers of surviving *Mandeville* manuscripts in England more than quadruple those of the *Devisement*.[20]

References made to John Mandeville in works by other writers of the fourteenth and fifteenth centuries also show that his book was influential and widely read. In England, information gleaned from *Mandeville* appears in the poem 'Cleannesse' by the *Pearl*-poet, the 'Morte Arthure,' and Geoffrey Chaucer's 'Squire's Tale.'[21] *Mandeville* was also popular in France, where it influenced Jean d'Arras's *Mélusine* and the work of Christine de Pizan. It is of some significance that manuscript collation patterns of *Mandeville* in England differed from those on the Continent. For instance, many *Mandeville* manuscripts produced in France appear as single-work productions containing that work alone.[22] In French versions where this is not the case, some manuscripts show *Mandeville* with another historical text, such as Ovid's *Heroides*, a history of the Old Testament, or a chronicle of the kings of France.[23] Other French manuscripts collate *Mandeville* with romances such as *The Seven Sages* and Gervais du Bus's *Roman de Fauvel* (with which it appears more than twice).[24] Another notable manuscript offers a particularly devotional reading list, placing *Mandeville* among religious treatises, political letters, and saints' lives.[25] One manuscript combines romance and devotion in a collection including *L'Image du Monde*, a voyage of St Brendan, the *Roman de Fauvel*, and *Advocacie Notre-Dame*.[26] French manuscripts containing works of exploration and political interest also featured the text, leading Röhl to suggest that *Mandeville* was especially popular among aristocratic audiences in France who obtained the book as a symbol of political, even royal, prestige.[27]

Of the *Mandeville* manuscripts written in English and collated in England, some appear with scientific works, such as Chaucer's *Treatise on the Astrolabe*. Romances, such as *The Seven Sages* or *Sir Gowther*, were also popular company.[28] Likewise, it appears with historical works, such as John Lydgate's *Destruction of Thebes*, a historical chronicle from Brut to Rouen, and a *Chronicon* from creation to the coronation of Richard II.[29] In the greater part of the English manuscripts, however, *Mandeville* features with devotional works such as *Piers Plowman* and treatises on visiting the sick; it also accompanies Robert Mannyng's *Handlyng Synne*, religious and moral works in Latin, the story of Susan, accounts of Daniel and the Flight into Egypt, and Chaucer's *Troilus*.[30] One manuscript shows *Mandeville* with William Staunton's *Vision of St. Patrick's Purgatory*; another production places it in with the Ten Commandments, an exposition on *De mirabilibus mundi* in Latin, a treatise on the Sacraments, and works by the Church Fathers.[31] Another manuscript includes *Mandeville* in company with *The Gospel of Nicodemus*, a letter by St Bernard, and other moral works.[32] Still another manuscript places it with *The Proverbs of Solomon* and Lydgate's *Life of St. Edmund*.

Another manuscript accompanies *Mandeville* with an English account of *The Translation of St. Anthony, Abbot of Constantiople*, and the *Long Charter of Christ*.[33] One manuscript with particularly striking moral content places *Mandeville* with *Ypotys, The Prick of Conscience, Guy of Werwyke, Seven Wise Masters*, and Chaucer's *Melibee*.[34] Of the devotional works, *Piers Plowman* appears several times with *Mandeville* in manuscripts, often in works planned as a single unit.[35] Among other devotional trimmings, one manuscript of *Mandeville* has added the passage: 'And oure holy fader hath graunted to al tho that redith or wrytith or heryth this boke with good devocion, an C dayes to pardon and goddis blessynge an hye. Explicit Maundevyle.'[36] The numerous appearances of *Mandeville* with other devotional material suggest that some English audiences received it as a book useful for promoting religious understanding and Christian spirituality. Further, this reception of *Mandeville*, in contrast to the French, offers distinctions which may be made between audience preferences in the late medieval period, and that may apply to English reception of other texts like Polo's *Devisement*.

Taking Bennett, Dutschke, and Röhl's manuscript evidence into account, a major difference that emerges between the English medieval reception of Pipino's translation and *Mandeville* in England is the consistent association of *Mandeville* with devotional material. If *Mandeville* was indeed considered in some way an 'improvement' on the *Devisement* because of such content, then this may suggest the English expectation of travel literature as a devotional medium. Such patterns lead one to speculate that the more incredible and miraculous content regarding the far reaches of the world was what English audiences enjoyed. By the fourteenth century, travel writing featuring monsters and miracles consolidated rather than challenged orthodox Christianity and invoked the powers of the human imagination to build faith. By comparison, the account by Polo and Rustichello, being comparatively drier and more factual, did not provide the imaginative view of the world which had been codified by previous Christian texts. Moving away from ecclesiastical, doctrinal explanations and into a trade-based, descriptive mode, Pipino transmitted Polo and Rustichello's world view, which focused primarily on political and anthropological knowledge. In order to further investigate these patterns, I contrast the content of the two works and assess those factors which may have affected audience reception.

The Texts' Shared Approaches to the Uses of Marvels

It is inconclusive whether the writer of *Mandeville* ever knew Polo's work or whether he used it as one of his sources. Higgins has discussed passages from Mandeville's text which appear to be an intentional 'response' to Polo; in spite of this responsive content, however, the *Devisement* is 'conspicuously absent' from Mandeville's own list of his work's sources.[37] Whether the Mandeville-writer was writing to correct Polo and Rustichello, or whether his views emerged coincidentally, both texts describe the East and its inhabitants as instrumental in increasing the membership of the Christian Church. Pipino, adding substantially to his Venetian source, writes that his work is aimed at learned people with ecclesiastical knowledge. He says that he translates the text into Latin because he was asked to do so by his masters 'qui amplius latino quam vulgari delectantur' ['who were more pleased by Latin than by common speech'] (1). Not coincidentally, then, the text is known to have circulated in England among monastic houses and in the universities. However, Pipino also suggests that his work is designed to attract people at all religious levels, and he relates the spiritual merits which may be earned by reading it:

> ex huius libri inspectione fideles viros posse multiplicis gracie meritum a domino promereri; sive quia ... mirabilia dei opera aspicientes ipsius poterint virtutem et sapientiam venerabilius admirari aut videntes gentiles populos tanta cecitatis tenebrositate tantisque sordibus involutos gracias deo agant, qui ... de tam periculosis tenebris vocare dignatus est in admirabile lumen suum.

> from reading this book, faithful people may earn from the Lord the reward of great grace; either because seeing the marvellous works of God ... they will be able to more reverently admire his power and wisdom or, seeing the pagan people enveloped in such darkness of blindness and such wretchedness, they may give thanks to God who ... has deigned to call them out of such perilous darkness into his marvellous light. (1; cf. I Peter 2:9)

Here, Pipino names the *fideles*, that is, worshippers of Christ, as his intended audience who may be positively affected by *mirabilia*. He then goes on to explain that he writes also for those Christians whose faith needs strengthening (1). Finally, he says that he hopes to inspire the Christian conversion of non-Christians:

> religiosorum aliquorum corda pervocari poterunt pro ampliacione fidei christiane, ut nomen domini nostri Jesu Christi portent ... ad occecatas infidelium naciones, ubi messis quidem multa, operarii vero pauci.

> that the hearts of some religious people may be moved for the spreading of the Christian faith so that they may carry the name of the Lord Jesus Christ ... to the blinded nations of the infidels, where indeed the harvest is great, but the workers are few. (1; cf. Matthew 9:37, Luke 10:2)

For Pipino, miracles in the *Devisement* will inspire into missionary activity those who are already Christians. His view of the East as a locus of religious conversion aligns with other episodes later in the narrative which can be construed as having similar views; these include the tale of the Caliph of Baghdad, who secretly converts for the piety of a Christian shoemaker, and the later depiction of the Khan, who harbours secret admiration for Christianity and only withholds conversion for want of ocular proof of Christian might. In his call for conversion, Pipino's addition to the Prologue perhaps heightens the impact of these later vignettes.

Like Pipino, Mandeville appears interested in assisting Christian devotion through his narrative; yet in contrast, Mandeville adopts an approach more substantially grounded in the fantastic. Certainly Pipino acknowledges the powers of *mirabilia* in his Prologue, but he does not proceed to deliver on this promise to describe them – at least to the degree that Mandeville does. As if he were fulfilling the promise made in Pipino's Prologue, Mandeville employs an abundance of the wonders of the East, foreign travel, and marvels; for, as he himself suggests, both *mirabilia* and marvels are significant as evidence of God and useful for strengthening Christian devotion. The most definitive statement on the use of these phenomena in aiding religious piety is seen in other Insular versions of *Mandeville* in a section which the Defective version may have contained at one time:

> For the myracles that God hath don and yit doth euery day ben the wytnesse of His myght and of His merueylles, as Dauid seyth in the Psaultere, *Mirabilia testimonia tua domine*, that is to seyne, Lord, Thi merueyles ben Thi wytness. (*Mandeville*, Cotton 44/25–9)[38]

Here, the conflated use of the words 'merueyle' and 'mirabilia' suggests that these terms, at least as far as Mandeville was concerned, con-
noted similar phenomena, and were based in biblical verses such as
Psalms 71:17–18. As Higgins has shown, Mandeville links earthly and
divine wonders in order to reflect the omnipotence of God; moreover,
Mandeville goes on to provide these marvels throughout his work,
making it understandable that most present-day scholars have placed
the book in the genre of the 'history of the imaginary' and 'imaginative
travels.'[39] Notably, the *Devisement* is rarely classified as such. Even
though Mandeville and Pipino differ in the content they deliver, they
both attest to their mutual goals of inspiring Christian faith through
their varied depictions of the East.

Along with supplying Christians with inspiration, *Mandeville* and
the *Devisement* reveal an interest in the conversion of eastern peoples.
As Mandeville puts it, certain similarities between Christianity and
Islam should make conversion from Islam to Christianity a simple
matter. Therefore he depicts Muslims as knowledgeable of the Christian faith:

> And þei graunte wel þe workis of Ihesu Crist to be goode and his wordis
> also and his vn[di]rstondyngis and his gospels and his myraclis to be
> soþe; and þat þe virgyne Marie is a goode mayde and holy bifore þe
> beryng of Ihesu Crist and after also; and þat þese þat trowiþ parfytly in
> God schal be saued. And for as myche as þei trowe nere oure fey, þei beþ
> liȝtlich conuertid to oure fey whanne men preche to hem of oure lawe and
> openeþ to hem þe prophecies. (58/19–26)

Polo likewise portrays the Mongols as a people ripe for western
Christian conversion. He writes that the Khan himself is not Muslim,
but that the people in Kublai Khan's lands are of diverse faiths, with
Muslims, Nestorian Christians, Jews, and 'idolaters' among them; by
'idolaters,' he almost certainly is referring to Buddhists and possibly
Daoists, or, depending on his location, Hindu peoples. In one scene,
the Khan appears so interested in Christianity that he invites missionaries into his lands:

> kaam … rogavit [Polos] … ut a more sui redirent ad papam … pro parte
> ipsius summum christianorum pontificem rogaturi querentes, [ut] ad
> eum centum sapientes christianos dirigeret, qui ostenderent sapientibus
> suis racionabiliter et prudenter, si verum erat, quod christianorum fides

esset melior inter omnes et quod dii tartaroum essent demones et quod ipsi et orientales alii erant decepti in suorum cultacione deorum.

The Khan ... asked the [Polos] ... that according to their custom they should return to the pope ... to ask the great pope of the Christians, requesting that he would send to [the Khan] one hundred wise Christian men who would show his learned men rationally and prudently, if it was true that the Christian faith was the best among all faiths and that they and other easterners had been deceived in the worship of their gods. (9–10)

Polo also presents the Khan as a man with Christian sympathies who asks the Polos to bring him oil from the lamps which burn in the Church of the Holy Sepulchre (10); such oil was considered a holy, miracle-working relic. The portrayal of the Khan as interested in this particular object may imply his general curiosity, and, together with surrounding material, depicts in the Khan a desire to access the power of the Christian God.

Through this discussion of non-Christian religions, both *Mandeville* and the *Devisement* share a reflective perspective on the state of western Christendom. Both narrators express dissatisfaction regarding the moral condition of western Europeans and place these criticisms in the mouths of eastern rulers. Mandeville relates a conversation in which the Sultan explains that the Christian loss of the Crusader states was a direct result of spiritual lapse (60/27–61/7). Likewise, Polo shows the Khan in the act of explaining orthodox Christian teaching regarding Christian defeat. In one instance, Naian, Kublai Khan's uncle, identified as a Christian, is defeated in his uprising against the Khan, and it is the Khan who places the loss in a Christian context. The Khan chastises Naian while simultaneously reassuring Naian's Christian army of their faith:

Si deus vester et eius crux noluit Nayam ferre presidium, nolite erubescere, quoniam dominus bonus iniusticie et iniquitati patrocinari non debet. Nayam domini sui proditor extitit et iniuste rebellis et dei vestri in sua malicia auxilium implorabat. Deus autem vester, quia bonus est noluit eius favere criminibus.

If your god and his cross did not wish to give Naian aid, do not feel ashamed since a good lord is not obligated to protect injustice and iniquity. Naian was a traitor to his lord and an unjust rebel and asked help of

your god in his (i.e., Naian's) malice. But your god, since he is good and
did not wish to reward crimes [did not aid him]. (77–8)

Such rationale of blaming the sins of western Christendom for military
losses also appears in ecclesiastical works and sermons written in western Europe and England after the Fall of Acre. This explanation placed
the defeat in a Christian framework which promised victory to those
favoured by God and punishment to those who sinned. Such justifica-
tions may have served as a textual balm to ease feelings of disillusion-
ment toward the Christian God by making the loss part of a divine plan.
These explanations would salvage their God's reputation as an omni-
scient power benevolent toward his people. By claiming a place for
Christian defeat in the economy of their religion, both the *Devisement*
and *Mandeville* texts indirectly explain the loss of the Crusader states and
may have appeared as calls for spiritual reform in western Europe.

The Texts' Divergent Approaches to Similar Sites and Peoples

Polo and Mandeville both claim to enjoy similar privileges and travel
opportunities; they even visit many of the same places. Yet although
they claim to share like experiences, they do not often interpret their
subject matter similarly. Regarding locations mentioned by both Polo
and Mandeville (that is, western and eastern Asia, including India), we
see that biblical interpretation is superimposed repeatedly on location
and history in *Mandeville*. This is not carried out to the same degree in
the text of the *Devisement* with which most English medieval audiences
would have been acquainted. For example, in Asia, Mandeville
emphasizes the relationship between the Khans and the Christian God.
Here, Mandeville describes Chinggis Khan's great-grandson, Mango
Khan, with reference to a specifically Latin Christian plan:

Mango Chan, that was a gode Cristene man and baptyzed, and yaf lettres
of perpetuelle pes to alle Cristene men … sente his brother Halaon with
gret multytude of folk for to wynnen the Holy Lond and for to put it into
Cristene mennes hondes and for to destroye Machametes lawe and for to
take the Calyphee of Baldak, that was emperour and lord of alle the Sara-
zines. (*Mandeville*, Cotton 165/21–7)

Historically, there was serious military action among the Khans against
the Caliphate; however, it is nowhere verifiable that this was undertaken

as a Christian initiative. Yet Mandeville locates the Khans fully within biblical history, explaining that they are the descendants of Ham, and that God sent Ghengis a vision appointing him the ruler of all Asia (94/ 25–98/11). Here, Mongolian greatness is explained as a function of salvation history, and the rise of this people is justified as a plan foreseen by the Christian God. In this way, Mandeville's Mongols work for the good of the Christians and their respective histories are intertwined. Unlike Mandeville, Polo's Mongols work for the profit of the Khans. Polo writes that 'Tartari' ['the Tartars'], not God, 'de communi consensus' ['by common consent'] chose Chinggis Khan as their ruler (52). For Polo, the Asian people, not the Christian God, shape their own histories, and the fate of non-Christian nations is thus depicted as separate from that of the Christians. According to Polo, the Mongols are not unwitting intermediaries in a divine plan designed for the betterment of Christians; instead, their history and religion develop independently of Christendom.

Regarding India and western Asia, Mandeville applies a Christian scriptural paradigm there as well. As if elaborating on Polo and Rustichello's brief account of the tomb of St Thomas in India, Mandeville extemporizes on the body of the saint. He declaims about the powers of the saint's arm – it being the arm supporting the hand with which Doubting Thomas touched the risen Christ's side. Unlike the relic in the *Devisement*, that in *Mandeville* has miraculous powers and assists in judicial decisions (75/25–76/24). However, when Polo and Rustichello account for the body of St Thomas, buried in the province of Maabar, they focus more on the region than on the saint, describing the area as unimportant for merchants (173). In spite of the scant possibilities for trade, Polo does mention that Christian pilgrims take away dust from the shrine, for it is known to heal the sick. While this dust is unlike the commodities usually listed elsewhere in the *Devisement*, it is significant that the earth of Maabar is considered an asset, as if it were a kind of merchandise similar to the jars of holy oil which the Khan wished to acquire.

As seen above, the Mandeville-writer is known to add devotional material to his sources; Higgins describes Mandeville's patterns of embellishment, explaining that the Mandeville-author establishes himself as the successor of Polo, paying Polo's work 'a kind of corrective homage by bringing its material under the aegis of Christian history.'[40] Likewise, when Mandeville and Polo discuss western Asia, their descriptions again diverge according to their priorities. Polo offers a merchant's view of the area, describing it in terms of its commodities, not pilgrim interests. Indeed, most of Polo's entries loosely follow a formula wherein he lists who is in control of the city, what language its inhabitants speak, what religion they uphold, and what commodities they export. The account of Balashan is typical of his urban descriptions:

> Reges habet ex una provincia sibi iure hereditario succedentes ... Ibi adoratur machometus. In montibus huius provincie inveniuntur lapides preciosi pulcri magnique valoris.

> [It] has kings succeeding each other from one province by hereditary law ... There Muhammad is worshipped. In the mountains of this province are found precious stones of great beauty and value. (34)

For those towns that have nothing to trade, Polo employs a different kind of description. For example, he describes how, in Su-chau, 'negotiatores non sunt' ['there are no merchants']; nevertheless, he says that the land is well provisioned, making it a pleasant place for merchants to pass through 'ad ceteras mundi partes' ['(on the way) to other parts of the world'] (49). If there are any restrictions on trade as there are in the city of Balashan, he carefully notes them (34). Not only does Polo show a detailed knowledge of trade regulations, but he also holds out the tantalizing detail that there are riches to be had in plenty. Although Pipino's Prologue suggests that the *Devisement* is useful for building Christian piety, the rest of the work appears to be just as interested in describing trade.

Several instances of scripturally related marvels subordinated to factual and economic information appear in Polo's descriptions of the East. In Greater Armenia he relates: 'In montibus huius armenie est archa noe' ['Noah's ark is in the mountains of this Armenia'] (18). What appear to be of greater interest to Polo and Rustichello, however, are the region's exportable products:

> ad aquilonem fons unus magnus est, ex quo liquor quidam scaturit oleo similis, pro cibo quidem inutilis, sed pro unctionibus et lampadibus optimus. Omnes naciones affines hoc liquore pro unctione et lampadibus utuntur. Tanta enim de fonte emanat huius liquoris copia, ut de ipsa naves centum aliquando onerentur.

> To the north is a great fountain from which streams a certain liquid like oil. However, it is not useful for food but is best for ointments and lamps.

All neighbouring nations use this liquid for ointment and lamps. For such an abundance of this fluid flows from the fountain that sometimes a hundred ships can be loaded from it. (18)

In this example, oil is not only a relic, as it was at the Holy Sepulchre, but also a financial boon. This is not to say that Polo and Rustichello never include the miraculous in their work. For example, they discuss the earlier-mentioned miracle of the mountain that moved at the request of a Christian shoemaker. Near Baghdad, they say, local *saraceni* asked their Christian neighbours to prove the biblical verse spoken by Christ in the Gospels: 'si habueritis fidem sicut granum sinapis dicetis monti huic transi hinc et transibit' ['if you have faith the size of a grain of mustard seed, and you say to this mountain "move here", it will move'] (Matthew 17:19; cf. Luke 17:6). In Polo and Rustichello's work, the Christians are threatened with death if their God fails them. When the prayers of the shoemaker, a 'devotus ... vir christianus' ['a devout Christian man'], were answered, and the mountain moved, many people were converted to Christianity (21–2). Thus Polo and Rustichello provide a solid example of the use of marvels: they are used to convert and strengthen individuals in the Christian faith. However, it is noteworthy that the Pipino translation of the tale is substantially abbreviated compared to the other manuscripts, such as the Franco-Italian version. [41] In contrast to *Mandeville*, episodes such as the miracle of the moving mountain are rare in the *Devisement*. Comparatively speaking, Polo and Rustichello rarely overlay the landscape and peoples of western Asia, greater Asia, or India with biblical history, and, perhaps more significantly, they omit description of Palestine altogether.

The Place of Jerusalem in Medieval Travel Literature

Apart from Polo and Rustichello's brief reference to Jerusalem as a pilgrimage site, they do not include a description of Palestine in the *Devisement*; this is worth comment for many reasons. Polo's collaborator on the *Devisement*, Rustichello of Pisa, at one time received the patronage of Prince Edward of England, later to become King Edward I. Some scholars believe that Rustichello had travelled in Edward's suite to Palestine; however, if he had done so, it is indeed curious that he does not show off his familiarity with the Holy Land by including descriptions of it in his work.[42] In addition to the possibility of Rustichello's first-hand experiences in Palestine, he could have drawn from almost one thousand years of devotional writing about the Holy Land. It is therefore all the more interesting that Rustichello and Polo not only skip Jerusalem but also do not employ biblical descriptions of the East which were popular throughout the medieval period. The Mandeville-writer, by contrast, relates much of his description of the world to events which biblical scripture located in Jerusalem. Drawing extensively from his sources, especially William of Boldensele and Odoric of Pordenone, Mandeville portrays the earthly city as a relic in its own right, consecrated through Christ's having inhabited it.

As Mandeville relates, the Passion events, above all others, gave Jerusalem its significance (3/2–10). Through the primary importance attributed to the Passion, events of the first century shape fourteenth-century devotion for a terrestrial place. In fact, Mandeville states explicitly that the place itself is to be accorded nearly the same rever-- ence as his God, suggesting that Christians felt that they could gain access to their God through that land:

> Ri?t wel au?te men to loue and worschipe and drede and serue siche a god and a lord, and worschipe and preyse siche an holy lond þat brou?t forþ siche fruyt, þur? þe whiche eche man is sauyd but it be his owne defaute. (4/8–12)

Likewise, placed as it is in the Prologue, this statement guides inter-pretation of the rest of the book. Mandeville's later chapter on Jerusa-lem, compared to other chapters, is quite lengthy and detailed, suggesting an effort to present a substantial amount of information which could have been used as devotional material for meditation on the Passion of Christ. The Church of the Holy Sepulchre is important in Mandeville's discussion of the Passion relics, and he makes clear its role as the spiritual centre of the holy city. Like most Christian pil-grim accounts, Mandeville values the Church of the Holy Sepulchre for housing the site of several major Passion events. As he says, 'when men go to Ierusalem, þei goþ þe firste pilgrimage to þe chirche whare is þe holy graue' (28/24–5). Along with the tomb, the Church of the Holy Sepulchre housed Mount Calvary, believed to be the site of Christ's crucifixion. Mandeville states that Calvary is engraved with the statement, 'þat þou seest is ground of alle þe world and of þis fey,' translated by him from Greek into Latin and English. Here, Mandeville recounts in rather bad Greek, 'Gros ginst rasis thou pestes *thoy thesmoysy,'* and comments 'þat is to say in Latyn, *Quod vides est fundamentum tocius mundi et huius fidei'* (29/26–8). Situating Calvary as the *fundamentum* or foundation of the world and Christian faith, Mandeville highlights the role of the Passion as the central focus of western medieval Christianity (29/28–9). Indeed, a spot on that mountain is referred to as such when Mandeville reports that the place where Joseph of Arimathea set Christ's body is 'þe myddel of þe world' (31/5–7).

The Church of the Holy Sepulchre is presented as a life-size 'store-house' of Passion memories both for Christians making the actual pilgrimage and for those visualizing the Passion at home. Like other relics, the fixtures of the Passion are described with exactitude: 'wiþynne þe mount of Caluarie at þe ri?t side is an auter whare þe pyler liþ to whiche oure lord was bounde when he was scourged' (30/10–12). Even the stones are held sacred for their proximity to the crucifixion (30/12–13). Likewise, other sites within the Church of the Holy Sepulchre are venerated as contact relics, such as the place of Helena's *inventio*, the wall where the four nails were hidden, the north side of the Church of the Holy Sepulchre where Christ was imprisoned, and part of the chain with which he was bound (30/14–20 and 31/5–11). Moving outward from the church, Mandeville mentions dozens of important Christian pilgrimage sites throughout the city, including another pillar where Christ was bound, and where Peter denied Christ (34/4–7). On Mount Sion he mentions more places made sacred by their role in the Passion events, such as the site where Christ gave the Last Supper, and the Garden of Gethsemane (38/7–8 and 39/30). Gradually Mandeville moves his description outside of Jerusalem, reporting how 'there' outside Bethany, Christ forgave Mary Magdalene, Lazarus was raised from the dead, the Virgin appeared to St Thomas, and Christ sat and preached (40/24–30). He describes the area where Judas hanged himself, the synagogue where Judas made his contract to betray Christ, and the field that was bought with the silver (39/10). In a round-about way, Mandeville pieces together the major events of the Passion as they occurred all over the landscape within and around Jerusalem. Though the pieces are not chronological, as is seen with his memory of Judas, together they make up the central events of medieval Christian faith and inscribe that land with a historical, theological definition.

Such descriptions suggest that, at least as far as Mandeville was concerned, contemporary fourteenth-century Palestine was not as important as the Palestine inhabited by Jesus. As for Polo, the immediacy of the Middle East, India, and Asia retained its contemporary cultural vitality. Thus while Mandeville both resurrects and reconstructs biblical history for his descriptions, Polo portrays a kind of textual present, based on actual occurrences in the thirteenth-century world. The focal points of Polo and Rustichello's book are trading centres, and for business purposes, their recommendations would have been considered the more valuable the more current they were. Perhaps it is possible to suggest, then, that had Mandeville included those ordinary, actual details that he might have seen in Palestine – for he does, after all, claim to have been there – then his audience might not have believed him. That is to say, English Christian medieval audiences seem to have had certain expectations about what they would see in Palestine; many of these preconceptions were cultivated by descriptions of the celestial, holy city in John's Revelation, the crusade chronicles, and ecclesiastical teaching. Because Mandeville satisfied these biblical and, at times, fabulous, expectations, his account may have been better received than the *Devisement*.

While descriptions of Jerusalem are absent from the *Devisement*, Polo and Rustichello do express an interest in describing how Asian and Indian cultures might be brought into a global economy. To that end, Polo's concomitant interest in the religious conversion of the people he encountered may be part of his rhetoric of trade, with the exportation of eastern goods to the West and the importation of Latin Christianity to the East. Polo's mercantile and political priorities thus explain why he does not mention Jerusalem and Paradise: western Asia would have been too difficult to wrest from the hands of its Muslim occupants, political instability injured trade, and Paradise was not considered humanly inhabitable. Mandeville calls Jerusalem the centre of the world and Eden its well-spring, in keeping with contemporary *mappae-mundi* that give pride of place to Jerusalem and Paradise. As work by Suzanne Conklin Akbari, Iain Higgins, and Scott Westrem has shown, these dual centres serve to orient the rest of the world according to a Christocentric framework.[43] Knowledge of the world in the *Devisement*, conversely, finds its *foci* in Venice and Khanbaliq – trade centres of a mercantile world.

Of the important cities in the *Devisement*, Polo and Rustichello do not describe Venice directly; however, it is always present throughout the narrative as a point of origin – it is home. In turn, Khanbaliq features as the Khan's favourite city, fit for the richest lord on earth, and for a ruler who is almost godlike in his powers (52–70). Even the translation of the city's name, 'Civitas domini' ['city of the Lord'], reflects the importance of the Khan (83). Just as Polo and Rustichello's depictions of the Khan make him appear godlike, their descriptions of Khanbaliq bear resemblances to medieval biblical depictions of Jerusalem. Like Jerusalem, Khanbaliq 'olim nobilis fuerat et regalis' ['once upon a time was noble and regal'] (83). Physically Khanbaliq mirrors the Celestial Jerusalem with its many walls:

> Est autem murus palacii grossus valde habens altitudinis passus X, cuius tota exterior facies undique colore albo et rubeo est depicta.

> The great wall of the palace is more than ten paces high, whose entire outer surface is painted everywhere with white and red color. (81)

This passage is reminiscent of John's vision of Jerusalem in the Apocalypse wherein he sees the city with white gates formed of a single pearl, whose foundations are bejewelled with precious stones, sapphires among them (Revelation 21:19–21). Another passage echoes Christ's description of his celestial kingdom in John 14:2: 'In my Father's house are many mansions.' This compares closely with the *Devisement*'s description of Khanbaliq: 'Intra urbem vero multa et pulcra palacia sunt. Et alie domus multe pulcre sunt valde' ['Indeed within the city there are many beautiful palaces. And the other houses are certainly beautiful'] (84).

As the language above suggests, Polo and Rustichello did not ignore Christian, religious concerns altogether, but used them in new ways to describe trade and universality. Here, I suggest that Polo and Rustichello used biblical models to increase the importance of their account, refashioning scriptural description in order to drive home the importance of the financial centres of the world in maintaining economic well-being. To this end, Khanbaliq, like Jerusalem, has a sacred centre: the Khan's palace (84). Like the Church of the Holy Sepulchre, which housed all of the historical events of the Passion, the Khan's palace is painted with the history of all of his past battles (82). Thus both city centres function as repositories of communal memory. Alongside Khanbaliq's quasi-divine status and historical functions are financial concerns. Instead of the names of the twelve sons of Israel which are depicted on the walls of the Celestial Jerusalem envisioned by John, we find descriptions of the city gates couched in terms of urban trade (Revelation 21:12–13):

Apud civitatem Cambalu sunt suburbia xii magna valde ante singulas portas, in quibus mercatores recipiuntur quique et viatores. Multus enim populus continue ad Civitatem confluit propter Curiam regis et mercaciones innumeras, que deferuntur illuc.

In the town of Khanbaliq there are twelve very great suburbs before single gates, in which merchants and travellers are received. For a great many people surge to the city continually on account of the royal curia and the innumerable trade goods which are brought there. (84)

As a chief city of governance and trade, Khanbaliq differs greatly from medieval Jerusalem, which occupied a poor trading position and was politically insubstantial compared to the port cities nearby, such as Tyre and Acre. Polo and Rustichello go so far as to call Khanbaliq the greatest trading city in all the world (85). It is also the financial heart of the Tartar Empire, since the Khan houses his mint there (97–8). Here, familiar biblical topoi have been exchanged; in their new currency they now reflect both the Khan's greatness, and a financial centre's fame. In these representations, the *Devisement* follows the conventions that place Jerusalem at the centre of the world, yet replace that centre with Khanbaliq; here, they design a new *mappamundi* centred on trade – a version of the world which some English medieval audiences may not have been ready to accept.

As I have discussed elsewhere, many Christian writers of medieval travel literature who journeyed eastward beyond Europe included Jerusalem in their accounts.[44] But certainly this depended upon whether the writer travelled primarily as a pilgrim, missionary, or functional emissary (the latter two seen, for example, in William of Rubruck or John of Plano Carpini). If the Pipino version really was intended strictly for a missionary audience, then it is curious that in the English reception of the text, one finds what appear to be attempts to situate the *Devisement* among pilgrim literature. Many pilgrim writers journeying in the Middle East saw Jerusalem as the ultimate goal of their travels. In omitting Jerusalem, the *Devisement* differs markedly from those texts in the medieval Christian pilgrim genre. However, manuscript evidence shows that medieval writers and manuscript collators often placed the *Devisement* together with works describing pilgrimage to the Holy Land. For example, of the five copies of Pipino's *Tractatus de locis terre sancte* which survive in the original Latin, four are transcribed in volumes that also contain the Pipino translation of the

Devisement.[45] Since it is known that Pipino composed the *Tractatus* at some time after he translated the *Devisement*, this medieval collation suggests that he either had intended the two pieces to go together or that medieval collators perceived them as part of a single unit. Although it is entirely possible that the pieces were placed together because they were composed by the same author, the fact that the Pipino text is continually included with other accounts of Jerusalem composed by other authors makes the pattern difficult to ignore. For instance, it is significant that Mandeville's work accompanies Polo and Rustichello's work in fifteen cases, whether in complete manuscripts or excerpts, or whether in Latin or in the vernaculars. Similarly, the Pipino text is joined with another pilgrim account, that of Ludolph von Suchem, in eight instances.[46] One manuscript in England even provides a T-O map with Jerusalem at its centre to accompany Pipino's text – notably this is the only surviving map accompanying a medieval Polo manuscript.[47] These consistent combinations of pilgrim literature with Polo's account of the East suggest that, for some English medieval Christian audiences, the addition of the Jerusalem material made the *Devisement* complete.

Along with extant manuscript material, historical events may also explain Polo and Rustichello's content choices. In response to the historical context in which they were writing, it is tempting to speculate that the falls of the last crusader states, Antioch and Acre, led to a shift in perception of the Holy Land and the East during the late thirteenth and early fourteenth centuries. The western gaze might have moved away from the reminders of its defeat in the Holy Land and toward more promising prospects in eastern Asia. Likewise, European ambitions of trade may have moved to the forefront, competing with the acquisitive ambitions of colonization and settlement. Moreover, western Europeans were becoming more aware of the Mongol peoples all the time: the increasing popularity of the *Letter of Prester John* after the loss of Jerusalem in 1187 fuelled the western European belief that the Mongols could be recruited as allies against the Turkish threat, and news of the Mongol invasion of eastern and central Europe in 1241 may have stimulated an interest in Polo's description of these areas. At the same time other areas of western interest were explored: one remembers that in 1271, Prince Edward and the Christian king of Armenia, together with the papacy, attempted an alliance with the Khan of Persia by sending Christian missionary and military embassies there from 1271 up until 1277. The exchange continued as the

Khan sent a Nestorian monk from Peipeng to Europe in 1287, 1290, and 1291, along with a Persian embassy in 1307 to see Edward. Negotiations seem to have broken off in 1316 when the Khan officially adopted Islam. Thus when the Mongols appeared on the scene in the thirteenth century, they were perceived by the West as potential allies and Christian converts against Islam; for western Christian Europeans, Mongol peoples were untapped resources.

Finally, commenting on the popularity of *Mandeville* over the Pipino text in England, Dutschke has suggested that along with the Mandeville-author's supposedly English nationality, the less didactic tone of *Mandeville* made it easier reading; in this sense, the Pipino translation of the *Devisement*, as the English saw it, was more moralizing than entertaining.[48] To Dutschke's assessment, I would add that *Mandeville*'s popularity was also attributable to its devotional information. It is this devotional focus, particularly surrounding *Mandeville*'s serious concern with the Holy Land, which worked to make it more popular than the Pipino text with English readers. By accessing the *mirabilia* and *miracula* abundant in pre-existing accounts of the Holy Land and Far East, Mandeville not only included the expected material, but also provided fodder for the imagination, and that fuel was vitally important to medieval devotion. Although the Pipino version of the *Devisement* may have been didactic and moralizing as Dutschke says, *Mandeville* was just as seriously concerned with Christian teaching and moral matters. The work fulfilled this purpose by proving to its medieval readers the greatness of their Christian God through evidence of his miracles far and wide. Thus, for Mandeville and writers of other 'wonder' works, truth claims were not an issue; rather, the object of the 'wonderful' accounts was to turn the audience's attention toward what was perceived as a higher truth: God in his glory among the world's monstrous and miraculous creation. By their looser adherence to this biblical template, Polo and Rustichello, via Pipino, may have lost credibility with later English medieval audiences. Perhaps had Polo recounted *more* than 'half of what [he] saw,' the *Devisement* might have joined Mandeville's work as a best-seller in England, establishing credibility through the incredible.

NOTES

I wish to thank Suzanne Conklin Akbari, Anindita Banerjee, Maria Fernandez, Sabine Haenni, Charles A. Peterson, Rachel E. Prentice, A.G. Rigg, Aminda Smith, and Scott D. Westrem for their thoughtful comments.

1 Giovanni Battista Ramusio, *Navigazioni e viaggi*, ed. Marica Milanesi, I. Praef., fol.6v.
2 For more on Polo's reliability, see Dutschke, 'Francesco Pipino and the Manuscripts of Marco Polo's *Travels*, 1: 1–32. Jacobo of Acqui, *Imago Mundi*, in Ambrosian MS D.526, fol. 77c, d; quoted in A.C. Moule and Paul Pelliot, ed. and trans., Marco Polo, *The Description of the World* 31–2; esp. 32n1.
3 On the use of the 'East–West' dichotomy and its limitations, see Akbari, 'From Due East to True North' 19–34.
4 Campbell, *The Witness and the Other World*; Higgins, *Writing East*; Larner, *Marco Polo and the Discovery of the World*.
5 *Mandeville* quotations throughout this chapter are from *The Defective Version of Mandeville's Travels*, ed. M.C. Seymour, by page and line number. Of the English versions of *Mandeville*, the Defective version is the oldest known.
6 Of these, nine are dated from the fourteenth century, four from the fifteenth century, and one from the sixteenth; see Dutschke, 'Francesco Pipino' 1: 242, and 3: 1219–20, n. 4. Quotations of the *Devisement* are taken from the Pipino version prevalent in medieval England: *Liber Marchi Pauli*, ed. Justin V. Prásek, in *Marka Pavlova Z Benátek: Milion*. This edition of the Pipino text does not correspond to any of the Pipino manuscripts extant in England; however, Prásek's text is the only published edition of Pipino's translation currently in circulation. Translations of the Prásek text, by page numbers, are my own.
7 Dutschke, 'Francesco Pipino' 1: 2, 9, 22–3.
8 John Critchley, *Marco Polo's Book* 137–57; Larner, *Marco Polo* 111–15.
9 Dutschke notes that John Frampton's copy made in 1579 was the first English translation of any Marco Polo redaction; this was based on San- taella's Spanish text, a derivative of the Venetian version which may have passed through a Latin intermediary.
10 For example: Berlin, Staatsbibliothek Preussischer Kulturbesitz, MS lat. qu. 70; cited in Dutschke, 'Francesco Pipino' 2: 535.
11 Oxford, Merton College, MS 312; BL, MS Harley 5115; and Cambridge, UL, MS Dd.1.17; in Dutschke, 'Francesco Pipino' 2: 807.
12 Cambridge, Gonville and Caius College, MS 162/83; in Dutschke, 'Francesco Pipino' 2: 538.

13 London, BL, MS Arundel 13; see Dutschke, 'Francesco Pipino' 2: 698.

14 Cambridge, UL, MS Dd.1.17 and MS Dd.8.7; London, BL, MS Royal 14.C.xiii; and Oxford, Bodleian Library, MS Digby 196. See Dutschke, 'Francesco Pipino' 1: 239–41 and 3: 1099. There may have been a fifth such manuscript at Westminster Abbey; see Dutschke 3: 1099–1100.

15 For *Mandeville* and *Piers Plowman*, Cambridge, UL, MS Dd.1.17. London, BL, MS Harley 5115 includes Polo alongside Geoffrey of Monmouth; see also London, BL, MS Royal 14.C.xiii. Cited in Dutschke, 'Francesco Pipino' 2: 538–9, 2: 699–700.

16 Dutschke, 'Francesco Pipino' 2: 807–9.

17 Moseley, 'The Availability of *Mandeville's Travels in England*' 125–33.

18 Scholars in favour of a 'Mandeville' persona include Seymour, *Sir John Mandeville* 1–24 and 173. John Larner has suggested the authorship of Jean de Langhe; see Larner, in this volume. Those who believe Mandeville to be a real, historical figure and the genuine author include Bennett, *Rediscovery* 10 and 179–80, and Howard, 'The World of *Mandeville's Travels*' 4n and *Writers and Pilgrims* 53–76.

19 Higgins, *Writing East* 6 and 271n18.

20 Röhl, *Der 'Livre de Mandeville' im 14. und 15. Jahrhundert* 207; and Bennett, *Rediscovery* 219 and 242–3.

21 Bennett, *Rediscovery* 221, 224–6.

22 See Röhl and Bennett's surveys of Mandeville manuscripts produced in French; *Livre* 27–141, and *Rediscovery* 265–86.

23 Regarding Ovid, see Paris, BN, MS Arsenal 3219 in Röhl, *Livre* 79; Old Testament history, see London, BL, MS Harley 3940 cited in Röhl, *Livre* 66–7; kings of France, see Paris, BN, MS Fonds., fr. 20145 and Aix-en-Provence BN, Méjanes, Nr. 437 (138) cited in Röhl, *Livre* 108 and 27–8. See also Bennett, *Rediscovery* 179, 274, and 277.

24 For *Seven Sages*, see Paris, BN, MS Fonds., fr. 5586 in Röhl, *Livre* 91–2; and for *Roman de Fauvel*, see Paris, BN, MS Fonds., fr. 24436; cf. Tours, Bibliothèque DE., MS No. 947 cited in Röhl, *Livre* 140. See also Bennett, *Rediscovery* 274, 279, and 282.

25 See Paris BN, MS, Fr, Nouv.acq.fr. 14 313; cited in Röhl, *Livre* 124.

26 *L'Image*, etc., see Tours, Bibliothèque DE., MS No. 947 cited in Röhl, *Livre* 140–1; see also Bennett, *Rediscovery* 274.

27 Regarding exploring interest, see Bern, MS Bergerbibliothek, Nr. 125, which includes Mandeville with Marco Polo, Odoric of Pordenone, and William of Boldensele, among others; see Röhl, *Livre* 39. Among political interests, see Brüssels, MS Bib. Royale, Albert Ier, Nr. 10437–40; see Röhl, *Livre* 44; see also Paris BN, MS, Fr. 20145; Röhl, *Livre*, 108 and 163–70.

28 For Chaucer, see Oxford, Bodleian, MS E. Museo 116 (3617); see Bennett, *Rediscovery* 289. For *Seven Sages* see Cambridge, UL, MS Dd.I.17; and *Sir Gowther* in London, BL, MS Royal 17.B.XLIII. See also Bennett, *Rediscovery* 289, 291.

29 For Lydgate, see Cambridge, UL, MS R.4.20; for historical chronicle from Brut, see Oxford, Bodleian, MS Rawlinson B.216; for *Chronicon*, see Oxford, Bodleian, MS Laud. 619. Cited in Bennett, *Rediscovery* 291–4.

30 See *Piers Plowman*, etc., in Cambridge, UL, MS Dd.I.17; *Handlynge Synne* in Devon, PA: Barbado Hill, MS Mr. Boies Penrose, Mannyng formerly bound with this manuscript. See religious Latin works in Oxford, Balliol, MS No. 239; for Susan, Daniel, Egypt, and *Troilus*, see San Marino, CA, Huntington Library, HM 114. See also Bennett, *Rediscovery* 289–92.

31 See *Vision* in London, BL, MS Royal 17.B.XLIII; Ten Commandments … Church Fathers, see Oxford, Bodleian, MS Laud. 619. See also Bennett, *Rediscovery* 291.

32 For *Gospel*, see Dublin, Trinity College, MS E5.6.15; and Bennett, *Rediscovery* 294.

33 For *Proverbs* and *Life*, see Oxford, Bodleian, MS Rawlinson B.216; for *Translation* and *Charter*, see London, R.H. Robinson MS 16 and 17, Pall Mall; see Bennett, *Rediscovery* 292, 294.

34 London, BL, MS Arundel 140; see Bennett, *Rediscovery* 293.

35 *Piers Plowman* with *Mandeville* in a manuscript planned as a single unit in London, BL, MS Harley 3954; San Marino, CA, Huntington Library HM 114; and Cambridge, UL, MS Ff.V.35. Cited in Bennett, *Rediscovery* 291–3.

36 Oxford, Bodleian, MS Rawlinson D101 (12919); and Bennett, *Rediscovery* 295.

37 Higgins, 'Defining the Earth's Center in a Medieval "Multi-Text"' 32.

38 Alternate readings to the Defective Version are taken from the Cotton Version represented in *Mandeville's Travels*, ed. M.C. Seymour.

39 Bennett, *Rediscovery* 1.

40 Higgins, *Writing East* 51–2.

41 Pipino's account of the miracle is shorter than those in other manuscripts; Dutschke, 'Francesco Pipino' 3: 1334–48. Compare with coverage of the moving mountain from an early fourteenth-century text in the Franco-Italian MS Paris, BN, fr. 1116, in Moule and Pelliot, eds., *Description*, 105–12. See also Ronchi's Tuscan and Franco-Italian edition, *Devisement* 30–2.

42 Ronald Latham, ed. and trans., *The Travels of Marco Polo* 16.

43 Suzanne Conklin Akbari, 'Locating Islam in "The Book of John Mandeville," Conference Paper, Medieval Academy of America, 8–10 April, 1999; see 8–18; expanded version in Akbari, *Idols in the East*. See also Higgins, *Writing East* 124–42; and Westrem, *Text* 1–4.

44 See Suzanne M. Yeager, *Jerusalem in Medieval Narrative* (forthcoming, Cambridge University Press, 2008) 1–60.

45 Dutschke, 'Francesco Pipino' 1: 137–8. Pipino visited the Holy Land in 1320–1; afterwards he composed the *Tractatus de locis terre sancte*. See Francesco Pipino, *Tractatus de locis terre sancte*; cited in Dutschke 1: 116–28.

46 Dutschke, 'Francesco Pipino' 1: 245.

47 Dutschke, 'Francesco Pipino' 1: 28n1.

48 Dutschke, 'Francesco Pipino' 1: 244.

8 Calvino's Rewriting of Marco Polo: From the 1960 Screenplay to *Invisible Cities*

MARTIN MCLAUGHLIN

> Throughout the centuries poets and other writers have been inspired by Marco Polo's *Il Milione* as though by a fantastic, exotic scenario, to produce new works: Coleridge's famous poem, Kafka's *The Emperor's Message*, Buzzati's *The Tartar Steppe*. Only *The Arabian Nights* can boast a fate similar to Polo's *Travels*: books which become imaginary continents, as it were, inside which other works of literature find their space.
>
> (From a lecture by Calvino, to the Graduate Writing Division of Columbia University of New York, 29 March 1983, now in Calvino, *Le città invisibili* viii)[1]

Italo Calvino's *Invisible Cities* (1972) is, according to the author himself, his most famous and best-selling work in North America ('Behind the Success' 232). It has also achieved cult status in the rest of the world, being enthusiastically read and quoted not just by the literary public but also by artists and architects. In fact, a major international conference held in Milan in 2002 to celebrate the thirtieth anniversary of the publication of the book brought together critics, artists, architects, and directors to discuss the work's influence (see Barenghi, Canova, and Falcetto). It is well known that the book was inspired by Marco Polo's *Il Milione* (*Travels*),[2] and is part of that fashion for the rewriting of classic older works that postmodern authors indulged in from the 1960s onwards (one of the earliest examples from the period would be Michel Tournier's rewriting of Defoe's *Robinson Crusoe, Vendredi* [1967], much admired by Calvino). Indeed, the author himself said of *Invisible Cities*: 'The book was a result of the fact that in those days I and some of my friends were fascinated by non-literary forms of narrative, and I was also interested in literary works that were re-writings of other works' (cited in Zancan 876). However, Calvino's is a highly original and illuminating kind of rewriting. *Invisible Cities* does not spring fully formed from the writer's head but has a lengthy and fascinating gestation which we are now able to study in some detail.

The fact is that Calvino first became interested in Polo's travels more than ten years before he wrote *Invisible Cities*. In July 1960, he agreed to write a screenplay for a film project on Marco Polo, and that substantial, eighty-page work, entitled *Marco Polo*, written between August and September 1960, is now available to scholars (it was published posthumously in 1994, in Calvino, *Romanzi e racconti* (henceforth RR) 3: 509–86). *Marco Polo* is not a definitive screenplay – it is too sketchy in places for that – but it is a substantial narrative, divided into thirteen sections containing sequences of description, narrative, and dialogue. In the end, the film was never made, and the screenplay has received little attention from scholars, apart from a brief but perceptive article by Bruno Falcetto. Exactly ten years later, in July 1970, Calvino wrote the first page of *Invisible Cities*, a much more complex and highly original work somewhere between a novel and a sequence of prose-poems, describing fifty-five imaginary cities that Marco Polo visits and recounts to Kublai Khan. The work has an elaborate, symmetrical structure, whereby the fifty-five cities are divided into eleven series of five cities each, and these are distributed across nine chapters (ten cities in chapters 1 and 9, and five cities in each of the intervening seven chapters). In addition, each chapter begins and ends with a piece of dialogue between Marco Polo and Kublai Khan on topics that will be illustrated by the five or ten cities in each chapter, topics such as the relationship between cities and fear or desire, the idea of cities of lightness, the analogy between a city and a game of chess. The complex, symmetrical shape of the book is effected by assigning the cities to eleven different categories of five cities each, such as Cities and Memory, Cities and Desire, Cities and Signs, and so on, arranged in such a way as to produce a diamond or lozenge shape, as in the two alternative diagrams on the next page.

In each case, reading the diagram from top to bottom and from left to right corresponds to the order in which the cities are described in the text. The numerical pattern on the left above, where the digits refer to the first, second, third, etc. appearance of a particular category of city, is the one first advocated by Milanini (130–1) and identical to that found amongst the author's own papers (RR 3: 1360). The use of letters, where *a* stands for all the cities of memory, *b* for all the cities of

1:	1	a
	21	ab
	321	abc
	4321	abcd
2:	54321	abcde
3:	54321	bcdef
4:	54321	cdefg
5:	54321	defgh
6:	54321	efghi
7:	54321	fghij
8:	54321	ghijk
9:	5432	hijk
	543	ijk
	54	jk
	5	k

desire, *c* for all the cities of signs, etc., makes a similar pattern but in an inverted form: the letters have a progressive sequence (*abcde*), the numbers a regressive sequence (*54321*). The structure is not gratuitous but closely reflects the thematics of the book, which is very much about the ideal pattern that lies beneath or above the Khan's empire and its cities.

The purpose of this essay is to examine the two-stage process whereby Polo's original text led first to Calvino's 1960 'screenplay' of *Marco Polo* and subsequently to *Invisible Cities*, charting the different kinds of inspiration that Marco Polo's account exercised on the modern novelist, in particular the creative chemistry that was to inspire one of the greatest cult works of recent times.

The Screenplay of *Marco Polo* and *Invisible Cities*

> To reach that minimum of arousal of the imagination that would allow me to work on this project, I had to read Marco Polo's *Il Milione* over and over again, even the bits that least lent themselves to narrative, in order to absorb that visionary charge that is the book's secret. In short, I tried to follow Coleridge's method: by smoking opium and reading Marco Polo he managed to compose in a dream-like trance 'In Xanadu did Kublai Kahn ...'. (Calvino, Letter to Suso Cecchi d'Amico, 2 September 1960, now in RR 3: 1264)

Calvino's lengthy letter to the screenwriter Suso Cecchi d'Amico, the beginning of which is cited above as the epigraph to this section, contains important insights into the poetics behind the film project, in particular with regard to the two central characters, Marco and Kublai Khan:

> Naturally the key to everything has to be Marco's character. ... There are essentially two things that interest him: rich merchandise (with a distinct propensity more for the marvellous than for the practical), and women and sexual mores. So here we already have his character: young Marco in Venice is a dreamer who goes crazy for everything that has a hint of the Orient: he wanders through the markets and every silk border or whiff of spices or glint of precious stones sets him off on a reverie, just as his dreams of the Orient's sexual freedom have him chasing every Saracen maidservant in Venice. ... Another character that has to be highlighted is Kublai Khan, this perfect ruler, full of absolute wisdom and a taste for the pleasures of life. And yet – and this is where we come in – melancholic and with barely perceptible psychological flaws, ambiguous and unfathomable, haunted by something between metaphysical despair and a secret perversity of mind just kept in check by reason. I want to turn him into an emblem of Shakespearean nobility and melancholy, a prince who is still young, handsome, refined, with a metaphysical sadness, a cross between the Duke in *Twelfth Night* (I think) and Marcus Aurelius. He rides on horseback with a tiger on his saddle and a falcon in his hand. (RR 3: 1265–6)

At this stage, then, Calvino's love of contrast has already identified the psychological traits that will characterize the two protagonists of both his screenplay and *Invisible Cities*. In the same letter, he also stresses the need for two female characters: Princess 'Cocacin' (or Kukachin), who is not opposed to Marco seducing her, but who is resigned to her destiny to be married to an Oriental prince; and the warrior princess Algiarne (or Agaruk in the screenplay), who on the contrary challenges all her suitors to a duel, and defeats every one of them. Here we are close to the contrasting chivalric characters of the novel that Calvino had just completed. In *The Non-Existent Knight* (1959), the female protagonist Bradamante challenges in combat and defeats all her suitors, symbolizing 'love as war,' while her opposite Sofronia is a passive, resigned woman, standing for 'love as peace' (for these symbolic roles, labelled as such by the author himself, see the 'postfazione' to the trilogy *Our Ancestors* [RR 1: 1217], written in June 1960 just before Calvino embarked upon the screenplay project [Falcetto 63]). Thus as far as characterization is concerned, the two male protagonists and their contrasting natures are already clear in the author's mind in 1960 and will remain the central psychological opposition in *Invisible Cities*, while the two female characters adumbrated at this stage will be elided in the later work.

Calvino's screenplay of *Marco Polo* opens with a first section ('Departure') in which fascinated crowds on the quayside watch the two elder Polo brothers sail back into port in Venice in a scene reminiscent of the opening page of another favourite Calvino text, Dumas's *The Count of Montecristo*. Calvino so admired the tale that he even went so far as to rewrite Dumas's story in 1967, in a story entitled 'The Count of Montecristo,' in *Time and the Hunter* (RR 2: 344–56). Young Marco, who had been encouraged by his family to become a monk, is however obsessed with women, and at the end of this first section hides in a barrel in order to be on board the elder Polos' ship as it sails back to the Orient. Marco's stratagem here demonstrates that if the section had opened with an evocation of Dumas's novel, it ends with a motif straight from another adventure classic well thumbed by Calvino, Stevenson's *Treasure Island* (for Calvino's fascination with the Scottish writer's work, see McLaughlin 29, 39, 81). Alongside these intertextual echoes, we also find elements that are more distinctive of Calvino's own works, and will remain constants in the later rewriting of the Polo story. In this first section, for example, Marco notes that the designs on the Persian carpet that he and the Moorish maid are sitting on at first appear not to have any meaning, but on closer inspection 'all these lines, all these colours, the way they emerge from one another, and meet up and overlay each other, all this seems to me to contain a whole world, cities with golden-roofed palaces and temples emerging from the thickest forests, and rivers, and bays, and seas full of islands' (RR 3: 515). We are close here to what will be two key moments in *Invisible Cities*: the first when the city of Eudoxia is said to be reflected and contained in the carpet that represents it (*Invisible Cities* 97–8), and the second when Marco is able to tell Kublai that even in the wood of the chessboard he is able to see how its fibres are arranged, and thus to deduce that that square came from a trunk that grew in a year of drought, and to see in each square a whole world of 'forests ... rafts laden with logs that come down the rivers, docks, women at the windows' (*Invisible Cities* 132).

The second section of the screenplay ('On the Threshold of the Orient') contains Marco's initial adventures in his travels with his father and uncle. Here the satire on the arbitrary nature of the religious customs of Muslims, Buddhists, and Brahmins is redolent of the early Calvino's attacks on other religious sects (in the satirical portrayal of Protestant capitalists in *The Cloven Viscount*, and the caricature of Jansenists and Jesuits in *The Baron in the Trees*, for instance).

In terms of content, section 3 ('The Old Man of the Mountain') is clearly based on the episode in chapter 31 of *Il Milione* concerning the Old Man of the Mountain and his sect of Assassins. However, it is also a harbinger of the key motifs in *Invisible Cities* in at least three aspects. First, there is a description of a city on the edge of a desert: 'What is that at the end of the endless stretch of sand? There is a shape like a city, yes, roofs of strange shapes, a tower, an arch, palm trees' (RR 3: 529). This image of the city bordering on the desert recurs in one of the first cities in the later work, the city of Despina, which sits on the edge of a desert and can be approached either by land or by sea: 'Each city receives its form from the desert it opposes; and so the camel driver and the sailor see Despina, a border city, between two deserts' (*Invisible Cities* 18). Secondly, when he is in the Old Man of the Mountain's false paradise, Marco's character is described in a way that will be strongly emphasized in the later work: 'Of all the beautiful things he sees, Marco instantly seeks out their opposite, the trick, the falsehood' (RR 3: 533). Similarly, in *Invisible Cities*, when Marco describes the city of Moriana, which consists of two halves, one half of which is glassy and crystalline, Marco is clearly just as interested in the other half, the obverse of the city, with its rusting metal and rotten beams: '[the city] has no thickness, it consists only of a face and an obverse, like a sheet of paper, with a figure on either side, which can neither be separated nor look at each other' (*Invisible Cities* 105). Finally, Kublai Khan, even after allying with Halogu Khan and defeating the Old Man of the Mountain, is portrayed as feeling paradoxically melancholic, as he muses: 'Every time an enemy is eliminated a kind of void opens up in the perennially provisory order of our lives. For us rulers our enemies are more important than our friends, alas. ... The destruction of an enemy leaves a void. And we are left even more on our own' (RR 3: 540). This last phrase recalls the very first sentences of *Invisible Cities*, the opening description of Kublai: 'In the lives of emperors there is a moment which follows pride in the boundless extension of the territories we have conquered, and the melancholy and relief of knowing we shall soon give up any thought of knowing and understanding them. There is a sense of emptiness that comes over us at evening' (*Invisible Cities* 5). Indeed, the theme of the void that permeates and surrounds the Khan's empire recurs on a number of occasions in the later text. The close of chapter 2 elaborates on this theme: 'But what enhanced for Kublai every event or piece of news reported by his inarticulate informer was the space that remained around it, a void filled with his words' (*Invisible Cities* 38). Similarly, cities like Armilla and Ottavia and Laudamia are suspended over a void, while the fullness and emptiness of the chess-pieces are a central contrast at the end of chapter 8: 'The quantity of things that could be read in a little piece of smooth and empty wood overwhelmed Kublai; Polo was already talking about ebony forests, about rafts laden with logs that come down the rivers, of docks, of women at the windows' (*Invisible Cities* 132). Consistently, then, the later work ignores the key action moments of Polo's account, such as the defeat of the Old Man of the Mountain and the Assassins, and there is no mention of the Old Man's false paradise, since *Invisible Cities* observes a strict unity of place (the Khan's palace) and concentrates not on military action and conquest but on character and stasis.

In the fourth section ('Marco the Fake Monk'), Marco is made to resist temptation along with other novice Buddhist monks in a temple. In a scene reminiscent of Torrismondo's attempt to pass the test to become a Knight of the Holy Grail in *The Non-Existent Knight* (RR 1: 147–9), Marco has to remain contemplating the void while an attractive girl dances a striptease. The first student passes the test and is made a novice. But, when it comes to Marco's turn, he at first resists because a beautiful butterfly flies into the temple and he concentrates on the butterfly, a recurrent symbolic animal in Calvino, usually denoting lightness (there is a brief but useful survey of this symbolism in Belpoliti 12–13). However, when the creature lands on the girl's breast and she gives a start, Marco leaps on her 'like a wolf.' The monks cry out at this sacrilege as Marco flees and a wry smile plays on the Khan's lips (RR 3: 544). This kind of comic eroticism will also be entirely absent from the later work.

In section 5 ('At the Grand Khan's Court'), Kublai makes a speech that could come straight out of *Invisible Cities*:

> The things of the earth are wonderful ... but when a man reaches the point of being able to say 'I possess all of them: there is no kind of precious stone, or weave of silk, or caged beast that I do not possess,' then the time has come when you would like all these things to come together to form a pattern, an order, a harmony ... reflecting a pattern in the heavens, an order, the music of the heavenly spheres. (RR 3: 547: Barenghi in a brief

note first drew attention to the significance of this passage for the later
work, in RR 2: 1364–5.)

Here, naturally, we think of the emphasis throughout *Invisible Cities* on
the contrast between chaos and pattern, order and disorder, reflected
both in the symmetrical structural pattern of the book and in its thematics. The end of the first page of the work contains the famous phrase:
'Only in Marco Polo's accounts was Kublai Khan able to discern,
through the walls and towers destined to crumble, the tracery of a pattern so subtle it could escape the termites' gnawing' (*Invisible Cities* 5–6).
Later, the Khan remarks to Marco: 'my empire is made of the stuff of
crystals, its molecules arranged in a perfect pattern. Amid the surge of
the elements, a splendid hard diamond takes shape, an immense, fac-
eted, transparent mountain' (*Invisible Cities* 60). Moreover, this emphasis on pattern and order continues to the end, notably the passage at the
start of chapter 8: 'Contemplating these essential landscapes, Kublai
reflected on the invisible order that sustains cities, on the rules that
decreed how they rise, take shape and prosper, adapting themselves to
the seasons, and then how they sadden and fall into ruin' (*Invisible
Cities* 122). Even the last chapter emphasizes no fewer than three times
the patterns of the empire that the Khan finds in his various atlases
(*Invisible Cities* 135–7). The more specific theme of the earthly pattern
reflecting a heavenly one is found in the whole sequence of 'Cities and
the Sky,' notably the last one of this series, Andria, whose buildings
'repeat the order of the constellations and the position of the most luminous stars' (*Invisible Cities* 150), and whose inhabitants are convinced
that it is the innovations in the city that modify the pattern in the sky
and not vice versa (*Invisible Cities* 151). If the heavens are one source of
the pattern, in both the screenplay and the later novel, what is unique to
the latter is another analogy of the pattern, namely the chessboard, that
favourite metaphor of linguistic structuralists in the 1960s and 1970s. At
the beginning of chapter 8 we are told that 'knowledge of the empire
was hidden in the pattern' drawn by the moves of the different chess-
pieces (*Invisible Cities* 122–3), but there is nothing structuralist or self-
referential in the 1960 screenplay.

Instead, the screenplay is very much concerned with action and
character. Still in section 5 of *Marco Polo*, there is a strong character contrast between Marco and Princess Cocacin, who is being brought up by
Kublai. Her fatalism and acceptance of destiny are the opposite of
Marco's desire to fashion his own destiny. She argues that if we do not

like our destiny it is because we are looking at it the wrong way; when we hold a leaf up to the sun we see only a dark shadow, not its beauty, but when we place it in the right position, we see its beauty and harmony. Marco points out, however, that we are the ones who move the leaf until it is in the right position. This contrast of character is subsumed in the later work into the opposition between Marco and Kublai, and instead of a leaf, the difference is symbolized in the famous discussion of the chessboard and its pieces that encloses chapter 8 (*Invisible Cities* 121–3, 131–2). Another element of dialogue transferred from Marco and Cocacin to Marco and Kublai in the later work is Marco's description of Venice, to which the Princess replies: 'My city, Hang-Kow, has all its roofs made of gold, and when the sun strikes them we are almost blinded. It is surrounded by a huge canal which goes all round the walls. At the spring festival we all go on boats with silken sails' (RR 3: 549–50). This implicit similarity between Venice and all cities, particularly the city of Hang Chow (or Quinsai as it appears in Polo's text), resurfaces at the beginning of chapter 6 of *Invisible Cities* (as pointed out by Bernardini Napoletano 171), but interestingly, in the later novel, Calvino chooses not to use the modern name but to return to its older form Quinsai, or Kin-sai in the English translation (*Invisible Cities* 85). The later, more poetic text adopts the more archaic form of nomenclature. Calvino spoke, in a letter of September 1970, about the self-consciously 'precious' nature of the novel he had just embarked upon: 'In the work I am writing this summer I am pushing myself as never before toward a precious, Alexandrian style, a sort of prose poem: it is a rewriting of Marco Polo's *Il Milione* all made up of brief descriptions of imaginary cities' (Calvino, *Lettere* 1089). The poetic prose of *Invisible Cities* is thus a deliberate effect pursued by the author, and is in stark contrast to the flat narrative of the screenplay.

Returning to Kublai's character, in the screenplay the Khan tells Marco that he constantly thinks of death (RR 3: 553), and even resorts to the kind of gnomic utterance that will be part of the prose music of *Invisible Cities*. When Marco asks him how many faiths he has studied, the Khan replies, 'The faiths are many; but there is only one heaven' (RR 3: 547). Later in the chapter, the Khan opines: 'What is our wisdom except a fragile covering which we don?' (RR 3: 551). One final key element in this section taken up in the later work is the episode in which the Khan is bored by the monotonous statistical accounts of his other ambassadors but is rapt by Marco, who captures the monarch's attention by moving from speech to pantomime (RR 3: 548; cf. *Invisible Cities* 21–2).

The sixth section ('Marco Polo's Embassies') recounts Marco's travels throughout the kingdom and, in a passage closely based on a recurrent feature of Polo's original text (*Milione*, chapters 43, 47, 99), emphasizes his amazement that in some towns, the rules of hospitality oblige the women to sleep with a stranger, and their husbands to leave the house as long as the stranger stays (RR 3: 553–4). This erotic motif surfaces only briefly in the later novel. In the city of Anastasia, Polo talks of the women bathing who invite passing strangers to disrobe and chase them in the water (*Invisible Cities* 12), while in Hypatia he describes 'the beautiful women who mount the saddle, thighs naked, greaves on their calves, and as soon as a young foreigner approaches, they fling him on the piles of hay or sawdust and press their firm nipples against him' (*Invisible Cities* 48). This sixth section also shows us that Marco too is able to reproduce gnomic maxims, as when he instructs Princess Cocacin, 'There is something else that makes travelling sweet. It is the thought of returning home' (RR 3: 556).

Section 7, entitled 'The King of Ceylon's Ruby,' is a fairy-tale elaboration of an episode from Polo's *Travels* but has no counterpart in the later work, in which the Khan's court remains the centre of narrative gravity and supplies a strict unity of place that would have been destroyed by locations such as Ceylon. Thus, although the erotic motifs are present in both of Calvino's reworkings of Polo's text (albeit toned down in the later work), the action and travel sequences that are another essential ingredient of the screenplay do not survive the transition to the novel form.

Sections 8 ('Agaruk, Warrior Princess'), 9 ('Cocacin Is Married') and 10 ('Agaruk Again') foreground the two contrasting female characters, the active, warrior princess Agaruk, and the resigned fatalistic Cocacin who is to be married to the Indian prince Argon, all characters who are present in the original of Polo's *Travels*. The characters of Cocacin and Agaruk, who are both used to provide the love interest for the screenplay, are missing entirely from the later novel. However, certain moments in Cocacin's tale find a particular resonance in *Invisible Cities*. When the Khan tells the princess that he is sending her as a bride to the Indian Prince Argon, this important conversation takes place in the 'observatory at the top of his tower, where he studies astronomy, amidst maps of the zodiacs, sextants, telescopes and planispheres' (RR 3: 570), all elements that will resurface at prominent points in *Invisible Cities*. The opening paragraph of the later work, for example, mentions the planispheres portraying the empire's rivers and mountains (*Invisible Cities* 5), while astrolabes are listed among the goods in the second city, Dorothea (*Invisible Cities* 9), and the opening section of the final chapter of the book repeatedly mentions Kublai's atlases: 'The Great Khan owns an atlas where ...' is the refrain that is repeated three times in this dialogue at the start of chapter 9 (*Invisible Cities* 135–9). Similarly, the lesson the Khan imparts to the princess is one that he will give to Marco in the later work: 'The stars too, the Khan says, merely trace in the heavens the lines of a complicated geometry. Yet in it is contained all that life can give us, the past and the future, good and evil, all the roads we follow on earth' (RR 3: 570). This analogy between the heavens and the earth is clearly the germ for the whole sequence of five 'Cities and the Sky' in *Invisible Cities*. In Eudoxia, there is the famous carpet which contains the city's design, and the oracle gives an ambiguous reply about the relation between these two objects, the carpet and the city: 'One of the two objects – the oracle replied – has the form the gods gave the starry sky and the orbits in which the worlds revolve; the other is an approximate reflection, like every human creation' (*Invisible Cities* 97). Further, the city of Beersheba has its reflection in a celestial city of the same name in the skies (*Invisible Cities* 111) and the blueprint for Thekla resides in the heavens (*Invisible Cities* 127). As for Perinthia: 'Summoned to lay down the rules for the foundation of Perinthia, the astronomers established the place and the day according to the position of the stars' (*Invisible Cities* 144). Finally, Andria, the city which reflects the heavens so perfectly that any change in the sky causes a change in the city, was 'built so artfully that its every street followed a planet's orbit, and the buildings and the places of community life repeat the order of the constellations and the position of the most luminous stars' (*Invisible Cities* 150).

The eleventh section ('Adventures at Sea') recounts what happens when Marco and Cocacin are shipwrecked on a cannibal island. While some moments of this episode have obvious Conradian resonances – 'The first sign of human life they find [on the island] plunges them into the deepest terror. They see shrunken human heads stuck on poles' (RR 3: 577) is an obvious echo of the climactic scene from *Heart of Darkness* (for the importance of Conrad throughout Calvino's oeuvre, see Calvo Montoro, and McLaughlin and Scicutella) – this is a sequence of adventures which contain too much action and are set in too different a location to remain in the later work. In the penultimate section 12 ('Orient Lost'), the Polos reach India, and when Marco is told that that Khan has committed suicide, he exclaims to the messengers: 'Him? The wisest of men! ... I have to go back to all of your countries, I have to understand everything you think, make you understand everything I think, to seek truth together, stop all this blood flowing!' (RR 3: 583). The Khan's dramatic end and Marco's rather melodramatic reaction are, of course, omitted in the restrained, polished prose of the later work. The final, thirteenth section ('Epilogue') returns to Venice and to the jocular tone of the opening, as well as alluding to the false etymology that is at the origin of the Italian title of Polo's work, *Il Milione*. We catch Marco courting a Venetian girl and constantly repeating: 'Well, just imagine, in the land of Cathay there are a million times more' (RR 3: 585).

Despite its unfinished state, the 1960 screenplay of *Marco Polo*, written for a film that was never realized, contains key elements in the creative itinerary that leads from Polo's original text to Calvino's *Invisible Cities*. The main constants in Calvino's two reworkings of *Il Milione* concern character and motifs. Marco's brilliant accounts and pantomimes, his restless pursuit of the marvellous but also his interest in the reverse side of things, are already in evidence, as are the Khan's melancholy and sense of emptiness lurking behind all his conquests and achievements. Motifs such as those of the pattern in the Persian carpet, or the design formed by the Khan's empire, are also adumbrated at this stage, as is the theme of the Khan's interest in astronomy and its tools (telescopes, sextants, maps), and the relationship between earthly cities and the sky.

However, more significant than the constants are the elements that are discarded by Calvino as he moves from the abortive screenplay to achieve the extraordinary poetic prose of *Invisible Cities*. Despite the different genres to which Calvino's two Polo texts belong, and their different audiences, these changes still constitute a representative sample of the divergences between 'early' and 'late' Calvino. Again, the chief differences concern characters and action: there is no room in the later work for any secondary character to distract from Marco and Kublai, whereas the screenplay contains two different female leads, Agaruk and Cocacin, as well as other important male characters such as the Old Man of the Mountain, Halogu Khan, and Prince Argon, not to mention lesser characters such as friars, soldiers, Assassins, and Huris. The only other characters in the later work apart from the two protagonists are the nameless ambassadors to the Khan's court, whom Marco clearly outshines, but they play a minimal role in the later text.

The absence of female characters also eliminates most (though not all) of the erotic elements from the later work, while the lack of secondary male characters elides most forms of action: instead, the emphasis is on contemplation. There is also a very tight unity of place that distinguishes the novel from the screenplay: the screenplay's secondary, exotic locations of Ceylon, Java, and India are nowhere in evidence in the later work, thus giving it a strict sense of unity of place, as the centre of narrative remains the Khan's court. If the screenplay contained intertextual homages to three of Calvino's favourite 'action' authors (Dumas, Stevenson, Conrad), the later book dispenses with all action except brief formulaic accounts, amounting to half a sentence, of Marco's journeys at the beginning of certain city descriptions: 'Beyond six rivers and three mountain ranges rises Zora ...' (*Invisible Cities* 15). The intertextual sources in the later work are not 'adventure' narratives, apart from *Il Milione*, but rather utopian and poetic works: More's *Utopia*, which talks of the island's fifty-five cities, and Coleridge's famous poem (for other utopian intertexts, from Campanella to Fourier, see Kuon, 'Critica e progetto dell'utopia'). The whole self-referential dimension of *Invisible Cities*, particularly the allusions to chess, to the arbitrary nature of the linguistic sign, as well as to how we look at the world, is entirely absent in the earlier 1960 text. The portrayal of Marco's father and uncle in the screenplay, with their ludicrous Venetian accents, allowed for a constant comic element to emerge, as also did Marco's mishaps with various Oriental religions. Indeed, the comic and the erotic come together in the episode when he tries to become a Buddhist monk and resist the temptations of the flesh. There are no such elements in *Invisible Cities*. In short, if the screenplay is about action and the body and has 'a cast of thousands,' the novel deals largely with meditation and the mind and concentrates exclusively on the Khan and Polo and their meta-literary discussions. Yet despite its pared-down nature, the later text paradoxically has a totalizing ambition: like many of Calvino's works of the 1970s and 1980s, it aspires to be a literary universe, and is organized into a much more complex structure.

Marco Polo's *Travels* and *Invisible Cities*

Marco describes a bridge, stone by stone.
'But which is the stone that supports the bridge?' Kublai Khan asks.
'The bridge is not supported by one stone or another,' Marco answers,

'but by the line of the arch that they form.'

Kublai Khan remains silent, reflecting. Then he adds: 'Why do you speak to me of the stones? It is only the arch that matters to me.'

Polo answers: 'Without the stones there is no arch.'

(*Invisible Cities* 82)

Turning to *Invisible Cities* itself and its relationship to Polo's *Il Milione*, it is worth recalling the important points made in an excellent essay on Calvino's text by Marina Zancan, '*Le città invisibili* di Calvino.' Zancan's conclusion is that while the screenplay *Marco Polo* is largely a reconstruction of the past, the novel is entirely concerned with the present. She identifies three main areas of divergence: the later work contains a meta-narrative discourse; it privileges the theme of the modern city; and it is concerned with redefining our gaze on the world. Her attention focuses in particular on the city of Quinsai (Hang Chow), which she claims is the only city from Polo's original text to be cited in *Invisible Cities* (Zancan 923). She notes the passage in Polo's *Travels* where he says, 'At the end of these three days' travel one reaches the noble city of Quinsai, which when translated means "the city of the heavens"' (Zancan 923), and it is this passage that she rightly sees as inspiring the important sequence of cities, 'The City and the Skies,' in Calvino's novel.

In this final section I would like to suggest some other important areas of contact between the two texts, the medieval and the modern. These areas divide into three broad categories: characters, descriptions, and structural elements. As far as the first category is concerned, we have noted how Calvino homes in, as in all his texts, on a central contrast of character: in this case, the lively, talkative Marco, recounting his various cities, and the sedentary, laconic, and melancholic Kublai, a contrast already adumbrated in the earlier screenplay. In fact, Marco's bravura was already featured in Polo's own account, in *Travels* chapters 10–11, where Marco's ambassadorial technique is shown to be superior to that of his rivals, since they concentrate solely on their embassies, whereas Polo also gives the Khan an account of 'the different customs of the world' (chapter 10), as well as 'all the marvels and the important and new things he had seen' (chapter 11).

The second group of links concerns description, and is most clearly visible in the descriptions of cities, especially the emphasis on numerical lists of the physical or architectural characteristics of the city. An obvious example here would be the very first city, Diomira: 'Leaving there, and proceeding for three days toward the east, you reach Diomira, a city with sixty silver domes, bronze statues of all the gods, streets paved with lead,[3] a crystal theater, a golden cock that crows each morning on a tower' (*Invisible Cities* 7). If this seems a rather formulaic account, with its list of different metals, many other cities are inspired by more complex mechanisms. Some of the most interesting ones are the 'specular' or double cities such as Sophronia, Eutropia, or Laudamia. Sophronia consists of two half-cities, one of which is devoted to fun-fairs and roller-coasters, while the other consists of the banks, factories, and schools; but the one half that is permanent is the fun fair, whereas the temporary half that is towed away each year for six months is the half-city of banks, factories, and schools (*Invisible Cities* 63). Similarly, when the inhabitants of Eutropia get tired of their jobs, relations, houses, and streets, they move into the adjoining empty city and take on different jobs, relations, houses, and streets (*Invisible Cities* 64–5). Moreover, the description of Laudamia begins 'Like Laudamia, every city has at its side another city whose inhabitants are called by the same names: it is the Laudamia of the dead, the cemetery' (*Invisible Cities* 141). These are typically Calvinian reversals of the description in Polo's own text of the Khan's capital Cambaluc (Beijing): in *Travels*, chapter 72, Polo tells how the capital Cambaluc has another city right beside it, separated only by a river, the reason for this being that 'the Khan, finding through his astronomers that this other city would rebel and cause great problems for his empire, consequently had this other city built beside it, and separated only by a river; and he decanted the people of one city into the other.' Another possible source for Calvino's moveable cities is the city of Sindafa, which is described in Polo's text as having 'several mansions where much merchandise is contained, and many trades are practised, but I tell you that these houses are made of wood, and they are taken down in the evening and put together again in the morning' (*Milione*, chapter 98). In addition, the famous dialogue between Marco and Kublai about whether it is the stone or the arch that supports the bridge, at the end of the central chapter 5 (*Invisible Cities* 82), is actually based on the emphasis in *Il Milione* on several stone bridges. First there is the bridge ten miles from Cambaluc: 'Over this river there is a very beautiful stone bridge. And I tell you that there is no other bridge like it in the world: it is a good three hundred paces long and eight wide, so that as many as ten horsemen can ride abreast along it' (*Milione*, chapter 89). There is also the bridge in the city of Sindafa, 'a bridge all made of stones, and it is a good half a mile long, and eight paces wide' (*Milione*, chapter 98). But the most relevant passage is the description of the bridges in Quinsai, since Quinsai is also mentioned in Calvino's text at the beginning of chapter 6 (*Invisible Cities* 85), immediately after the dialogue about the stone bridge at the end of chapter 5 (*Invisible Cities* 82). In Polo's *Travels*, we find this description:

> The city of Quinsai extends fully one hundred miles in circumference, and contains twelve thousand stone bridges; and under the arches of most of these bridges a large ship could pass, and the other bridges would be big enough for a ship half that size. And no one should be amazed by this, because the whole city sits on the water and is surrounded by water, and consequently has to have so many bridges to allow people to pass over its territory. (*Milione*, chapter 131)

Needless to say, the Venetian Polo is struck by this city that sits on the waters and requires so many bridges. This is picked up by Calvino in his text, since it is at this same point (the beginning of chapter 6) that Kublai asks Marco why the one city he never mentions is Venice. Marco replies, 'Every time I describe a city I am saying something about Venice' (*Invisible Cities* 86).

Zancan's suggestion that Quinsai is the only city mentioned in Calvino's novel is not quite accurate, because the text mentions at the outset that the ambassadors return to the Khan's court at Kemenfu (Kai-ping-fu in the English translation; *Invisible Cities* 21), just as the Polos are described in *Il Milione* as first coming to the Khan at Kemenfu (chapter 8), although it is also possible that Kemenfu is mentioned in Calvino because Polo's longer description of the city (in chapter 63) occurs at a structurally strategic point, just before the description of Kublai Khan and his exploits (chapters 64–71). We have seen that Quinsai is mentioned in the middle of *Invisible Cities*, and Calvino's text mentions a third city, Cambaluc (or Kambalu, in Weaver's translation), at the opening of the final chapter 9 (*Invisible Cities* 135). The modern text thus reflects the order in which Polo's text mentions these same three cities (Kemenfu, Quinsai, Cambaluc), and this final emphasis on Cambaluc probably derives from the many chapters devoted to that city in Polo's original text. There is the description of the palace and garden (*Milione*, chapter 71), the mention of the adjoining city (chapter 72), and the description of the city's feasts and use of paper money (chapters 79–83, especially chapter 81). Polo's interest in money and exchange systems in his text probably also suggested to Calvino the sequence of five 'Città e gli scambi' (rather narrowly translated by Weaver as 'Trading Cities' [see *Invisible Cities* 36, 51, 64, 76, 88], even though such cities are also about semiotic and linguistic exchange).

Lastly, we should consider the important structural elements that Calvino takes from the ancient text and transforms within his own. First of all, the very title *Invisible Cities* derives from a characteristic Calvinian inversion, since some of the first words of Polo's *Travels* concern the visible evidence of what he saw: 'And all this will be recounted in this book in due order just as Messer Marco Polo, a wise and noble citizen of Venice, recounted them, and he himself saw these things' (Prologue). Indeed, throughout Polo's text there is an emphasis on what he saw with his own eyes (chapters 89, 131, 133, 139). Calvino reverses Polo's emphasis on the visible both in his title and in the description of each city, which follows a format of first itemizing the visible elements of the city, then stating that what is really striking about the city is something other than the visual. A good example of the technique is the city of Zaira:

> In vain, great-hearted Kublai, shall I attempt to describe Zaira, city of high bastions. I could tell you how many steps make up the streets rising like stairways, and the degree of the arcades' curves, and what kind of zinc scales the roofs; but I already know this would be the same as telling you nothing. The city does not consist of this, but of relationships between the measurements of its space and the events of its past. (*Invisible Cities* 10)

Another key structural element is Calvino's use of Polo's journey formula. In the early part of the *Travels*, Polo talks at first of shorter journeys of seven days (chapters 24, 25, 28, 32), or three days (chapters 34, 62). Similarly, we find in the early descriptions in Calvino mentions of three days (*Invisible Cities* 7, 12), and indeed at the beginning of chapter 6 the words Marco addresses to the Khan – 'Di là l'uomo si parte e cavalca tre giornate tra greco e levante' ['You leave there and ride for three days between the northeast and east-by-northeast winds'] (*Città* 88; *Invisible Cities* 85) – are a verbatim quotation from Polo's *Travels* (chapters 24, 34). Bernardini Napoletano (175–6) points out that Calvino echoes Polo in stressing the huge distances covered in each journey, using words such as 'lungamente' or 'finalmente,' but it is also interesting to note that at a later stage, when the journeys become longer, Polo's text switches from days to miles: thirty miles (chapter 90), fifteen miles (chapter 126), and even a thousand miles (chapters 150, 152, 167). Similarly, in Calvino, the early mentions of three days' or seven days' travel are later replaced by distances such as eighty miles (*Invisible Cities* 36). Calvino's text thus follows Polo's original faithfully in these spatial particulars.

Perhaps the most striking recurrent structural feature of *Invisible Cities* is the fact that all the cities have female names. Although some critics have noted this and advanced plausible reasons for it, nobody has suggested that this feature may also derive from the fact that, in the important chapter 63 of Polo's *Travels*, the description of Kemenfu, Polo says that in that city all the gods in the temples have female names. That this is a key chapter is underlined by the fact that the very next sentence states, 'Now we leave here, and I will tell you of the great lord of all the Tartars, namely the noble Khan who is called Kublai' (chapter 63).

Finally, even the elaborate, patterned structure of *Invisible Cities* is probably also inspired ultimately by Polo's own fascination with statistics and numbers. This numerical obsession is then creatively transformed into a structural feature of the later text as Calvino opts for a highly symmetrical shape of fifty-five cities divided into eleven series of five cities each, distributed among nine chapters; the total of fifty-five and nine then give the number sixty-four, which amounts to the number of squares on a chessboard, one of the themes of the book. The shape of the work is thus like the diamond mentioned by Kublai as the secret pattern of his empire (*Invisible Cities* 60). Thematics and structure are tightly and symmetrically interwoven in *Invisible Cities*, as opposed to the rambling, asymmetrical 173-chapter account of his travels by Polo himself.

In short, the secret chemistry behind *Invisible Cities* appears to be this: Calvino takes an old text and makes it (post)modern. He suppresses action for contemplation, downgrades mercantile description for an analysis of mental states, replaces irregularity with symmetry, and dispenses with objective non-literary narration in favour of an introspective, highly polished, meta-literary text. As Calvino tells us in his Harvard essays, published posthumously, *Invisible Cities* was one of the texts with which he was most satisfied, since in it he had managed to say the maximum number of things in the smallest number of words. He thus was able to concentrate all his meditations on a single symbol, and its multifaceted structure allowed multiple, non-hierarchical readings, both sequential (page after page) and ramified (following any of the different sequences of cities: see Calvino, *Saggi* 1: 689–90; *Six Memos* 71). Its influence and appeal have been enormous, and part of that appeal must lie in its conciliation of opposites: the brevity that encompasses infinity (a lesson learned from Borges), the prose that borders on poetry (*Saggi* 1: 671; *Six Memos* 49), the mixture of imaginary and real cities (see Barenghi), and the single work that embraces all his own previous works, as well as alluding to many other canonical texts (the Bible, classical literature, medieval texts, oriental literature, and utopian/dystopian literature from More to Huxley). Calvino, as we saw in the epigraph to this chapter, considered that Polo's *Travels* was one of those books that become imaginary continents, inside which other works of literature find their space. *Invisible Cities* is a highly literary work that has found its space inside Polo's work, and in turn has also become another continent of the imagination capable of inspiring other writers and artists (see, for instance, Bonsaver). And yet, however unique Calvino's modern masterpiece may be, its main inspiration was Marco Polo's *Travels*, which also inspired the substantial 1960 screenplay. Calvino's Polo tells us that there is no arch without the stones; similarly, without *Il Milione*, there would have been no *Invisible Cities*.

NOTES

1 All quotations from Calvino and from Polo's *Il Milione* have been given in my own English translation, except for quotations from William Weaver's 1974 translation of *Invisible Cities*.
2 The edition I have used is Marco Polo, *Il libro di Marco Polo detto Milione nella versione dell''ottimo'*, ed. Daniele Ponchiroli (1954. Turin: Einaudi, 1962), since this Einaudi edition is the one that Calvino himself read when working on the screenplay and on his novel.
3 Actually the Italian original reads 'stagno' not 'piombo,' so should be translated 'tin.'

9 From Alterity to Holism: Cinematic Depictions of Marco Polo and His *Travels*

AMILCARE A. IANNUCCI AND JOHN TULK

I content myself with noting the fact that somehow or other the Oriental generally acts, speaks, and thinks in a manner opposite to the Europeans.
(Lord Cromer quoted in Said, *Orientalism* 39)

[T]o know the Other is a process of *Bildung*, of learning and self-cultivation, which is neither projecting the self onto the Other nor erasing the self with the Other's alterity. It is rather a moment when self and Other meet and join together, in which both are changed and enriched in what Gadamer calls 'the fusion of horizons.'
(Zhang, *Mighty Opposites* 53)

Marco Polo and his *Travels* have been the subject of many adaptations, including numerous films of the sound era; among these is an aborted film whose script was written by none other than Italo Calvino, discussed in McLaughlin's essay in this volume. Many are the genres these adaptations encompass, from swashbuckling adventure through documentary and historical docudrama, to fantasy, the musical, and television mini-series, and many are the resultant views of the Venetian traveller and the lands and the people he encountered. Two overriding views of Polo predominate, however: namely, the romantic/adventuresome and the historical/cultural. These views, in turn, predetermine the way in which the other is filmed and portrayed. This essay explores the cinematic reception of Marco Polo, investigating various cinematic views by examining two films in depth, although other films are used as points of reference: Archie Mayo's *The Adventure of Marco Polo* (1938), and Giuliano Montaldo's *Marco Polo* (1982). These films permit, in turn, a close study of the filmic reception of Marco Polo by focusing attention on four key questions: (1) How is Marco Polo presented and how does this portrayal agree or not with what is recorded in the *Travels*? (2) How is the other, the object of encounter, presented? (3) How do the cinematic conventions of a particular film genre affect the depiction of the self (that is, 'Marco Polo') and the other? (4) How are the various cinematic interpretations shaped by the historical, political, and cultural conventions of the times?

In 1923, legendary movie mogul Samuel Goldwyn became an independent producer and formed Samuel Goldwyn Inc. Becoming friends with other independents, he began releasing his films through United Artists in 1926 (Thompson and Bromwell 217–18). The 1930s saw the height of his fame. He had a fine eye for talent and discovered or bought some of the best talent for the production of his movies – talent such as the directors Cecil B. DeMille, John Ford, and William Wyler, the writers Ben Hecht, Sidney Howard, and Lilian Hellman, and the stars Ronald Coleman and Gary Cooper. Goldwyn's credo was shaped by the belief that the single driving force behind any great movie was the storytelling. He was therefore most receptive to a story idea brought to him by his friend Douglas Fairbanks, Sr, who suggested making an adventure film based on the exploits of Marco Polo. Undoubtedly, Fairbanks wanted to direct the movie himself and have his son star in it. Through some rather tricky negotiating, Fairbanks Sr was removed and Goldwyn won all rights to the film (Berg 317). *The Adventures of Marco Polo* was born.

Goldwyn knew the kind of film he wanted to make and knew who would be the film's principals. Goldwyn envisioned a swashbuckling adventure (see the movie poster, figure 9.1). This was a natural choice given the nature of many Hollywood films of this time. For example, in roughly the same time period as the release of *The Adventures of Marco Polo* (April, 1938), the silver screen was ablaze with adventures such as *Wells Fargo* starring Joel McCrea, *Captains Courageous* starring Spencer Tracy, *Test Pilot* starring Clark Gable, *Three Comrades* starring Robert Taylor, and *The Adventures of Robin Hood* starring Errol Flynn – the swashbuckler *par excellence*. Goldwyn was also sure of his star, Gary Cooper. Cooper, the iconic embodiment of all things American, had already contributed mightily to the national passion for adventure (especially adventure of an American kind, that is, the western) and had starred in such box office successes as *Arizona Bound* (1927), *The Last Outlaw* (1927), *The Virginian* (1929), *The Texan* (1930), and *A Man*

Figure 9.1: Gary Cooper as Marco Polo in *The Adventures of Marco Polo* (1938), produced by Samuel Goldwyn, directed by Archie Mayo. ©1938, The Samuel Goldwyn, Jr., Family Trust. All rights reserved. By permission of MGM Clip and Still Licensing, inc.

from Wyoming (1930), as well as other non-western roles such as *A Fare-well to Arms* (1932) and *Mr. Deeds Goes to Town* (1936). So great was Goldwyn's commitment to Cooper that he withstood criticism from a number of quarters that Cooper was all wrong for the part. Goldwyn commissioned a script from Robert Sherwood, a veteran screenwriter who had already contributed to the snappy dialogue of *The Scarlet Pimpernel* (1934) and who had received rave reviews for his script of *The Petrified Forest* (1936), a film directed by Archie Mayo. It was the latter who also got directing nods from Goldwyn after a number of false starts with other directors, described below. Mayo, known for his flair for melodrama (cf. Thomson, who pans even *The Petrified Forest* for its theatricality and its principal actors who 'are unlikely trees in an unlikely forest' [579]), had directed a string of B movies in the 1930s, including *Desirable* (1934), *Bordertown* (1935), and *Call It a Day* (1937), and would later direct more critically acclaimed movies such as *The House across the Bay* (1940), *Confirm or Deny* (1941), and *Orchestra Wives* (1942). He is, perhaps, best remembered for directing one of the most famous scenes in comic film history, that of Harpo Marx leaning against a building in *A Night in Casablanca* (1946). No money was spared on the lavish sets for the film, especially the Great Khan's palace, and Goldwyn assembled what the theatrical trailer for the film describes as a cast of five thousand contributing to the film's 'magnitude, scope and spectacular sweep' (again from the trailer). Production costs exceeded two million dollars.

The plot of the movie follows the conventions of the adventure/romantic drama rather than the dictates of the *Travels*. The film opens with cast credits appearing on a running scroll which seems to suggest the primacy of the text, but the text is quickly sacrificed in favour of adventure and romance as the film's major themes. A brief prologue provides an introduction to Marco, his character, and the travel to China. In Venice, various Polo relatives examine the magnificent treasures of China and muse about trade. Puzzled as to who will be able to travel there on their behalf, Marco's father announces that it will be his son, the one Venetian 'strong enough and clever enough' to make this perilous journey. One relative complains that Marco knows nothing of business, but Marco's father retorts: 'perhaps not, but in him burns the spirit of adventure and romance like a sacred flame,' adding flippantly that the women of China will appeal to his romantic bent. In a funny scene, the Polos' bookkeeper Binguccio (Ernest Truex) scours the canals of Venice in search of the young Polo (Gary Cooper), turning his name into a gondolier's song (very bad) and asking various pretty courtesans if they have seen him. Discovered in one such locale where the ladies' man is engaged in gambling, Marco is brought to his father, who commissions him and Binguccio to travel to China, giving him a letter for Kublai Khan and a small pouch in which to store whatever he sees on the route. Short scenes convey the travel to China: a violent storm at sea en route to Acre reduces the merchant party to Marco and Binguccio, the trek across Persia is a single scene of Marco and Binguccio on horseback caught in a violent desert sand storm (and the loss of one horse), and the crossing of Tibet is a single scene of a blinding Himalayan blizzard (and the loss of the other horse). Quickly they reach Cathay and Peking.[1]

They arrive on foot at the Great Wall, which appears in much better repair than it actually was in the thirteenth century (Larner 59), and enter Peking where scores of Chinese walking the streets are not the least surprised to see them and where a beatitude-reciting philosopher, Chen Tsu (H.B. Warner), invites them into his home. The subsequent dinner consists of a food, we are told, eaten by China's poor, named by the philosopher 'spaghett.' After dinner the philosopher gives some dried 'spaghett' to Marco, who adds it to his pouch, and the two discourse on the golden rule. An ugly street scene is witnessed by the two and in answer to Marco's questioning of the emperor's justice the philosopher responds: 'Kublai Khan is a good man, a just man, but he is dominated by an adviser who has little respect for the sanctity of human life ... a Saracen named Ahmed, a foreigner, the emperor's Minister of State. Watch out for him.' Afterward Chen leads Marco to his workshop where he demonstrates the power of gunpowder (seen only as a toy), and Marco adds a firecracker to his pouch.

Reaching the palace of Kublai Khan, Marco and Binguccio are given quarters and we are introduced to the Khan (George Barbier) in his spectacular reception hall. He is, thanks to the advice of Ahmed (superbly portrayed at his evil best by Basil Rathbone), planning an invasion of Japan, and has promised his daughter, Princess Kukachin, to the king of Persia, a promise he reiterates to the Persian ambassador (Ferdinand Gottschalk). While waiting for an audience, Marco stumbles upon Princess Kukachin (portrayed by Sigrid Gurie) in the royal courtyard and romance quickly blooms (see figure 9.2). In the first of three key romantic scenes, the princess is immediately captivated by

Figure 9.2: Gary Cooper as Marco Polo with Sigrid Gurie as Princess Kuchakin in a romantic scene from *The Adventures of Marco Polo*. ©1938, The Samuel Goldwyn, Jr., Family Trust. All rights reserved. By permission of MGM Clip and Still Licensing, inc.

Marco's youthful attractiveness and literally examines his body from foot to head, in a slow pan shot of a Gary Cooper suffused in light. Marco reciprocates and tells the princess she is like no other, describing her as 'lovely' and 'exquisite' and asking her: 'Has any man ever looked at you as I'm looking now?' When she answers negatively, he replies: 'Then the men of this country don't appreciate their own treasures.' The scene ends with Cooper, in a cinematic move he perfected over the years, becoming romantically flustered, tongue-tied, and close-lipped.

Marco is brought before the emperor, who introduces him to Ahmed. The Khan is surprised to learn from Kukachin that she has already conversed with his Venetian guest, a conversation that vexes Ahmed, who quite clearly favours the princess. The Khan then has Marco serve as the judge in an oriental beauty pageant to determine which girls will serve in his harem. Upon its conclusion, Ahmed shows Marco and Binguccio the palace, including his own quarters which are replete with the torture-loving servants Bayan (Stanley Fields) and Tocktai (Harold Huber), man-eating vultures, and a lion pit into which a hapless spy is thrown for the benefit of the visitors.

A second romantic scene follows in the courtyard, this time at night, in which the princess tells Marco of her betrothal. Romantic bantering leads to a number of ultra-romantic lines, all spoken by Marco ('The reason I am going is, well, there are warnings of danger sounding in my heart. I've heard such warnings before but never so strongly. You see. You may be a princess but when I look at your eyes I see deep beauty and when I touch you I feel warm life') and the development of new romantic techniques such as Marco's teaching the princess how to kiss, something to which she takes rather too eagerly. A spy reports their kissing antics to Ahmed, who has the emperor send Marco into the robber territory of Kaidu as a spy and possible assassin. When Marco complains that he has no experience of killing, Ahmed retorts: 'That is not necessary. We only want to make use of your remarkable gifts for intrigue.' He gives assurances to Marco that he will be protected and that he need have no thought for his well being.

The third romantic scene takes place in the princess's boudoir. She is distressed that Marco is being sent to bandit territory and tells him that Ahmed is plotting against him, adding: 'He's afraid of you because you're strong.' She expresses deep fear for his safety and the two hug extremely closely in a shot suffused, once again, with deep lighting. At the end of the scene, Marco says that his mission may bring some good and encourages her to look to the future: 'Then perhaps the Moon god-dess might tell you that you don't have to travel all the way to Persia to find your love.' The princess replies, 'She doesn't have to tell me.' More kissing follows, kissing which is interrupted by Ahmed, who grabs the princess and closes the door on Marco.

Marco and Binguccio no sooner enter Kaidu's territory than they are captured and taken before Kaidu (Alan Hale), a womanizing warlord desperately trying to escape the attentions of his possessive wife Nazama (Binnie Barnes). Kaidu questions Marco, who protests his innocence ('we are only commercial travellers from Venice'), and instantly recog-nizes that his wife is attracted to the young Venetian. He therefore keeps him as a distracting foil against his wife for his numerous romantic trysts, especially with Nazama's maid (the seventeen-year-old bombshell from Idaho, Lana Turner). Eventually, however, events in Peking take over. The emperor has lost most of his army in Japan and returns in disgrace. Ahmed seizes his opportunity and forces the emperor to abdicate in favour of himself, claiming the princess as his bride. She sends a note via eagle to Marco, who convinces Kaidu to let him return to Peking. Kaidu also agrees to rouse his troops and attack Ahmed in Peking. Returning in disguise to Peking, Marco encounters Chen Tsu, from whom he learns that the marriage of Ahmed to the princess is to take place that very night and with whom he hatches a plot to strike at Ahmed.

The final scenes bring to a resounding conclusion the adventure and romance themes. Marco returns to the palace to find the princess about to commit suicide. Reunited, they pledge their love and Marco leaves her, encouraging her to do whatever she can to delay the mar-riage ceremony. Kaidu's forces attack Peking, but due to Ahmed's clever plans, are splintered, some remaining outside the walls and the rest bogged down within the city's gates. Marco comes to the res-cue with a massive load of gunpowder provided by Chen Tsu and blows up the city's main gate, thus allowing Kaidu's forces to strike at the enemy. Marco rushes to Ahmed's quarters to find the ceremony all but completed. A no-holds-barred fight ensues between Ahmed and Marco, at the conclusion of which Ahmed is pushed into the lions' pit. The next scene sees the emergence of Kaidu as the friend of the Khan and his being rewarded handsomely. In the final scene, Marco and the princess discuss her upcoming marriage to the king of Persia and Marco promises to accompany her on what he describes as 'a very long journey.'

It is clear that this movie is a liberal adaptation of the *Travels* that bears little or no resemblance to the original, except in name only. The prologue to the *Travels* (33–45)[2] makes it clear that two Polo brothers (Niccolò, the father of the author of the *Travels*, and Maffeo) had already travelled to the court of Kublai Khan around 1260 (*Travels* 34–5; for date cf. Larner, *Marco Polo* 33) and had returned to Venice in the late 1260s, around 1269 (Larner 35). They returned to the Great Khan around 1271, taking the seventeen-year-old Marco with them (*Travels* 38 ff.). This second Polo expedition was undoubtedly mounted so that the Polo brothers could report to the Great Khan on their progress, for the Khan had entrusted them with a letter to the pope requesting a hundred men educated in the liberal arts who could act as missionaries within his domain, along with some holy oil from the Church of the Holy Sepulchre in Jerusalem (*Travels* 36). There is therefore nothing in the *Travels* to suggest that young Marco had undertaken a voyage on his own and there is no mention of the bookkeeper Binguccio. It is true that the *Travels* mentions 'bad weather and severe cold' (*Travels* 39) as contributing to the inordinately long time for their journey (some three and a half years), but does not provide the movie's details of the storm at sea which destroyed most of the party, the desert sandstorm, or the blizzard in the Himalayas.

It is really with Marco's entry into China that the cinematic details become more and more fanciful. Thus, while the *Travels* make no mention of the Great Wall (a fact often adduced to argue that Marco Polo never travelled to China at all), the very first scene of the arrival in China has Marco and Binguccio approaching it on foot. There is no mention in the *Travels* of Chen Tsu. And while we know that Marco met the Great Khan, and while the *Travels* state that he achieved high rank in his court (*Travels* 40 ff.), there is nothing to suggest Marco was ever dispatched as a spy to the territory of Kaidu. The latter does make an appearance in the *Travels* (114 ff.) as a nephew of the Great Khan and a powerful lord who rebelled against him with Nayan, Kublai's uncle, but without success. Moreover, while Ahmed the Saracen does figure in the *Travels* (131 ff.) as a powerful and ruthless governor of Peking and confidante of the Great Khan, he is killed by a conspiracy of Cathayans, and is not involved in a long-running feud with Marco Polo. Moreover, while there is a Princess Kukachin in the *Travels* (42–3), she is adamantly not a love interest of Marco Polo. Rather, she is a seventeen-year-old beauty who is given by the Great Khan to King Arghum of the Levant and who is accompanied on her journey of betrothal by Marco, Maffeo, and Niccolò on their return to Venice. Finally, there is no evidence in the *Travels* for the extremely far-fetched details that Marco Polo brought back 'spaghett' or gunpowder from his trip to China.

Just as telling as the plot discrepancies between movie and text is the emphasis placed in both on Marco's character. Through the *Travels* Marco is revealed as a traveller, a merchant, a geographer, and a keen observer of people and places. In the movie, conversely, Marco becomes a young swashbuckler whose major interests are adventure and romance. The travel is thus handled in a cursory manner with little description of people or places: the only geography is provided by ongoing updates on a filmed map. As for the merchant aspect, Marco deliberately keeps hidden his mercantile interests for no apparent reason, a fact made all the more puzzling because Binguccio is forever filmed as tending to his books. In this respect, it is interesting to note that the *Travels* and *The Adventures of Marco Polo* share a hybrid style. The *Travels* consist of two interwoven styles: the mercantile and matter-of-fact objective style of Marco Polo and the romance style provided by Marco Polo's co-author, Rustichello of Pisa (Larner 46 ff.). Thus, while Marco Polo brought the bare details, Rustichello brought the themes of romance and adventure to the enterprise of the composition of the *Travels*, employing the conventions of popular chivalric literature. Likewise, but in an altogether skewed manner, *The Adventures of Marco Polo* takes this chivalric style to deliberately exaggerated heights to produce a film which is a radical departure from the original text. The story that results is one that even Rustichello would not recognize.

What then of the film's portrayal of alterity, the experience and recognition of the other? It is clear that the film presents the other through a series of dichotomies that emphasize the difference between East and West, civilized and primitive, active and passive, noble and wicked, male and female, dominant and submissive. The opening shots of the film make clear the fundamental binarism of East and West. Marco's father prefaces his commission to Marco by telling him: 'The Orientals are a curious people. They do not trade as we do.' When they reach China, this dichotomy is maintained. Marco is astounded to discover that the philosopher Chen Tsu knows of the Beatitudes and equally astounded to hear him recite the golden rule, 'Thou shalt love thy neighbour as thyself.' China is thus represented as an eastern civilization that must be based on other non-western principles, rather than kindness and love. Similarly, although China is seen as ancient and highly developed, it is mired in the primitive, a primitiveness that confers on it a passivity, an inability to act. Kublai Khan laments that the Chinese have thousands of years of history, but that it takes them forever to reach decisions, while Marco has to goad Chen Tsu to give him gunpowder, a commodity the philosopher relegates to the rank of a child's toy. Only Marco, the film makes clear, sees the potential of this technology and only Marco can take effective action. In a telling scene he chides Chen Tsu, 'There's no time for philosophy, Chen Tsu; we need action.' The West, therefore, is pragmatic, while the East remains stagnated in idle philosophical speculation.

A major theme of the movie is the contrast between noble and wicked. Marco is a noble man. He does not take life indiscriminately, he does not torture, he does not lord it over other people, he does not force himself upon women. In contrast, Ahmed, a 'Saracen,' does all of these things in the Khan's service and seems to have a free hand to do so. Ahmed is the wicked easterner so feared by the West, ruthlessly resourceful and cruel, who cements his power by means of a system of well-developed espionage. As the palace guard tells Marco on his arrival: 'It is a country where no one is so important as not to be watched … constantly.' China therefore appears as an Orwellian country, teeming with intrigue and unjust acts. Finally, in contrast to the dominant male westerner is the passive eastern female: Marco Polo is not only the hero but also the conquering lover. From the beginning, Marco Polo takes the lead, teasing the princess at court, teaching her how to kiss, and saving her from the brink of suicide. He is resolutely the dominant force throughout, and through his eyes – the eyes of the western male subject – we are privileged to see the feminine and emasculated East. In a nutshell, the film's view of alterity is blatantly racist and sexist, built on the most extreme stereotypes imaginable.

Alterity is clearly a major problem for the movie, since everyone in it is pretending to be someone he/she is not. Thus Marco Polo is not Venetian, not even Italian, but a young American from Helena, Montana. Similarly, and more glaringly, the Princess Kukachin is not 'oriental': she is none other than Sigrid Gurie, whom Goldwyn had billed as the 'Norwegian Garbo' and the 'siren of the fjords.' It hurt the film and Goldwyn's reputation considerably when it was discovered that Sigrid Gurie had been born Sigrid Haukelid on 11 May 1911 in Brooklyn, New York, right in the middle of Flatbush (Berg 317). Equally risible are H.B. Warner from London, England as Chen Tsu, George Barbier from Philadelphia as Kublai Khan, Basil Rathbone

from Johannesburg (via England) as Ahmed, and Alan Hale, an Irish-
man from Washington, as Kaidu. The film is a veritable cultural melt-
ing pot of Anglo-Saxons. Frank Nugent in *the New York Times* (8 April
1938) captured the rather inane casting as follows:

> The Khan speaks with George Barbier's nasal Philadelphian, the Venetian
> Marco Polo with Mr. Cooper's Montana drawl, the Saracen Ahmed with
> Basil Rathbone's clipped Londonese, the Princess Kukachin with Sigrid
> Gurie's Garboesque Norwegian, the servant Binguccio with Ernest Truex's
> Burbanked-Kansas-Broadway. And we're not counting Binnie Barnes's
> Cockney, Stanley Fields' growling Pennsylvanian, Ferdinand Gottschalk's
> whatever-it-is.

In a similar way the film's make-up artists go to great lengths to make
the principals resemble either Venetians or Mongols, but with disas-
trous results. Thus, Gary Cooper's one claim to being Venetian is provided by his wardrobe, which alternates between (in Venice) a tunic
over which is a fur-lined coat, or (Peking) a long tunic which gives way
to shirt over pants and a head scarf for the battle scenes. He looks fairly
foppish: to Cooper's subsequent dismay, his sartorial elegance in the
film set a new trend in women's clothing (Myers 131). Sigrid Gurie is a
pastiche of multiple layers of plastic-looking embalming fluid, clad in
a kimono and pearls, with her hair in a bun kept in place by vast quantities of ornamental jewellery. No amount of make-up can disguise
Alan Hale as the Mongol Kaidu: toying incessantly with his glued-on
sideburns/tails and beaming through his deliberately squinty eyes, he
resembles a displaced American Falstaff more than a Mongol bandit.
Finally, there is Lana Turner, who, although she has only a small role in
the film, was hurt by Goldwyn's attempts to make her an exotic Oriental and commented harshly on the process:

> I was a Eurasian handmaiden who had caught the eye of a warrior chief,
> played by Alan Hale. I wore a fancy, black oriental wig which had to be
> glued around my face with spirit gum. I didn't mind the wig so much ...
> but the costume made me feel undressed. And, worse yet, they shaved
> off my eyebrows and replaced them with false slanting black ones.
> (Myers 131)

All of the characters, therefore, resemble the other they seek to represent in no meaningful way.

Such a skewed view of alterity is based in the nature of narrative film itself, of which the adventure film is a leading proponent. As Laura Mulvey points out in her seminal essay 'Visual Pleasure and Narrative Cinema,' associated with such an 'illusionistic narrative film' as *The Adventures of Marco Polo*, there are three 'looks,' that of the camera, that of the audience, and that of the characters: 'The conventions of narrative film deny the first two and subordinate them to the third, the conscious aim being always to eliminate intrusive camera presence and prevent a distancing awareness in the audience' (25). Therefore, the looker in a narrative adventure film is not only the object of the visual work but also the privileged owner of the film. The looker is the dominant force and all other objects are inferior and are viewed from the looker's vantage point. Thus, the looker is typically, especially in Hollywood adventure films, a white, young, attractive heterosexual male. His opposite, a woman, is portrayed as a female sex object, and outsiders, those of ethnic or cultural diversity, are either portrayed by white actors or are assigned highly stereotypical roles. Thus, in *The Adventures of Marco Polo*, Marco is the virile, male hero. He dominates the action of the film and everything is seen through his eyes. He pursues and captures the heart of the Asian sex object figured as an exotic delight. He is the principal doer and his character sets him apart. Charming, shrewd, beguiling, and capable of superior powers of intrigue (cf. Basil Rathbone's line, 'We only want to make use of your remarkable gifts for intrigue'), Marco Polo wins over Kublai Khan, enamours the Princess Kukachin, outwits Kudai, and is victorious over Ahmed. He is, in a word, superior and his superior (read, imperial) gaze reduces all of the other film presences to secondary entities. Gary Cooper's Marco Polo is all-encompassing, a larger-than-life character who subsumes all others. Such a character may make for a good adventure film, but it radically skews the portrayal of alterity and is totally out of keeping with the Marco Polo of the *Travels*, where 'impersonality, that pronounced lack of interest which Marco has in telling us anything about himself, is one of the most obvious and remarkable characteristics of his Book' (Larner 64).

The treatment of alterity in *The Adventures of Marco Polo* has also been shaped by the historical and cultural sensibilities of the times. Historically, America and China were not on good terms for most of the early twentieth century. In the peace negotiations after the First World War, the Americans refused to support China, a war ally, concerning the return of Shangdong, which had been seized by the Japanese, with the result that China refused to sign the Treaty of Versailles in 1919. This event caused a huge outpouring of anti-American protests in China, especially in Beijing, where a massive student protest took place on 4 May 1919 (Haw, *Traveller's History,* 181; Fairbank and Goldman 267–8). This tenuous situation was exacerbated by political chaos in China during the 1920s and 1930s and by the fledgling Chinese republican government's inability to wrest control of the country from numerous local warlords (cf. Fairbank and Goldman 279 ff.; Roberts 214 ff.). America was then shocked by the formation of the Chinese Communist Party in 1921 and by the admission of communists in 1923 into Sun Yat-sen's Nationalist Party of China or Kuomintang, a move which helped it hang on to power (cf. Fairbank and Goldman 285; Roberts 219–20). Subsequent developments such as the rise of Mao Zedong in the 1920s and 1930s, the Long March of 1934, and the alliance in 1937 between the Kuomintang and the Chinese Communist Party in the face of Japanese aggression all made America wary of its far eastern neighbour (cf. Fairbank and Goldman 301 ff.; Roberts 219 ff.).

Culturally, early twentieth-century Americans tended to view 'Orientals' as outsiders, labourers who had originally come to America in the 1850s and who took menial jobs working as part of the gold rush or on the building of the Central Pacific railway (Chang 38 ff.). As American resentment grew over Chinese immigration and migrants' willingness to take on low-paying jobs in restaurant or laundry work, people of Chinese extraction were perceived as a threat embodying the so-called yellow peril. They were viewed as 'coolies,' low-life labourers defined by an exclusive society that was riddled with dark and foreboding Chinatowns, opium dens, loose women, and dangerous secret societies (Chang 204 ff.). It is no accident that the Chinese Exclusion Act, which excluded all Chinese labourers from immigrating to the United States, was passed in 1882 and was not repealed until 1943. At the same time, both historically and culturally, America was enamoured of the East: not necessarily as it really is, but as America imagined it to be. The East was thus envisioned as exotic and alluring, possessing treasures of unknown beauty: as Cooper's Polo exclaims, 'Well, I was told that if I travelled far over hot deserts and cold mountains, I would see what no man of my world has ever seen before.' The cinematic portrayal of alterity is the inevitable result of these polarities. Thus, the Great Khan, although magnificent in his surroundings and eminently wise, is also scheming and bellicose, his energies taken up with mounting a war against Japan. In addition, the country teems with warlord bandits and is ruled by an evil outsider, Ahmed; but it also has great beauty, personified by the exotic Princess Kukachin, and is rich in a tradition, exemplified by Chen Tsu, shaped by thousands of years of history and thought.

Goldwyn's *The Adventures of Marco Polo* was doomed from the start. The original director, John Cromwell, failed to please Goldwyn and withdrew after only a week (Berg 317). Goldwyn's friend William Wyler refused the job. John Ford agreed to direct a few shots, including the blizzard and the crossing of the Himalayas. Finally, Archie Mayo was brought in to direct (Berg 317–18). Unfortunately, Mayo does not seem to have grasped Sherwood's tongue-in-cheek humour, which involved twentieth-century dialogue being mouthed by thirteenth-century characters. The result is that the picture fell flat on its face, having neither a recognizable style nor a convincing cast. Some reviews, such as that of the *Illustrated London News*, were kind, declaring the film 'irresistible and splendid' (Dickens 154), but most were not, and the film failed to win critical and audience approval. Goldwyn knew it was a flop and passed out notices seeking audience feedback, describing the film as being in 'rough form' (Myers 132). Years later, Goldwyn admitted, 'The Marco Polo picture was the biggest flop I produced – yes, more than *Nana*' (Swindell 111). The film lost over $700,000.

Once the image of the adventurous Marco Polo was formed, it governed most of the subsequent Marco Polo films. The 1961 adventure film *Marco Polo* was an Italian production with the original title of *L'avventura di un italiano in Cina* (*An Italian's Adventure in China*). Directed by Hugo Fregonese and Piero Pierotti, it is a lacklustre version of the Polo tale in which much of the plot detail is identical to the 1938 movie. Marco Polo (Rory Calhoun) is a young adventurer who goes to China and battles with the emperor's evil servant (Robert Hundar) in order to win the hand of the princess Amurroy (Yoko Tani), with the added bonus that Marco Polo even gets to build a cannon. As Marco Polo, Venetian hero and ladies' man, Rory Calhoun, the veteran western actor (*River of No Return* [1954] and the television series *The Texan* [1959–60]), is even less convincing than Cooper. The movie shares with the earlier film its fanciful treatment of Marco Polo and the *Travels* and its stereotypical approach to the depiction of alterity. Above all, the films share a forced dichotomy between the West as good and the East as scheming and bad, a dichotomy fuelled historically by post-war developments in China and the onset of the Cold War. These events included the establishment in 1949 of the People's Republic of

China, a communist one-party state, the war in North Korea (1950–3) in which the Chinese fought with the north against the American and UN forces supporting the south, and Mao Zedong's repressive policies including the 'Hundred Flowers' campaign of 1957 and the 'Great Leap Forward' of 1958 (Roberts 254 ff.).

Moreover, the West was further estranged owing to the growing cooperation between China and Russia, which began with Mao's visit to Stalin in 1949 and which reached its apex in the period 1953–8 (cf. Roberts 256–62). The film's lavish sets, however, and its huge cast of extras proved useful. Riccardo Freda, director of the highly regarded *Maciste* strongman films, was brought in to fashion yet another sword-and-sandal muscleman flick entitled *Maciste alla corte del gran Khan* (*Maciste at the Court of the Great Khan* [1961]), which came to be regarded as one of the better films of the *Maciste* genre. The 1961 Marco Polo, by contrast, was not very successful, either critically or commercially, nor was its immediate French descendant *La fabuleuse aventure de Marco Polo* (*Marco the Magnificent*) of 1965, which was an all-star production directed by Denys de la Patellière, Raoul Lévy, and Noel Howard. Filmed on location in France, Italy, Yugoslavia, Egypt, and Afghanistan, the film stars Horst Buchholz as Polo, who is figured as an ambitious and adventuresome young voyager who, accompanied by his faithful servant Akerman (Orson Welles), ventures to China, where he aids (once again, through gunpowder) Mongol Emperor Kublai Khan (Anthony Quinn) in his fight against rebelling forces. The film was started in 1962 by the imaginative Christian-Jaque, who had ambitious plans to produce a movie on a grand scale with a finale featuring a giant chess game (hence the earlier title of *God's Chessboard*) starring Alain Delon, Dorothy Dandridge, Michel Simon, and Bernard Blier, but production plans went amok and the film was shelved until 1963 when it was entrusted to other directors. The film is most uneven. The cinematography of Vladimir Ivanov, Claude Renoir, and Armand Thirard produces absolutely beautiful external shots, but the casting is even more outrageous than the 1938 and 1961 films. Horst Buchholz is horribly miscast as the young Marco, Orson Welles looks decidedly out of place, and Anthony Quinn inhabits his usual jovial pan-eastern persona. Once again, the film is fanciful and even more stereotypical in its presentation of alterity than its predecessors (a German Horst Buchholz as an Italian, a Mexican-American Anthony Quinn as the Mongol Khan, and an Egyptian of Lebanese/Syrian descent, Omar Sharif, as 'The Desert Wind'). The net result is a laughable mini-epic.

The 1996 adventure film *Marco Polo: Haperek Ha'aharon* (*Marco Polo: The Missing Chapter*) is a full-length feature directed by Rafi Bukai, a young Israeli filmmaker who died young. The film opens promisingly, with shots of Rustichello (Peter Firth) in a Genoese prison, but it quickly deteriorates: there is a trade war between Venice and Genoa, and the Genoese are keen to have Rustichello obtain a confession from the Venetian Marco Polo (Shuli Rand) so that he can be declared a heretic by the Inquisition, causing the pope to issue a papal interdiction against Venice, thus giving Genoa control of the trade routes. Polo consents to dictate the final missing chapter of his travels to Rustichello. The plot then focuses on this missing chapter, which involves a complicated story about Marco's return from China to the Middle East, his numerous marital problems with his oversexed wife Tamara (Avitel Dicker), her involvement with an Arab Bedouin, and a bizarre subplot of the search and retrieval by two crusaders of the casket of Jesus from the Church of the Holy Sepulchre. At the film's end, just as the declared heretics Marco and Rustichello are about to be burned alive, they are freed by the authority of the pope. In a closing scene, the Doge of Venice, standing with Marco on a high cliff, hurls down the manuscript of the missing chapter and says, 'The last chapter is too much for me. It was never written.' Would that the same sentiment had been applied to this inane piece of movie-making. Finally, there is the 1998 adventure flick *The Incredible Adventures of Marco Polo*, directed by George Erschbamer. In it, Marco Polo (*The Young and the Restless*'s Don Diamont) is sent by his uncle to find his missing father, and, along the way, makes amazing discoveries, meets exotic characters, and experiences non-stop excitement. The fact that there is a supporting character named Beelzebub (Jack Palance), son of the devil and ruler of Romania, gives some idea of how far-fetched the movie is.

Little better are the fantasy/musical genre films. All of these, which make Marco an adventurer facing danger in the East, are Marco Polo films in name only. Thus, the fantasy film *Marco Polo Versus the Red Dragon* (1972), directed by Eric Porter, is an extremely good piece of film animation (Australian), but bears little resemblance to Polo or his *Travels*. The hero, Marco, is a distant descendant of the thirteenth-century explorer who travels to Xanadu bearing one half of the Golden Medallion of Friendship passed down by his ancestors. He must slay the Red Dragon, which has enslaved the country, and rescue the princess, both of which tasks he accomplishes with the assistance of fantastic friends such as Guru and the Delicate Dragon. A remake of this film, *Marco Polo: Return to Xanadu* (2001), directed by Ron Merk, was nominated for a Best Animated Feature Oscar, but was critically panned, being deemed family entertainment at its worst. It has basically the same plot as the first and recycles animation from that film, blending into it new sequences and songs. Thus, young Marco journeys to Xanadu in order to reunite the kingdom. Along the way, he encounters many dangerous traps set by the evil sorcerer Foo-Ling. Once again, however, Marco has a special medallion and enough support from his friends to overcome his evil nemesis. The kung fu film, *Ma Ko Po Lo* (1975), directed by Cheh Chang, was a box-office smash, grossing more than HK 1,000,000. Action sequences aside, however, it is a dreadful and boring film. The plot concerns Marco Polo (Richard Harris), who travels to Cathay, meets with Kublai Khan, and is made governor of Yangchow. After two thugs attack the Khan, Marco must hunt them down, tracing them eventually to Tien Tao Mansion, where an insidious group of conspirators is practising their kung fu techniques and where the final fight sequences are choreographed in an awesome manner. Finally, in the musical *Marco* (1972), directed by Seymour Robbie, we have a Marco Polo portrayed by Desi Arnaz and a Great Khan portrayed by Zero Mostel, in a Japanese environment, in a Xanadu that never was. Although the sets are extravagant and the music often funny and upbeat, the film is pedestrian and soon gets bogged down in its own escapism.

Meriting separate brief discussion is a piece of pornography of the hardcore genre, *Marco Polo: La storia mai raccontata* (*Marco Polo: The Story Never Told* [1995]), directed by Joe D'Amato (Aristide Massaccesi), the quintessential sexploitation filmmaker, sometimes known as 'Italy's worst film director.' The film is an over-the-top romp about a lustful Marco Polo who likes to explore more than land on his numerous travels. D'Amato, having started in gore with films such as *Buio Omega* (*Beyond the Darkness* or *Blue Holocaust* [1979]), turned more and more in the 1980s and 1990s to hardcore sex films, which all have a formulaic structure: exotic locations, little plot, acting reduced to costume wearing (or, more often than not, no costume wearing), and lots of sex. His *Marco Polo: La storia mai raccontata* is typical. Marco (Rocco Siffredi) is presented as a clever young man who travels to China, beds the emperor's wife, and completes the Great Wall of China. In all of these endeavours he is manly, a quality epitomized by his exceptional sexual prowess. The emperor, on the other hand, is impotent and is only restored to virility by an elixir provided by Marco Polo. This film, therefore, presents a more extreme form of the mythologically adventurous Polo and pits East against West in a battle of epic sexual proportions. Polo is a hero possessed of a virility unknown in the East. He can have any woman he wants, and so he does. The racism and sexism apparent in the adventure genre come to the surface and are explicitly acknowledged as western assets. *Marco Polo: La storia mai raccontata* was very popular and did well at the box office, but it is a horrible film, trading on the worst stereotypical images, although this time of a decidedly sexual nature.

On a far different level is Giuliano Montaldo's 1982 television miniseries *Marco Polo*. The film was initiated by the Chinese government, which made inquiries through Italy's ambassador if the Italian government would be interested in making a film version of the *Travels* which would have access rights to sites not previously viewed (Patterson 470). This was therefore the first film produced with Chinese backing since the founding of the People's Republic in 1949. The Italian government immediately began negotiation with China and brought in RAI (Radio Audizioni Italiane), the Italian public service broadcaster.[3]

The first order of business was the choice of producer and director. RAI entrusted the project to executive producer Franco Cristaldi (along with Vincenzo Labella and Giovanni Bertolucci), one of the most successful, if not the most successful, of the post-war producers in the Italian cinema (cf. Morandini 595). Over the years, many Cristaldi productions, such as Monicelli's *I soliti ignoti* (1958), Germi's *Divorzio all'italiana* (1961), and Fellini's *Amarcord* (1973), had garnered a slew of international film awards, and Cristaldi, well respected for his intelligence and taste, had worked with leading Italian directors such as the three above, as well as Rosi, Bellocchio, Pontecorvo, Petri, and Tornatore. He had also branched into television and had just completed work on the popular mini-series *Jesus of Nazareth*. Giuliano Montaldo was brought in as director, albeit Genoese (for the irony, see Crespi 124). Montaldo was a veteran who had begun as an actor in Carlo Lizzani's *Achtung! Banditi!* (1950), but had turned to direction in the 1960s. He made a succession of films including *Una bella grinta* (1965), which was awarded the special jury prize at Berlin, and achieved international recognition for his film trilogy on power (*Gott mit uns* [1969], *Sacco e Vanzetti* [1971], *Giordano Bruno* [1973]). Montaldo quickly assembled a talented film team, including himself, David Butler, and Vincenzo Labella (writing), Pasqualino De Santis (cinematography), Ennio Morricone (music), John Martinelli (editing), Bruno Cesari (set design), and Enrico Sabbatini (costume design). He also brought together an international cast consisting of both eastern and western stars. The film took three years to make. A scouting trip by Montaldo and Labella was undertaken in 1979 and this was followed by a full year of pre-production in Rome plus the actual shooting (consisting of more than a million and a half feet by De Santis) which took place in Italy, Morocco, and China. The result was one of the costliest budgets in television history, some thirteen billion lire (Bondanella 383), and a ten-hour television mini-series which is one of the most sumptuous and opulent Marco Polo films, including incredible on-site sets which had never been seen before and some four thousand lavish costumes, which were designed for their authenticity.

The film begins with the shot of a Venetian galley in 1298. Jump cuts quickly follow. Above deck, a sombre and reflective Marco Polo (Ken Marshall) is in charge. Below deck, a rambling crew member regales his mates with tall tales. Quickly, the ship is set upon by a Genoese boat and during the ensuing battle the cast credits begin to roll. Just as quickly, we are transported to a Genoese prison where Dominican brothers, Damian (Patrick Mower) and Philip (John Dicks), summarily visit Marco Polo and then rush to the cell of Rustichello (David Warner), whose cell mate is the above teller of tall tales. Brandishing some disorganized papers, Damian throws them on a table and shouts: 'We want you to explain what you have written down on these pages, seductive tales that you and the Venetian Marco Polo have been fabricating during the eight months you have spent in this cell.' Stressing the gravity of the situation, he pointedly asks Rustichello 'What in these tales is the Venetian's fantasy and what is your own contribution?' The brothers wish to get at the truth and, in a derogatory manner, Philip dismisses Rustichello as 'a Pisan and a storyteller,' to which the latter snaps 'Writing is my trade.' The brothers are not to be deterred, for the 'notes' contain tales that could corrupt the young and innocent. Since deciphering the pages seems out of the question, they demand that Rustichello tell them what he knows. Rustichello, in flashback mode, now recounts: 'It all began in the year of our Lord, 1254, when Marco Polo was born in Venice.'

The story line unfolds in four parts (each part is preceded by a scene of Rustichello in prison as he continues the narration). The first part deals with events prior to Marco's leaving Venice in 1271. Through Rustichello's narration, we are transported via some magnificent shots of the harbour of Venice to Marco as a boy (Alexander Picolo). His father Niccolò and his uncle Matteo have left some time in the past and are still away. Marco's mother (Anne Bancroft) is ill (she dies shortly afterwards in a tearful farewell with her young son) and he comes under the care of his aunt Flora (Sada Thomson) and uncle Zane (Riccardo Cucciolla). Marco spends his time at the harbour, where he listens to the tales of wandering seafarers and anxiously hopes to hear of his father. Family tensions are exposed as Flora reveals that she is no admirer of the boy's adventurous father, while the repressively enclosed atmosphere of the in-laws' house is established by means of a film technique that treats Marco's surroundings as an aquarium.

Fast forward several years (1269) to Marco as a young adult. Although he works for his uncle in the cloth trade, he still dreams of travel. He constantly reminds his in-laws that there is much more to the world than Venice, an attitude that gets him into further trouble, causing the young Marco to turn to an independent and pretty young friend, Caterina (Georgia Stowe), to whom he confides his dreams. There follows an amorous plot as Marco tries to see her, is brought before the authorities, then escapes with Caterina on a home-built boat only to end in disaster. Returning home, he is astounded to find that his father Niccolò (Denholm Elliott) and uncle Matteo (Tony Vogel) have returned. Joyfully, son welcomes father and listens to his tales about his journey, the 'years' it took to get there and back, and the wondrous sites he has seen, especially the vastness of China, the extraordinary realm of the Great Khan, and its immeasurable riches.

Eventually, in 1271, the Polo brothers appear before the Doge of Venice (John Gielgud) and the assembled senate, surrender the *paiza* or gold tablet the Great Khan had given them, and tell him of their mission: to return to the Khan with one hundred doctors of the Church. The Patriarch of Aquileia (John Houseman) opposes the idea, ruling out any contact with 'barbarians' and 'Mongols ... a race of blood-thirsty savages.' He is reluctant to enter into arrangement with 'the enemy of the one true God' and speaks only of conversion or conquest. The Doge, however, is more sympathetic to the possibility of a peace with the Khan and mindful of the importance of mercantile interests. He secretly encourages the Polos to continue on their mission, informing them that the election of a new pope is stalled interminably: 'Go now. Go with Venice and St Mark.'

In the second part, the Polo brothers begin their preparations and secure a crew whose leader is Jacopo (F. Murray Abraham). Niccolò is reluctant to take Marco with him, but after consistent lobbying by the young man, coupled with the rather troubling disclosure of the indelicate tryst between Marco and Catarina, agrees to take the boy with him. Marco takes his leave of Catarina, realizing that his destiny is fixed. There follows the voyage through the Middle East. Against a mist-filled morning, the ship plies the waters on its way to Acre, where the Polos arrange an audience with the prominent ecclesiastic Archdeacon Teobaldo Visconti (magisterially portrayed by Burt Lancaster). He is most liberal, open to the possibility of contact with the Great Khan and understanding of other people and their ways. He is progressive and has a deep appreciation of the prevailing attitude of fear and ignorance: 'We should clear roads, build bridges, open doors.' The archdeacon condemns the myopia of the patriarch and, indeed, the senate of Venice for not furthering the Polos' mission and decries the dilatory process for electing the new pope. He arranges safe passage for the Polos to Jerusalem, including Marco, whose father had wanted to leave him in Acre, but who had relented in this decision thanks to Teobaldo.

En route to Jerusalem they come upon a tribe of Muslim Bedouins filmed beautifully against the desert wild. Marco is fascinated, especially by the arrival of some crusaders whom he describes as 'splendid.' His fascination quickly turns to disbelief and revulsion when the crusaders murder the tribespeople and burn their simple dwellings. Extreme close-ups of the faces of women and children emphasize the horrors of war. Later, in an olive grove outside of Jerusalem, Marco is haunted by the slaughter. As soon as the Polos visit the Church of the Holy Sepulchre to obtain some holy oil, they are summoned back to Acre where they meet with Pope Gregory X, the former Teobaldo Visconti, who names them his ambassadors and commissions them with the letter, the oil, and the first apostolic visitors, brothers Nicholas (Tony Lo Bianco) and William (Hal Buckley).

The Polo party (Niccolò, Matteo, Marco, the two brothers, and three crew members) crosses the Armenian and Persian deserts, where they suffer from lack of water, and Marco is shown taking notes on the various things he witnesses, including a second scene of the carnage of war. Warring 'Saracens' overrun the party, kill Marco's friend Giulio (Bruno Zanin), and take them to the Saracen camp at Tabriz, where they are imprisoned. Brought before a Christian-turned-Muslim leader, Ali Ben Yousuf (*Deadwood*'s Ian McShane), they are freed after they are given a lecture by Ali on understanding and the primacy of Allah, a lecture which has a deep impact on Marco. The Dominican brothers desert the party and the others head for Hormuz on the Persian Gulf, which they reach in the autumn of 1272. Barred from travelling at sea by the outbreak of plague (which Marco contracts but survives), the party travels north up the Oxus to Badakhshan, which is shot mainly through the myriad faces of its inhabitants, largely Tajik peoples. From here they cross the Pamirs in scenes which are breathtaking in terms of raw beauty, serenity, and harsh reality. In the Pamirs, an avalanche overtakes the party and Marco, upon waking, sees a levitating lama and finds himself in a Tibetan lamasery being taken care of by a young Tibetan novice (Jesse Dizon) on Mount Muztagata (winter 1273). The novice gives Marco a primer on Buddhism and stresses that his destiny has just begun. The party, reunited, then skirts the southern edge of the Takla Makan desert to Lop Nur, crosses the Gobi Desert, and continues on to Gansu in northern China (spring 1275). Falling in with a group of Mongols, the party is treated to local food, drink, and customs, such as dances, horsemanship, courting practices, and wrestling (some comic relief is provided by a slightly tipsy Marco and his wrestling antics), and eventually meets Caidu Khan (Shaokang Yu), the nephew of Kublai. Through him we see that there are tensions in the Mongol kingdom, as when he tells Marco directly that 'Caidu would never accept his orders, never.' From here the party reaches Shang-Du (summer 1275) and the summer court of Kublai Khan.

The third part focuses on Marco in China. Quickly, Marco meets the Great Khan (Ruocheng Ying, resembling the general description provided by the *Travels* [121–2]) who responds to his 'active mind' and who has him report up-to-date information to Phags-pa (James Hong), a Tibetan lama and the keeper of records. The Khan even relaxes etiquette for him, allowing Marco to stand or sit in the Great Khan's presence. Marco also wins favour with the Empress Chabi (Beulah Quo), who is grateful for the oil from the Holy Sepulchre and who marvels at Marco's ability to tell stories. Most importantly, he forms a close friendship with Prince Chinkin (Junichi Ishida), the Khan's eldest and heir apparent, a friendship that draws the mounting enmity of Phags-pa. On a hunting outing, Marco witnesses Chinkin having an epileptic seizure and, later, confronted by the Khan over what he has seen, instructs him on the benign nature of the 'falling sickness,' correcting his interpretation of it as 'the plague' and 'a weakness' and telling him 'many people have suffered from it, famous men, Alexander the Great, Julius Caesar, the noblest of Romans. It's an affliction, it didn't destroy them, it didn't affect anything else in their lives.' For this insight the

Great Khan rewards Marco with a position of authority in his court, a position which further draws the jealousy of Phags-pa.

The court then returns to Khanbaliq. En route, Marco and Chinkin visit the Great Wall. The regent Achmet (Leonard Nimoy) welcomes the Khan and tells him that his armies have been victorious in the south, and 'have defeated the last resistance of the Sung.' Accordingly, Achmet tells the Khan that his empire is now 'one ... the greatest empire under the sun.' The Khan enters The Forbidden City and there, enthroned in high splendour, receives General Bayan (Lao Li), the leader of his armies, to whom he entrusts the throne of the Sung. Marco is introduced to Achmet, who offers his friendship, but appears highly suspicious.

The rest of the third part is taken up with the tensions, factions, and conflicting opinions over a possible campaign against Japan. Both the empress and Chinkin discuss the failure of past campaigns and the rumours surrounding the present one. Outside the palace with Chinkin, Marco visits an astronomical observatory where he is given a brooding prophecy that is left unexplained. Two conferences, involving the Khan's relatives (including Kaidu and Nayan [Erkang Zhao]) and the King of Korea, surround a visit to a Japanese potter. In the first, the King of Korea proposes a naval invasion of Japan followed by a ground offensive. The Khan's in-laws disagree. Achmet advises war for the great profit of gold, 'more gold than any other kingdom has known,' while Phags-pa says that 'perhaps the last word should be left to the stars.' But the last word is the Great Khan's, for he explains that his envoys have been sent to demand submission and they must wait for their return. Marco then visits a blind Japanese potter, Saiamon (Tetsuro Tamba), and inquires about Japan. The potter explains that while his country is divided, in the face of a common enemy, Japan turns into a fist, 'united and strong': 'No foreigner will ever dominate our country. The only domination we accept is from our own lord ... to protect our land. Every man is ready to sacrifice everything, even the sight of the glorious sun.' He also interprets the ambiguous prophecy as meaning certain death for the Khan's armies and encourages Marco to go to the Khan and make reason prevail. Subsequently, the second conference opens with the Khan's revelation that his envoys have been beheaded. While he is keen on war, his in-laws again advise restraint; even Chinkin asks his father to listen. Marco attempts to explain the prophecy, but the Khan cuts him short. He has made up his mind, and dismisses 'the quibbling and the caution' of his advisers as being simply 'fear and cowardice.' He therefore proposes war. Marco, because of his outspokenness and the suspicious jealousy of Phags-pa, is sent by Achmet on a mission with Matteo to Yanzhou in the south in order to undertake a tax census.

The fourth part focuses on the revolt of Nayan and Kaidu against the Great Khan (*Travels* 114–19), the departure of the Polos from China, and (in a closing film coda) the release of Marco from prison. The revolt is situated within a subplot at the centre of which is Marco. In the south, Marco encounters the actor Yang-Zhu (Soon-Tek Oh) and the poet Yang Ku (Tang Bowen). Through them he becomes aware of the iniquity of the tax system for the conquered Chinese, is introduced to The Immortal (Tad Horino), a reclusive monk who provides a primer on Daoism, including its development as a form of hygiene, and develops a relationship with Monica (Kathryn Dowling), Yang Ku's adopted Caucasian daughter. Yang-Zhu's sweetheart, Mai Li (Agnes Chan), is kidnapped by soldiers and Marco returns to Khanbaliq to denounce the corruption of the south and to plead with Achmet for the safe return of Mai Li. Meanwhile, the Great Khan is grieved to learn that his invading armies against Japan have been horribly ravaged by a typhoon, a kamikaze, which has wreaked havoc and destruction on his ships and soldiers. Achmet is no sooner seen by Marco than he is slain by Yang-Zhu after having his way with Mai Li. The Great Khan, furious over the corruption of his ministers and the assassination of Achmet, orders all conspirators to be put to death or driven into exile. Among the latter is Monica. Then the Great Khan turns his attention to the revolt of Nayan and Kaidu. He refuses to listen to Marco's call for mercy and understanding. Instead, he leads a vast army against the camp of Nayan before Nayan can join forces with Kaidu. Incredibly large forces battle it out on the plains of Mongolia so as to do full justice to the *Travels*' account (117): 'Enough that this was the most hazardous fight and the most fiercely contested that ever was seen.' Nayan and his forces are defeated, Nayan is executed, and the Khan returns home. Here he reluctantly agrees to let the Polos return to Venice (1292), accompanying the Princess Kukachin, who is betrothed to the Ilkhan Arghun. In a film coda Marco and Rustichello are released from prison in Genoa in 1299 and Marco returns to Venice where, a voice-over informs us, he remained until his death in 1324.

It is abundantly clear that this film is a serious attempt at recreating the words and world of Marco Polo. Both at its beginning and at select moments, the film establishes that the *Travels* is a privileged intertext by focusing on three pivotal issues: the primacy of the text, its joint authorship, and its formative status within the culture of the times. The primacy of the text is apparent from the opening of the film. When Brother Damian visits Rustichello in his prison cell, he throws some disorganized papers on a table. In almost all of the flashback scenes which follow, the papers are present, and many times they are used to emphasize a point of contention, as when Rustichello holds a page up to the camera and mouths the word 'Badakhshan' to reinforce his description of the Polos' voyage to China. It is also clear that these papers have been produced from Marco's memory and his own notes. Rustichello explicitly says that he produced these papers from Marco's memory of events and places: 'It all happened so fast. I found Marco Polo blessed with such a prodigious memory and such a vast quantity of tales I couldn't resist the temptation to write them down.' Moreover, Marco is filmed throughout as taking copious notes, sometimes in the field, sometimes in his study, so much so that Chinkin jokes that Marco has seemingly become a scholar and should be assigned to the Archives. And the thread of 'notes' is carefully woven into the prison flashbacks, Rustichello at one point pleading for the return of Marco's notes so that he may produce more accurate work. In short, the film makes clear that memory and notes produced the *Travels*, and that the *Travels* qua text is what is most important. It is also a nice cinematic touch that the text is presented as a series of *disiuncta membra* or scattered papers, thereby foreshadowing the complicated issues of textual transmission which have been front and centre in much Marco Polo research.

Also given prominence is the joint authorship of the text: Marco Polo and Rustichello are the authors of the *Travels*, Marco providing the raw material of his travels and Rustichello shaping it into an adventurous whole. Marco insists to the Dominicans that 'he recorded only what he saw without adding or taking anything away,' while Rustichello keeps Marco's contribution before us by reminding his listeners that the *Travels* contain Marco's account of everything he saw during his travels: 'Marco Polo says it's all true and that he can prove it if only he had his notes.' At the same time, Rustichello also makes it clear that he is not a traveller, but a writer ('Writing is my trade ... I am very widely read') of 'stories ... ventures, romances, comedies, tragedies.' In the film's coda, Rustichello admits his dramatic flair and begs Marco's forgiveness 'for a few inventions, some background of colour my pen allowed itself to scribble. You will understand when

you read what I've written. Don't hate me for it.' He also acknowledges that Marco's is the lion's share of the work - '*The Book of Wonders*
is truly yours' – to which Marco replies 'Ours.' The film thus
establishes that, although the *Travels* was shaped by diverse hands,
with different stylistic registers, the *Travels* is nevertheless a single
book that was produced by a joint undertaking of Marco Polo and
Rustichello while they were prisoners at Genoa (cf. *Travels* 33–4). This
dual authorship, once established, is then developed cleverly to
account for certain textual anomalies, such as the introduction of fantastical elements or the presence of lacunae. Marco repeatedly dis-
avows knowledge of any fantastic elements, ascribing everything to
what he witnessed as fact. Rustichello, on the other hand, repeatedly
lets slip that he may have invented certain details of fancy, confessing
that 'he may have written them by mistake' or questioning their inclusion because 'they are not proper.' Similarly with the lacunae that
have caused some to deny that Marco ever went to China, such as the
Great Wall, fishing with cormorants, printing, acupuncture, and tea
houses. All of these are actually shown being witnessed by Marco
Polo in the course of the film. Why then are they not mentioned in the
Travels? In a pivotal scene, Rustichello provides the answer. He says
that he suppressed reference to the Great Wall because he thought that
it was too fanciful, a thought that could easily be applied to other fanciful sights. Although such an explanation is not as convincing as others, such as the possibility that Marco was simply indifferent to the
customs of the conquered Chinese (cf. Larner 59), it still cleverly uses
joint authorship to account for a number of textual problems.

The film also makes the *Travels* a formative text for its times, insert-
ing the *Travels* into the religious ferment of the period and showcasing
its broad human appeal. Against the backdrop of the crusades of the
thirteenth century and the establishment of the Inquisition in 1231, the
Travels is presented as a potentially dangerous book. When the Dominican brothers visit Rustichello in prison at the film's beginning, they
make it clear that they are scandalized by the content of the papers that
they have seen, since they contain tales that 'could pervert the mind of
the reader ... for they contain pages of pagan places, sinful practices
that could easily lead to the corruption of the young and innocent.'
And in the film's coda, prior to the final decision of the Inquisitorial
Office, the charges against the accounts of the *Travels* are set out in
detail: they contain descriptions of pagan peoples, pagan places, pagan
practices, pagan religions, pagan astronomy. The flashbacks to prison

therefore constantly remind us that the *Travels* is a dangerous text and that the text's milieu is a battleground between religion, superstition, and ignorance on the one hand, and secularism, reason, and tolerance on the other. Not only Marco and his work are portrayed as suspicious, but so is anyone who has contact with the 'infidel.' When, for example, Niccolò and Matteo appear before the Venetian senate to plead for approval for another journey to China, they are given short shrift by the Patriarch of Aquileia, who decries contact with 'the enemy of the one true God' and rules out any contact with 'barbarians' and 'Mongols … a race of blood-thirsty savages.' Against such ignorance Marco and his *Travels* are positioned within the film as voices of reason, of humanity. In the film's coda, Rustichello sings the praises of his association with Marco and his memories which have brought him 'a new faith, a new faith in man, a creature born to overcome frontiers and prejudice. He made me see that violence, hatred, suspicion are mere shadows in the light of reason's sun. Marco Polo made me free. From his long journeys across lands known and unknown he returned the champion of a new mankind.' It is this humanity of the text which, at least in part, accounts for its broad popular appeal and which provides a *modus operandi* for the filmic encounter of self and other.

Given the primacy of the *Travels* in the film, it is no surprise that the film follows the text very closely, not only historically and geographically but also in its portrayal of Marco Polo and of the world he encountered in China. Historically, the film begins accurately with Niccolò and Matteo away and Marco as a boy in Venice. They return in 1269, make preparatory arrangements, and begin travel to China in 1271, taking the seventeen-year-old Marco with them. They consult with Teobaldi Visconti in Acre in 1272 and, after he becomes Pope Gregory X, are commissioned by him with letters and the oil from the Church of the Holy Sepulchre to travel with two Dominicans to the Great Khan. After sundry experiences and a rather circuitous journey, they reach China in 1275. After accomplishing various important missions, Marco returns with his father and uncle from China in 1292 and reaches Venice in 1295. He then takes part in the naval battle between Venice and Genoa, is imprisoned in 1298, and released shortly afterwards in 1299. All of these film details accord generally with the description of the travel of Marco and his relatives in the *Travels* (cf. 33 ff.; for dates cf. Larner 39–44) and all of the film dates are well researched and carefully presented to the audience as a series of ongoing intertitles before decisive events (i.e., 'Shang-Du, summer 1275,' 'Khanbalic, 1292').

Geographically, we do not know exactly from the *Travels* what route the Polos followed, but the rough one given in the film (from Acre through Persia to Hormuz, north through Persia to the Oxus River, up the Oxus to the Pamirs, across the mountains, around the southern edge of the Takla Makan Desert to Lop Nur, and across the Gobi Desert to China) closely follows Marco's westward geographical account of lands en route to Cathay (*Travels* 46ff.). Moreover, geography, the essential characteristic of the *Travels*, is front and centre throughout the film, although it is limited, making no mention of Burma (*Travels* 188–9), India (*Travels* 260–94), Ceylon (*Travels* 258–9; 281–4), etc. Since this film was shot on location and not in a studio, the audience gets a close-up view of physical geography, the terrain and its beauty and difficulties. This is especially true of the shots (even if Morocco fills in for Persia) of desert wilderness (*Travels* 68–70), of the flora and fauna of the mountainous terrain of Badakhshan (*Travels* 76–9), of the plains-dwelling Tartars (*Travels* 97 ff.), and, especially, of the cities and places of the Great Khan's domain (*Travels* 108 ff.). In short, this film version is a welcome relief from the historical and geographical distortions and oversights of its 1938 counterpart.

The film's depiction of Marco Polo is consistent with what little we know of him from the *Travels*: he is from Venice and his relatives are Venetian merchants. He does not see his father until he is fifteen years old (*Travels* 37) and sets off to China with his father and uncle in 1271 (*Travels* 38). There, he meets the Great Khan, who prizes his 'alert mind,' his ability to remember details, that is, the 'novelties and curiosities' of a particular place (*Travels* 41): for, as Marco maintains in the film, 'I remember what interests me.' And the film makes clear that what is of interest is exceedingly broad: customs, beliefs, practices, crops, teaching, care for the old, asbestos, wild sheep in the Pamir mountains, mining, weaving. In one telling scene, Marco and the Great Khan become much closer as Marco relates that he observes 'what makes a people strong or weak, determined or uncertain. I make the notes to help me, especially the principal products of a district, how many days it took to cross it, or the distance between towns ... [E]very place, every city sends out signals to your eyes, the way the paths and streets are traced, the alignment of the trees, the pattern of the furrows in the fields.' The Khan responds warmly to Marco's ability to remember detailed information and Marco goes on to serve the Khan on various missions for nearly two decades:

What need to make a long story of it? You may take it for a fact that Messer Marco stayed with the Great Khan fully seventeen years; and in all this time he never ceased to travel on special missions. For the Great Khan, seeing that Messer Marco brought him such news from every country and conducted so successfully all of the business on which he was sent, used to entrust him with all the most interesting and distant missions. He continued to conduct his business with great success and to bring back word of many novelties and curiosities. And the Great Khan was so well satisfied with his conduct of affairs that he held him in high esteem and showed him such favor and kept him so near his own person that the other lords were moved to envy. (*Travels* 41)

Both in film and text, therefore, Marco is not an adventurer, not an amorous westerner who is an expert on kissing. He is, first and foremost, a recorder of information, most of it of a geographical/topographical/anthropological nature, and a civil servant in the Khan's administration. Although the previously quoted passage from the *Travels* probably exaggerates the importance of Marco in the service of the Khan (as does the non-factual assertion of the *Travels* [206] that Marco Polo 'governed the city of Yanzhou for three years,' as well as the claim that the surrender of Siang-yang-fu was due to the Polos' construction of siege weapons called mangonels [*Travels* 208]), the film follows the *Travels* in depicting Marco as highly regarded by the Khan (cf. Achmet's complimentary reference to Marco's 'talents for observation that the Khan so highly values') and shows him being assigned missions such as a trip to Yanzhou in order to draw up a tax census, and one to Nayan to avoid an all-out clash, missions which arouse the envy of lords such as Phags-pa. These missions, of course, are perfectly consistent with the Khan's policy of using foreigners in his administration, an administration in which 2.1 per cent of the foreign population held the most important positions (Lovell 176).

Outside of his civic duties, Marco throughout the film is portrayed as an inveterate traveller, a characteristic that must have been an intimate part of his personality. In the shots of his youth he is filmed as a boy who dreams of exotic and distant lands and who cautions his relatives against the vice of being too smug: 'everybody here thinks that all this, the lagoon, the square, is all that's worth knowing, but there's a whole world out there, beyond the lagoon, vast as the sky.' He confides his love of travel to Caterina and, when he is reunited with his father and creates an opportunity for himself to travel to China, he relishes the experience. Along the way, the desire for travel does not abate. Even in China, Marco longs to see more. He tells Chinkin that the nighttime sound of horses 'makes me think about travel … I almost smell the dust in the road.' He wants to experience the world, and expresses some small regret over the static nature of Khanbaliq, a city where 'everything is so quiet, so calm, so imperial.' Achmet tells Marco that the mission to the south should be welcome to him, for 'you have not tried to hide your impatience to travel again.' In short, then, Marco is a traveller, for whom travel is inextricably bound with destiny. The young Buddhist monk who nurses Marco back to health after the avalanche pointedly says to Marco: 'I understand you, Marco. Your destiny is to travel. You will go from land to land with your mind and body.'

The film accordingly portrays Marco as a traveller, a recorder, and a civil servant in the service of the Mongol Great Khan. Since these are the aspects of Marco's character most germane to his sojourn in China, and since the *Travels* is almost totally reticent about details of Marco's life before, during, and after his stay in China, the director Giuliano Montaldo may be allowed some leeway in adding some dramatic touches to flesh out a televisual character (whose character in the *Travels* is marked by 'stoic silence' and 'impersonality' [Larner 183]) and to fashion some creative details to propel his narrative epic for the small screen. This he does most tastefully. The boyhood and adolescence in Venice includes nothing intrinsically illogical, and is notable for the introduction of Marco's mother. The theme of family tensions is kept deliberately low-keyed, even if the filming technique foregrounds claustrophobia. True, the romance with Caterina is fanciful, but the details are kept to a bare minimum and avoid overly romantic undertones. Most importantly, Caterina is portrayed as an independent woman who can stand her own ground against Marco and who understands, when he does not, that his life is destined to be different. The travel to China accords with the *Travels* and the only jarring scenes seem to be the rather strained defence of Islam by Ali Ben Youssuf and the levitating lama witnessed by Marco during his convalescence after the avalanche. The character depiction of Marco in China follows the *Travels* in its main details, and incidental details such as Marco's friendship with the Empress Chabi and with Prince Chinkin, his loose association with Achmet, his eventual friendship with Phags-pa, his missions, his extraneous involvement in the plot of Yang-Zhu, and his being present at the councils of the Great Khan are not totally improbable. The only false notes are the romance between Marco and Monica and certain details of the friendship with Phags-pa. It is a bit of a strain to introduce a Caucasian woman who is the adopted daughter of a Chinese poet and to have her meet by chance the Venetian traveller. The nagging question persists: why not a Chinese actress as a love-interest, as abhorrent a thought as that was, apparently, to the Chinese co-sponsors of the film? It further strains credulity that her father's name is 'millione.' Just as important is the manner of her exit, for Monica, though horribly wronged, is exiled with Marco's agreement for being involved in a plot of which she has no apparent knowledge. The film also depicts Marco as an object of jealousy, at first, and, much later, as a friend to Phags-pa. This presents some chronological difficulties, as the lama Phags-pa died in Tibet in 1280 (Rossabi 221; Man 151) after a life of distinguished service to the Khan, and most of his accomplishments, including the Buddhist-Daoist debates and the famous Phags-pa script, took place before Marco's arrival in China (Rossabi 41–2; 155–60). The scene, therefore, in which Phags-pa takes his leave of Marco and announces his plan to help the Polos in their desire to leave China, clearly occurring long after Marco's mission to the south which the film places in 1280 and toward the end of Marco's stay – say somewhere in 1292 – cannot have taken place.

Just as noteworthy as its depiction of Marco's character is the cinematic vision of the world which Marco experienced, a world demarcated by the splendours of the court of Kublai Khan (*Travels* 113 ff.) and his limitless power. Marco is shown as awe-struck at the 'stately pleasure-dome' and the splendours of the imperial summer court at Shang-Du (cf. *Travels* 108–9), even if the summer palace of Emperor Qian Long substitutes for the palace of Shang-Du, which is now little more than an eroded mound. Film shots include ornate palaces with magnificent chambers, intricate ritual and etiquette, lavish outdoor banquets (shot against the beauty of the evening sky), entertainments, especially fantastic magicians, acrobatic sword dances and spectacular firework displays, parks, groves, hunting parties, numerous retainers, and luxuries, such as baths in hot water prepared by burning coal. Although many of these shots are culled from details applied in the *Travels* to palace locales other than Shang-Du, their juxtaposition in the filming of Shang-Du displays an attentive reading of the text and reinforces the munificence of the Great Khan. Then follows the cinematic portrayal of the court at Khanbaliq. The Khan's majesty is reinforced by the opening magnificent procession into the city. It consists of thousands of extras forming long lines of family members, horsemen, retainers, guards, and advisers, and its apex is a litter carrying the Great Khan, borne by sixty-four servants. The Khan then enters the great palace (*Travels* 124 ff.) – filmed within The Forbidden City, a significant anachronism – with its vast hall, its high roof, its endless decorated chambers (cf. *Travels* 125). Here the Khan holds court, and the film focuses repeatedly on the ornate councils including the barons, ambassadors, military advisers, and clerks (*Travels* 149–50). In this place, the Khan's word is absolute: he decides to send his armies to the south, he decides on war with Japan, he decides to mount a campaign against Nayan, he decides the life or death fate of his generals and his subjects. In short, his authority is supreme. On those few occasions when the Khan leaves the confines of his palaces, his power and magnificence remain also cinematically front and centre. So, when he takes to the field at the head of his army, as he does against Nayan, he is conveyed in a golden mobile battle station, a veritable fortress, leading an army of innumerable forces filmed on location against the broad sweep of the vast plains of Xilin Hot of Inner Mongolia. In sum, everything about the filmic depiction of the Great Khan's realm and person presents the Khan as 'the mightiest man ... who is in this world today or who ever has been' (*Travels* 113). Such a presentation is perfectly in accord with the *Travels*, in which 'Marco is above all else a champion of the glories of Kublai Khan' (Larner 94).

Given that this *Marco Polo* is far more textually accurate, how does it present alterity, the meeting with the other? As is to be expected from a film with a strong humanistic bias, the 'other' is depicted as human, that is, as an extension of the self. The film's principal other, the Great Khan, is not exclusively other: he is not a doddering old man, or a savage Mongol, or a fanatic eastern potentate, but a complex character of deep human appeal, an appeal reinforced by the masterful performance of Ruocheng Ying, one of China's most illustrious actors. True, he is arrogant, opinionated, stubborn, given to having his every wish fulfilled, and, above all else, bellicose in the extreme. As Achmet reminds Marco, 'The sword is never far from its scabbard,' and the film gives great precedence to Kublai's conquest of the Sung in 1273 and his campaigns against Japan in 1274 and 1281 (the latter appear in the *Travels* 244–7, treated as one). But he is also a benevolent ruler whose 'thoughts are directed toward helping the people who are subject to him' (*Travels* 155), thereby cutting into the perception of Mongol as other. In a telling scene which highlights his personality, the Great Khan is filmed, in a slow circular shot, having a conversation with Marco and Chinkin, aboard a water enclosure in

Shang-Du. He compliments Marco on his 'alert mind' and his ability to remember detailed information, talents necessary to any ruler:

> This is the information a ruler needs to understand the very soul of his people. The way of life behind the walls of their houses, their ability to farm land, so that, if famine should hit certain areas, one would know where there may be food to share. What we need are accurate records and we must study them. We must know our land and people better.

Such a preoccupation with the demands of proper rule accords well with the portrayal of the Khan in the *Travels* (cf. 155–8), which places great emphasis on the Khan's 'bountiful' nature, so much so that Marco tells us that 'all the people hold him in such esteem that they revere him as god' (*Travels* 158). Thus, the Khan is a humane visionary who manages the military, economical, social, legal, and religious lives of his subjects through a well-oiled bureaucratic system. Constant film shots of the Khan in council or of his ministers and clerks at work make this abundantly clear, reflecting the *Travels'* depiction of the Khan as 'the wisest man and ablest in all respects, the best ruler of subjects and of empire and the man of the highest character of all that have ever been in the whole history of the Tartars' (*Travels* 124). The Khan is also intellectually curious and eager for knowledge (*Travels* 36), a mirror image, in some ways, of the inquiring Marco. In the same scene, he carefully questions Marco about the lamasery and the roads leading outwards from there, and displays a keen interest when Marco corrects the official map with his own memory of the route. The Khan also values the truth and likes open disagreement, telling Marco, 'Do not be afraid. Too many people are only too ready to agree with me. To find someone who can speak frankly is refreshing.' The Khan combines this thirst for knowledge with a deep sense of culture and religious tolerance. When he is presented with an ornate cross by the Polos, he carefully examines it and says pointedly, 'Strange ... yours is the only religion to turn an instrument of death into an object of beauty.' In his realm, all religious practices seem to mingle (cf. *Travels* 119–20): the Christianity of the Polos, the Buddhism of Phags-pa, the Islam of Achmet, the Daoism of Yang-Zhu and the Immortal, the Confucianism of Yang Ku, the necromancy/quasi-Christianity of Chabi. Moreover, in spite of his Mongol bombast, he is a devoted husband and loving father, who does not hesitate to consult with Chabi about important matters and who exercises great care in the personal formation of

Chinkin, adding at one point close to film's end, 'Everything I did was for Chinkin.' The film even draws a parallel between the love of both fathers, Niccolò and the Great Khan, which is presented as almost identical in its caring and normative role, recognizing the flightiness of youth in both Marco and Chinkin and endeavouring to guide them to new positions of awareness. Finally, the Great Khan is portrayed as a noble man, generous and hospitable, ever eager to welcome the other – that is, Marco himself – and to embrace the other in true and lasting friendship (*Travels* 40). In the film's most touching scene, the Great Khan Kublai is filmed taking his leave of Marco in 1292. He tells Marco that his departure will cause him great suffering and accepts a promise that Marco will return, but adds, 'I will not be here to greet you. Something of you will remain behind, in this land, though, as long as men have memory. People coming here in your name will need no safe conduct. You have proved yourself a friend and they will be welcome as friends.' He rues what is happening to his empire, the absence of unity and the loss of blood it entails. Too old and too weak to mount his favourite steed by himself, he enlists the help of Marco, and from the saddle tells him that in the future 'Nostalgia will seize me and I will think of you as a faraway son.' He then extends his hand to Marco, saying, 'Take my hand, Marco. Remember that when a Mongol takes your hand some of his spirit passes over to you.' With this deeply human and moving touch the Great Khan rides slowly away from the Venetian traveller for the last time.

What is true of the principal other is likewise true of all the minor characters. Where information from the *Travels* is sparse or non-existent, Montaldo and his writers turn to other sources such as the *Yuan-shih* or Chinese annals and other travel accounts by foreigners such as Rashid al-Din for their character portrayal. For example, Chabi is a loyal wife who is aware of her husband's weaknesses, especially his penchant for war. Of him she says coolly there is 'always a new frontier to be crossed ... a new land to conquer.' She is also coy and has a good sense of humour. When Kublai approaches her in her chamber and complements her beauty, she teases him and reminds him of their initial encounter: 'Your hair is more beautiful than my horse's mane, you said ... [C]oming from a Mongol, there could be no higher compliment.' But she also has a serious side and is at the heart of palace decisions: Kublai consults with her before he invades Japan and clearly pays attention to her advice, a fact in keeping with what is known of the Empress historically (Rossabi 41; 67–9). Like her husband, Chabi is open to new ideas: she willingly accepts the oil from the Church of the Holy Sepulchre and deposits it in a receptacle she had made especially for this purpose. She also welcomes the tales of Marco and asks him pointed questions about other lands, taking particular delight in his description of Rome. Although ostensibly a Buddhist (Man 20), she practises necromancy and admires Christianity. In all, Chabi is not a distant other, a subservient Oriental, or a scheming eastern empress, but a decent human being, the lifelong companion of the Great Khan, with whom she spends forty-one years of her life, and the loving mother of Chinkin, to whom she is especially devoted.

Chinkin himself is not other, but a reflection of the young Marco, with whom he develops a close bond. It is appropriate, given the meticulous Chinese education prepared for him by his father (Rossabi 137–8), that Chinkin (mentioned in the *Travels* [123] as 'Chinghiz') is depicted by the film as being aware of the history and sufferings of the other: that is, the subject Chinese. When Marco and Chinkin visit the Great Wall, Chinkin tells him that the Wall was built to keep out the 'the deadly barbarians ... the Mongols.' When Marco inquires who built it, Chinkin says that people would say the Emperor had done so but, in reality, 'It was hundreds of thousands of slaves, prisoners, a hundred years of forced labour ... and untold thousands of deaths ... [T]heir tomb is this wall ... these stones are cemented with their blood ... they were the builders ... theirs should be the glory.' Chinkin is both principled and deeply aware of the disparity in his father's realm: as he reminds Marco, 'Order and peace do not dwell long among us.' He is also philosophical – one might say, Confucian. Chinkin believes that emperors should be just and should lead by the power of example. He is guided by respect for his father and strives to be kind, upright, decorous, wise, and faithful. He is also a realist, aware of his mortality and his place in history. He knows the reality of petty intrigues at court and cautions Marco against being too naïve in matters of government: 'To them you are just a pawn on a chessboard. Who knows which of them will gain more by moving you. But remember, Marco, that the pawn is the last to find out.' Chinkin, therefore, is not other, but a mirror image of the young Marco, who is equally principled and who strives to follow the same virtues as his Mongol counterpart. Like Chinkin, Marco comes to experience the suffering of the conquered Chinese and to empathize deeply with their lot.

Phags-pa is not a scheming eastern court official who is eager to plot against Marco and have him killed or removed from the realm, but evolves in the course of the film into a man of deep spirituality and kindness. True, at times he seems jealous of Marco's favour with the Khan, but his underlying motivation is loyalty to the Khan and his empire. He wants peace for his country and decries the wanton wars and destruction. Phags-pa even comes to like and admire Marco, telling him, 'We should have been friends a long time ago.' When Marco laments that this friendship has come too late, Phags-pa retorts, 'Friendship is a bridge that reaches across space and time, even when you're home in Venice.' Once again, the other is not who he or she seems to be, but is, in the end, a human being who often turns out to be more human than the observer.

Lastly, Achmet is not an 'other' stereotype. True, he is immoral, scheming, and ruthless, just as the *Travels* portray him (131–5). But he is also 'a man of great energy and ability' (*Travels* 131) and deserves the kind of objective historical treatment that Rossabi (178–84) accords him. He is obviously valued by the Khan, who gives him a free hand to act as he pleases. The film, in fact, portrays him as an 'agent,' in many respects, of the Mongol court. He also has his human, if forced, side, showing the Polos hospitality and offering his hand in friendship ('If you should ever need any help or advice, do not hesitate to come to me before you approach anyone else'), although one suspects a high degree of self-ingratiating scheming on his part. A little later, for example, he tells Marco that Phags-pa is the cause of the emperor's displeasure and that he suspects Marco of 'distracting Chinkin from his duties,' of poisoning him 'with ideas foreign to the Mongol spirit, ideas as foreign as yourself.' Achmet's powers of intrigue, however, finally get the better of him. He justifies his immorality with the glib line, 'I spend my days solving the Khan's problems. I am entitled to spend my nights solving my own,' and proceeds to seduce Mai Li in one of the most frightening film scenes in movie history. Shortly afterwards, he is assassinated in the manner described in the *Travels* (133–4).

Thus, throughout the film *Marco Polo*, there is an absence of stereotyping in its presentation of the other. Characters are presented as three-dimensional, having both positive and negative qualities. Above all else, it is the humanity of the characters which is front and centre. This is true not only of the characters listed above, but also of the innumerable 'other' extras – the Muslim Bedouins, the Mongols, the Chinese – who are captured on film for their humanity, whether that humanity is being expressed by simple labour (the rice harvesting and fishing sequences), entertainment (the slow pan shot of the faces of

Chinese peasants at the pantomime performance), joy (the close-ups of the Chinese wedding sequence), sorrow (the shots of anguished faces of Bedouins after being attacked by the crusaders), or family life and traditions (the myriad shots of Mongol life and Mongol celebrations). All of these things Marco experiences and, through them, comes to perceive the other as simply an extended self. True, there are differences of facial features, of language, of culture, of customs, of history, of politics. These are explicitly acknowledged as differences in several key scenes, as when Marco faces the etiquette of the imperial court with its constant kneeling before the emperor; or witnesses forms of justice alien to him; or learns of the ways that people of different cultures express their love; or observes the plight of his Chinese servant versus that of his Mongol overlords. None of these differences, however, is an impediment to discovering the value of the human. The film *Marco Polo* has therefore been described as an extraordinary human experience: '*Marco Polo* was to be not only a spectacular piece of entertainment but the embodiment of a kind of humanity that reaches across national barriers of political differences in a gesture of cooperation and respect' (Patterson 471).

The human and humane vision of *Marco Polo* has been shaped by its film genre and by historical developments in China. Marco Polo is a film of discovery, of the 'journey' film genre. In all such movies[4] the protagonist is pictured on a life quest, which, after all sorts of twists and developments, leads to some fundamental realization. In the process, unlike the traditional adventure flick, the protagonist's gaze is no longer exclusive, but is now extended to include the camera, the director, and the audience, who, like the protagonist, are privileged to view the various discoveries. Moreover, the discoveries are not grasped as alien, as 'other,' but fundamentally as one with the protagonist. This is the case with *Marco Polo*, in which the production itself and the film are figured as expeditions comparable to Marco's original journey. So, through an international crew and cast, we are transported to Marco's world of discovery, and realize what he undoubtedly realized: that is, a sense of a profoundly abiding humanity that binds us all together. This is reinforced in one particularly telling scene. After Jacopo, the Polos' servant and chief crew member, has been caught in a fire and is horribly burnt, he is comforted by Marco and Matteo with the thought of returning to Venice. But he refuses to entertain the thought and instead says, 'No. I'm staying here. I want to stay with these people. The flames took half my face away. I am crippled. If I return to Venice, I would be seen as some sort of monster. But here they treat me with affection, like an unfortunate brother. So, leave, leave. I am staying here … [T]his is my true home.' Marco sees, in this moment, that China is also his home, the place where he is truly one with himself and with the other. Grasping this realization, he tearfully bids Jacopo good-bye. Marco, therefore, discovers who he is, and in the process of discovery we are given what is missing in the travels, namely the development of a personality in the Venetian which is grounded in the transformation of a boyish naïveté in Italy into a humane maturity in China. In a sense, Montaldo guided Ken Marshall in a condensed version of Marco's physical and spiritual journey. Accordingly, *Marco Polo* 'is the struggle of a man of limited experience and education to absorb wonders and to rise above culture shock to an understanding that makes the change in character so fascinating' (Patterson 467). Thus does the film genre of 'journey' leave an indelible stamp on the film and on its portrayal of the other.

Crucial to the film's vision is the historical development of China at that time. After the isolation of China of the 1950s and 1960s, a new era of openness started to dawn in the 1970s. In 1971, the People's Republic of China was given the China seat in the United Nations, replacing the nationalist government on Taiwan, which had held the seat since 1945. In the same year, Henry Kissinger, the National Security Adviser of the United States, made a secret trip to China, followed in 1972 by an official visit by President Richard Nixon, which brought to an end the 'aberration [from 1949 to 1971] that could not last' (MacMillan 329). This 'was, after all, the first-ever visit of an American president to China, an end of the long stand-off during which neither country had recognized the other. It was an earthquake in the Cold War and meant that the Eastern Bloc no longer stood against the West' (MacMillan 1). As a result of this visit and its mutually agreed upon need for contact and withdrawal of troops from Taiwan, China became more integrated within the world community and many other nations now switched their allegiance from Taiwan. China normalized many of its diplomatic relations, including, in 1972, Japan. After the death of Mao in 1976, Deng Xiaoping initiated a series of overdue economic and social reforms that involved modest political changes and the adoption of a market economy (Roberts 285–6). These reforms, in turn, led to an economic boom which saw China's industrial output nearly double in the period 1981–6 (Roberts 287). Such improvements were accompanied by an open-door policy by which the Chinese government made known its wish to engage in trade and cultural exchange. It is a direct result of the latter policy that the Chinese inaugurated the Marco Polo film. Moreover, the Chinese made clear that they would make available whatever was needed in the way of travel visas, travel arrangement, film extras, and logistical support. They also did not exercise any direct censorship of the film, retaining only a right to a limited voice in matters of scripting, such as not portraying Genghis Khan as a savage but as a statesman and leader. As a result of such openness, the film was made and amply repaid its debt of gratitude by a filmic portrayal of other as inclusive and non-stereotypical, a reminder of the humanity of us all.

In addition to Montaldo's *Marco Polo*, three other factual films are worthy of note. All are short and cast in documentary/docudrama mode. *La Croisière jaune* (1932), directed by Léon Poirier, is part of the 'croisières' series of films pioneered by André Citroën, founder of the French automobile factory. Billed as 'technical, humane and diplomatic adventures,' these films opened up worlds barely known and were closely followed by the public. The first 'croisière' took place in 1922 in the vast region of the Sahara. This was followed by many others, including the expedition of 1932, *La Croisière jaune*, which was an attempt to retrace the steps of Marco Polo from Beirut to Peking and tell the story in fifty-five minutes. The expedition was undertaken by George-Marie Haardt and led by Citroën himself. The film follows Haardt through Persia, Afghanistan, and the Himalayas and was compiled from the more than forty thousand metres of film shot during the trek. Unfortunately, Haardt died while en route. The film provides an excellent introduction to the terrain of many locations described by Polo, but is not primarily concerned with him. *La Route des Épices* (1953), directed by William Novik, is only fifteen minutes long, and presents Marco Polo's journey to China and back by means of images from European illuminated manuscripts, Indian miniaturists, and Chinese paintings. The film has two parts: in the first, we are treated to the Muslim conquests, the crusades, the campaign of the Mongols, and the journey of the Polos. In the second, Marco describes the wonders he has seen and there is a tension kept before us between wonder and exaggeration. Beyond the inherent beauty of the images, the film is very flat and too brief to be little more than a classroom aid.[5] A completely different sort of short film (thirty-five minutes) is the independent and avant-garde *A Description of the World* directed by Mike Eaton (1981). Made at the New Cinema Workshop at Nottingham, England

and funded by local authorities, the film is a postmodern reflection on the pervasive human need for fiction. The title appears on a magic screen toy and is followed by shots of a modern city's streets, superimposed over which are rhetorical captions. The body of the film is taken up with conversations between Marco Polo (Tim Leggatt) and Rustichello (Hugh Curriston), in a Genoese prison, which explore the tension in their collaboration, the former aiming for factual reporting and the latter devoted to the exposition of the fantastic. Marco argues for truth for truth's sake and responds to Rustichello's cynicism by resorting to his own fictive self, boasting of wonders he has left untold, and reminding Rustichello of his nickname 'Il millione.' Interrupting these conversations are shots of an exotic upscale building and an interview with a tattoo artist. The film is clever, drawing attention to the space between the spoken word of the traveller and the written word of the romance writer, but is limited by its subject matter. Besides these three brief films there are no other feature films of the factual kind. Most recent of these docudramas is the 2007 American-backed mini-series *Marco Polo*, directed by Kevin Connor with Ian Somerhalder as Marco Polo and Brian Dennehy as Kublai Khan, testifying to the ongoing centrality of the *Travels* in modern reimaginings of the encounter of East and West.

Through the many films of Marco Polo, a constant theme has been the kind of person Marco Polo was and the kind of people he encountered. From the perspective of the adventure film, to which most Marco Polo films belong, Marco is a youthful hero who goes to the exotic East, where he discovers both romance and the ability to excel in combat with threatening Asian enemies. The depiction of Montaldo's *Marco Polo*, by contrast, is the one serious attempt at presenting a historical Marco according to the *Travels*, a boy who was taken by his father and uncle on an eastern journey to the court of Kublai Khan and who there came to maturity, discovering his common bond with the 'other' in spite of profound cultural differences. This cinematic journey from alterity to holism has not been easy, nor has it occurred quickly. In fact, the issues underlying cinematic alterity and holism are still with us today. In 1972, the incomparable Michelangelo Antonioni made his three-and-a-half-hour-long documentary of China, *Chung Kuo*. It was subsequently shown at the Venice Biennal Exposition, where it created a furor. Antonioni was convinced that he had made a creative and compelling documentary based on the evidence made available to him by his Chinese hosts. The Chinese, however, saw the film as an anti-Chinese piece of Fascist/Soviet revisionism and American imperialist propaganda, and consequently did everything in their power to have it banned.

In an aptly entitled article ('*De Interpretatione*, or The Difficulty of Being Marco Polo'), Umberto Eco pleaded for reason and calm on both sides. He correctly surmised that the underlying problem was due to the cinematic depiction of holism and alterity. Antonioni had wanted to stress the holism of the Chinese encounter, to show persons 'who are calm and much more human than we are, at times [coming] close to our ideal of serenity, harmony with nature' (Eco 10). But Antonioni, being more interested in personal relationships than ideological questions, created a film that alienated by its portrayal of alterity. Antonioni did not hesitate to use such loaded words as 'povera' (i.e., 'arte povera,' 'medicina povera'), or to make the political statement that Shanghai was built by colonial powers (an Italian flyer corrected this statement with 'Shanghai was built by People's China with the help of the imperialists'), or to depict the Chinese in ethnic terms instead of the revolutionary ideal, thereby promulgating stereotypes as offensive as Italians in Sardinian peasant garb (Eco 10). Underlying Eco's analysis is the realization that it is not easy to navigate the cinematic space between the 'other' and its depiction. Any lack of sensitivity, no matter how small, can vitiate the final product and lead to controversy. Too little attention to holism results in broad stereotyping, while too little attention to alterity sugarcoats essential differences. Such a delicate balancing act makes us all the more aware of how masterful a job Montaldo has done in recreating the world of Marco Polo, its inhabitants, their differences, and, above all else, their shared humanity.

Eco appreciated Antonioni's vision of shared humanity; at the same time, however, he also stressed a sensitivity to differences, concluding that 'The dialogue between peoples (and between persons of the same class who live in different cultures) must be sustained by a historical and social conscience of cultural differences' (Eco 11). The three following essays in this volume, which stress the need to move beyond dichotomous thinking, might disagree with Eco's conclusion. Such a sentiment, however, is a sober reminder of the differences that continue to separate us, but which nonetheless never blind us to our shared humanity. To return to the opening quotation from Longxi Zhang, 'to know the Other is a process of *Bildung*, of learning and self-cultivation, which is neither projecting the self onto the Other nor erasing the self with the Other's alterity. It is rather a moment when self and Other meet and join together, in which both are changed and enriched in what Gadamer calls "the fusion of horizons"' (53). One can only hope that future cinematic visions of Marco Polo and the world he encountered will respond to these determining words.

NOTES

1 The names of places and people are those contained in scripts/cast credits/ intertitles and are not necessarily consistent, nor has any attempt been made to transliterate consistently according to one system such as pinyin.

2 All references to the *Travels* are from *The Travels of Marco Polo* translated by R.E. Latham. On this essay's citation of a modern translation in preference to the medieval text, see the Introduction, p. 10.

3 For a condensed history of the film's genesis, development, and success, see the interview with Montaldo in Crespi 107–15 and 123–7.

4 The list is exhaustive and includes Dennis Hopper's *Easy Rider* (1969), Wim Wenders's *Im Lauf der Zeit* (1976), Bill Forsyth's *Local Hero* (1983), Aki Kaurismaki's *Ariel* (1989), David Lynch's *The Straight Story* (1999), Olivier Ducastel and Jacques Martineau's *Drole de Felix* (2000), Sofia Coppola's *Lost in Translation* (2003), Walter Salles's *Diarios di motocicleta* (2004), Alexander Payne's *Sideways* (2004), and Jim Jarmusch's *Broken Flowers* (2005).

5 The issue of classroom movies is outside the scope of this paper, but there is a large number of such films which are readily available.

PART THREE

Cross-Cultural Currents

10 The Perils of Dichotomous Thinking: A Case of Ebb and Flow Rather Than East and West

SUSAN WHITFIELD

The brief of this paper – which was originally given as a keynote address in a conference that called for 'cultural encounters in the various humanistic disciplines' – is to be provocative. But it is not intended to be flippant. Although I do not have clear answers to the dilemmas I pose, I think they need to be addressed sooner rather than later if we are to make headway in understanding world history. So I will start by asking, 'What are we doing still talking in terms of East and West?' In our post-orientalist times, should we not be moving beyond the dichotomy 'East and West'?[1] This is even more pressing today when, as I will argue, Central Asia is again beginning to be acknowledged and studied. Where does Central or Inner Asia[2] fit into the dichotomous model of East and West? In the West and the East – that is, Europe and China – the peoples of Central Asia have often been dismissed as barbarians or nomads, in a display of still more oversimplifying, dichotomous models (barbarians versus civilized; nomads versus sedentary). They were neither West nor East but occupied what, for some of these same historians, has been easiest to classify as a void, only definable in terms of the space or cultures around it. But if we move beyond comfortable, familiar dichotomies, how do we categorize the world? How do we define Central Asia, unfamiliar to most, if not in contrast to a familiar category and using familiar terminology? This paper examines these dichotomies and their limitations and argues that we need to move beyond the comfortable certainties they offer to new, more flexible models for exploring and understanding world history.

The arguments of those who defined Orientalism have been strongly challenged and are now rejected by many. Yet the Orientalist debate has changed the way we look at the world, while its terminology has permeated our language and continues to define many of our debates. It cannot be ignored. Several of the papers in this collection are concerned with the post-medieval world – when Europe, for the first time in world history, became dominant. This is where the attack on Orientalism was targeted; that is, on post-medieval Europe and its narratives of Islam. And this gave rise to one of its most ubiquitous dichotomies, Self and Other. Marshall Hodgson was the first to offer a sustained attack on the western narratives of Islamic history in his three-volume *The Venture of Islam*. Others followed, notably scholars like Tibawi, but it was Edward Said's attack, making use of Foucault's theories, which sparked the greatest debate.

In recent years, some scholars have started to spread the Orientalism debate wider to include attacks on western narratives of China, India, and East Asia, not traditionally Islamic countries.[3] Several Chinese scholars have further broadened its scope, notably Zhang Longxi. In his excellent study of the Orientalist debate, *Mighty Opposites*, he shows how modern China subverted the Orientalist argument by adopting with alacrity the role of the Other in relation to the West as it served the anti-imperialist, nationalist political agenda of those in power. Instead of denouncing the characteristics of the 'Other' as a fabrication of corrupt western Orientalists, they instead turned the argument on its head, accepting China's passivity and backwardness as a sign of the unavoidable harm that western imperialism had wrought upon modern China. This served the very useful purpose of blaming outside forces for internal problems.

What Said's attack on Orientalism succeeded in achieving, at least to some extent, was to make what had previously been seen as good in the European narrative be seen as bad, and this included, among other things, ethnocentricity, racial pride, service to the state, and national pride. In this interesting subversion of the original argument, China adopted its attack on Orientalism to promote these very same values. And, of course, by accepting the attacks on Orientalism, China also tacitly accepted its theoretical foundations, which, as Macfie pointed out, 'were either based on, or assumed the existence of, a European philosophy or thought system, derived from the most part from the work of ... Hegel ... and Nietzsche' (6–7). But then modern Chinese historiography is also based on a European thought system – Marxism – which is yet another theory riddled with dichotomies. China's reaction to the Orientalist debate is thus replete with ironies, as Zhang points out in an insightful chapter in his book.[4]

Zhang is concerned with modern Chinese historiography, but if, as Said postulates, the capitalist West from its position of perceived superiority in both might and culture could not study the Other dispassionately, then might not his argument be applicable to other cultures in similar situations at other times in history? Specifically, what about China when it was a major world power in the Han (206 BC–AD 220) and Tang periods (618–907) before Islam, Marco Polo, and the rise of Europe? How did the Han- and Tang-period historians characterize the world outside the remit of the Chinese culture which was, in a very real sense, their 'Other'?

According to Said, European scholars characterized the Orient in their narratives as 'irrational, aberrant, backward, crude, despotic, inferior, inauthentic, passive, feminine and sexually corrupt' (Macfie 8). We only have to read a few accounts of China's neighbours from the chapters on the 'Western Regions' in the early histories to come across very similar characterizations, as Zhang shows in his paper in this volume. Foreigners were certainly often described as 'feminine,' being 'yin' as opposed to 'yang,' and also inferior, backward, and crude. Deviant sexual practices are also often ascribed to them. But does this language imply acceptance of models of the Self and the Other as in Said's definition of Orientalism (that is, absolute dichotomies), or does it reflect something closer to the Chinese concept of yin and yang, expressing two ends of a continuum?

From early times the Chinese emperor was expected to set a moral example as a civilizing influence, both for his own people (and several early Chinese philosophers made clear that the 'ordinary' people of China were in need of such influences) and for peoples beyond the boundaries of China. Once China started to expand and colonize the west and south, this remit extended to foreign peoples within its boundaries as well. Foreigners could come to China and be transformed or 'laihua.' Once they had accepted the Chinese way and had, in effect, been transformed, they were considered to be Chinese, now civilized or 'hua.' This was not an empty concept; although it is open to doubt whether Marco Polo ever became an official in China, there are many instances of foreigners being accepted into the inner sanctum of the civil service and not solely in lowly positions. Thus we see the paucity of this dichotomous framework, Self and Other, when applied to narratives of pre-modern China and, indeed, to those of the pre-modern world in general. Clearly, there was no absolute dichotomy in medieval times between the Self and the Other in either China or Europe.

The framework also fails when applied to modern China, as Zhang recognizes:

> It is indeed the image of the Self that appears through the mirror that we call the Other, and this is no less true of the Chinese than of the Europeans or Americans. But there is perhaps this essential difference: while the Westerners tend to see the Chinese as fundamentally Other, sometimes the Chinese would think the Westerners eager to become like the Chinese themselves. In the minds of Chinese rulers and officials, China was the sole centre of civilisation where all foreigners were barbarians. What we find in this inadequate picture of the Other is of course nothing but the incredible ignorance and arrogance of the Chinese ruling elites. (40–1)

Should we therefore reject entirely the dichotomy of Self and Other, or may it still have some function in helping us to interpret pre-modern Chinese historiography? Is it a viable conceptual tool for some narratives? If we accept that there are always 'Others' by which we define ourselves, and if the dominating 'Other' for the post-capitalist Christian West has been Islam, China's dominant other in pre-modern history is the 'nomad,' the 'barbarian' from the West.

This raises another problem, however, with the dichotomy as applied to pre-modern times. The Orientalist argument was predicated on both the West and the 'Orient' as having essences, essences that were displayed in their Great Books: their texts. Said criticized specifically the essentialist approach rather than the study of the languages, societies, and peoples themselves. As Burke says: 'The textualist position foreshortens history, annihilates changes, and levels difference the better to represent an image of the past in dramatic form' (xv). China's own past is certainly presented in this form, one that suits political leaders – and not only those of the modern era. The Tang emperors, whose ancestors came from the steppes, sought to link their genealogy with the father of Daoism, Laozi, claiming to be descended from the same clan. But most of China's 'Others' were, for much of the first millennium, cultures without books. How, then, are their essences to be defined? Without essence, moreover, can there be anything approaching 'Orientalism' as Said defined it or, for that matter, 'Occidentalism,' as it should probably be termed from a Chinese viewpoint? For these and the other reasons argued above, the dichotomous model of the Self and the Other as defined by Said is redundant for interpreting pre-modern Chinese historiography.

So what about other dichotomies as interpretative tools, such as the nomad and the agriculturalist? Here is one example from a very eminent historian of Inner Asia, typifying attitudes widespread in western historiography only a few decades ago. He describes the nomads of Central Asia as little known and unpredictable peoples living in a land of 'immense wastes' surrounded by civilizations. These people, he continues, 'can only be defined by comparison: the Brother of the Civilised ... They are opposed but complimentary.' Once they have conquered the civilizations, they themselves become civilized and 'prefer to lose their identity rather than to return to their nomadic state.' 'Historical circumstance,' he says, 'may force a human group to remain or to return to barbarism, but it never does so of its own free will.' He ends with a rhetorical flourish: 'Who would like to leave the flesh pots and go forth into the wilderness? There are no volunteers for the Outer Darkness. To be a barbarian is a moral as well as an economic and political state. The history of Central Eurasia is a history of the barbarian' (Sinor I: 94–5). Surely this rhetoric exemplifies the pitfalls of dichotomous thinking, yet the narrative of this dichotomy between the nomad and the farmer in Central Asia continues today. For example, a book published as recently as 2001 states that 'the roots of a basic duality between the nomadic and sedentary ways of life exist[ed] here from the earliest times' (Knobloch 34). It must be acknowledged, however, that there has also been a sophisticated debate in recent years challenging the absolute distinction between the nomad and the agriculturalist, and more subtle analyses are starting to appear which show that the boundaries between the two are blurred. For example, *An End to Nomadism*, by Humphrey and Sneath, has gone some way toward rejecting the dichotomy.

The cases reviewed above show how readily historians slip into dichotomous models and how they continue to be used by both Chinese and western historians of China, especially when discussing China's relationships with her western neighbours. As soon as we characterize Central Asia in contrast to China, however, it becomes almost impossible to avoid thinking of it as opposite to how we think of China. Central Asia is viewed as an uncivilized, backward, and thus an uninfluential place, except perhaps militarily; even then, as Sinor suggests, its influence is also seen as entirely negative, destroying rather than building. It has been too easy to define this region in terms of the surrounding 'civilizations.' To quote Sinor again: 'The definition of Central Eurasia that can be given in space is negative. It is part of the

continent that lies beyond the borders of the great sedentary civilisa-
tions' (I: 95). The idea of Central Asia as a void, a place outside, is also
implied by the dichotomy 'East and West.' Some scholars have challenged this negative definition; Andre Gunder Frank, for example,
presents Central Asia and the steppe as central to the rise of world civilization and the source of many of the most important inventions of
early world history, including the development of agriculture, domes-
tication of animals, the chariot, horseback riding, stringed instruments,
and more. All these had a profound impact on both China and Europe
and their development. The preponderance of the negative view must
be owing in large part to the absence of an 'essence' or large corpus,
but, as Frank shows, the absence of a written history does not mean the
absence of influence.

The influence of Central Asia continued to be pervasive throughout
the first millennium, yet modern histories of China, whether in Chinese or English, hardly mention the region. Tang China is presented as
unequalled and unchallenged, as virtually the only civilization in East
Asia. In these narratives, China's neighbours may have posed a temporary military threat, but they could not threaten the power of Chinese
civilization. In recent years, this has started to change. Books like the
collection of papers *China among Equals,* edited by Morris Rossabi,
Barfield's *The Perilous Frontier,* Valerie Hansen's *The Open Empire*, and
Joanna Waley-Cohen's *The Sextants of Beijing: Global Currents in Chinese
History* challenge the view of China as unequalled. One hopes that this
new outlook will seep into classrooms and university lecture halls
and educate a new generation of scholars to be more sceptical of
traditional historiography.

However, dichotomies are difficult to avoid. In *The Perilous Frontier*,
Barfield explains Chinese foreign policy in terms of the Self and Other,
the Agriculturalist versus the Nomad:

> It was no accident that the steppe and China tended to be mirror images
> of each other. Ultimately the state organisation of the steppe needed a sta-
> ble China to exploit ... a weak T'ang dynasty was actually preserved by
> the nomads and protected from internal revolts and invasions because of
> the benefits it provided. A relationship that began as predatory became
> symbiotic. When the Uighurs fell in 840, the T'ang dynasty lost its protec-
> tor and collapsed in internal revolt within a generation. (131)

In his contribution to *China among Equals,* Tao Jingshen provides a more
subtle challenge to one of the mainstays of the narratives of Chinese

foreign policy: 'The tribute system does not adequately describe these fluctuations in China's relations with foreigners.' He goes on to note that 'even the tribute system masked what were really relations between equal and independent states. The relationship between the Han and the Hsi-ung-nu, for example, was at first conducted on the basis of equality ... in the T'ang, Sino-Turkish and Sino-Tibetan relations were often marked by a sense of equality between the parties' (66). As Tao's argument suggests, the idea that China in its arrogance disregarded knowledge of the outside at this time is a myth. There were few Chinese who learned and studied the languages, literatures, and religions of their neighbours (with the notable exception of Buddhism from India, which became absorbed into Chinese culture), let alone who wrote books on the subject. It is calculated that sixty thousand books were written on the languages and culture of Islam by western scholars between 1800 and 1950, but this was a different time; one might say, a more literate time. There is no shortage of travel narratives, such as Faxian's and Xuanzang's travels to India. Nor were such accounts restricted to journeys to near neighbours: a prisoner of war captured in the 751 battle between the Arabs and Chinese was subsequently sent to Damascus, capital of the Arab caliphate. He returned twelve years later to Chang'an, where he wrote an account of the Arab lands and their customs. Though most of these accounts are no longer extant, traces remain in the official histories or other such works, and they were not uninfluential in their time. As Rossabi points out, 'Chinese envoys often returned to China with valuable accounts of their travels, which occasionally included useful military intelligence ... Using this information ... [the Chinese rulers] differentiated among the various "barbarians," treating each one according to its presumed power and wealth. Some rulers and envoys were addressed as equals, whereas others were clearly dealt with as subordinates' (*China among Equals* 9). In other words, their view of their neighbours was dictated by a political pragmatism: there was no single 'Other.'

It was not only politicians who studied foreigners and their customs. Monks, medical men, merchants, musicians, and others all studied foreign forms and customs and incorporated them into their body of knowledge. There is no need to attempt to summarize here the multifarious influences, for Schafer's study, *The Golden Peaches of Samarkand*, gives details of all areas of Tang life affected by foreign ideas, goods, and technologies, while Kieschnick's recent study looks at the influences of Buddhism on Chinese material culture, from chairs to bridges. One can argue without much dissent that China is a richer and more interesting culture because of this openness. In *China Turning Inward*,

Liu has developed this argument further to suggest that the conservatism of the Song (960–1279) led to an ossification of Chinese culture
which, ultimately, led to its downfall.

The roots of another stultifying dichotomy, that separating Chinese
and non-Chinese, can be traced back to the period following the Song
conservatism. To modern China, this dichotomy serves a political
agenda which seeks to promote 'racial' and national pride by presenting a unified historical narrative. This dichotomy is expressed using
the terms 'Han' (that is, the Chinese) versus everyone else, non-Han.
This nomenclature is now widely used in all writings on China,
whether journalistic or scholarly, or written by Chinese or others. What
does the category 'Han' signify? It was the Mongol rulers who used
'Hanren' – 'Han' people – to name one of the four peoples they ruled in
China. The Han were distinguished from the Mongols, the Central
Asians, and the Southerners ('Nanren'), but they also included the Khi-
tan and other groups living in northern China.

Dikotter argues that it is misleading to think of such a categorization
as akin to a racial distinction and suggests that the dichotomy between
race and culture is inappropriate when applied to pre-modern Chinese
history: 'It introduces an opposition so far not supported by historical
evidence, and tends to project a modern perception into a remote
phase of history' (3). Recent studies have shown that the distinction
between Han and non-Han certainly bears no clear and unequivocal
relationship to genetic make-up. Northern Chinese are genetically closer
to their northwestern 'barbarian' neighbours than to southern Chinese,
who are closer to their southeastern Asian neighbours (Bowring).
Dikotter further argues that it was only during the Qing dynasty
(1644–1911) that 'Han' became a racial categorization in China. It is
arguable that it is still used this way in China, despite 'race' having
been rejected as a meaningless concept by many. The adoption of the
same nomenclature among western historians of China during the
twentieth century would make an interesting study, but it is beyond
the remit of this paper. It is, however, now firmly entrenched in their
vocabulary, and while many scholars and journalists would defend
their use of it in terms of ethnicity and culture (Saussy 21), very few
challenge it. The dichotomy is therefore now ubiquitous in non-
Chinese and Chinese narratives of both modern and pre-modern
China, whether political, journalistic, or scholarly.

The use of the term 'Han' suggests a unified, homogenized cultural
tradition and confuses our perceptions and insights into pre-modern

China. This is shown by the reaction to the relatively recent archaeological finds from the Bronze Age Shu culture in the southwest of China with their gilt-covered metal masks with protruding eyes. Robert Thorp, in his catalogue from one of the several exhibitions showing these finds, expresses his disquiet: 'An exceptional archaeological context … means that archaeologists have few rules of thumb to guide their interpretations. When a find is made within an archaeological culture only recently recognized, the challenges are greater still, "Common knowledge" does not exist, and each new report may alter even basic information' (in Yang, *The Golden Age* 206). The problem is not this material, however; it is our categorization of it. Despite the fact that this is clearly a new archaeological culture, it is only exceptional if considered as part of a five-thousand-year continuum of Chinese culture. Yet this is how it is packaged. For example, in the same catalogue, Zhang Wenbin, then Director General of the State Administration of Cultural Heritage in China, states: 'Each work of art exhibited here will help the visitor along the path that leads towards understanding the profundity and grandeur of Chinese civilisation … The present China is the extension of the historical China, which is a country with a history of five thousand years of history and civilisation' (10). This exemplifies the problem. We have all, to some extent, been hoodwinked into accepting the concept of a homogenized 'Han' culture, that represented by oracle bones, restrained Shang bronzes, Confucian texts, beautiful ceramics, and a literati tradition with a clear link to the present. As Galambos puts it in his challenge to one such narrative, the standardization of Chinese characters, it is necessary to deny the 'ideologically motivated unilateral genealogy of traditional historiography which traced the mandate of Heaven from mythical emperors' (1). This is our narrative of China, one that has been presented to us by the rulers of China past and present. This narrative of a unified culture does not correspond to the complex reality as exemplified by these finds. It is not surprising that scholars struggle to contextualize them within this narrative. We should realize that the history of the geographical area now called China is far too complex to fit into a unified narrative.

If this modern dichotomy Han/non-Han has stunted our understanding of the diversity of the world encompassed by the 'Han,' then it has also forced us to think of the 'non-Han,' including the Central Asians, in terms of negative definitions – what the 'Han' are not. The rejection of this dichotomy would liberate our approach to both Chinese and Central Asian history. But any such progress would also require greater concentration on Central Asia as a field of study. In 1979, Luc Kwanten suggested this was already happening: 'For a long time Central Asia remained a neglected field of study, the domain of a few brilliant, eccentric scholars and a host of unenlightened amateurs. It is a field where misinformation is still more readily available than accurate documentation. During the last three decades there has been a remarkable change ... and it now appears that the study of Central Asia in general, and of the Mongol empire in particular, is an important constituent element of integrative and comparative world history' (1). But the late twentieth-century scholars were not the first in this field. The importance of Central Asia was recognized by the archaeologists and scholars who followed in the wake of the Great Game in the late nineteenth and early twentieth century. Central Asian studies flourished for these few decades in western scholarship. A new society was founded, the Central Asian Society (now the Royal Society for Asian Affairs), and, far from neglecting this region, the major academic journals of the time carried articles in every issue on its geography, archaeology, history, and manuscript finds. Translations were made of all the major known travel accounts, the relevant chapters of the Chinese histories, and, where available, other historical sources.

Unfortunately this momentum was not maintained. Although the tradition continued in some centres, notably among German philologists and French sinologists, these became islands of excellence as knowledge, interest, and the skills needed for the study of this area waned.[5] The demands are considerable. Open any account of Central Asian history and one is bombarded with names of unknown peoples, regions, cultures, all moving across a vast landscape and living lives on which it is almost impossible to get a grip, speaking languages which are now understood by only a handful of people worldwide, practising any number of religions and in any number of social and political frameworks. The main sources for their history are through those of the cultures located on their peripheries. Although there are primary manuscript sources, these are in numerous different languages and scripts, while the growing body of archaeological and epigraphical data is still comparatively underexploited.

Is Kwanten right to suggest that we are seeing a renaissance in Central Asian studies? There is no doubt a resurgence of interest in this area, only encouraged by events of the early twenty-first century which have refocused political attention on the region. There are any number of organizations, talks, symposia, and conferences on Central

Asia and even UNESCO Silk Road initiatives. Cataloguing of the primary sources has reached a momentum not seen since the early decades of the twentieth century, and historians worldwide are finally working together on researching some of the key areas of Central Asian history, such as that of the Sogdians. But to counter this, the use of the binary of East and West is still pervasive, used to name departments, universities, conferences, and books. The number of courses on Central Asian history and culture is still lamentably small, while history in Europe and China is still taught as if Central Asia is peripheral, not only in space but also importance. To change this we need to make Central Asian history more accessible.

Writing history often entails choosing what to leave out, determining which events show a larger picture. Historians, for example, talk of movements at a certain period of history of peoples from the northeast to the southwest Central Asian steppes, or of changes from Iranian to Turkic cultural influences in the region. To borrow a term from Buddhism, this is *upaya*: an expedient means to get an initial grasp of the subject. Of course, there will be exceptions, and once we have a general grasp we can move on to those. So is there perhaps a role for the old dichotomies in our expedient means? Might they offer a way in for scholars perplexed by Central Asian complexity? I would argue against this. As we have seen, dichotomies are dangerous. They offer too much simplification, as Knobloch suggests: 'The History of Afghanistan is so complex that every attempt at simplification must inevitably lead to superficiality and confusion' (187). He is arguing the case for just one area of this vast region, so how much more valid is his argument when we consider the region as a whole?

In a discussion of Orientalism, Tønnesson argues passionately for a more universal approach:

East and West have so much in common, and both East and West differ so much internally that any attempt to understand the world from the standpoint of an East-West divide is bound to fail. We should thus reject Samuel Huntington and Hassan Hanafi's contention that humanism always serves as a smokescreen for Western domination. It must be possible to do what Liu Binyan suggests: to use 'the best of all civilizations, not emphasizing the differences between them' (49), to promote global civilization, create or build one world on the basis of shared human values, fight seclusiveness and protectionism without also promoting domination. Bridges can be built on the basis of drawings from architects on both sides, and bridges can be crossed by people from both sides. The basic idea behind the humanist approach is that in essence every human being is alike. The differences highlighted by cultural relativists should be seen as exceptions to the general rule, and should never be exaggerated.

However, thinking is not changed easily. Conservatism lies at the heart of scholarship, so to make a major change in thinking, it is necessary to offer a practical model which will reflect this new way of looking at the problem. One thing is clear: to reach an understanding of Central Asian history, we can no longer work in the old model of scholarship in the humanities, as isolated and independent scholars. There are too many data for individuals to collect and process, so we must work in collaboration. This is a new departure for historians, although one long followed by scientists and, indeed, by social scientists. Perhaps we can learn from science in their use of modelling as well as their working practices.

In his 1970 essay on Central Eurasia in *Orientalism and History*, Sinor used the analogy of a volcanic eruption to describe the region:

> Surrounded by this 'crust' of civilisation lie the immense wastes of Central Eurasia, little known, and unpredictable in their reactions – the Magma, the molten core around which most of world history has been built. When it comes to the surface, then it breaks through the shell within which the sedentary civilisations endeavour to contain it, man, horror-stricken, speaks of catastrophe ... And when the eruption calms down ... the molten lava is added to the crust and helps to contain the forces that brought it to the surface. The solid crust becomes thicker and thicker. The eruptions become less frequent. ... (I: 93)

This is again following the old mode of seeing Central Asia, the land of nomads, as a blank or, even worse, as a negative which made its presence felt only through catastrophes. We hope we have moved beyond this. But perhaps there are more useful analogies from the natural world. In a previous work, I compared Central Asia to a great ocean, but I still made the mistake, as I see it now, of suggesting that the various, literate surrounding civilizations were like the great land masses on the shores of which the currents of the enclosed ocean brought influences from other shores, mixed along the way by the ebb and flow of ocean currents. But this distinction between the land and the water again inevitably establishes a hierarchy between the two, separating sedentary civilization from nomadic barbarism. This model, once again, has a dichotomous model at its foundation. I now think it is more appropriate to think of a cultural world as being like a world only of water, a world where great currents ebb and flow, sometimes interacting and sometimes (like the Gulf Stream) retaining a distinct identity, but where there is no distinction. All is water, whether warm current, cold currents, deep or shallow; each supports its own distinctive natural life, its own culture, but there are constant interactions and exchanges, and blurred or permeable and constantly shifting boundaries. The interaction and effects of actual ocean currents are now described by oceanologists using complex computer animations. Perhaps we can make use of these dynamic geospatial models in the humanities.

Attempts to use computer models for mapping ocean circulations began in the 1960s, but it took three decades before the oceanologists had acquired sufficient data and before computers were powerful enough to process it quickly. Collecting data and building suitable models were essential to a new understanding of ocean currents, as Weart explains, but now oceanologists are able to predict future changes as well as to understand past ones. Similar although much cruder models are just starting to be used by some in the humanities, although this work is still in its infancy. The Electronic Cultural Atlas Initiative (ECAI) has been trying to encourage such modelling among humanities scholars for a decade by providing some of the necessary tools and support, but as yet has made few inroads. ECAI's website shows various attempts at such models, including a relatively early and crude model showing an animation of the growth of the Mongol empire between 1100 and 1400 as well as a more sophisticated later model showing the growth and decline of the Mughal empire (ECAI). In the latter example, the empire is shown in red and one can see how it behaves in a curious way: it looks rather like a film of oil or ink on water that can only cover so much surface area before breaking up. Of course, we all know there is a logistic limit on empires, but this computer model displays it in a very immediate and compelling way. It also shows how the empire is constricted by geography, especially by the Himalayan Mountains to the north.

These two examples show single empires and are very crude compared to models used by oceanologists. The power of such systems is that they can show multiple layers and multiple interactions in space and time. Mapping the movements of peoples, languages, cultures, technologies, and ideas, alongside the rise and fall of political and economic entities such as empires, cities, and trade routes, is all possible. The model both is genuinely cross-disciplinary and also, of course, shows no boundaries or distinctions between East and West. When we have more complex and animated models displaying layers of data over time, how much more will our understanding of the complexities of human history be changed? So, while we understand in some sense that a movement at one end of the steppes would, as Knobloch put it, 'bring about quite unexpected consequences, continuously subjecting this immense area to migratory movement' (15), can we really conceptualize this with our current models, which are merely written words and static maps?

This is just one model which we could use almost immediately in our teaching and research to start to present a more complex reality than one modelled using dichotomies. This approach will not be realized, however, until scholars and students are encouraged to collate data and develop computer models, activities not yet generally recognized as scholarship in the humanities. Computers are still used as scribes, but, as I hope I have indicated, words coined as shorthand to express complex ideas all too often end up suppressing the complexity and limiting our thinking. If we are to move beyond stultifying dichotomous thinking, we need to exploit the available technology to help us find better ways to conceptualize history's complexities and to move into a world no longer divided into East and West.

NOTES

1 See Said's definition of Orientalism: 'Orientalism is a style of thought based upon ontological and epistemological distinction made between "the Orient" and (most of the time) "the Occident." Thus a very large mass of writers, among whom are poets, novelists, philosophers, political theorists, economists, and imperial administrators, have accepted the basic distinction between East and West as the starting point for elaborate accounts concerning the Orient, its people, customs, "mind," destiny, and so on ... the phenomenon of Orientalism as I study it here deals principally, not with a correspondence between Orientalism and Orient, but with the internal consistency of Orientalism and its ideas about the Orient despite or beyond any correspondence, or lack thereof, with a "real" Orient' (1–3, 5).
2 There is a lively debate on nomenclature and boundaries of this region, but since my paper is concerned with finding models that do not constrain us

to fixed boundaries, I simply use Central Asia here as a recognizable term for most readers. For further discussion and references, see my article 'Was There a Silk Road?'

3 For example, see Haun Saussy, *Great Walls of Discourse*, Prasenjit Duara, *Rescuing History*, and Ranajit Guha, *History at the Limit*.

4 Other non-western countries are also using the precedent of Orientalism, but to argue that western civilization is unnatural and decadent – that is, inherently base and depraved. This 'Occidentalism' is discussed by Ian Buruma and Avishai Margalit in their recent book. They point out that Said himself dismissed such a scenario: 'Nobody is likely to imagine a field symmetrical to [Orientalism] called Occidentalism.'

5 The World Wars must have had a detrimental effect not only in interrupting the training of new scholars but also in shifting attention to a new world arena and new world powers.

11 Marco Polo: Meditations on Intangible Economy and Vernacular Imagination

YUNTE HUANG

As befits the genre of meditation, this essay proceeds in incomplete circles and ponders the intangibility of sound and the increasingly acoustic quality of value, truth, and reality in the twenty-first century. I begin with a return, or re-tune, to the frequently read but seldom heard Prologue to Marco Polo's book, a passage in which the speaker makes a plea that we *listen* to the book. The acoustic truth, to which Polo's speaker has begged us to attend, finds reverberations throughout this essay in Italo Calvino's *Invisible Cities*, Kublai Khan's paper money, British Romanticists' poetic imagination, George Soros's global capitalism, twenty-first-century virtual money, and so on. Whether it is in the case of cities that are invisible but audible, of the emperor's words that have acquired gold-like quality, or of a financial market where reality is not objectively visible like signals, but intersubjective like echoes, my primary concern is with the intangible economy, which constantly eludes the grasp of our logic-based, vision-biased rationality. In the fantastic tales of Calvino, we already witness the pitfall of an empire built on the principles of spatial conquest – the Great Khan insists on hearing the cities he has conquered, as if only sound could reveal the ultimate truth of those dots already visible on his imperial map. Poetic imagination as defined by the Romanticists, while taking us closer to the intangible economy, shares with the imperial conquest the same preference for vision. To escape such vision-ary constraints, I propose vernacular imagination as a description of a mode of being in the world built on both vision and sound. In this acoustic space, we hear the sound-bites of reality as echoes of dreams, moneyed thoughts uttered in local currencies, and clashes of empires as a result of a few misheard words.

Cordier 1: 111). The foreignness of the proper names creates tre-
ous difficulties for annotators to ascertain the exact reference, as
referents existed only in sound. 'Falsehood is never in words,'
s Calvino's Marco Polo, 'it is in things' (*Invisible Cities* 62). Com-
ng on the French – supposedly the first – copy of the narrative,
y Yule notices that in the book's style, apart from grammar or
ulary, there is 'a rude angularity, a rough dramatism like that of
narrative.' The frequent change in spelling of the same proper
es, occurring sometimes within only a few lines, is especially
ative of 'the unrevised product of dictation,' a tale caught by ear
and fixed by pen later (Yule-Cordier 1: 83–4).
e acoustic markers that draw us into the presence of the narration,
disappear faster than they appear, meet their echoes in 'a marvel-
thing' that Polo describes about a desert in China:

hen travelers are on the move by night, and one of them chances to lag
ehind or to fall asleep or the like, when he tries to gain his company
gain he will hear spirits talking, and will suppose them to be his com-
ades. Sometimes the spirits will call him by name; and thus shall a trav-
ler ofttimes be led astray so that he never finds his party. And in this
vay many have perished. [Sometimes the stray travelers will hear as it
vere the tramp and hum of a great cavalcade of people away from the
eal line of road, and taking this to be their own company they will fol-
ow the sound; and when day breaks they find that a cheat has been put
on them and that they are in an ill plight.] Even in the day-time one hears
those spirits talking. And sometimes you shall hear the sound of a variety of musical instruments, and still more commonly the sound of
drums. (Yule-Cordier 1: 197)

is striking that Polo here describes an acoustic illusion rather than
optical one. A mirage, which travellers often encounter in deserts,
an illusory image of something that actually exists ('a deceptive
nage of a distant object formed by light that is refracted as it passes
rough air of varying temperature' – *Oxford English Dictionary*, s.v.
nirage'). But this 'sound mirage,' which occurs in a desert known in
hina by the name of *Lew-sha*, i.e., 'Quicksand,' or 'Flowing Sands'
1: 198), cannot be seen but only heard in one's head, not verifiable but
ntensely hypnotizing.
In *The Global Village: Transformations in World Life and Media in the
Twenty-First Century* (1989), Marshall McLuhan and Bruce R. Powers

1. Acoustic Truths

The book of Marco Polo, as one of his most
sounds like 'a Chinese whisper translated fron
ness of the language, which Frances Wood and
the evidence that the infamous Merchant of Ven
to China, speaks nonetheless to the acoustic trut
genesis of the book, as we know it, lies in dictati
in Genoa, Polo asked his fellow inmate, Messer I
his oral narratives to writing. In case the reader s
tics of the book, the Prologue duly contains a 1
a caveat:

> Great Princes, Emperors, and Kings, Dukes and
> Knights, and Burgesses! and People of all degrees who
> edge of the various races of mankind and of the diver
> regions of the World, take this Book and *cause it to be rea*
> find therein all kinds of wonderful things ... according t
> Messer Marco Polo, a wise and noble citizen of Venice, a
> *his own eyes*. Some things indeed there be therein which
> these he *heard* from men of credit and veracity. And v
> things *seen as seen*, and things *heard as heard* only, so that r
> may mar the truth of our Book, and that all who shall rea
> may put full faith in the truth of all its contents. (Yule-Co
> italics mine)

The speaker here is careful to distinguish between 't
'things heard,' between cognizable facts and reliable he
to intensify the effects of the latter, he recommends that
the book with ears, as does the Great Khan in Italo Ca
book, who prefers to hear (about) the 'invisible cities.'
does not condemn the cities to the realm of nowhere; cit
may be audible, or tactile, existing in what Marshall I
called the 'acoustic space.'

The book of Marco Polo, then, is built on acoustic signa
on visual signs. Names of places, persons, and objects are
in their Persian, Mongol, or Turkish sounds rather than C
even though they often have Chinese equivalents: *Cathe*
Pulisanghin, Tangut, Chagannor, Saianfu, Kenjanfu, Tenduc, A
jan, Zardandan, Zayton, Kemenfu, Brius, Caramoran, Chorcl

(Yule-
mend
if the
asser
ment
Henr
vocal
oral
nam
indi
first
Tl
that
ous

W
b
a
r
e

It
a
i
t

try to differentiate acoustic space from visual space: 'The left-hemisphere [of the human brain] places information structurally in visual space, where things are connected sequentially – having separate centers with fixed boundaries. On the other hand, acoustic space structure, the function of the right brain in which processes are related simultaneously, has centers everywhere with boundaries nowhere.' The nature of the human eye, which gave birth to linear logic, encourages reasoning by exclusion: Something is either in that space or it isn't. By contrast, sounds can be neither inside nor outside and they function less like signals than replies. If the visual space may be compared to a painting or a photograph, the acoustic space may be likened to a symphonic surround (McLuhan and Powers 8; 39).

2. From the Invisible (Cities) to the Intangible (Economy)

The visible world is no longer a reality and the unseen world is no longer a dream.

(William Butler Yeats)

The Great Khan waged a battle against the uncertainties in the entanglement between an acoustic signal and its even more elusive referent. In Calvino's *Invisible Cities*, the Khan begins by listening to the Venetian Merchant's tales with some scepticism: 'Kublai Khan does not necessarily believe everything Marco Polo says when he describes the cities visited on his expeditions, but the emperor of the Tartars does continue listening to the young Venetian with greater attention and curiosity than he shows any other messenger or explorer of his' (5). Soon the emperor becomes impatient and interrupts Polo: 'From now on I shall describe the cities and you will tell me if they exist and are as I have conceived them' (43). If there is still something iffy in the Khan's conception – his voiced words may or may not materialize in real cities, because they are still subject to the listener's verification – then the other scheme of his would make his words 'achieve cities too probable to be real' (Calvino 69). And that scheme is the making of paper money.

In this famous chapter in Marco Polo's narrative, the Khan becomes an alchemist, a conjuror, who causes his words to be equivalent to all the treasure in the world:

The Emperor's Mint then is in this same city of Cambaluc, and the way it is wrought is such that you might say he hath the Secret of Alchemy in perfection, and you would be right! For he makes his money after this fashion.

He makes them take of the bark of a certain tree, in fact of the Mulberry Tree, the leaves of which are the food of the silkworms, – these trees being so numerous that whole districts are full of them. What they take is a certain fine white bast or skin which lies between the wood of the tree and the thick outer bark, and this they make into something resembling sheets of paper, but black. When these sheets have been pre-pared they are cut up into pieces of different sizes. The smallest of these sizes is worth a half tornesel; the next, a little larger, one tornesel; one, a little larger still, is worth half a silver groat of Venice; another a whole groat; others yet two groats, five groats, and ten groats. There is also a kind worth one Bezant of gold, and others of three Bezants, and so up to ten. All these pieces of paper are [issued with as much solemnity and authority as if they were of pure gold or silver; and on every piece a vari-ety of officials, whose duty it is, have to write their names, and to put their seals. And when all is prepared duly, the chief officer deputed by the Kaan smears the Seal entrusted to him with vermilion, and impresses it on the paper, so that the form of the Seal remains printed upon it in red; and Money is then authentic. Any one forging it would be punished with death.] And the Kaan causes every year to be made such a vast quantity of this money, which costs him nothing, that it must equal in amount all the treasure in the world. (Yule-Cordier 1: 423–4)

The secret of the Khan's alchemy lies in the 'as if' effect: 'as if they were of pure gold or silver.' And the key to the success of the poetic confla-tion is to get rid of the 'iffiness' and turn 'as if' into simply 'as.' This is a verbal trickery Calvino's Khan is unable to perform because his futuristic descriptions of cities have yet to be verified by Marco Polo: 'It is not the voice that commands the story: it is the ear' (Calvino 135). In Polo's narrative, however, the Khan becomes King Midas; his words, as deputed by his officials, change into gold when they fall onto sheets of paper. His voice is not just golden; it is as good as gold.

That voices, words, and other intangible things acquire the power of creating wealth or become wealth itself is not just a socio-economic reality in Khan's empire or in any society where there is an uneven power structure; it is an essential feature of what we in the twenty-first century have called the 'intangible economy.' In our postindustrial age, an identifiable shift from the tangible to the intangible has taken place: The economic landscape is no longer shaped by physical flows of material goods and products, but by ethereal streams of data, images, and symbols. Whereas at the core of the agricultural economy was a relationship between man, nature, and natural products, and at the core of the industrial economy was a relationship between man, machine, and machine-created artificial objects, the intangible economy is structured around relationships between man and ideas and symbols. Today, the source of economic value and wealth is no longer the production of material goods but the creation and manipulation of intangible content (Goldfinger 93).

The Khan is apparently a forerunner of such intangible economy with his boundless ability to create and manipulate signs and their relationship to reality/value. In some sense the name of the Khan is a most precious intangible asset. Like a name brand in our postindustrial age, the value of such an asset is beyond calculation, or is indeed, as Polo observes admiringly and jealously, 'equal in amount to all the treasure in the world.' In the case of the Khan, value is determined not by the weight of gold and silver, but by his words, voices, seals, etc.; in the case of a postindustrial company, value is calculated not by its output of material production, but by its brand, human capital, intellectual property, knowledge, and above all the ever-fickle pricing of its stocks.

Such dematerialization of value is deeply unsettling because it runs squarely against some of the key tenets of the conventional logic of economy: 'Conventional logic is concerned with scarcity, dematerialization logic with abundance. The former stresses equilibrium; the latter, disequilibrium. Obsolescence, redundancy and volatility, perceived in the past as pernicious epiphenomena, now constitute essential and necessary vectors' (Goldfinger 98). Most unsettling about such dematerialization, however, is the emergence of the concept of truth that is no longer cognizable, but fleeting, flying, audible, tactile, and above all, participatory.

In his reflections upon the crisis of global capitalism, billionaire and philanthropist George Soros points out that truth nowadays is not – even if it ever were – cognizable, but instead is participatory. 'We have come to treat correspondence as the hallmark of truth. But correspondence can be brought about in two ways: either by making true statements or by making an impact on the facts themselves. Correspondence is not the guarantor of truth' (14–15). Especially in the world of global capital, cognizable truths, something the narrator in Polo's book painstakingly tries to differentiate from audible hearsays, become interactive mirages that change according to the actions of the observer: 'Physical objects move the way they move irrespective of what anybody thinks.

But financial markets attempt to predict a future that is contingent on the decisions people make in the present. Instead of just passively reflecting reality, financial markets are actively creating the reality that they, in turn, reflect. There is a two-way connection between present decisions and future events, which I call reflexivity' (Soros xxiii).

Such reflexivity would place value and truth less in the visual space, which is dominated by linear logic and abstraction, than in the acoustic space, where sounds, to quote McLuhan and Powers again, flow more like replies than signals. In their study of the history of media, McLuhan and Powers consider the invention of paper money as a major step toward the acoustic and intangible: 'Cash money and the compass, leading technologies of the fifteenth century, illustrate early figure-ground transformations of visual space archetypes to the acoustic, from the tangible to the intangible, from hardware dominance to software dominance – analogous to the present role of the computer. Current shift from visual space to acoustic space technologies in society is accelerating' (35). And their investigation of the 'global village' concludes with a description of the Electronic Funds Transfer System (EFTS) as an acoustic space, a world of the simultaneous, whose centre is everywhere and whose margin is nowhere (121). It is in this acoustic world that a modern-day Cinderella was born – virtual money.

3. From 'Flying Money' to 'Daylight Money'

> When evening came Cinderella wanted to leave, and the prince tried to escort her, but she ran away from him so quickly that he could not follow her. The prince, however, had set a trap. He had had the entire stairway smeared with pitch. When she ran down the stairs, her left slipper stuck in the pitch. The prince picked it up. It was small and dainty, and of pure gold.
>
> (Jacob and Wilhelm Grimm, 'Cinderella')

Virtual money is a kind of money that circles around the globe without a permanent, cognizable interface but whose effect is world-changing. It enabled, for instance, Soros to make a fortune of five billion dollars within a few months in 1992 by successfully shorting the British pounds. It is a money that is never to be touched, held, or seen; that is always in motion, 'in the form of brief pulses of light that glide outward through cyberspace like ripples in a pond'; and that also includes plastic money, credit and debit cards, and the e-money used in the internet trade (Solomon ix). Virtual money is often compared to a virtual particle in quantum mechanics, a particle that, according to Stephen Hawking, 'can never be directly detected, but whose existence does have measurable effects' (187). And virtual money's effects are indeed astonishing if we would just consider these facts: The value of foreign currency trading, which is conducted almost exclusively in cyberspace, averaged $1.1 trillion a day in 2000, more than fifty times greater than the daily physical trade volume and thirty times larger than the combined volume of all US equity markets. The relative weight of non-cash monetary transactions now exceeds the value of cash money by a factor of ten. Money and payments are almost entirely delivered via electronic networks as data bits and database entries (Goldfinger 92–3).

That mobile digital bits have replaced cash money is not, however, such a far cry from the invention of the so-called flying money, which existed in China almost two thousand years ago and to which historians have attributed the origin of Khan's paper money. The Chinese *feiqian*, or 'flying money,' was essentially a draft to transmit funds to distant places. In the Tang dynasty (618–907), there emerged large-scale commercial activities, of which the most spectacular was the tea trade between south China and Chang'an, the Tang capital, in the north. The tea merchants wished to transfer profits realized from the sale of tea in the north back to the south, but found the shipment of cash both cumbersome and perilous. The same problem of transfer faced the provincial authorities who were obliged to send monetary tribute and gifts to the imperial court. These authorities maintained in the capital liaison offices known as 'memorial-presenting courts,' whose duty in part was to expedite presentation of gifts. The transfer problem was solved by the institution of 'flying money,' whereby merchants deposited cash with the 'memorial-presenting courts,' in return for vouchers guaranteeing reimbursement in designated provinces. Thereby a double transfer of cash was realized without an actual physical transfer. Hence the picturesque name 'flying money' (Yang, *Money* 51–2).

Almost all forms of modern-day virtual money are 'flying money' of sorts because they all share the feature of mobility. But the queen among them, the form that represents the epitome of intangible economy, is 'daylight money.' Imagine a bank sending money by wire but being over its credit cap; in the US (and in many other countries) the bank can borrow on overdraft but must pay back the sum within the day. These funds, existing only as figures on computer screens, live essentially on borrowed time. But before their inevitable end-of-day demise, they can buy and sell just as 'real' money does. 'Like Cinder-ella at the ball,' writes Elinor Harris Solomon, the daylight money 'has but a certain length of time in which to play. It buys and sells assets, whether currencies or thirty-year Treasury bonds. It stirs things up in markets and responds to expectations shifts. In a brief time span, it captures not a prince but a profits prize' (205). When the bell rings – not the midnight bell at the prince's ball, but the closing bell of a business day – the virtual money vanishes in a cloud of settlement smoke, only to arise again like the sun the next (business) morning.

4. Imagination: A Romantic Detour

In Xanadu did Kubla Khan
A stately pleasure-dome decree:
Where Alph, the sacred river, ran
Through caverns measureless to man
   Down to a sunless sea.
So twice five miles of fertile ground
With walls and towers were girdled round:
And there were gardens bright with sinuous rills
Where blossomed many an incense-bearing tree;
And here were forests ancient as the hills,
Enfolding sunny spots of greenery.
                (Samuel Taylor Coleridge, 'Kubla Khan')

Like money that is mobile, a romantic poet's mind can also travel long distances. For the poem 'Kubla Khan,' Coleridge provided a note of explanation: 'In the summer of the year 1797, the Author, then in ill health, had retired to a lonely farm house between Porlock and Linton, on the Exmoor confines of Somerset and Devonshire. In consequence of a slight indisposition, an anodyne had been prescribed, from the effect of which he fell asleep in his chair at the moment that he was reading the following sentence, or words of the same substance, in *Purchas's Pilgrimage*: "Here the Khan Kubla commanded a palace to be built, and a stately garden thereunto: and thus ten miles of fertile ground were inclosed with a wall"' (*Complete Poems* 249).

The poet is meticulous about the local details, 'a lonely farm house between Porlock and Linton, on the Exmoor confines of Somerset and Devonshire,' partly because he wants to foreground the poetic mind's extraordinary capacity to travel across space and time and land itself in an oriental palace centuries ago. Coleridge uses the phrase 'words of the same substance' because his quote from Purchas is not exact.[2] If faithful duplication is the mode of validation of a culture of print, to which Coleridge rightly belongs, here he is apparently more concerned with the 'substance' that underlies words, visions, dreams, and realities.[3] He disregards the laws of print for a good reason: He is following a higher law, the law of imagination. Coleridge is the one who has provided us with the quintessential Romanticist definition of 'imagination,' which he also calls the 'esemplastic power.' He coined the word 'esemplastic' and used it to mean 'moulding into unity.' Imagination, according to Coleridge, is 'the living power and prime agent of all human perception' and 'a repetition in the finite mind of the eternal act of creation in the infinite I AM ... It struggles to idealize and to unify. It is essentially vital, even as all objects (as objects) are essentially fixed and dead' (*Biographia* 167).

That Coleridge in his opium reverie would dream of the palace of the Khan may be a result of his reading of Purchas's book, or it can be a staged performance of Romantic exoticism or Coleridge's trademark mysticism. But there could be an even deeper reason. If Khan is, as I have suggested, a forerunner of intangible economy, the Romanticists are certainly its early advocates. Intangible economy, as we know, is structured around relationships between man and ideas and symbols, rather than between man, nature, and natural products as in agricultural economy, or between man, machine, and machine-created artificial objects as in industrial economy. Likewise, the Romanticists ran up against the centuries-old poetic theory of mimesis, which takes as its central concern the relationship between art and nature, and turned exclusively to imagination, whose interface is between man, his mind, and his poetic work. As M.H. Abrams puts it in his classic *The Mirror and the Lamp*, 'Instead of imitation ... the orientation is now toward the artist, the focus of attention is upon the relation of the elements of the work to his state of mind' (47). Like the Great Khan, who envisions cities and wealth at will and in his mind, a Romantic poet, as Coleridge put it, expresses 'intellectual purposes, thoughts, conceptions, sentiments, that have their origin in the human mind' (qtd. in Abrams 48). In his opium reverie, Coleridge states that 'The author continued for about three hours in a profound sleep, at least of the external senses, during which time he has the most vivid confidence, that he could not have composed less than from two to three hundred lines; if that indeed can be called composition in which all the images rose up before him as things, with a parallel production of the correspondent expressions, without any sensation or consciousness of the effort' (*Complete Poems* 439). Images, things, and expressions – all of them are interchangeable with each other.

Such a Romantic sublimity in the poet's head may now be recreated in a computer's brain: Virtual money, information, access codes, and intellectual property all share a common technological substratum of digital storage in networked computers. It is, therefore, 'easy and cheap to exchange money for information, information for access, access for intellectual property acknowledgement, and so on. Each of these can be used alternatively as a store of value and/or exchange medium' (Goldfinger 110). Call that the digital sublime.

5. The Return of Polo: The Ear versus the Eye

'The other ambassadors warn me of famines, extortions, conspiracies, or else they inform me of newly discovered turquoise mines, advantageous prices in marten furs, suggestions for supplying damascened blades. And you?' the Great Khan asked Polo, 'you return from lands equally distant and you can tell me only the thoughts that come to a man who sits on his doorstep at evening to enjoy the cool air. What is the use, then, of all your traveling? ... My gaze is that of a man meditating, lost in thought – I admit it. But yours? You cross archipelagoes, tundras, mountain ranges. You would do as well never moving from here.'

(Italo Calvino, *Invisible Cities*)

The Khan's scepticism over the worth of Polo's travel is completely understandable from a Romanticist's viewpoint. Indeed, if Coleridge could see the Khan's palace without having to move an inch from his chair, 'What is the use, then, of all your traveling?' It was in this context that the Khan told the Venetian, 'From now on, I'll describe the cities to you ... in your journeys you will see if they exist' (Calvino 69). Both the Khan and Coleridge turned inward to seek reality. 'Perhaps, Kublai thought, the empire is nothing but a zodiac of the mind's phantasms' (Calvino 22). Why, then, did the Khan want to hear Polo's stories? Could it be that there is something in hearing that even the most powerful imperial vision would not be able to, forgive the tautology, envision?

The Mongol emperor was a foreigner (who wouldn't be?) to the vast empire he had built; the dominant language in this empire, namely

Chinese, was a foreign tongue to him. 'The foreignness of what you no longer are or no longer possess lies in wait for you in foreign, unpossessed places' (Calvino 29). An empire, boundless as it appears, exists in the visual space, which is ruled by boundaries; sound, however, is difficult to conquer. Could it be, then, that Polo's book, so far as it is a description of the empire, already exists in the Khan's mind, since he has indeed conquered all the cities; but it is the acoustic space, where cities exist in their invisibility, that constantly eludes his grasp? '"On the day when I know all the emblems," he asked Marco, "shall I be able to possess my empire, at last?" And the Venetian answered: "Sire, do not believe it. On that day you will be an emblem among emblems"' (Calvino 22–3). Polo's answer is enigmatic; a clearer answer would be: It depends on what you mean by 'know,' because there is seeing, and then there is hearing.

Curiously enough, the only piece of Chinese evidence – if it is indeed evidence – that may lend credibility to Polo's narrative exists in sound, or at least it requires one to listen across languages in order to hear the acoustic connections among a Chinese document, a Persian record, and Polo's narrative. Since the story of Marco Polo was first introduced into China in 1874, Chinese historians had tried in vain to uncover any evidence among the vast arrays of Chinese historical records to authenticate Polo as a reliable narrator. In 1941, Chinese historian Zhijiu Yang published an article in which he announced his discovery of a passage in Chinese concerning Marco Polo's departure from China. On the basis of an official note recorded in the 19,148th volume of the encyclopedic *Yongle dadian*, Yang proves that the names of the three emissaries the note refers to are the same as those of the three emissaries dispatched by Argon mentioned in Polo's book.

In Book One, Chapter XVII of the Yule-Cordier edition, there is a passage that reads:

> Now it came to pass in those days that the Queen Bolgana, wife of Argon, Lord of the Levant, departed this life. And in her Will she had desired that no Lady should take her place, or succeed her as Argon's wife, except one of her own family [which existed in Cathay]. Argon therefore dispatched three of his Barons, by name respectively Qulatay, Apusca, and Coja, as ambassadors to the Great Khan, attended by a very gallant company, in order to bring back as his bride a lady of the family of Queen Bolgana, his late wife. (1: 32)

Polo told us that he, his father, and his uncle were able to persuade the Khan to allow them to accompany the three Barons and the chosen

Lady, Kukachin, back to the Levant, and from there they went back to Europe. In the Chinese record that Yang uncovered, the passage reads in English translation (provided by Francis Woodman Cleaves, who published an article in the *Harvard Journal of Asiatic Studies* in 1976 to reassess in part Yang's evidence): 'In the 3rd moon of this year there was received an Imperial Directive [to the effect] that Wu-lu-tai, A-pi-shih-ha, and Huo-che be dispatched to proceed to the domain of the Ta-wang, A-lu-hun, via Ma-pa-erh' (Cleaves 186–7). Cleaves further quotes a crucial passage from a Persian text: 'And after one moon the royal flags faced in the direction of Xurasan and into the city of Abhar came Xwajah and the party of messengers whom Aryun Xan had sent to the servitude of Qa'an in order that they bring one of the kinswomen of the Great Buluyan and seat her in her place' (195–6).

If the eye cannot find traces of connection when gliding over the vast terrain of scriptural differences, the ear can hear the echoes in *Coja*, *Huoche*, and *Xwajah*. Coja, it seems, was the sole survivor of the three emissaries sent by the Great Khan after the long journey, and Polo's narrative also speaks of the loss of many lives on this journey. The sinologists who are willing to lend Polo a sympathetic ear seem to concur that no one who has not heard the name spoken can provide such a seemingly flimsy but acoustically unmistaken line of connection despite the name's different appearances in different texts and languages.

Of all the episodes of Polo's adventure, it is this voyage from China to Persia that Eugene O'Neill chose as the basis for his 1927 play *Marco Millions*. In the Foreword, O'Neill laments that his protagonist has been called a liar in history. But he blames this injustice on Polo himself: 'The failure to appraise Polo at a fair valuation is his own fault. He dictated the book of his travels but left the traveler out. He was no author. He stuck to a recital of what he considered facts and the world called him a liar for his pains' (v). The undervaluation only shows the extent to which O'Neill himself is a prisoner of print culture and its attendant visual biases. Even Henry Yule, Polo's most sympathetic editor, admits that 'in his Book impersonality is carried to excess; and we are often driven to discern by indirect and doubtful indications alone, whether he is speaking of a place from personal knowledge or only from hearsay' (Yule-Cordier 1: 107–8).

In a culture of vision and silent reading, repetitions of such formulaic descriptions as 'the people are idolaters, burn their dead, use paper money, and have a peculiar language' in a series of chapters not only seem unbearably verbose and monotonous, but they also expose the dire lack of visual evidence. But in a culture of orality and vocalized reading, they sound rhythmic and reverberant like an echo chamber. 'One can look at seeing,' says Marcel Duchamp, '[but] one can't hear hearing' (23). If applied to Polo, Duchamp's statement would sound more like a lament than a description. In a world where vision is predominant, hearing is not personal witness. As if he had foreseen such a future verdict on him, Polo's prologue begs us to hear the book read to us, to sound it out: Huo-che, Xwajah, Coja. Indeed, 'a Chinese whisper translated from Persian.'

6. Vernacular Imagination

Huo-che, the Chinese version of Coja, literally means 'fire person,' a person who carries a fire. This fire is the verbal energy that flows through an otherwise fractured landscape of multiple graphic signs. Our ability to listen across linguistic boundaries constitutes what I would call the 'vernacular imagination.' The Romanticist notion of imagination as 'the living power and prime agent of all human *perception*' carries a profound preference for vision; 'transcendence' is above all a visualized, spatial metaphor. While the Romanticists may have taken us a step closer to the world of intangibility (you *see*, I am using a visual metaphor, 'a step closer,' to describe the intangible), they also have left us a legacy of imperialist vision, an esemplastic power that moulds everything into unity. The coupling of 'vernacular' with 'imagination,' then, is my attempt to describe a relationship to the world that is predicated as much on hearing as on vision and a mode of being that is at once local and global.

In an essay entitled 'Cosmopolitan and Vernacular in History,' Sheldon Pollock studies the different historical trajectories of two cosmopolitan vernaculars, Latin and Sanskrit, and comes to the conclusion that 'if the cosmopolitanisms [of the two vernaculars] were similar in transcending the local and stimulating feelings of living in a large world, their modalities were radically different: the one coercive, the other voluntaristic.' What justifies Pollock's conclusion is a small but telling sign, 'the graphic sign itself': 'Roman script was constitutive of Latin literature: *arma virumque cano* could be written in only a single alphabet. The graphic forms of Sanskrit literature, by contrast, were innumerable: *vagarthau iva samprktau* could be inscribed in Javanese script; in Thai, Sinhala, and Grantha in Tamil country; and in Sharada in Kashmir – a substitutability unique among Benedict Anderson's "immense communities" of premodernity'

(28–9). In other words, whereas Latin imposed universality in both sound and vision, Sanskrit at least allowed graphic variations. Whereas Latin 'traveled where it did as the language of a conquest state,' Sanskrit 'never sought to theorize its own universality,' a feature Pollock deems consistent with Sanskrit being 'an alternative form of cosmopolitanism in which "here," instead of being equated with "everywhere," is equated with "nowhere in particular"' (24). It seems that the world of Sanskrit is such an invisible empire built in acoustic space.

Here I would like to draw an analogy between vernacular and money. Money may be a universal language, but currencies speak vernaculars of their own. Curiously enough, currencies are usually called in their native tongues: dollar, pound, yuan, yen, won, mark, franc, lira, ruble, baht, etc. We may change their graphic appearance when we transliterate them into English, but their sounds remain. It is as if we must have our own *terms*, with their sounds as measures, in order to understand, to *come to terms* with the world and its meaning. In Polo's narrative, the reader/listener is constantly asked to look at things in terms of Venetian currency:

> The smallest of these sizes is worth a half tornesel; the next, a little larger, one tornesel; one, a little larger still, is worth half a silver groat of Venice; another a whole groat; others yet two groats, five groats, and ten groats. There is also a kind worth one Bezant of gold, and others of three Bezants, and so up to ten. (Yule-Cordier 1: 423–4)

Or,

> First there is the salt, which brings in a great revenue. For it produces every year, in round numbers, fourscore tomans of gold; and the toman is worth 70,000 saggi of gold, so that the total value of the fourscore tomans will be five million and six hundred thousand saggi of gold, each saggio being worth more than a gold florin or ducat. (2: 171)

Or,

> And you must know that Messer Marco Polo, who relates all this, was several times sent by the Great Kaan to inspect the amount of his customs and revenue from this ninth part of Manzi, and he found it to be, exclusive of the salt revenue which we have mentioned already, 210 tomans of gold, equivalent to 14,700,000 saggi of gold. (2: 172)

It seems that unless Polo renders everything in Venetian terms, such as tornesels, groats, saggi, florins, and ducats, his European contemporaries will have no way of imagining what he has seen. Monetary terms, besides being called in their vernacular sounds, are often themselves related to sounds. The Venetian ducat of Polo's times, for instance, bears an inscription 'SIT.T.XRE.DAT.Q.TV.REGIS.ISTE. DUCAT,' which is meant to be read aloud as 'Sit tibi Christe datus, quem tu Regis, iste ducatus' ('Let this duchy, which thou rulest, be dedicated to thee, O Christ') (Shell 69). The issuing of a new coin is technically called an 'utterance.' To utter, according to the *Oxford English Dictionary*, means 'to give currency to; to put into circulation,' as well as 'to send forth as a sound; to speak, say, or pronounce.'[4]

7. Rhubarb, Opium, and Coleridge's Dysentery: A Loose End

> This fragment with a good deal more, not recoverable, composed, in a sort of Reverie brought on by two grains of opium, taken to check a dysentery, at a Farm House between Porlock & Linton, a quarter of a mile from Culbone Church, in the fall of the year, 1797.
>
> (Coleridge's note found on a manuscript copy of 'Kubla Khan')

Coleridge took the poetically inspiring opium to cure his dysentery (*Complete Poems* 525). In 1839, on the eve of the first Opium War, China was imagining the opposite problem for the population of Great Britain: constipation. In his official letter to Queen Victoria, the high imperial commissioner Lin Zexu tried to persuade Her Majesty to stop dumping opium in the Chinese market–the British had engaged in such aggressive drug dealing in order to balance the huge trade deficit created by their excessive fondness for Chinese tea. Couched within the diplomatic niceties of the letter was a threat: 'Has China (we should like to ask) ever yet sent forth a noxious article from its soil? Not to speak of our tea and rhubarb, things which your foreign countries could not exist a single day without, if we of the Central Land were to grudge you what is beneficial, and not to compassionate your wants, then wherewithal could you foreigners manage to exist?' (qtd. in J.T.C. Liu 234). In other words, if you don't stop selling opium in China, we will stop exporting tea and rhubarb to you. Lin was imagining that with all the excessive consumption of tea, the British populace must be suffering from constipation, which may be alleviated by rhubarb, a medicinal root whose great abundance in China was keenly noted by Marco Polo.[5]

If Lin's threat may be construed as a one-sided perception of the problem, the British were not any better: they wilfully misread the letter and heard something far more offensive. Lin's letter was written in Chinese, and the above-quoted passage can be translated differently as: 'Is there a single article from China which has done any harm to foreign countries? Take tea and rhubarb, for example; the foreign countries cannot get along for a single day without them. If China cuts off these benefits with no sympathy for those who are to suffer, then what can the *barbarians* rely upon to keep themselves alive?' (qtd. in Liu 234). The crucial substitution of 'barbarians' for 'foreigners' as translation of the Chinese term in Lin's letter, 'yiren,' could be deeply offensive to the queen. As Lydia Liu has argued in her study of the politics of translation during China's clash with the West in the nineteenth century, *yiren* was a supersign that has entangled and embattled etymologies. While the Chinese term may be neutral and can be simply translated as 'foreigner,' the Western countries often translated it as 'barbarian' and thereby regarded Chinese documents that use this word in their originals as deeply insulting (31–69). One nation exaggerated the other's bowel problem, and one nation misheard the other's speech (the Greek term *barbaros* mimics the sound of incomprehensible speech). So the war broke out and we know the rest of the story.

Fast forward one and a half centuries, and we have another story that also makes use of vernacular imagination, but with a happy ending. On 1 April 2001, while doing reconnaissance in the South China Sea, a US navy spy plane collided with a Chinese military aircraft. The Chinese plane disappeared and its pilot was supposedly dead. The US plane was also damaged and had to perform an emergency landing in China without authorization. The US crew was detained by the Chinese, triggering a diplomatic crisis. What eventually resolved the issue was an intentional mistranslation, a purposeful realignment of the equivalence of words in English and Chinese as they are used in diplomatic exchanges. In his half-hearted letter of apology to the Chinese government, the US ambassador Joseph W. Prueher states, 'Please convey to the Chinese people and to the family of pilot Wang Wei that we are very sorry for their loss... We are very sorry the entering of China's airspace and the landing did not have verbal clearance' (Prueher). When reported in Chinese media, however, the English phrase 'very sorry,' which sounds almost too simple or casual for an event of such magnitude, was translated into Chinese as 'shenbiao-qianyi.' Meaning literally 'expressing the deepest regret,' the Chinese phrase carries a weight of formality that goes way beyond the English colloquial term. It was this Chinese phrase that was published in bold as headlines in the Chinese media, and it effectively quieted the raging anti-US sentiments. The crew was released and the spy plane returned. Despite the perennial US complaint of China's pegging of its currency against the dollar (as of today, 19 May 2005, the exchange rate of one US dollar to one Chinese yuan is 1 : 8.2765), this is one pegged, uneven linguistic trade that the US is more than happy to allow: 'very sorry' for 'shenbiaoqianyi.'

Somewhere the Merchant of Venice is whispering to the ears of his listeners because the secret is almost too good to be true: 'In the mountains belonging to this city, rhubarb and ginger grow in great abundance; insomuch that you may get some 40 pounds of excellent fresh ginger for a Venice groat' (Yule-Cordier 2: 181). We can almost hear the jingling of the moneyed mind, some hearsay by a self-labelled cosmopolite who tries to help the locals imagine a world of wonder in their own terms.

NOTES

1 Frances Wood, *Did Marco Polo Go to China?* 63. See also John W. Haeger, 'Marco Polo in China?' and Craig Clunas, 'The Explorer's Tracks.'
2 The lines from Samuel Purchas, *Purchas his Pilgrimage* (1613), read: 'In Xamdu did Cublai Can build a stately Palace, encompassing sixteene miles of plaine ground with a wall, wherein are fertile Meddowes, pleasant Springs, delightful Streams, and all sorts of beasts of chase and game, and in the middest thereof a sumptuous house of pleasure, which may be removed from place to place' (qtd. in Coleridge, *Complete Poems* 526).
3 For an insightful discussion of duplication as a literate, visual preference, see Vanessa Smith, *Literary Culture and the Pacific.*
4 I am indebted to Stephen Deng for pointing me to the term 'utterance' used in this context.
5 About the province of Sukchur, which he would later confuse with the city of Suju, Polo says, 'Over all the mountains of this province rhubarb is found in great abundance, and thither merchants come to buy it, and carry it thence all over the world' (Yule-Cordier 1: 217).

12 Marco Polo, Chinese Cultural Identity, and an Alternative Model of East-West Encounter

LONGXI ZHANG

When Marco Polo returned to Venice from the East with his father and uncle in 1295 after a long absence of twenty-four years, they were not recognized by their own family members until they ripped open the seams and linings of their well-worn coats cut in the exotic fashion of the Tartars and pulled out a large quantity of rubies, sapphires, and other kinds of precious stones that they had brought back from China. This legend, told by the geographer Giovanni Battista Ramusio (1485–1557) in his *Navigazioni e viaggi*, situates the return of the Polos in the age-old framework of narrative conventions, of which the recognition of Odysseus by the old nurse Euryclea in Book XIX of the Homeric epic provides the archetype of what Northrop Frye called 'the theme of the *nostos* or return home in the *Odyssey*' (319). The establishment of credibility, which is the whole point of this legend, has often been a problem with Marco Polo's remarkable story. Many of his contemporaries regarded him as a 'braggart,' and throughout the centuries the account of his adventurous journey to the East has not gone unchallenged by sceptical scholars who either denied him the experience of having actually gone to China or questioned the veracity of his extraordinary tale.[1] In perhaps the most comprehensive study of Marco Polo's book so far, John Larner has rigorously defended Marco against his detractors, dismissing their sceptical charges as 'nothing outside fantasies of 'jiggery-pokery' and a wholly imaginary hostility between Maffeo and Marco, compounded in a mass of unbridled conjecture' (63). Insofar as the presence of the Polos in China is concerned, however, Larner has no choice but to acknowledge with regret that 'No Chinese source can be used to gain evidence of them' (41).

It is true that Chinese documents of the Mongol-ruled Yuan dynasty have no records either of Marco Polo, or of his father Niccolò and uncle

Maffeo, but the absence of record cannot be taken as proof that the Polos never went to China. As Francis Woodman Cleaves remarks, 'If we were to draw up a list of historical figures who are not mentioned in sources in which we might justifiably expect to encounter their names, it would be excessively long' (192). Yang Zhijiu, a Chinese historian and expert on the Mongol dynasty, also observes that of those other Western travellers to the East before and after Marco Polo, such as Giovanni di Pian di Carpini, William of Rubruck, Prince Hetoum of Little Armenia, and Odorico da Pordenone, there is no Chinese record, either (Yang, *Make Bole* 157). 'If we judge by whether their names appear in Chinese records,' says Yang, 'should we conclude then that none of these people had gone to China, and that their writings were all hearsay or plagiarism? If not, why should we single out Marco Polo for such harsh treatment?' (158). Among Chinese scholars, Yang Zhijiu is indeed the most eloquent of Marco's defenders.

In 1941, while researching the history of the Muslims in the Yuan dynasty, Yang Zhijiu came upon a brief and banal piece of official document, preserved in *juan* (literally a scroll, hence a chapter or volume) 19,418 of the *Yongle dadian* or *Great Compendium Composed during the Yongle Reign*, a multi-volume fourteenth-century encyclopedia. The document is a report sent from Quanzhou (Marco's Zaiton) through the postal relay system under the Mongol rule, in which an official named Sha-bu-ding (Persian or Arabic Sahāb al-Dīn) stated that in the third month of the twenty-seventh year of the Zhiyuan reign (1290), an imperial decree was issued 'to dispatch Wu-lu-dai, A-bi-shi-ke and Huo-zhe to the court of the Great Prince A-lu-hun via Ma-ba-er' (*Yongle dadian* 8: 7211). Yang Zhijiu immediately realized that these foreign-sounding names corresponded perfectly with what Marco Polo mentioned in an important passage of his book: Wu-lu-tai is Marco's Ulatai, A-bi-shi-ke is Abushka, and Huo-zhe is Koja, the Great Prince A-lu-hun is Arghun, lord of the Levant, and Ma-ba-er is Maabar, the Coromandel Coast of India. According to Marco, Lord Arghun's wife Bulagan died, and in her will she stipulated that no lady other than from her own family clan in Cathay should be her successor. Lord Arghun thus sent Ulatai, Abushka, and Koja to Kublai the Great Khan, and Kublai chose a young lady named Kukachin of the lineage of Arghun's late wife for his marriage. When Arghun's Persian emissaries were ready to return to their country with Lady Kukachin, they requested the company of the three Polos, who were experienced in sea voyages. 'The Great Khan, who was very fond of the three,' according to Marco, 'granted this favor with some reluctance and gave leave to the three Latins to travel with the three lords and the lady' (Polo, *Travels* 29). That was how, according to Marco, the Polos were able to take leave of the Great Khan and finally return to Venice. Short of naming Marco Polo directly, this piece of a Yuan dynasty official document offers the best corroborative evidence in a Chinese source to support Marco's claims and thus goes a long way toward establishing the credibility of Marco's narrative about his life in China under Kublai's rule. Although F.W. Cleaves already discussed Yang Zhijiu's discovery of the Chinese document as supporting evidence of Marco's departure from China in an article published in the *Harvard Journal of Asiatic Studies* in 1976, Yang's work seems still largely unknown in the West, and therefore it is necessary to emphasize the importance of his discovery of the hidden relationship between Marco's book and that short piece of official document buried in the huge amount of materials preserved in the Chinese encyclopedic *Yongle dadian*. I believe that Yang's work deserves much wider circulation and better appreciation in the field of Marco Polo scholarship.[2]

Insofar as his contemporaries were concerned, Marco's story was unbelievable not because it was too extravagant in speaking of fabulous creatures or supernatural beings, but because it presented such a plausible picture of China under the rule of Kublai Khan as a civilized and prosperous society beyond the boundaries of medieval Christendom. Of Kublai Marco says: 'all the emperors of the world and all the kings of Christians and of Saracens combined would not possess such power or be able to accomplish so much as this same Kublai, the Great Khan' (Polo, *Travels* 78). It is statements like this that would sound incredible to European readers at the time. As Martin Gosman observes, Marco Polo 'was considered a liar mainly because he contradicted the traditional image of the Mongols. People just could not believe that those barbarians who had threatened to destroy Europe in 1240–1, had reached the level of civilization and organization Marco described in his book' (76–7). That does not mean, however, that Marco's book was not popular at the time, because many manuscripts in various European languages survive to testify to Marco's 'contemporary fame,' 'an unparalleled record in the Middle Ages for translations effected during the life of the author' (Larner 44).

For modern readers with expectations of adventures and medieval legends or fantasies, Marco's book may prove to be disappointing. Despite some strange episodes like Prester John, the Old Man of the

Mountains, and a few other legends and tales, and despite the French title *Le Livre des Merveilles* in a manuscript that includes a version of it, Marco's book is not one of marvels or adventures, but its narrative is very often matter-of-fact in tone, particularly in comparison with texts of medieval travel literature such as the immensely popular *Book of John Mandeville*. Nor is it a guide to trade in the East or a detailed account of the various regions for missionary purposes. In delineating the itineraries of his journey, Marco or his collaborator Rustichello often glossed over details of various places in schematic and formulaic ways, but when he described some of the places in the north, especially Kublai's palaces in Beijing (the Mongolian Khanbaliq), or the famous city of Hangzhou (Marco's Quinsai) in the south, his accounts suddenly gained momentum and became quite vivid and detailed, bearing the marks of lived experience and eyewitness narration. Indeed, there is often a clear sense of genuine admiration, even identification. Marco Polo, as John Larner argues, 'is not an adventurer, a merchant, or a Christian missionary; he is rather a minor Mongolian civil servant who during his years in the East has been an observer or student of the topography and human geography of Asia, of its customs and folklore, of, above all, the authority and court of the Great Khan, all seen from a Mongol point of view' (85). Putting him in contrast with the French friar Jourdain of Serverac, who returned from India in the 1330s to declare that the best place on earth, after all his travels and journeys, was still home 'in our own Christendom,' Larner shows how different Marco Polo was in his stance and perspective:

> The splendours of Khubilai's court, the magnificence of his autocratic rule (in such contrast to the spirit of Venetian republicanism), the great cities of Khanbalikh and 'the paradise' of Quinsai, seem, as we read of them, to surpass anything in the western world. This is not simply because the cities of thirteenth-century China outshone Venice and Pisa, but because 'East-West, home's best', and for Marco home was China. (86)

This is a striking statement, particularly in view of the currently predominant model of East-West encounter based on the opposition between West as colonizer and East as the colonized, an unequal relationship that obtained in more recent times, above all the nineteenth century, when European colonialism was at the height of its expansion. Given the prevailing force of that oppositional model, however, it is only predictable that Marco Polo's book would come to be read, sooner or later, in the theoretical framework of Edward Said's notion of Orientalism regardless of whatever historical gaps there might be in social reality and political outlook between the thirteenth and the nineteenth centuries. That is exactly what Syed Manzurul Islam did when he read Marco's book as an exemplary text that 'registers the full range of the tropes of othering that shaped the Western sense of identity and difference' (123), a text that 'exudes a sense of specialist knowledge about other cultures that would be the hallmark of Orientalism in its institutional phase, which Edward Said has so scrupulously mapped' (124). But Said's *Orientalism* deals largely with European discourse on the Arabic world in the eighteenth and the nineteenth centuries, and its argument cannot be extended to cover all time and all space as a sort of catchall universal theory. Comparing Syed Islam's claims with the actual text of Marco's book, I find it difficult to support those claims. For example, Islam maintains that 'Marco Polo travelled to tell a fantastic story. He is singularly obsessed with difference and the desire to represent it. The world that sprouts from Marco Polo's pen is as strange as the dreamscape of old fables' (123). That is surely a gross exaggeration! If anything, Marco's text is, as I mentioned above, mostly descriptive in a matter-of-fact tone, with very little sensational stuff typical of medieval fables of the marvellous and the fantastic. Larner observes that 'in comparison with the time-hallowed portrait which for so long constituted the agreed popular and general knowledge of the subject, Marco's Asia is strikingly deprived of wonders' (107–8). Yang Zhijiu, himself a Chinese Muslim and a specialist in the Mongol-ruled Yuan dynasty, never takes Marco's book for a dreamscape or idle fantasies. 'Marco Polo's book,' says Yang, 'has recorded a large amount of information about the political, economic and social conditions of China, about its people and customs, of which much can be verified in Chinese documents and books, and will continue to be verified as scholarship develops further. It does have some inevitable defects of overstatements and factual errors, but by and large it can be said to provide a true account' (116). The point is that Marco's book was written at a time and from a perspective remarkably different from that of colonialist explorers of later times, and it is Marco's different outlook on Asia that has made his book so very valuable to us today in rethinking the possibilities of understanding and interactions between the East and the West.

Difficult as it may be for us to imagine in a postcolonial time, it was indeed possible for Marco the Venetian in the thirteenth century to adopt a Mongol's point of view and identify himself with Kublai's court. Marco was genuinely impressed by the vast Mongol empire, the magnificence of Kublai's palaces, the wealth of China, both the northern Cathay and the southern Mangi, and he thought of himself as at the Great Khan's service, though his claim to have governed the city of Yangzhou for three years was groundless and has been dismissed by almost all commentators. The Yuan dynasty in China was ruled by the Mongols as conquerors, who employed in their government what the Han Chinese called 'people with coloured eyes' (*semu ren*) – Muslims, Nestorian Christians, and other foreigners from regions to the west of China. That peculiar situation in Chinese history made it rather easy for people like Marco to integrate into the system, and that may also explain why he was ignorant of the Chinese language and did not mention such well-known facts about Chinese culture and customs as the Great Wall, tea, women's bound feet, fishing with cormorants, Confucianism, Chinese writing, and so on. As Henry Yule argued long ago, Marco gave readers the impression 'that his associations in China were chiefly with foreigners' (intro. to Polo, *Book* 1: 111). Such associations made it possible for Marco to culturally adopt a Mongolian perspective and present to his European readers a picture of China and the East blessed with incredible wealth, sophisticated culture, and social organization, thus offering an alternative model of East-West encounter very different from the Orientalist model of conflict and domination. If Marco had some knowledge of the Han majority, of their language and culture, particularly the idea of Chineseness defined in cultural terms, with which I shall be concerned later in this essay, he might have found it compatible with his own desire and effort to integrate into a different culture and society, and to adopt a different perspective.

As for the marvellous or the fantastic in his book, it is often not Marco himself but his early illustrators who are chiefly responsible for depicting scenes and creatures more grotesque and stranger than Marco described. In a recently published French version based on a fifteenth-century manuscript, *Le Livre des Merveilles*, we find some imaginary pictures that take a hint from Marco's text and push it to the limits of credibility. To be sure, Marco had his own prejudices, stereotypes, and wild imagination largely shaped by his time and his background. In describing the inhabitants of Andaman in the Bay of Bengal, for example, he said that those people 'vivent comme des bêtes, sans être gouvernés par un roi' ['live like beasts, without being governed by a king'], and that 'Tous les hommes de cette île ont une méchante tête de chien, avec des yeux et des dents de chien aussi' ['all the men of this island have ugly heads of dogs, and eyes and teeth of dogs as well'] (Polo, *Livre* 158). In the French manuscript illustration (folio 76v, figure 1; reproduced in this volume as fig. 2.14, p. 47), the metaphorical expression in Marco's text ('comme des bêtes') was taken literally and turned into a surreal picture of several dog-headed figures. These fabulous dog figures are seen engaged in 'l'exercice du commerce des fruits et des céréales' ['exercises of trade in fruits and cereals'] (Polo, *Livre* 158). In another section, Marco speaks of his journey eastward: 'Depuis Campitiu, l'on traverse cinq jours durant, en direction du Levant, une région où maints esprits parlent la nuit' ['From Campitiu, one travels for five days, in the direction from the Levant, across a region where many spirits are heard talking during the night'] (Polo, *Livre* 76). What we find in the French illustration here (folio 29r, figure 2; reproduced in this volume as fig. 2.13, p. 46) is again a fantastic picture of wooded hills and three specimens of mythical creatures: a Cyclops holding a cudgel and a shield, a Sciopod with his big foot up in the air, and one of the Blemmyae, the monstrous race famously described by Shakespeare as 'men whose heads / Do grow beneath their shoulders' (*Othello*, 1.3.143).[3] These fantastic creatures, as Marie-Thérèse Gousset comments, are hardly warranted by Marco's text ('il n'est guère question dans le texte'), but they are nonetheless painted 'évoquent la contrée sauvage entre la province de Campicion et le royaume d'Erguiul dans le Gansu, une région où l'on entend "parler maints esprits de nuit"' ['to evoke the wilderness between the province of Campicion and the kingdom of Erguiul in Gansu, a region where one hears "many spirits of the night talking"'] (Polo, *Livre* 73). Obviously, there is a discrepancy between Marco's text and its illustrations in illuminated manuscripts, which shows that Marco's perspective was difficult for the medieval artists to grasp. Miniaturists commissioned to illustrate Marco's book, as Larner argues, 'though not finding [those fantastic creatures] in the text, decided none the less to include images of them; a work about the East *must* have such things in it!' (82).

The imagining of the Other as barbarian and monstrous, however, is by no means uniquely European or Western, for every civilization, be it Greek or Chinese, in the East or the West, tends to construct its self-identity in differentiation from what is imagined to be the foreign and the uncivilized. The sense of belonging or the notion of a collective identity is always formed in such conceptual oppositions. Therefore it is not coincidental that those fabulous creatures in French illustrations of Marco's book can find almost exact counterparts in an ancient Chinese book, *Shan hai jing* or the *Classic of Mountains and Seas*. Most scholars agree that *Shan hai jing* was compiled during the Warring States period (403–221 BCE), but it contains materials that date back to a much earlier time. It combines geographical knowledge with mythical lore, and its strange and monstrous creatures may represent different tribes and ethnic groups in fabled forms. This book briefly describes a kingdom where people have 'only one eye in the middle of the face,' similar to the Cyclops in Greek mythology (figure 3, Ma 461). To the east of these one-eyed people is another kingdom where the inhabitants 'have one arm and one leg, with inverted knees so that the arm and leg can bend upward' (figure 4, Ma 463). This sounds like just the right description of the Sciopod in *Le Livre des Merveilles*. Then we have the figure Xing Tian, which etymologically may mean 'the beheaded one.' The book records an ancient legend that 'Xing Tian contended with the Yellow Emperor. The Emperor cut off his head and buried him in the Changyang Mountains, but he used his nipples as eyes, his navel as mouth, and continued to hold his weapons and fight,' looking very much like a Blemmye (figure 5, Ma 438). From an anthropological point of view, that ancient myth may symbolically represent the struggle of different tribes and ethnic groups for the control of land and resources, as well as for cultural and political authority.

Like the Greek myth of the war of the Titans against Saturn or the Giants against Jupiter, mythological battles finally resulted in the establishment of cosmic order with the Yellow Emperor as the supreme ruler and the ancestor of Chinese civilization, while his defeated enemies gradually moved from the north and central plains to the south and southwest, and became ancestors of marginalized minority tribes represented in *San hai jing* as half-human, half-animal barbarians. The geographical migration of the defeated thus also marked them as barbaric (*man*), foreign (*yi*), and even nonhuman creatures dwelling in mountainous regions far away from the civilizing influence of the Central Kingdoms. The word barbaric (*man*), referring to the south, was etymologically the origin of what Marco called, perhaps after Mongolian or Persian transliteration, Mangi, but of course by the thirteenth century, the south of China had long developed into a vast and prosperous region, having cities like Quinsai, which Marco declared to be 'without doubt the finest and most splendid city in the world' (Polo, *Travels* 179). In the Confucian classic *Zhou li* or *Rites of Zhou*, we read that men from barbarian tribes were appointed to minor offices in charge of royal horses and cattle, because they were thought to be able to communicate with wild creatures as though they were kindred families, or, as the commentator Zheng Zhong put it succinctly, they were able 'to know the language of birds and animals' (Ruan Yuan 1: 884). The difference in language always marks the boundaries of ethnicity and cultural identity, and what identifies the Chinese is first and foremost the powerful social institution of the Chinese language, the language of the ethnic majority known in modern time as the Han people.[4] The minorities in the south or southwest, or the nomadic tribes in the north or northeast, would be marked as alien barbarians because they speak languages different from the Han Chinese, known as *Han yu*, the language of the Han majority, or *Hua yu*, the standard or Mandarin Chinese. Let me quote just one example from the works of Ouyang Xiu (1007–72), a famous eleventh-century literati-official and poet. When he travelled to the south, where the ancient state of Chu was located, he wrote a poem to his friend, the poet Mei Shengyu, trying to describe what he perceived to be a country of the barbarians and their strange rituals and customs. Ouyang Xiu writes:

> Without end blue mountains sprawl chaotic all around;
> A few houses with fowls and dogs scattered far and near.
> It's southern custom to worship diverse ghosts in different seasons,
> The barbarian tongue mumbles unintelligible to a Chinese ear.
>
> (Ouyang Xiu 1: 75)

To the poet's ear, the language of the south was an unintelligible mumble, failing to communicate, and 'diverse ghosts' populated the country of the barbarians at different times of the year in strange rituals. It is precisely the 'diverse ghosts' in various parts of Chinese territory that the words and pictures of the *Shan hai jing* try to describe. By mapping different tribes and ethnic groups onto various regions of mountains and seas, this ancient book thus also tells the story of how ethnic and cultural identities were constructed as imagined communities, how boundaries were drawn between the Chinese and the foreign, the civilized and the barbarian, and how culture played a significant role in such conceptual oppositions.

The differentiation of the Chinese and the barbarian is of course a complicated issue with a long and complicated history. In the *Analects*, in which we find many of Confucius's remarks recorded by his disciples dating back to the fifth century BCE, there is a rather revealing statement: 'Barbarian tribes with their rulers are inferior to Chinese states without them' (Confucius 67). Here the belief in the superiority of the Chinese to the barbarians comes out quite clearly, and the sense of superiority was based on Confucius's understanding of the relative degrees of cultural development. 'The Chinese view of other peoples, which evolved over many centuries of extensive contact with foreigners within China, on China's borders, and beyond,' as Richard J. Smith observes, 'was based on the essentially unchallenged idea of China's cultural superiority to all other states' (137). In a narrower formulation of the idea of Chineseness, racial and ethnic differences become decisive factors, as we see articulated, for example, in this famous phrase in a Confucian classic, *Chunqiu zuozhuan* or *Zuo's Commentaries on the Spring and Autumn Annals*: 'Whoever is not of our kin must have his heart different from ours' (Ruan Yuan 2: 1901). In the original context, this refers to people in the southern state of Chu, the same region Ouyang Xiu wrote about in the poem quoted above; the speaker here regarded those southerners as barbaric and having totally different interests from his own state of Lu in the north, for the two states were of different lineage and had no kinship relations with one another. This phrase and its emphasis on kinship and ethnicity were often used later to differentiate the Chinese (*hua*) from the foreign (*yi*), particularly in periods when China was under the reign of non-Han rulers like the Mongols in Marco Polo's time, or the Manchu emperors in China's last imperial dynasty of Qing. When the Han Chinese rose against the Mongolian rulers and established the Ming dynasty in the fourteenth century, or more recently when the Han Chinese tried to overthrow the Manchu emperor in the late nineteenth century and the early twentieth, the rhetoric of ethnic and racial distinction often became prominent and widely used to serve political purposes. In the twentieth century, particularly when China was weakened and under the threat of western colonization, the consciousness of Chinese identity came to be sharply defined in nationalistic, that is, racial and ethnic, terms. This is true in modern times when the Chinese realize that China is a nation among many nations of the world, and as a result, the traditional idea of the Central Kingdoms as inclusive of 'All under Heaven' quickly gave way to the ideas of China as a nation-state and Chineseness as a national identity.

In Chinese history and tradition, however, the distinction between the Chinese and the barbarian is not sharply drawn along racial or ethnic lines. In fact, some scholars argue that the idea of Chineseness has always been open, inclusive, and culturally defined. Qian Mu, for example, compares Chinese and Greco-Roman antiquities and, by sorting out the intermarriage and kinship relations among different ancient states in China, he comes to the conclusion that, unlike the diversity of races, nations, and ethnicities in Europe, the concept of China has been more or less consistent throughout the centuries as a unifying and inclusive idea, constantly assimilating new elements of various tribes or ethnic groups and their cultural characteristics. Through intermarriage of princely families, many of the ancient states have kinship relations and therefore cannot be differentiated from one another by racial or ethnic criteria. 'In ancient conceptualization,' says Qian Mu, 'the barbarians in the four directions and the Chinese at the centre had in fact a different sort of criterion, and that criterion was not "kinship", but "culture." It is an old saying that "when Chinese lords adopt barbarian rituals, one should treat them as barbarians; and when the barbarians bring themselves to behave like the Chinese, one should treat them as Chinese." This may serve as clear evidence that culture was the criterion for differentiating the Chinese from the barbarian.' He goes on to specify 'culture' in terms of an agrarian mode of life. 'China was the general name for all city-states grounded in agricultural life,' says Qian Mu, 'and all others were called barbarians who did not engage in agriculture and had no city-states' (41). Such a cultural understanding of Chinese identity can find support in numerous ancient Chinese books as textual evidence. The important Confucian thinker Mencius (372–289 BCE), for example, mentioned a man by the name of Chen Liang from the kingdom of Chu – the same southern barbarian country that Ouyang Xiu wrote about in his poem, – and praised that man as a better follower of the Confucian way than many northern scholars. 'Chen Liang was a native of Chu,' says Mencius. 'Being delighted with the way of the Duke of Chou and Confucius, he came north to study in the Central Kingdoms. Even the scholars in the north could not surpass him in any way. He was what one would call an outstanding scholar' (*Mencius* 103). Perhaps the strongest and most famous evidence of the cultural concept of Chinese identity beyond racial or ethnic denominations comes from another passage of the *Mencius*, in which we read:

Mencius said, 'Shun was an Eastern barbarian; he was born in Chu Feng, moved to Fu Hsia, and died in Ming T'iao. King Wen was a Western barbarian; he was born in Ch'i Chou and died in Pi Ying. Their native places were over a thousand *li* apart, and there were a thousand years between them. Yet when they had their way in the Central Kingdoms, their actions matched like the two halves of a tally. The standards of the two sages, one earlier and one later, were identical.' (128)

By identifying their native birthplaces, Mencius pointed out that Shun and King Wen were originally barbarians from the East and the West, outside the Central Kingdoms, which in Mencius's original is *Zhong-guo*, what we now translate as China. It would be of some interest to speculate: Why did Mencius make such a remark? Why did he think it necessary to reveal the origins of Shun and King Wen as natives of bar-barian countries? Now Shun and King Wen are both legendary sage kings at the beginning of Chinese civilization, whose presence in the Confucian classics and the commentary tradition is ubiquitous, partic-ularly admired by Confucius himself as models of moral virtue and humane rule. That is to say, they are ancient cultural heroes at the very core of Chinese civilization, the very source of many basic ideas and values about Chinese culture and tradition. In effect, they largely define what is Chinese culture and tradition, and therefore it would be utterly unthinkable to have any sense of a Chinese identity that excludes Shun and King Wen. Apparently, even in the time of Mencius, they were already so closely identified with the culture and tradition of the Central Kingdoms that their origin as natives from a barbarian country had become an obscure fact that few people knew about or took notice of. By reminding us that Shun and King Wen were non-Chinese barbarians in origin, Mencius drove home the important idea that Chi-neseness has nothing to do with one's ethnic origin, that Chinese iden-tity is culturally defined rather than racially or ethnically determined, and that culture is not an inborn essence, but something one adopts, assimilates, and cultivates, something we may perhaps call a sort of *Bil-dung*. For this edificatory idea of cultural identity, Mencius points to Shun and King Wen as shining examples. According to Mencius, then, no matter who we are or where we originally come from, even if from some barbarian region outside the Central Kingdoms, we can be unequivocally Chinese if our actions measure up to the moral stan-dards 'like the two halves of a tally.'

This concept of Chineseness is distinctly cultural, and its bounda-ries are so porous that the Chinese and the foreign, the civilized and the barbarian, do not form a mutually exclusive opposition. After all, even Confucius once expressed his desire to go abroad and 'to settle amongst the Nine Barbarian Tribes of the east' (Confucius 98). The assimilation of Buddhism in China may serve as a successful example of cultural transformation and enrichment. When the Buddhist monks first came from India and the other regions to the west of China, the encounter was a fruitful process of exchange and adaptation. The Sanskrit language was definitely foreign to the Chinese, but it was not considered barbaric. An interesting poem by the Tang Emperor Xuanzong (reigned 712–56) on the difficulty of Sanskrit may express a sense of amused marvelling rather than any kind of xenophobic rejection:

> Like standing cranes and twirling snakes, this writing
> Baffles ghosts from all spheres, or even a god.
> No Confucian scholar finds it easy to decipher;
> The green-eyed foreign monk smiles with a nod.
>
> (Wang Chongmin et al. 1: 6)

Since the Tang, many Buddhist sutras have been translated into Chinese and many special Sanskrit terms have found their way into the Chinese language. Though it takes generations to integrate, the spread of Buddhism in China shows the receptiveness of the Chinese tradition in cultural terms. In a discussion of the concepts of nation-state and national consciousness, Yu Ying-shih also argues that 'insofar as Chinese conceptualization is concerned, culture far exceeds nation. Whether we are speaking of "All under Heaven" or "Central Kingdoms," these were all inclusive cultural notions in antiquity, far transcending purely political or ethnic boundaries' (18). It is indeed a widely accepted view among most China specialists that there was very little self-consciousness of China as a nation in pre-modern times, that is, before the end of the dynastic history in the late nineteenth and the early twentieth centuries. In traditional understanding of the situation, the emperor of China ruled over 'All under Heaven,' and Chinese culture was the only culture worth having. It was taken for granted that barbarians outside the Central Kingdoms would benefit from acculturation and could become Chinese when they adopted Chinese cultural values and habits, particularly the teachings of Confucianism. But at the same time, Chinese culture itself constantly assimilated elements of non-Chinese cultures and became an all-embracing umbrella of universal cultural values.

For the Chinese, the realization of China as a nation among other nations was not only relatively recent and modern, but also a painful

Bibliography

Marco Polo: Editions and Translations

Polo, Marco. *The Book of Ser Marco Polo the Venetian concerning the Kingdoms and Marvels of the East*. Edited and translated by Sir Henry Yule and rev. Henri Cordier. 1871. 2 vols. 3rd ed. New York: Charles Scribner's Sons, 1929. Reissued as *The Travels of Marco Polo: The Complete Yule-Cordier Edition*, Vols. 1 and 2. New York: Dover, 1993.

– *La Description du Monde*. Edited and translated by Pierre-Yves Badel. Lettres Gothiques. Paris: Livre de Poche, 1998.

– *The Description of the World*. Edited by A.C. Moule and Paul Pelliot. 2 vols. London: Routledge and Sons, 1938. Reprint, New York: AMS, 1976.

– *Le Devisement du Monde*. Edited by Philippe Ménard, M.-L. Chênerie, and M. Guéret-Laferté. Vol. 1, *Départ des voyageurs et traversée de la Perse*. Textes Littéraires Français 533. Geneva: Droz, 2001.

– *Le Devisement du Monde*. Edited by Philippe Ménard. Vol. 2, *Traversée de l'Afghanistan et entrée en Chine*, edited by Jeanne-Marie Boivin, Laurence Harf-Lancner, and Laurence Mathey-Maille. Textes Littéraires Français 552. Geneva: Droz, 2003.

– *Le Devisement du Monde*. Edited by Philippe Ménard. Vol. 3, *Khoubilai Khan*, edited by Jean-Claude Fouconm, Danielle Quéruel, and Monique Santucci. Textes Littéraires Français 568. Geneva: Droz, 2004.

– *Le Devisement du Monde*. Edited by Philippe Ménard. Vol. 4, *Voyages à travers la Chine*, edited by Joël Blanchard and Michel Quereuil. Textes Littéraires Français 575. Geneva: Droz, 2005.

– *Le Devisement du Monde*. Edited by Philippe Ménard. Vol. 5, *À travers la Chine du Sud*, edited by Jean-Claude Delclos and Claude Roussel. Textes Littéraires Français 586. Geneva: Droz, 2007.

– *Il libro di Marco Polo detto Milione nella versione dell''ottimo.'* Edited by Daniele Ponchiroli. Turin: Einaudi, 1962.
– *Le Livre des Merveilles. Extrait du Livre des Merveilles du Monde (Ms. fr. 2810) de la Bibliothèque nationale de France.* Translated into modern French by Marie-Hélène Tesnière. Commentary by François Avril and Marie-Thérèse Gousset. Tournai: La Renaissance du Livre, 1999.
– *Milione/Le Divisament dou monde. Il Milione nelle redazioni toscana e franco-italiana.* Edited by Gabriella Ronchi. Milan: Mondadori, 1982.
– *Il Milione.* Edited by Luigi Foscolo Benedetto. Florence: L.S. Olschki, 1928.
– *Il Milione con le postille di Cristoforo Colombo.* Edited by Luigi Giovannini. Rome: Edizioni Paoline, 1985.
– *Milione: Versione toscana del Trecento.* Edited by Valeria Bertolucci Pizzorusso. Milan: Adelphi, 1982.
– *The Most Noble and Famous Travels of Marco Polo together with the Travels of Nicolò Conti.* Translated by John Frampton (1579). Edited by N.M. Penzer. London: Argonaut Press, 1929. Reprint, London: Adam and Charles Black, 1937.
– *The Travels of Marco Polo.* Translated and edited by Ronald Latham. New York and London: Penguin Books, 1958. Reprint, London: The Folio Society, 1968.
– [Version of Francesco Pipino]. *Itinerarium.* Antwerp, 1485. Reprint, Tokyo: Otsuka Kogeisha, 1949.
– [Version of Francesco Pipino]. *Marka Pavlova Z Benátek: Milion.* Edited by Justin V. Prásek. Prague: Nákladem Ceské Akademie, 1902.

Primary Sources

d'Ailly, Pierre. *Imago mundi.* Edited by Edmund Buron. 3 vols. Paris: Maison-neuve Frères, 1930–1.
Alexandre de Paris. *Le Roman d'Alexandre.* Edited by E.C. Armstrong et al. Translated by Laurence Harf-Lancner. Lettres Gothiques. Paris: Livre de Poche, 1994.
Ambrose. 'De paradiso.' In *Il paradiso terrestre and Caino e Abele.* Edited by Paolo Siniscalco and Agostino Pastorino. Milan: Biblioteca Ambrosiana/Rome: Città nuova, 1984.
Augustine. *De Genesi ad litteram.* Edited by J.-P. Migne in *S. Aurelii Augustini Hipponensis Episcopi, De Genesi ad litteram libri duodecim.* Patrologia Cursus Completus, Series Latina 34. Paris, 1844–55. Translated by Ronald J. Teske in *On Genesis: Two Books on Genesis against the Manichees and On the Literal Inter-pretation of Genesis, an Unfinished Book.* Fathers of the Church 84. Washington, DC: Catholic University of America Press, 1991.

– *Sermones*. Edited by J.-P. Migne. Patrologia Cursus Completus, Series Latina 38. Paris, 1844–55.

Calvino, Italo. *Le città invisibili*. Milan: Mondadori, 1993. Translated by William Weaver as *Invisible Cities*. New York: Harcourt Brace and Company, 1974.

– 'Dietro il successo.' In *Eremita a Parigi. Pagine autobiografiche*, 249–64. Milan: Mondadori, 1994. Translated by Martin McLaughlin as 'Behind the Success,' in *Hermit in Paris. Autobiographical Writings*, 221–33. London: Cape, 2003.

– *Lettere 1940–1985*. Edited by Luca Baranelli. Milan: Mondadori, 2000.

– *Romanzi e racconti*. Edited by Claudio Milanini, Mario Barenghi, and Bruno Falcetto. 3 vols. Milan: Mondadori, 1991–4.

– *Saggi*. Edited by Mario Barenghi. 2 vols. Milan: Mondadori, 1995.

– *Six Memos for the Next Millennium*. Translated by Patrick Creagh. London: Vintage, 1996.

– *Time and the Hunter*. Translated by William Weaver. London: Picador, 1993.

da Canal, Martin. *Les Estoires de Venise: Cronaca veneziana in lingua francese dalle origini al 1275*. Edited and translated by Alberto Limentani. Florence: Leo S. Olschki, 1972.

Chronica monasterii Sancti Bertini auctore Iohanne Longo. Edited by O. Holder-Egger. Monumenta Germaniae Historica, Scriptores 25. 1880.

Chronica sive Historia Monasterii sancti Bertini. In *Thesaurus novus anecdotorum*, vol. 3, edited by E. Martène and U. Durand, 747–860. Paris, 1717. Reprint, New York: Farnborough, 1968.

Chunqiu zuozhuan zhengy [The Correct Meaning of Zuo's Commentaries on the Spring and Autumn Annals]. In Ruan Yuan, *Shisan jing zhushu*, 2: 1697–2188.

Cocito, Luciana, ed. *Anonimo genovese: Poesie*. Officina romanica 17. Rome: Edizioni dell'Ateneo, 1970.

Coleridge, Samuel Taylor. *Biographia Literaria; or, Biographical Sketches of My Literary Life and Opinions*. Edited by George Watson. New York: Everyman's Library, 1956.

– *The Complete Poems*. Edited by William Keach. New York: Penguin, 1997.

Confucius. *The Analects*. Translated by D.C. Lau. Harmondsworth: Penguin, 1979.

Duchamp, Marcel. *The Writings of Marcel Duchamp*. Edited by Michel Sanouillet and Elmer Peterson. New York: Da Capo Press, 1973.

Foppens, J.F. *Bibliotheca Belgica*. Brussels, 1739.

Freud, Sigmund. 'General Introduction: Lectures on Psycho-Analysis.' Translated by W.J.H. Sprott in *The Major Works of Sigmund Freud*, edited by Robert D. Gwinn, 807–84. Chicago, 1952. Reprint, Chicago: Encyclopaedia Britannica/University of Chicago Press, 1991.

– *Vorlesungen zur Einführung in die Psychoanalyse*. 1916–17 [1915–16]. Studien-ausgabe 1. Frankfurt am Main: S. Fischer, 1969.

Gesta Romanorum. Edited by Hermann Oesterley. Hildesheim: Georg Olms, 1963.

Glossa Ordinaria. In Walafridus Strabo [attrib.], *Liber Genesis*, edited by J.-P. Migne. Patrologia Cursus Completus, Series Latina 113. Paris, 1844–55.

Grimm, Jacob and Wilhelm. 'Cinderella.' Translated by D.L. Ashliman. http://www.pitt.edu/~dash/grimm021.html.

Gui, Bernard. *Manuel de l'inquisiteur*. 2 vols. Paris: G. Mollat et G. Drioux, 1926–7.

Hakluyt, Richard. *The Principal Navigations, Voiages and Discoveries of the English nation, made by Sea or ouer Land*. Hakluyt Society Extra Series 39. Cambridge: Hakluyt Society, 1939.

'Johannes Iperii Continuatum S. Bertini Chronicon.' In *Veterum scriptorum et munimentorum historicorum ... opera*, vol. 6, edited by E. Martène and U. Durand. Paris, 1729.

John of Plano Carpini. *Historia Mongalorum*. In *Giovanni di Pian di Carpine: Storia dei Mongoli*. Edited by Enricò Menesto. Translated by Maria Christiana Lungarotti. Spoleto: Centro Italiano de Studi Sull'Alto Medioevo, 1989.

– In *Mission to Asia*. Edited and translated by Christopher Dawson. Medieval Academy Reprints for Teaching 8. Toronto: University of Toronto Press, 1980.

Kircher, Athanasius, ed. *China monumentis ... Illustrata*. Amsterdam, 1667.

Leland, John. *Commentarii de scriptoribus britannicis*. Edited by A. Hall. Oxford, 1709.

[Letter of Prester John.] *La lettere del Prete Gianni*. Edited by Gioia Zaganelli. Parma: Pratiche editrice Parma, 1990.

– 'Littera Presbyteri Johannis.' Edited by Friedrich Zarncke. In *Königlich-sächsische Gesellschaft der Wissenschaften Philologisch-historische Classe* 7, 909–24. Leipzig, 1879.

– In Vsevolod Slessarev, *Prester John: The Letter and the Legend*, 67–79. Minneapolis: University of Minnesota Press, 1959.

Mandeville, John. *The Bodley Version of 'Mandeville's Travels.'* Edited by M.C. Seymour. Early English Text Society Original Series 253. London: Oxford University Press, 1963.

– *The Book of John Mandeville: An Edition of the Pynson Text*. Edited by Tamarah Kohanski. Tempe: Arizona Center for Medieval and Renaissance Studies, 2001.

– *The Defective Version of Mandeville's Travels*. Edited by M.C. Seymour. Early English Text Society Original Series 319. Oxford: Oxford University Press, 2002.

– *Le Livre des Merveilles du Monde*. Edited by Christiane Deluz. Paris: CNRS, 2000.
– *Mandeville's Travels*. Edited by M.C. Seymour. Oxford: Clarendon Press, 1967.
– *Mandeville's Travels*. Edited by P. Hamelius. Early English Text Society Original Series 154. Oxford: Oxford University Press, 1923. Reprint, 1961.
– *Mandeville's Travels: Texts and Translations*. 2 vols. Edited by Malcolm Letts. London: Hakluyt Society, 1953.
– *The voiage and travaile of Sir John Maundeville, kt., which treateth of the way to Hierusalem; and of marvayles of Inde, with other ilands and countryes. Reprinted from the ed. of A.D. 1725*. With an introduction, additional notes, and glossary by J.O. Halliwell. London: E. Lumley, 1839.
La manière et les faitures des monstres des hommes qui sont en Orient et le plus en Inde. Eine altfranzösische moralisierende Bearbeitung des Liber de Monstruosis Hominibus Orientis aus Thomas von Cantimprés, De Naturis Rerum. Edited by Alfons Hilka. Abhandlungen der Gesellschaft der Wissenschaften zu Göttingen: Philologisch-Historische Klasse 7. Berlin: Weidmannsche Buchhandlung, 1933.
Marvels of the East. Edited by Montague Rhodes James. Oxford: Roxburghe Club, 1929.
Mayer, Iacopus. *Commentarii sive annales rerum Flandricarum Libri septendecim*. Edited by Antonius Mayer. Antwerp, 1561.
Ma Changyi. *Guben Shan hai jing tushuo [Old Editions of the Classic of Mountains and Seas with Illustrations]*. Jinan: Shandong huabao chubanshe, 2001.
Mencius. *Mencius*. Translated by D.C. Lau. Harmondsworth: Penguin, 1970.
Montecorvino, Giovanni. 'Letter of Fra Giovanni Montecorvino.' In van den Wyngaert, *Sinica Franciscana*, 1: 349.
Odoric da Pordenone [Odoricus de Portu Naonis]. 'Relazione.' In van den Wyngaert, *Sinica franciscana*, 1: 381–495.
O'Neill, Eugene. *Marco Millions: A Play*. New York: Boni and Liveright, 1927.
Ouyang Xiu. *Ouyang Xiu quanji [Ouyang Xiu's Complete Works]*. 2 vols. Beijing: Zhongguo shudian, 1986.
Peters, Edward, ed. *The First Crusade: The Chronicle of Fulcher of Chartres and Other Source Materials*. Philadelphia: University of Pennsylvania Press, 1971.
Pipino, Francesco. *Tractatus de locis terre sancte*. In *Dritte Wanderung nach Pälestina*, edited by T. Tobler. Gotha, 1859.
Pliny [Plinius Secondus, Gaius]. *Naturalis Historiae*, Lib. VII. Edited by Robert König et al. Zürich and Düsseldorf: Artemis Verlags-AG, 1996.
Prueher, Joseph W. 'The Ambassador's Letter.' 10 February 2006. http://www.pbs.org/newshour/bb/asia/china/plane/letter_4–11.html.
Raleigh, Walter. *The Discoverie of Guiana*. Edited by Joyce Lorimer. Hakluyt Society, 3rd series, 15. Aldershot, Hants and Burlington, VT: Ashgate Publishing for the Hakluyt Society, 2006.

Ramusio, Giovanni Battista. *Navigazioni e viaggi*. Edited by Marica Milanesi. 6 vols. Turin: G. Einaudi, 1980.

The Romance of Alexander: A Collotype Facsimile of MS. Bodley 264. Edited by M.R. James. Oxford: Roxburghe Club, 1933.

Ruan Yuan, ed. *Shisan jing zhushu [The Thirteen Classics with Annotations]*. 2 vols. Reprint. Beijing: Zhonghua, 1980.

Shakespeare, William. *Othello: A New Variorum Edition of Shakespeare*. Edited by Horace Howard Furness. New York: Dover Publications, 1963.

Simon de Saint-Quentin. *Histoire des Tartares*. Edited by Jean Richard. Paris: Librairie Orientaliste Paul Geuthner, 1965.

Spuler, Bertold, trans. and ed. 1961. *History of the Mongols Based on Eastern and Western Accounts of the Thirteenth and Fourteenth Centuries*. Translated from the German by Helga and Stuart Drummond. London: Routledge and Kegan Paul/Berkeley: University of California Press, 1972.

van den Wyngaert, A., ed. *Sinica franciscana, Itinera et relationes fratrum minorum saeculi XIII et XIV*. 3 vols. Ad Claras aquas: Collegium S. Bonaventurae, 1928.

Voragine, Jacobus de. *[Legenda Aurea] The Golden Legend: Reading on the Saints*. Vol. 1. Translated by William Granger Ryan. Princeton: Princeton University Press, 1993.

Le Voyage de Charlemagne à Jérusalem et à Constantinople. Edited by Paul Aebischer. Geneva: Droz, 1965.

Wang Chongmin, Sun Wang, and Tong Yangnian, eds. *Quan Tang shi waibian. [Supplements to the Complete Tang Poems]*. 2 vols. Beijing: Zhonghua, 1982.

William of Rubruck. 'Itinerarium.' In Van den Wyngaert, *Sinica Franciscana*, 1: 206–7.

Yongle dadian [Great Compendium Composed during the Yongle Reign]. 10 vols. Beijing: Zhonghua suju, 1986.

Yule, Henry, trans. and ed. *Cathay and the Way Thither: Being a Collection of Medieval Notices of China*. 4 vols. London: Hakluyt Society, 1911–14.

Zhou li zhushu [The Rites of Zhou with Annotations]. In Ruan Yuan, *Shisan jing zhushu*, 1: 631–940.

Secondary Sources

Abrams, M.H. *The Mirror and the Lamp: Romantic Theory and the Critical Tradition*. London: Oxford University Press, 1953.

Abu-Lughod, Janet L. *Before European Hegemony: The World System A.D. 1250–1350*. New York: Oxford University Press, 1989.

Akbari, Suzanne Conklin. 'From Due East to True North: Orientalism and Orientation.' In *The Postcolonial Middle Ages*, edited by Jeffrey Jerome Cohen, 19–34. New York: Palgrave, 2001.

- *Idols in the East: European Representations of Islam and the Orient, 1100–1450.* Ithaca: Cornell University Press, 2009.
- 'The Diversity of Mankind in *The Book of John Mandeville.*' In *Eastward Bound: Travel and Travellers, 1050–1550,* edited by Rosamund Allen, 156–76. Manchester: Manchester University Press, 2004.
Alexander, J.J.G. *Medieval Illuminators and Their Methods of Work.* New Haven: Yale University Press, 1992.
- 'Painting and Manuscript Illumination for Royal Patrons in the Later Middle Ages.' In Scattergood and Sherborne, *English Court Culture,* 141–62.
Allsen, Thomas T. 'The Cultural Worlds of Marco Polo.' *Journal of Interdisciplinary History* 31, no. 3 (Winter 2001): 375–83.
Amin, Samir. *Eurocentrism.* Translated by Russell Moore. New York: Monthly Review Press, 1989.
Ashtor, Eliyahu. 'The Crisis of Levant Trade (1291–1344).' In *Levant Trade in the Later Middle Ages,* 3–63. Princeton: Princeton University Press, 1983.
Avril, François. 'Le Livre des Merveilles: Manuscrit Français 2810 de la Bibliothèque Nationale de France.' In Tesnière et al., eds. *Le Livre des Merveilles,* 204–15.
Barenghi, Mario. 'Gli abbozzi dell'indice. Quattro fogli dall'archivio Calvino.' In Barenghi et al., *La visione dell'invisibile,* 74–95.
Barenghi, Mario, Gianni Canova, and Bruno Falcetto, eds. *La visione dell'invisibile. Saggi e materiali su 'Le città invisibili' di Italo Calvino.* Milan: Mondadori, 2002.
Barfield, Thomas J. *The Perilous Frontier: Nomadic Empires and China, 221 BC to AD 1757.* Cambridge, MA and Oxford, UK: Blackwell, 1989.
Barthold, W. *Turkestan Down to the Mongol Invasion.* Translated by T. Minorsky and C.E. Bosworth. 3rd ed. London: Luzac, 1958. Reprint, New Delhi: Munshiram Manoharlal, 1992.
Bartlett, Robert. *Gerald of Wales, 1146–1223.* Oxford: Clarendon Press, 1982.
- *The Making of Europe, 950–1350.* Princeton: Princeton University Press, 1993.
Baumgärtner, Ingrid. 'Weltbild und Empirie. Die Erweiterung des kartographischen Weltbilds durch die Asienreisen des späten Mittelalters.' *Journal of Medieval History* 23 (1997): 227–53.
Beaugendre, Anne-Caroline. *Les Merveilles du monde ou Les Secrets de l'histoire naturelle.* Arcueil: Anthèse, 1996.
Bellamy, J.G. *The Law of Treason in England in the Later Middle Ages.* Cambridge: Cambridge University Press, 1970.
Belpoliti, Marco. 'Calvino's Colours.' In *Image, Eye, and Art in Calvino: Writing Visibility,* edited by Birgitte Grundtvig, Martin McLaughlin, and Lene Waage Petersen, 12–25. Oxford: Legenda, 2007.
Benedetto, Luigi Foscolo. *La tradizione manoscritta del 'Milione' di Marco Polo.* Turin: Bottega d'Erasmo, 1962.

Bennett, John. 'The Case of Sir John Mandeville.' Paper presented at 37th International Congress on Medieval Studies, Western Michigan University, Kalamazoo, MI, 3–6 May 2004.

Bennett, Josephine Waters. *The Rediscovery of Sir John Mandeville*. New York: Modern Languages Association, 1954.

Berg, A. Scott. *Goldwyn: A Biography*. New York: Knopf, 1989.

Bernardini Napoletano, Francesca. *I segni nuovi di Italo Calvino. Da 'Le Cosmicomiche' a 'Le città invisibili.'* Rome: Bulzoni, 1977.

Bernheimer, Richard. *Wild Men in the Middle Ages: A Study in Art, Sentiment, and Demonology*. Cambridge, MA: Harvard University Press, 1952.

Bertolucci Pizzorusso, Valeria. 'Enunciazione e produzione del testo nel Milione.' *Studi Mediolani e Volgari* 25 (1977): 5–43.

Bezzola, G.A. *Die Mongolen in abendländischer Sicht (1220–1270): Ein Beitrag zur Frage der Völkerbegegnungen*. Bern: Francke, 1974.

Bibliotheca Sanctorum. Edited by F. Caraffa. 13 vols. Rome: Istituto Giovanni XXIII della Pontificia Università lateranense, 1961–9.

Bisaha, Nancy. *Creating East and West: Renaissance Humanists and the Ottoman Turks*. Philadelphia: University of Pennsylvania Press, 2004.

Boase, T.S.R. 'The History of the Kingdom.' In *The Cilician Kingdom of Armenia*, edited by T.S.R. Boase et al., 1–33. New York: St Martin's, 1978.

Bondanella, Peter. *Italian Film from Neorealism to the Present*. New York: Continuum, 1990.

Bonsaver, Guido. 'Cities of the Imagination: Traces of Italo Calvino in Jeanette Winterson's Fiction.' *Italianist* 15 (1995): 213–30.

Bowring, Philip. 'It's Not a Chinese World after All.' *International Herald Tribune*, 12 July 1999.

Boyle, J.A. 'The Journey of Het'um I, King of Little Armenia, to the Court of the Great Khan Möngke.' *Central Asiatic Journal* 9 (1964): 175–89. Reprint, Article X in *The Mongol World Empire 1206–1370*. London: Variorum, 1977.

Brownlee, Kevin. 'The Conflicted Genealogy of Cultural Authority: Italian Responses to French Cultural Dominance in *Il Tesoretto*, *Il Fiore*, and *La Commedia*.' In *Generation and Degeneration: Tropes of Reproduction in Literature and History from Antiquity through Early Modern Europe*, edited by Valeria Finucci and Kevin Brownlee, 262–86. Durham: Duke University Press, 2001.

Brückner, W. 'Drei Könige. Verehrung.' *Lexikon des Mittelalters*, vol. 3. Munich: Deutscher Taschenbuch Verlag, 2002. c.1388–9.

Bryer, Anthony. 'The Grand Komnenos and the Great Khan at Karakorum in 1246.' In *Itinéraires d'Orient: Hommages à Claude Cahen*, edited by Raoul Curiel and Rika Gyselen, 257–61. Bures-sur-Yvette: Groupe pour l'étude de la civilisation du Moyen-Orient, 1994.

Bucher, Bernadette. 'Die Phantasien der Eroberer: Zur graphischen Repräsentation des Kannibalismus in de Brys *America*.' In *Mythen der Neuen Welt: Zur Entdeckungsgeschichte Lateinamerikas*, edited by Karl-Heinz Kohl, 75–91. Berlin: Frölich und Kaufmann, 1982.

Buettner, Brigitte. 'Profane Illuminations, Secular Illusions: Manuscripts in Late Medieval Courtly Society.' *Art Bulletin* 74 (1992): 75–90.

Bunim, Miriam Schild. *Space in Medieval Painting and the Forerunners of Perspective*. New York: Columbia University Press, 1940.

Burke, Edmund, III. 'Introduction.' In *Rethinking World History: Essays on Europe, Islam and World History*, by Marshall G.S. Hodgson, ix–xxi. Cambridge: Cambridge University Press, 1993.

Burnett, Charles, and Patrick Gautier Dalché. 'Attitudes towards the Mongols in Medieval Literature: The XXII Kings of Gog and Magog from the Court of Frederick II to Jean de Mandeville.' *Viator* 22 (1991): 153–67.

Buruma, Ian, and Avishai Margalit. *Occidentalism: The West in the Eyes of Its Enemies*. New York: Penguin Press, 2004.

Bynum, Caroline Walker. *Metamorphosis and Identity*. New York: Zone Books, 2001.

– 'Miracles and Marvels: The Limits of Alterity.' In *Vita Religiosa im Mittelalter: Festschrift für Kaspar Elm zum 70. Geburtstag*, edited by Franz J. Felten and Nikolas Jaspert, 803–7. Berlin: Duncker and Humbolt, 1999.

– 'Wonder.' *American Historical Review* 102 (1997): 1–26.

Calvo Montoro, María J. 'Joseph Conrad/Italo Calvino, o della stesura di una tesi come riflessione sulla scrittura.' *Forum Italicum* 31, no. 1 (Spring 1997): 74–115.

Camille, Michael. *The Gothic Idol: Ideology and Image-Making in Medieval Art*. Cambridge: Cambridge University Press, 1989.

Campbell, Mary B. 'The Object of One's Gaze: Landscape, Writing, and Early Medieval Pilgrimage.' In Westrem, *Discovering New Worlds*, 3–15.

– *The Witness and the Other World: Exotic European Travel Writing, 400–1600*. Ithaca: Cornell University Press, 1988.

Cardona, Giorgio R. 'Indice ragionato.' In *Marco Polo. Milione. Versione toscana del Trecento*, edited by Valeria Bertolucci Pizzorusso, 491. Milan: Adelphi, 1975.

Cary, George. *The Medieval Alexander*. Edited by D.J.A. Ross. Cambridge: Cambridge University Press, 1956.

Chang, Iris. *The Chinese in America: A Narrative History*. New York: Viking, 2003.

Chow Kai-wing. 'Imagining Boundaries of Blood: Zhang Binglin and the Invention of the Han "Race" in Modern China.' In *The Construction of Racial Identities in China and Japan: Historical and Contemporary Perspectives*, edited by Frank Dikötter, 34–52. London: Hurst, 1997.

Christianson, C. Paul. *A Directory of London Stationers and Book Artisans, 1300–1500*. New York: Biographical Society of America, 1990.

Ciccuto, Marcello. 'Le meraviglie di Marco. Il *Milone* alla corte di Borgogna.' *Rara volumina* 1 (1997): 5–34.

Cleaves, Francis Woodman. 'A Chinese Source Bearing on Marco Polo's Departure from China and a Persian Source of His Arrival in Persia.' *Harvard Journal of Asiatic Studies* 36 (1976): 181–203.

Clunas, Craig. 'The Explorer's Tracks.' *Times China Supplement*, 14 April 1982.

Coens, M. 'L'auteur de la vita Erkembodonis.' *Analecta Bollandiana* 42 (1924): 126–36.

Cohen, Warren I. *East Asia at the Center: Four Thousand Years of Engagement with the World*. New York: Columbia University Press, 2000.

Coleman, John E. 'Ancient Greek Ethnocentrism.' In *Greeks and Barbarians: Essays on the Interactions between Greeks and Non-Greeks in Antiquity and the Consequences for Eurocentrism*, edited by John E. Coleman and Clark A. Walz, 175–220. Bethesda: CDL, 1997.

Coleman, Joyce. *Public Reading and the Reading Public in Late Medieval England and France*. Cambridge: Cambridge University Press, 1996.

Connell, C.W. 'Western Views on the Origin of the "Tartars."' *Journal of Medieval and Renaissance Studies* 3 (1973): 115–37.

Coopland, G.W. *The Abbey of St Bertin and Its Neighbours, 900–1350*. Oxford Studies in Social and Legal History 4. Oxford: Clarendon Press, 1914.

Cordier, H. 'L'Extrême-Orient dans l'Atlas Catalane de Charles V, roi de France.' *Bulletin de géographie historique et descriptive* 14 (1895): 19–63.

Cornish, Alison. 'Translatio Galliae: Effects of Early Franco-Italian Literary Exchange.' *Romanic Review* 97 (2006): 309–30.

Crespi, Alberto. *Dal Polo all'equatore. I film e le avventure di Giuliano Montaldo*. Venice: Marsilio Editori, 2005.

Critchley, John. *Marco Polo's Book*. London: Variorum, 1992.

Crosby, Ruth. 'Oral Delivery in the Middle Ages.' *Speculum* 11 (1936): 88–110.

Cummins, John. *The Hound and the Hawk: The Art of Medieval Hunting*. London: Weidenfeld and Nicolson, 1988.

Cutler, Anthony. 'Gifts and Gift Exchange as Aspects of the Byzantine, Arab, and Related Economies.' *Dumbarton Oaks Papers* 55 (2002): 247–78.

Dawson, Christopher. *Mission to Asia*. Medieval Academy Reprints for Teaching 8. Toronto: University of Toronto Press, 1980.

De Clercq, Charles. 'Hugues de Fouilloy, imagier de ses propres oeuvres?' *Revue du nord* 45 (1963): 31–42.

de Rachewiltz, Igor. 'Marco Polo Went to China.' *Zentralasiatische Studien* 27 (1997): 34–92.

Deluz, Christiane. *Le Livre de Jehan de Mandeville: Une 'Géographie' au XIVe Siècle.* Louvain-la-Neuve: Institut d'Études Médiévales de l'Université Catholique de Louvain, 1988.

– 'Villes et organisation de l'espace: La Chine de Marco Polo.' In *Villes, bonnes villes, cités et capitales. Études d'historie urbaine (XIIe–XVIIIe siècle) offertes à Bernard Chevalier*, edited by M. Bourin, 161–8. Caen: Paradigme, 1993.

Dickens, Homer. *The Films of Gary Cooper.* Secaucus, NJ: Citadel Press, 1970.

di Cosmo, Nicola. 'Mongols and Merchants on the Black Sea Frontier in the Thirteenth and Fourteenth Centuries: Convergences and Conflicts.' In *Mongols, Turks, and Others: Eurasian Nomads and the Sedentary World*, edited by Reuven Amitai and Michal Biran, 391–424. Brill's Inner Asian Library. Leiden: Brill, 2005.

Dikötter, Frank. *The Discourse of Race in Modern China.* Hong Kong: Hong Kong University Press, 1992.

DiMarco, Vincent. 'The Amazons and the End of the World.' In Westrem, *Discovering New Worlds*, 69–90.

Doyle, A.I. 'English Books in and out of Court from Edward III to Henry VII.' In Scattergood and Sherborne, *English Court Culture*, 163–81.

Duara, Prasenjit. *Rescuing History from the Nation: Questioning Narratives of Modern China.* Chicago: University of Chicago Press, 1995.

Dufresne, Laura Jean. 'An Assembly of Ladies: The Fifteenth-Century Pictorial Tradition of Christine de Pizan's *La cité des dames* and *Le trésor de la cité ses dames*.' PhD diss., University of Washington, 1989.

Durand, D.B. *The Vienna-Klosterneuburg Map Corpus of the Fifteenth Century: A Study in the Transition from Medieval to Modern Science.* Leiden: E.J. Brill, 1952.

Dutschke, Consuelo W. 'Francesco Pipino and the Manuscripts of Marco Polo's *Travels*.' PhD diss. 3 vols., University of California, Los Angeles, 1993.

– 'The Truth in the Book: The Marco Polo Texts in Royal 19.D.I and Bodley 264.' *Scriptorium* 52 (1998): 278–300.

Eco, Umberto. '*De Interpretatione* or the Difficulty of Being Marco Polo.' *Film Quarterly* 30, no. 4, Special Book Issue (Summer 1977): 8–12.

Edson, Evelyn. *Mapping Time and Space: How Medieval Mapmakers Viewed Their World.* London: British Library, 1997.

Electronic Cultural Atlas Initiative (ECAI). 'Mongol Empire CE 1100–1400' and 'Mughal Empire CE 1500–1850.' *TimeMap Open Source Consortium.* http://www.timemap.net/index.php?option=com_content&task=view&id=124&Itemid=130.

Elliott, J.H. *The Old World and the New, 1492–1650.* Cambridge: Cambridge University Press, 1970.

Emersleben, Otto. *Marco Polo.* Reinbek bei Hamburg: Rowohlt Taschenbuch, 2002.

Engels, Odilo. 'Die Reliquien der Heiligen Drei Könige in der Reichspolitik der Staufer.' In Zehnder, *Die Heiligen Drei Könige*, 33–6.

Epstein, Steven A. *Genoa and the Genoese, 958–1528*. Chapel Hill: University of North Carolina Press, 1996.

Fairbank, John King, and Merle Goldman. *China: A New History*. Cambridge, MA: Belknap Press, 2006.

Falcetto, Bruno. 'Le cose e le ombre. *Marco Polo*: Calvino scrittore per il cinema.' In Barenghi et al., *La visione dell'invisibile*, 62–73.

Fleming, John. *The Roman de la Rose: A Study in Allegory and Iconography*. Princeton: Princeton University Press, 1969.

Foltz, Richard C. *Religions of the Silk Road: Overland Trade and Cultural Exchange from Antiquity to the Fifteenth Century*. New York: St Martin's, 1999.

Frank, Andre Gunder. *The Centrality of Central Asia*. Comparative Asian Studies 8. Amsterdam: VU University Press for Centre for Asian Studies, 1992.

Freiesleben, Hans-Christian. *Der katalanische Weltatlas von Jahre 1375*. Stuttgart: Brockhaus Komm.-Gesch., 1977.

Friedman, John Block. *The Monstrous Races in Medieval Art and Thought*. Cambridge, MA: Harvard University Press, 1981.

Frugoni, Chiara. *A Distant City: Images of Urban Experience in the Medieval World*. Translated by William McCuaig. Princeton: Princeton University Press, 1991.

Frye, Northrop. *Anatomy of Criticism: Four Essays*. Princeton: Princeton University Press, 1957.

Fuss, Diana. *Essentially Speaking: Feminism, Nature and Difference*. New York: Routledge, 1989.

Galambos, Imre. 'Dunhuang Characters and the Dating of Manuscripts.' In *The Silk Road: Trade, Travel, War and Faith*, edited by Susan Whitfield with Ursula Sims-Williams, 72–80. Chicago: Serindia Publications, 2004.

Gladney, Dru C. *Dislocating China: Muslims, Minorities and Other Subaltern Subjects*. Chicago: University of Chicago Press, 2003.

– *Muslim Chinese: Ethnic Nationalism in the People's Republic*. Cambridge, MA: Harvard University Press, 1991.

Goldfinger, Charles. 'Intangible Economy and Electronic Money.' In *The Future of Money*, edited by the Organisation for Economic Co-operation and Development (OECD). Paris: OECD, 2002.

Goodman, Jennifer R. *Chivalry and Exploration, 1298–1630*. Woodbridge: Boydell, 1998.

Gosman, Martin. 'Marco Polo's Voyages: The Conflict between Confirmation and Observation.' In *Travel Fact and Fiction: Studies on Fiction, Literary Tradition, Scholarly Discovery, and Observation in Travel Writing*, edited by Zweder von Martels, 72–84. Leiden: E.J. Brill, 1994.

Gow, Andrew. 'Gog and Magog on Mappaemundi and Early Printed World Maps: Orientalizing Ethnography in the Apocalyptic Tradition.' *Journal of Early Modern History* 2 (1998): 61–88.

Grabar, Oleg. 'The Shared Culture of Objects.' In *Byzantine Court Culture from 829 to 1204*, edited by Henry Maguire, 115–29. Washington, DC: Dumbarton Oaks, 1997.

Green, Richard Firth. *Poets and Princepleasers: Literature and the English Court in the Late Middle Ages*. Toronto: University of Toronto Press, 1980.

Greenblatt, Stephen. *Marvelous Possessions: The Wonder of the New World*. Chicago: University of Chicago Press/Oxford: Oxford University Press, 1991. Translated as *Wunderbare Besitztümer: Die Erfindung des Fremden: Reisende und Entdecker*. Darmstadt: Wissenschaftliche Buchgesellschaft, 1994.

Guha, Ranajit. *History at the Limit of World History*. New York: Columbia University Press, 2002.

Gumilev, L.N. *Searches for an Imaginary Kingdom: The Legend and Kingdom of Prester John*. Translated by R.E.F. Smith. Cambridge: Cambridge University Press, 1987.

Guzman, Gregory G. 'Reports of Mongol Cannibalism in the Thirteenth-Century Latin Sources: Oriental Fact or Western Fiction?' In Westrem, *Discovering New Worlds*, 31–68.

Haeger, John W. 'Marco Polo in China? Problems with Internal Evidence.' *Bulletin of Sung and Yuan Studies* 14 (1979): 22–30.

Hall, Edith. *Inventing the Barbarian: Greek Self-Definition through Tragedy*. Oxford: Clarendon Press, 1989.

Hamilton, Bernard. 'Continental Drift: Prester John's Progress through the Indies.' In *Prester John, the Mongols, and the Ten Lost Tribes*, edited by Charles F. Beckingham and Bernard Hamilton, 237–69. Brookfield, VT: Variorum, 1996.

– 'Prester John and the Three Kings of Cologne.' In *Studies in Medieval History Presented to R.H.C. Davis*, edited by Henry Mayr-Harting and R.I. Moore, 177–91. London: Hambledon Press, 1985.

Hansen, Valerie. *The Open Empire: A History of China to 1600*. New York: Norton, 2000.

Harf-Lancner, Laurence. 'From Alexander to Marco Polo, from Text to Image: The Marvels of India.' In *The Medieval French Alexander*, edited by Donald Maddox and Sara Sturm-Maddox, 235–57. Albany: State University of New York Press, 2002.

Harrell, Stevan, ed. *Cultural Encounters on China's Ethnic Frontiers*. Seattle and London: University of Washington Press, 1994.

Harris, Kate. 'Patrons, Buyers and Owners: The Evidence for Ownership and the Rôle of Book Owners in Book Production and the Book Trade.' In *Book*

Production and Publishing in Britain, 1375–1475, edited by Jeremy Griffiths and Derek Pearsall, 163–200. Cambridge: Cambridge University Press, 1989.

Harvey, P.D.A. *Medieval Maps.* London: British Library, 1991.

– 'The Sawley Map and Other World Maps in Twelfth-Century England.' *Imago Mundi* 49 (1997): 33–42.

Hassig, Debra [Debra Higgs Strickland]. 'The Iconography of Rejection: Jews and Other Monstrous Races.' In *Image and Belief,* edited by Colum Hourihane, 25–37. Princeton: Princeton University Press, 1999.

Haw, Stephen G. *A Traveller's History of China.* New York: Interlink Books, 1997.

– *Marco Polo's China: A Venetian in the Realm of Khubilai Khan.* London: Routledge, 2006.

Hawking, Stephen W. *A Brief History of Time: From the Big Bang to Black Holes.* New York: Bantam Books, 1988.

Heers, Jacques. *Marco Polo.* Paris: Fayard, 1983.

– 'De Marco Polo à Christophe Colomb: comment lire le *Devisement du Monde?' Journal of Medieval History* 10 (1984): 125–43.

Higgins, Iain Macleod. *Writing East: The 'Travels' of Sir John Mandeville.* Philadelphia: University of Pennsylvania Press, 1997.

– 'Defining the Earth's Center in a Medieval "Multi-Text": Jerusalem in *The Book of John Mandeville.'* In *Text and Territory,* edited by Sylvia Tomasch and Sealy A. Gilles, 29–53. Philadelphia: University of Pennsylvania Press, 1998.

Hilka, Alfons, ed. *La manière et les faitures des monstres des hommes qui sont en Orient et le plus en Inde. Eine altfranzösische moralisierende Bearbeitung des Liber de Monstruosis Hominibus Orientis aus Thomas von Cantimpré, De Naturis Rerum.* Abhandlungen der Gesellschaft der Wissenschaften zu Göttingen: Philologisch-Historische Klasse 7. Berlin: Weidmannsche Buchhandlung, 1993.

Hindman, Sandra. 'The Roles of Author and Artist in the Procedure of Illustrating Late Medieval Texts.' *Acta* 10 (1986): 27–62.

Hodgen, Margaret T. *Early Anthropology in the Sixteenth and Seventeenth Centuries.* Philadelphia: University of Pennsylvania Press, 1971.

Hodgson, Marshall G.S. *Rethinking World History: Essays on Europe, Islam and World History.* Cambridge: Cambridge University Press, 1993.

– *The Venture of Islam: Conscience and History in a World Civilization.* 3 vols. Chicago: University of Chicago Press, 1974.

Hofmann, Hans. *Die Heiligen Drei Könige. Zur Heiligenverehrung im kirchlichen, gesellschaftlichen und politischen Leben des Mittelalters.* Bonn: Roehrscheid, 1975.

Housely, Norman. *The Later Crusades, 1254–1580: From Lyons to Alcazar.* Oxford: Oxford University Press, 1992.

Howard, Donald R. 'The World of *Mandeville's Travels.' Yearbook of English Studies* 1, no. 1 (1971): 1–17.

- *Writers and Pilgrims: Medieval Pilgrimage Narratives and Their Posterity.* London: University of California Press, 1980.

Huang, Yunte. *Transpacific Displacement: Ethnography, Translation, and Intertextual Travel in Twentieth-Century American Literature.* Berkeley and Los Angeles: University of California Press, 2002.

Hubala, Erich. *Reclams Kunstführer.* Vol. 2, *Venedig. Stuttgart: Philipp, 1974.*

Humphrey, Caroline, and David Sneath. *The End of Nomadism?: Society, State, and the Environment in Inner Asia.* Durham, NC: Duke University Press, 1999.

Huot, Sylvia. *The Romance of the Rose and Its Medieval Readers: Interpretation, Reception, Manuscript Transmission.* Cambridge: Cambridge University Press, 1993.

Husband, Timothy. *The Wild Man: Medieval Myth and Symbolism.* New York: Metropolitan Museum of Art, 1980.

Hyde, J.K. *Literacy and Its Uses: Studies on Late Medieval Italy.* Edited by Daniel Waley. Manchester: Manchester University Press, 1993.

- 'Ethnographers in Search of an Audience.' In Hyde, *Literacy and Its Uses*, 162–216.

- 'Medieval Descriptions of Cities.' In Hyde, *Literacy and Its Uses*, 1–32.

Islam, Syed Manzurul. *The Ethics of Travel: From Marco Polo to Kafka.* Manchester: Manchester University Press, 1996.

Jackson, Peter. 'The Crusade against the Mongols (1241).' *Journal of Ecclesiastical History* 42 (1991): 1–18.

James, M.R. *Marvels of the East.* Oxford: Roxburghe Club, 1929.

- *The Romance of Alexander: A Collotype Facsimile of MS. Bodley 264.* Oxford: Roxburghe Club, 1933.

Jensen, Jørgen. 'The World's Most Diligent Observer.' *Asiatische Studien* 51 (1997): 719–727.

Jones, W.R. 'The Image of the Barbarian in Medieval Europe.' *Comparative Studies in Society and History* 13 (1971): 376–407.

Kahane, Henry and Renee. '*Lingua Franca*: The Story of a Term.' *Romance Philology* 30 (1976): 25–41.

Kay, Sarah. 'The Middle Ages: From the Earliest Texts to 1470.' In *A Short History of French Literature,* by Sarah Kay, Terence Cave, and Malcolm Bowie, 13–95. Oxford: Oxford University Press, 2003.

Keen, Maurice H. *The Laws of War in the Late Middle Ages.* London: Routledge and Kegan Paul, 1965.

Kieschnick, John. *The Impact of Buddhism on Chinese Material Culture.* Princeton: Princeton University Press, 2003.

Kinoshita, Sharon. 'Almería Silk and the French Feudal Imaginary: Toward a "Material" History of the Medieval Mediterranean.' In *Medieval Fabrications: Dress, Textiles, Cloth Work, and Other Cultural Imaginings*, edited by E. Jane Burns, 165–76. The New Middle Ages. New York: Palgrave Macmillan, 2004.

– *Medieval Boundaries: Rethinking Difference in Old French Literature*. The New Middle Ages. Philadelphia: University of Pennsylvania Press, 2006.

– 'The Poetics of *Translatio*: French-Byzantine Relations in Chrétien de Troyes's *Cligés*.' *Exemplaria* 8, no. 2 (1996): 315–54.

Knefelkamp, Ulrich. *Die Suche nach dem Priesterkönig Johannes*. Gelsenkirchen: Müller, 1986.

Knobloch, Edgar. *Monuments of Central Asia: A Guide to the Archaeology, Art and Architecture of Turkestan*. London and New York: I.B. Tauris, 2001.

Knowles, C. 'Jean de Vignay. Un traducteur du XIVe siècle.' *Romania* 75 (1954): 353–86.

Komaroff, Linda, and Stefano Carboni, eds. *The Legacy of Genghis Khan: Courtly Art and Culture in Western Asia, 1256–1353*. New York: Metropolitan Museum of Art, 2002.

Kubiski, Joyce. 'Orientalizing Costume in Early Fifteenth-Century French Manuscript Painting (*Cité des Dames* Master, Limbourg Brothers, Boucicaut Master, and Bedford Master).' *Gesta* 40 (2001): 161–80.

Kuon, Peter. 'Critica e progetto dell'utopia: *Le città invisibili* di Italo Calvino.' In Barenghi et al., *La visione dell'invisibile*, 24–41.

Kwanten, Luc. *Imperial Nomads: A History of Central Asia, 500–1500*. Philadelphia: University of Pennsylvania Press, 1979.

Lane, Frederic C. *Venice: A Maritime Republic*. Baltimore: Johns Hopkins University Press, 1973.

Lane, George. *Early Mongol Rule in Thirteenth-Century Iran: A Persian Renaissance*. Studies in the History of Iran and Turkey. London: RoutledgeCurzon, 2003.

Larner, John. *Marco Polo and the Discovery of the World*. New Haven: Yale University Press, 1999.

Lawton, Lesley. 'The Illustration of Late Medieval Secular Texts, with Special Reference to Lydgate's "Troy Book."' In *Manuscripts and Readers in Fifteenth-Century England: The Literary Implications of Manuscript Study*, edited by Derek Pearsall, 41–69. Cambridge: D.S. Brewer, 1983.

Lecouteux, Claude. 'Les Cynocéphales: Étude d'une tradition tératologique de l'Antiquité au XIIe s.' *Cahiers de civilisation médiévale* 24 (1981): 117–28.

Ledyard, Gari. 'Cartography in Korea.' In *The History of Cartography*, vol. 2, bk. 2, *Cartography in the Traditional East and Southeast Asian Societies*, edited by J.B. Harley and David Woodward, 235–345. Chicago: University of Chicago Press, 1994.

– 'The Kangnido: A Korean World Map, 1402.' In *Circa 1492: Art in the Age of Exploration*, edited by Jay A. Levenson, 329–32. New Haven: Yale University Press, 1991.

Le Goff, Jacques. 'L'Occidente medievale e l'Oceano Indiano: Un orizzonte onirico.' In *Tempo della Chiesa e tempo del mercante: e altri saggi sul lavoro e la cultura nel Medioevo*, edited by Jacques Le Goff, 257–77. Turin: Einaudi, 1977.

– *Phantasie und Realität des Mittelalters*. Translated by Rita Höner. Stuttgart: Klett Cotta, 1990.

Lejeune, Rita, and Jacques Stiennon. *La légende de Roland dans l'art du Moyen Âge*. Brussels: Arcade, 1966.

Lewis, Bernard. *The Assassins: A Radical Sect in Islam*. London: Weidenfeld and Nicolson, 1967.

Lewis, Martin W., and Kären E. Wigen. *The Myth of Continents: A Critique of Metageography*. Berkeley and Los Angeles: University of California Press, 1997.

Lewis, Suzanne. *The Art of Matthew Paris in the 'Chronica Majora.'* Berkeley and Los Angeles: University of California Press, 1987.

Lexikon des Mittelalters. 11 vols. Munich and Zürich: Deutscher Taschenbuch Verlag, 1977–99.

Lipton, Sara. *Images of Intolerance: The Representation of Jews and Judaism in the Bible moralisée*. Berkeley and Los Angeles: University of California Press, 1999.

Liu Binyan. 'Civilization Grafting: No Culture Is an Island.' In *The Clash of Civilizations? The Debate*, edited by Samuel P. Huntington, 46–9. New York: Foreign Affairs, 1996.

Liu, James T.C. *China Turning Inward: Intellectual-Political Change in the Early Twelfth Century*. Harvard East Asian Monographs 132. Cambridge, MA: Harvard University Press, 1988.

Liu, Lydia H. *The Clash of Empires: The Invention of China in Modern World Making*. Cambridge, MA: Harvard University Press, 2004.

Lodén, Torbjörn. 'Nationalism Transcending the State: Changing Conceptions of Chinese Identity.' In *Asian Forms of the Nation*, edited by Stein Tønnesson and Hans Antlöv, 270–96. Richmond: Curzon, 1996.

Lovell, Julia. *The Great Wall: China against the World, 1000 B.C.–A.D. 2000*. Toronto: Viking, 2006.

Luz, Ulrich. *Das Evangelium nach Matthäus*. Evangelisch-Katholischer Kommentar zum Neuen Testament. Vol. 1. 5th ed. Zürich: Benzinger Verlag/Neukirchen-Vluyn: Neukirchener Verlag, 2002.

Macfie, A.L. *Orientalism*. London and New York: Longman, 2002.

MacMillan, Margaret. *Nixon in China: The Week That Changed the World*. Toronto: Viking, 2006.

314   Bibliography

Mair, Victor H., and J.P. Mallory. *The Tarim Mummies: Ancient China and the Mystery of the Earliest Peoples from the West.* London: Thames and Hudson, 2000.

Mallette, Karla. *The Kingdom of Sicily, 1100–1250: A Literary History.* The Middle Ages. Philadelphia: University of Pennsylvania Press, 2005.

Man, John. *Kublai Khan: From Xanadu to Superpower.* Toronto: Bantam Press, 2006.

March, K.N., and K.M. Passman. 'The Amazon Myth and Latin America.' In *The Classical Tradition and the Americas*, vol. 1, *European Images of the Americas and the Classical Tradition*, edited by W. Haase and M. Reinhold, 285–338. Berlin and New York: Walter de Gruyter, 1994.

Martin, Henry. *Catalogue des manuscrits de la Bibliothèque de l'Arsenal.* Vol. 5. Paris: Librairie Plon, 1889.

Mason, Peter. *Deconstructing America: Representations of the Other.* London: Routledge, 1990.

Matar, Nabil. *Turks, Moors, and Englishmen in the Age of Discovery.* New York: Columbia University Press, 1999.

McLaughlin, Martin. *Italo Calvino.* Edinburgh: Edinburgh University Press, 1998.

McLaughlin, Martin, and Arianna Scicutella. 'Calvino e Conrad: dalla tesi di laurea alle *Lezioni americane.' Italian Studies* 57 (2002): 113–32.

McLuhan, Marshall, and Bruce R. Powers. *The Global Village: Transformations in World Life and Media in the 21st Century.* New York: Oxford University Press, 1989.

Meiss, Millard. *The Boucicaut Master.* London: Phaidon, 1968.

– *The Late Fourteenth Century and the Patronage of the Duke.* 2 vols. London: Phaidon: 1967.

Meiss, Millard, and Elizabeth H. Beatson. *The Belles Heures of Jean, Duke of Berry.* New York: George Braziller, 1974.

Mellinkoff, Ruth. *Outcasts: Signs of Otherness in Northern European Art of the Late Middle Ages.* 2 vols. Berkeley and Los Angeles: University of California Press, 1993.

Ménard, Philippe. 'L'Illustration de *Devisement du Monde* de Marco Polo: Étude d'iconographie comparée.' In *Métamorphoses du récit du voyage*, edited by François Moureau, 17–31. Geneva: Slatkine, 1986.

– 'Réflexions sur l'illustration du texte de Marco Polo dans la manuscrit fr. 2810 de la Bibliothèque Nationale de Paris.' In *Mélanges in memoriam Takeshi Shimmura*, edited by N. Fukumoto, T. Matsumura, and Y. Otaka, 81–92. Tokyo: Comité de Publication, 1998.

Menesto, Enricò, ed. *Giovanni di Pian di Carpine: Storia dei Mongoli.* Translated by Maria Christiana Lungarotti. Spoleto: Centro Italiano de Studi Sull'Alto Medioevo, 1989.

Milanesi, Marica. 'I regni del Prete Gianni.' In *Africa: Storie di viaggiatori italiani*, edited by Giovanni Benzoni et al., 42–50. Milan: Electa, 1986.

Milanini, Claudio. *L'utopia discontinua. Saggio su Italo Calvino*. Milan: Garzanti, 1990.

Monneret de Villard, Ugo. *Le leggende orientali sui Magi Evangelici*. Studi e Testi 163. Vatican City: Biblioteca Apostolica Vaticana, 1952.

Morandini, Morando. 'Franco Cristaldi, 1924–1992.' In *The Oxford History of World Cinema*, edited by Geoffrey Nowell-Smith, 595. Oxford: Oxford University Press, 1996.

Morgan, David O. 'Marco Polo in China – or Not.' *Journal of the Royal Asiatic Society* 3, no. 6 (1996): 221–25.

– *The Mongols*. The Peoples of Europe. Oxford: Blackwell, 1986.

– 'The Mongols and the Eastern Mediterranean.' *Mediterranean Historical Review* 4 (1989): 198–211.

Moseley, C.W.R.D. 'The Availability of *Mandeville's Travels* in England.' *Library* 30, no. 5 (1975): 125–33.

– 'Behaim's Globe and Mandeville's Travels.' *Imago Mundi* 33 (1981): 89–91.

– 'Introduction.' In *The Travels of Sir John Mandeville*, by John Mandeville, v–xiv. Harmondsworth: Penguin, 1983.

– 'The Metamorphoses of Sir John Mandeville.' *Yearbook of English Studies* 4 (1974): 5–25.

Moule, A.C. 'Marco Polo's Description of Quinsai.' *T'oung Pao* 33 (1937): 105–28.

Mulvey, Laura. 'Visual Pleasure and Narrative Cinema.' In *Visual and Other Pleasures*, 14–26. London: Macmillan, 1989.

Münkler, Marina. *Marco Polo. Leben und Legende*. Munich: Beck, 1998.

Myers, Jeffrey. *Gary Cooper: An American Hero*. New York: William Morrow and Co., 1998.

Needham, J., with Wang Ling. *Science and Civilisation in China*. Vol. 3, *Mathematics and the Sciences of the Heavens and the Earth*. Cambridge: Cambridge University Press, 1959.

Nicholas, D. *Town and Countryside: Social, Economic, and Political Tensions in Fourteenth-Century Flanders*. Bruges: De Tempel, 1971.

Nichols, J.G. 'Inventory of Reliques at St Omer 1465.' *Gentleman's Magazine*, November 1842.

Nowell, C.E. 'The Old Man of the Mountain.' *Speculum* 22 (1947): 475–89.

Nowell-Smith, Geoffrey. *The Oxford History of World Cinema*. Oxford: Oxford University Press, 1996.

Oesterley, Hermann, ed. *Gesta Romanorum*. Hildesheim: Georg Olms, 1963.

Olschki, Leonardo. 'Asiatic Exoticism in Italian Art of the Early Renaissance.' *Art Bulletin* 26 (1944): 95–106.

– 'Der Brief des Presbyters Johannes.' *Historische Zeitschrift* 144 (1931): 1–14.

– *Marco Polo's Asia: An Introduction to His 'Description of the World' Called 'Il Milione.'* Berkeley and Los Angeles: University of California Press, 1960.

– 'Ponce de Léon's Fountain of Youth: History of a Geographic Myth.' *Hispanic American Historical Review* 21 (1941): 261–385.

Omont, Henri. *Livre des merveilles. Reproduction des 265 miniatures du manuscrit français 2810 de la Bibliothèque Nationale.* 2 vols. Paris: Berthaud Frères, 1908.

Orchard, Andy. *Pride and Prodigies: Studies in the Monsters of the 'Beowulf'-Manuscript.* Cambridge: D.S. Brewer, 1995.

Origo, Iris. 'The Domestic Enemy: The Eastern Slaves in Tuscany in the Fourteenth and Fifteenth Centuries.' *Speculum* 30 (1955): 321–66.

Orlandini, G. 'Marco Polo e la sua Famiglia.' *Archivio Veneto-Tridentino* 9 (1926): 1–68.

Pächt, Otto. 'René d'Anjou Studien. 1, 2.' *Jahrbuch der kunsthistorischen Sammlungen in Wien* 69 (1973): 85–126; 73 (1977): 7–106.

Pächt, Otto, and J.J.G. Alexander. *Illuminated Manuscripts in the Bodleian Library Oxford.* Vol. 3, *British, Irish, and Icelandic Schools.* Oxford: Clarendon Press, 1973.

Palmer, Martin. *The Jesus Sutras: Rediscovering the Lost Religion of Taoist Christianity.* London: Piatkus, 2001.

Park, Katherine. 'The Meanings of Natural Diversity: Marco Polo on the "Division" of the World.' In *Texts and Contexts in Ancient and Medieval Science: Studies on the Occasion of John E. Murdoch's Seventieth Birthday,* edited by Edith Sylla and Michael McVaugh, 134–47. Leiden and New York: Brill, 1997.

Park, Katherine, and Lorraine Daston. *Wonders and the Order of Nature, 1150–1750.* New York: Zone, 1998.

Patterson, Richard. 'The Filming of Marco Polo.' *American Cinematographer* 63, no. 5 (May 1982): 465–71.

Perrig, Alexander. 'Erdrandsiedler oder die schrecklichen Nachkommen Chams: Aspekte der mittelalterlichen Völkerkunde.' In *Die andere Welt: Studien zum Exotismus,* edited by Thomas Koebner and Gerhart Pickerodt, 31–87. Frankfurt am Main: Athenäum, 1987.

Perroy, Édouard. *La Guerre de Cent Ans.* Paris: Gallimard, 1945.

Phillips, J.R.S. *The Medieval Expansion of Europe.* Oxford: Oxford University Press, 1988.

Plummer, John. *The Last Flowering: French Paintings in Manuscripts 1420–1530 from American Collections.* Oxford: Oxford University Press, 1982.

Pochat, Gotz. 'Das Fremde im Spiegel der Kunst des Mittelalters.' In *Bild und Abbild vom Menschen im Mittelalter,* edited by Elisabeth Vavra, 113–46. Klagenfurt: Wiester, 1999.

Pollock, Sheldon. 'Cosmopolitan and Vernacular in History.' In *Cosmopolitanism,* edited by Carol A. Breckenridge et al., 15–53. Durham: Duke University Press, 2002.

Porter, Vicki. *The West Looks at the East in the Late Middle Ages: The 'Livre des Merveilles du Monde.'* Ann Arbor: University Microfilms, 1977.

Qian Mu. *Zhongguo wenhua shi daolun [Introduction to the History of Chinese Culture]*. Taipei: Taiwan shangwu, 1993.

Raiswell, Richard. 'Before the Company: English Perceptions of India in the Sixteenth Century.' PhD diss., University of Toronto, 2003.

Ravenstein, E.G. *Martin Behaim*. London: G. Philip, 1908.

Reichert, Folker. 'Marco Polos Buch: Lesarten des Fremden.' In *Fiktion des Fremden: Erkundung kultureller Grenzen in Literatur und Publizistik*, edited by Dietrich Harth, 180–202. Frankfurt am Main: Fischer Taschenbuch Verlag, 1994.

Richard, Jean. 'Les Navigations des occidentaux sur l'Ocean Indien et la Mer Caspienne (XIIe–XIVe siècles).' In *Sociétés et compagnies de commerce en Orient*, 353–63. Paris, 1970. Reprint, Article 31 in *Les Relations entre l'Orient et l'Occident au moyen âge*. London: Variorum, 1977.

Richard, Jean, ed. *Simon de Saint-Quentin: Histoire des Tartares*. Paris: Librairie Orientaliste Paul Geuthner, 1965.

Rieger, Dietmar. 'Marco Polo und Rustichello da Pisa. Der Reisende and rein Erzähler.' In *Reisen und Reiseliteratur im Mittelalter und in der frühen Neuzeit*, edited by Xenja von Ertzdorff, Dieter Neukirch, and Rudolph Schulz, 289–312. Amsterdam and Atlanta, GA: Rodopi, 1992.

Roberts, J.A.G. *A History of China*. New York: Palgrave Macmillan, 2006.

Röhl, Susanne. *Der 'Livre de Mandeville' im 14. und 15. Jahrhundert. Untersuchungen zur handschriftlichen Überlieferung der kontinentalfranzösischen Version*. Mittelalter Studien 6. Munich: Wilhelm Fink, 2004.

Roncaglia, Aurelio. 'Le Letteratura franco-veneta.' In *Storia della letteratura italiana*, edited by Emilio Cecchi and Natalino Spegno, vol. 2, *Il Trecento*, 745–82. Rome: Garzanti, 1987.

Ross, D.J.A. 'Methods of Book-Production in a XIVth Century French Miscellany (London, B.M., MS. Royal 19.D.I).' *Scriptorium* 6 (1952): 63–75.

Rossabi, Morris. *Kublai Khan: His Life and Times*. Berkeley and Los Angeles: University of California Press, 1988.

Rossabi, Morris, ed. *China among Equals: The Middle Kingdom and Its Neighbors, 10th–14th Centuries*. Berkeley: University of California Press, 1983.

Rossbach, Nikola. 'Ästhetische Bewältigung von Landlosigkeit. Schlaraffische Perspektiven in Marco Polos und Christoph Kolumbus' Reiseberichten.' In *Exterritorialität. Landlosigkeit in der deutschsprachigen Literatur*, edited by Carsten Jakobi, 15–48. Munich: Martin Meidenbauer, 2006.

Rouse, R.H., and M.A. Rouse. 'The Commercial Production of Manuscript Books in Late-Thirteenth-Century and Early-Fourteenth-Century Paris.' In

A Potencie of Life: Books in Society, edited by Nicolas Barker, 45–61. London: British Library, 1993.

Rubiés, Joan Pau. *Travel and Ethnology in the Renaissance: South India through European Eyes, 1250–1625.* Cambridge: Cambridge University Press, 2000.

Runcimann, Steven. *The History of the Crusades.* 3 vols. Cambridge: Cambridge University Press, 1954.

Runte, H.R. 'The Scribe and Miniaturist as Reader.' In *Essays in Early French Literature Presented to Barbara M. Craig,* edited by Norris J. Lacy and Jerry C. Nash, 53–64. York, SC: French Literature Publications Company, 1982.

Ruotsala, Jussi Hanska-Aniti. 'Berthold von Regensburg, OFM, and the Mongols: Medieval Sermon as a Historical Source.' *Archivum Franciscanum Historicum* 89 (1996): 425–45.

Saenger, Paul. *Space between Words: The Origins of Silent Reading.* Stanford: Stanford University Press, 1997.

Said, Edward W. *Orientalism.* New York: Vintage, 1979.

Sand, Alexander. 'Drei Könige. Biblisch-Theologische Voraussetzungen.' *Lexikon des Mittelalters,* vol. 3. Munich: Deutscher Taschenbuch Verlag, 2002. c. 1384–5.

Saunders, Corinne. *The Forest of Medieval Romance.* Cambridge: Cambridge University Press, 1993.

Saunders, J.J. *The History of the Mongol Conquests.* London: Routledge and Kegan Paul, 1971.

– 'Matthew Paris and the Mongols.' In *Essays in Medieval History Presented to Bertie Wilkinson,* edited by T.A. Sandquist and M.R. Powicke, 116–32. Toronto: University of Toronto Press, 1969.

Saussy, Haun. *Great Walls of Discourse and Other Adventures in Cultural China.* Harvard East Asian Monographs 212. Cambridge, MA: Harvard University Press, 2001.

Scattergood, V.J., and J.W. Sherborne, eds. *English Court Culture in the Later Middle Ages.* London: Duckworth, 1983.

Schafer, Edward H. *The Golden Peaches of Samarkand: A Study of T'ang Exotics.* Berkeley: University of California Press, 1963.

Schäfer, Werner. 'Die Wallfahrt zu den Heiligen Drei Königen.' In Zehnder, *Die Heiligen Drei Könige,* 73–80.

Schiller, Gertrud. 'Die Weisen (Magier) aus dem Morgenland. Die heiligen drei Könige.' In *Ikonographie der christlichen Kunst,* vol. 1, edited by Gertrud Schiller, 105–21. Güterloh: Güterloher Verlagshaus Gerd Mohn, 1981.

Scott, Kathleen. *Later Gothic Manuscripts, 1390–1490.* 2 vols. London: Harvey Miller, 1996.

Segre, Cesare. 'Introduzione.' In *Marco Polo. Milione: Le Divisament dou monde,* edited by Gabriella Ronchi, xi–xxix. Milan: Arnoldo Mondadori, 1982.

Seymour, Michael C. *Sir John Mandeville*. Authors of the Middle Ages 1: English Writers of the Late Middle Ages. Aldershot: Variorum, 1993.

Shell, Marc. *The Economy of Literature*. Baltimore: Johns Hopkins University Press, 1978.

Silverberg, Robert. *The Realm of Prester John*. London: Phoenix, 2001.

Sinor, Denis. *Inner Asia and Its Contacts with Medieval Europe*. London: Variorum Reprints, 1977.

Slessarev, Vsevolod. *Prester John: The Letter and the Legend*. Minneapolis: University of Minnesota Press, 1959.

Smith, Richard J. *China's Cultural Heritage: The Qing Dynasty, 1644–1912*. 2nd ed. Boulder: Westview, 1994.

Smith, Vanessa. *Literary Culture and the Pacific: Nineteenth-Century Textual Encounter*. Cambridge: Cambridge University Press, 1998.

Snoek, G.J.C. *Medieval Piety from Relics to the Eucharist: A Process of Mutual Interaction*. Leiden and New York: E.J. Brill, 1995.

Solomon, Elinor Harris. *Virtual Money: Understanding the Power and Risks of Money's High-Speed Journey into Electronic Space*. New York and Oxford: Oxford University Press, 1997.

Soros, George. *The Crisis of Global Capitalism: Open Society Endangered*. New York: Public Affairs, 1998.

Soucek, Svat. *A History of Inner Asia*. Cambridge: Cambridge University Press, 2000.

Sprunger, David A. 'Wild Folk and Lunatics in Medieval Romance.' In *The Medieval World of Nature: A Book of Essays*, edited by Joyce E. Salisbury, 145–63. New York: Garland, 1993.

Stakosch-Grassmann, Gustav. *Der Einfall der Mongolen in Mitteleuropa in den Jahren 1241 und 1242*. Innsbruck: Wagnerischen Universitäts-Buchhandlung, 1893.

Stehkämpfer, Hugo. 'Könige und Heilige Drei Könige.' In Zehnder, *Die Heiligen Drei Könige*, 37–51.

Steinicke, Marion. 'Apokalyptische Heerscharen und Gottesknechte. Wundervölker des Ostens in abendländischer Tradition vom Untergang der Antike bis zur Entdeckung Amerikas.' PhD diss., Freie Universität Berlin, 2005. http://www.diss.fu-berlin.de/2005/290/index.html.

– 'Sprachohnmacht und Bewusstseinswandel in Reiseberichten des Spätmittelalters.' In *Begegnung und Verhandlung. Möglichkeiten eines Kulturwandels durch Reise*, edited by Christian Berkmeier, Katrin Callsen, and Ingmar Propst, 107–18. Münster: Lit-Verlag, 2004.

Stookey, Laurence Hull. 'The Gothic Cathedral as the Heavenly Jerusalem: Liturgical and Theological Sources.' *Gesta* 8 (1969): 35–41.

Strickland, Debra Higgs. 'Artists, Audience, and Ambivalence in Marco Polo's *Divisament dou monde*.' *Viator* 36 (2005): 493–529.

- [As Debra Hassig]. 'The Iconography of Rejection: Jews and Other Monstrous Races.' In *Image and Belief*, edited by Colum Hourihane, 25–37. Princeton: Princeton University Press, 1999.
- *Saracens, Demons, and Jews: Making Monsters in Medieval Art*. Princeton: Princeton University Press, 2003.

Sumption, Jonathan. *Pilgrimage: An Image of Medieval Religion*. London: Faber and Faber, 1975.

Swindell, Larry. *The Last Hero: A Biography of Gary Cooper*. Garden City, NJ: Doubleday, 1980.

Tattersall, Jill. 'Anthropophagi and Eaters of Raw Flesh in French Literature of the Crusade Period: Myth, Tradition and Reality.' *Medium Aevum* 57 (1988): 240–53.

Tao Jing-shen. 'Barbarians or Northerners: Northern Sung Images of the Khitans.' In Rossabi, *China among Equals*, 66–88.

Taylor, E.G.R. *Tudor Geography, 1485–1583*. London: Methuen, 1930.

Thomas, Marcel, François Avril, and Wilhelm Schlag. *The Hunting Book of Gaston Phébus*. London: Harvey Miller, 1998.

Thompson, Kristin, and David Bromwell. *Film History: An Introduction*. Boston: McGraw-Hill, 2003.

Thomson, David. *The New Biographical Dictionary of Film*. New York: A. Knopf, 2002.

Thorp, Nigel. *The Glory of the Page: Medieval and Renaissance Illuminated Manuscripts from Glasgow University Library*. London: Harvey Miller, 1987.

Tolan, John Victor. *Saracens: Islam in the Medieval European Imagination*. New York: Columbia University Press, 2002.

Tønnesson, Stein. 'Orientalism, Occidentalism and Knowing about Others.' http://www.multiworld.org/m_versity/decolonisation/saidres.htm (accessed 11/11/2005; article no longer available).

Tooley, Marian J. 'Bodin and the Mediaeval Theory of Climate.' *Speculum* 28 (1953): 64–83.

Trotter, D.A. 'Introduction.' In *Les Merveilles de la Terre d'Outremer: Traduction du XIVe siècle du récit de voyage d'Odoric de Pordenone*, by Jean de Vignay, v–xxxix. Exeter: University of Exeter, 1990.

Tucci, U. 'Marco Polo, andò veramente in Cina?' *Studi Veneziani* 33–4 (1997): 49–59.

Tucker, Jonathan. *The Silk Road: Art and History*. London: Philip Wilson Publishers, 2003.

Tzanaki, Rosemary. *Mandeville's Medieval Audiences: A Study on the Reception of the 'Book' of Sir John Mandeville (1371–1550)*. Aldershot and Burlington, VT: Ashgate, 2003.

van der Essen, L. 'Jean d'Ypres ou de Saint-Bertin: Contribution à l'histoire de l'hagiographie médiévale en Belgique.' *Revue Belge de Philologie et d'Histoire* 1, no. 3 (1922): 475–94.

Vitullo, Juliann M. *The Chivalric Epic in Medieval Italy.* Gainesville: University of Florida Press, 2000.

Voiret, J.P. 'China, "Objektiv" Gesehen: Marc Polo als Berichterstatter.' *Asiatische Studien* 51 (1997): 805–21.

von den Brincken, Anna-Dorothee. *'Fines terrae': Die Enden der Erde und die vierte Kontinent auf mittelalterlichen Weltkarten.* Monumenta Germaniae Historica, Schriften 36. Hannover: Hahnsche, 1992.

– 'Gog und Magog.' In *Die Mongolen*, edited by Walther Heissig and Claudius C. Müller, 27–9. Innsbruck: Pinguin-Verlag, 1989.

Waldron, Arthur. *The Great Wall of China: From History to Myth.* Cambridge: Cambridge University Press, 1990.

Waley, Daniel, ed. *Literacy and Its Uses: Studies on Late Medieval Italy.* Manchester: Manchester University Press, 1993.

Waley-Cohen, Joanna. *The Sextants of Beijing: Global Currents in Chinese History.* New York: Norton, 1999.

Wang Gungwu. 'The Rhetoric of a Lesser Empire: Early Sung Relations with Its Neighbors.' In Rossabi, *China among Equals*, 47–65.

Warner, George F., and Julius P. Gilson. *British Museum Catalogue of Western Manuscripts in the Old Royal and King's Collections.* 4 vols. London: British Museum, 1921.

Weart, Spencer. 'Ocean Currents and Climate.' *Climate Change: The Discovery of Global Warming.* http://www.aip.org/history/climate/oceans.htm#L_1988.

Weatherford, Jack. *Genghis Khan and the Making of the Modern World.* New York: Crown, 2004.

Weckmann, L. 'The Middle Ages in the Conquest of America.' *Speculum* 26 (1951): 132–3.

Weiers, Michael. 'Von Ögödei bis Möngke. Das mongolische Großreich.' In *Die Mongolen. Beiträge zu ihrer Geschichte und Kultur*, edited by Michael Weiers, 192–216. Darmstadt: Wissenschaftliche Buchgesellschaft, 1986.

Westrem, Scott. 'Against Gog and Magog.' In *Text and Territory: Geographical Imagination in the European Middle Ages*, edited by Sylvia Tomasch and Sealy Gilles, 54–75. Philadelphia: University of Pennsylvania Press, 1998.

– *The Hereford Map: A Transcription and Translation of the Legends with Commentary.* Turnhout: Brepols, 2001.

– 'Medieval Western European Views of Sexuality Reflected in the Narratives of Travelers to the Orient.' In *Homo Carnalis: The Carnal Aspect of Medieval Life*, edited by Helen Rodnite Lemay, 141–56. Binghamton: Center for Medieval and Early Renaissance Studies, State University of New York at Binghamton, 1987.

Westrem, Scott, ed. *Discovering New Worlds: Essays on Medieval Exploration and Imagination.* New York: Garland, 1991.

White, David Gordon. *Myths of the Dog-Man*. Chicago and London: University of Chicago Press, 1991.

Whitfield, Susan. *Life along the Silk Road*. Berkeley: University of California Press, 1999.

– 'Was There a Silk Road?' *Asian Medicine: Tradition and Modernity* 3.2 (2007): 2001–13.

Whitfield, Susan, ed., with Ursula Sims-Williams. *The Silk Road: Trade, Travel, War and Faith*. Chicago: Serindia Publications, 2004.

Willard, Charity Cannon. *Christine de Pizan: Her Life and Works*. New York: Persea Books, 1984.

Windschuttle, Keith. 'Edward Said's "Orientalism Revisited."' *New Criterion online*, January 1999. http://www.newcriterion.com/archive/17/jan99/said.htm.

Wittkower, Rudolph. *Allegory and the Migration of Symbols*. Boulder: Westview Press, 1977. Translated by Benjamin Schwarz as *Allegorie und der Wandel der Symbole in Antike und Renaissance*. Cologne: DuMont, 1984.

– 'Marco Polo and the Pictorial Tradition of the Marvels of the East.' In *Allegory and Migration of Symbols*, 76–92.

– 'Die Wunder des Ostens: Ein Beitrag zur Geschichte der Ungeheuer.' In *Allegorie und der Wandel der Symbole in Antike und Renaissance*, 87–150.

Wood, Frances. *Did Marco Polo Go to China?* London: Secker and Warburg/ Boulder: Westview, 1995.

Woodward, David. 'Medieval *Mappaemundi*.' In *The History of Cartography*, vol. 1, *Cartography in Prehistoric, Ancient, and Medieval Europe and the Mediterranean*, edited by J.B. Harley and David Woodward, 286–370. Chicago: University of Chicago Press, 1987.

Wunderli, Peter. 'Marco Polo und der Ferne Osten: Zwischen "Wahrheit" und "Dichtung."' In *Reisen in reale und mythische Ferne: Reiseliteratur in Mittelalter und Renaissance*, edited by Peter Wunderli, 124–96. Düsseldorf: Droste, 1993.

Xue Fucheng. *Chou Yang chuyi: Xue Fucheng ji [Xue Fucheng's Works: Preliminary Proposals for Managing Foreign Affairs]*. Edited by Xu Suhua. Shenyang: Liaoning renmin chubanshe, 1994.

Yang Lien-sheng. *Money and Credit in China: A Short History*. Cambridge, MA: Harvard University Press, 1952.

Yang Xiaoneng, ed. *The Golden Age of Chinese Archaeology: Celebrated Discoveries from the People's Republic of China*. New Haven and London: Yale University Press, 1999. Catalogue of an exhibition held at the National Gallery of Art, Washington, DC, 19 September 1999–2 January 2000; Museum of Fine Arts, Houston, 15 February– 7 May 2000; Asian Art Museum of San Francisco, 17 June–11 September 2000.

Yang Zhijiu. 'A Passage in Chinese Concerning Marco Polo's Departure from China.' In *Zhongxi wenhua jiaoliu xianqu–Marco Polo*, edited by Lu Guojun et al., 17–25. Beijing: Commercial Press, 1995.

– *Make Bole zai Zhongguo [Marco Polo in China]*. Tianjin: Nankai daxue chuban-she, 1999.

Yeager, Suzanne M. 'England's Quest for Jerusalem: Fourteenth-Century Literature of Crusade and Pilgrimage.' PhD diss., University of Toronto, 2004.

Young, John, and P. Henderson Aiken. *A Catalogue of the Manuscripts in the Library of the Hunterian Museum in the University of Glasgow*. Glasgow: James Maclehose and Sons, 1908.

Yule, Henry. 'Marco Polo and His Book: Introductory Notices.' In *The Travels of Marco Polo: The Complete Yule-Cordier Edition*, by Marco Polo, edited by Henry Yule, 3–12.

Yule, Henry, trans. and ed. *Cathay and the Way Thither: Being a Collection of Medieval Notices of China*. 2nd ed. revised by Henri Cordier. Hakluyt Society, 2nd series, 33. 1913. Rpt. Nendeln, Liechtenstein: Kraus Reprint, 1967.

Yu Ying-shih. *Wenhua pinglun yu Zhongguo qinghuai [Cultural Criticism and Chinese Sensibilities]*. Taipei: Yongchen, 1993.

Zacher, Christian K. *Curiosity and Pilgrimage: The Literature of Discovery in Fourteenth-Century England*. Baltimore: Johns Hopkins University Press, 1976.

Zaganelli, Giovanna. 'La Terra Santa e i miti dell'Asia.' In *L'Oriente: Storie di viaggiatori italiani*, edited by Gino Benzoni et al., 13–27. Milan: Electa, 1985.

Zancan, Marina. 'Le città invisibili di Calvino.' In *Letteratura italiana: Le opera*, vol. 4, *Il Novecento*, part 2, *La ricerca letteraria*, 828–930. Turin: Einaudi, 1996.

Zehnder, Frank Günter, ed. *Die Heiligen Drei Könige. Darstellung und Verehrung*. Cologne: Wallraf-Richartz Museum, 1982. Catalogue of an exhibition of the Wallraf-Richartz-Museums held at the Josef-Haubrich-Kunsthalle, Cologne, 1 December 1982–30 January 1983.

Zhang, Longxi. *Allegoresis: Reading Canonical Literature East and West*. Ithaca: Cornell University Press, 2005.

Zhang, Longxi [as Lung-hsi Chang]. *Mighty Opposites: From Dichotomies to Differences in the Comparative Study of China*. Stanford: Stanford University Press, 1998.

Zink, Michel. 'Références.' In *Introduction à la littérature française du Moyen Age*, 157–86. Paris: Livre de Poche, 1993.

Contributors

Suzanne Conklin Akbari is Associate Professor of English and Medieval Studies at the University of Toronto. She has published *Seeing through the Veil: Optical Theory and Medieval Allegory* (2004) and has a forthcoming study titled *Idols in the East: European Representations of Islam and the Orient, 1100–1450*.

Yunte Huang is professor of English at the University of California, Santa Barbara. He is the autor of *Transpacific Displacement: Ethnography, Translation, and Intertextual Travel in Twentieth-Century American Literature* (2002) and *Shi: A Radical Reading of Chinese Poetry* (1997), and the translator into Chinese of Ezra Pound's *The Pisan Cantos*. Huang's newest book is titled *Transpacific Imaginations: History, Literature, Counterpoetics* (2008); he is currently at work on *Global Poetics: A Thick Description*.

Until his untimely death, **Amilcare A. Iannucci** was Professor of Comparative Literature and Founding Director of the Humanities Centre at the University of Toronto. Among his many publications are *Forma ed Evento nella Divina Commedia*, *Dante e la 'bella scola' della poesia*, *Dante: Contemporary Perspectives*, and *Dante, Cinema and Television*.

Sharon Kinoshita is Professor of World Literature and Cultural Studies at the University of California, Santa Cruz. She has recently published *Medieval Boundaries: Rethinking Difference in Old French Literature* (2006) and is at work on a new book titled *Paying Tribute: Eastern Empires and the Medieval French Imaginary* as well as other projects in medieval Mediterranean Studies.

The late **John Larner** was Professor Emeritus in History and Honorary Research Fellow at the University of Glasgow. In addition to his widely influential study *Marco Polo and the Discovery of the World* (1999), he was the author of *Italy in the Age of Dante and Petrarch, 1216–1380, Culture ans Society in Italy, 1920–1420*, and *The Lords of Romagna: Romagnol Society and the Origins of the Signorie*. In 1993, John Larner was awarded the Henry Allen Moe Prize in the Humanities by the American Philosophical Society for his work on Christopher Columbus.

Martin McLaughlin is Fiat-Serena Professor of Italian Studies and Fellow of Magdalen College at the University of Oxford. He is the author of *Italo Calvino* (1998), co-editor of *Image, Eye and Art in Calvino: Writing Visibility* (2007), and translator of Calvino's *Why Read the Classics?* (1999) and *Hermit in Paris* (2003).

Marion Steinicke is a member of the research faculty at the University of Heidelberg, Germany. She is the author of *Apokalyptische Heerscharen und Gottesknechte* (2002) and the co-editor of *Investitur- und Krönungsrituale: Herrschaftseinsetzungen im kulturellen Vergleich*. Her current work centers on ritual inventions in the Italian Trecento.

Debra Higgs Strickland is Deputy Director of the Glasgow Centre for Medieval and Renaissance Studies at the University of Glasgow. In addition to her study *Saracens, Demons, and Jews: Making Monsters in Medieval Art* (2003), she is (as Debra Hassig) the author of *Medieval Bestiaries: Text, Image, Ideology* and the editor of *The Mark of the Beast: The Medieval Bestiary in Art, Life, and Literature*.

John Tulk is a research associate at the University of Toronto and longstanding Assistant to the Director of the Humanities Centre. A former Roman Catholic priest and Professor of Historical Theology in the Toronto School of Theology, he is the author of several articles on topics including Iron Age Greece, the early Christian Fathers, Martin Luther, and Christian Humanism.

Susan Whitfield is Director of the International Dunhuang Project at the British Library. She is the author of *Life along the Silk Road* (1999) and *Aurel Stein on the Silk Road* (2004), and the editor of *The Silk Road: Trade, Travel, War and Faith* (2004), *Dunhuang Manuscript Forgeries* (2002), and *Dunhuang and Turfan: Contents and Conservation of Ancient Documents from Central Asia* (1996).

Suzanne Yeager is Assistant Professor of English and Medieval Studies at Fordham University. Her book *Jerusalem in Medieval Narrative* is forthcoming from Cambridge University Press, and she has written articles on medieval religious identity, crusade romance, and pilgrimage. Her new project explores the relationship between the rhetoric of alterity and Christopher Columbus's interactions with the 'New World.'

Longxi Zhang is Chair and Professor of Comparative Literature and Translation at the City University of Hong Kong. His English-language publications include *Unexpected Affinities: Reading across Cultures* (2007) and *Allegoresis: Reading Canonical Literature East and West* (2005), and (as Lung-hsi Chang) *Mighty Opposites: From Dichotomies to Differences in the Comparative Study of China* (1998) and *The Tao and the Logos: Literary Hermeneutics, East and West* (1992).

Index